THE REIGN OF JAMES VI

The Reign of James VI

Edited by

JULIAN GOODARE

and

MICHAEL LYNCH

TUCKWELL PRESS

First published in Great Britain in 2000 by
Tuckwell Press
The Mill House
Phantassie
East Linton
East Lothian EH40 3DG
Scotland

ISBN 1 86232 095 0

British Library Cataloguing in Publication Data
A catalogue record for this book is available
on request from the British Library

Printed and bound by Cromwell Press, Trowbridge, Wiltshire

CONTENTS

PREFACE

The reign of James VI, one of the longest and most important in Scottish history, still lacks full, systematic or authoritative treatment. This book is intended to go some way towards remedying that need.

The idea for the book arose among a group of historians at the University of Edinburgh in the mid-1990s, and it has been extended to include a number of scholars from elsewhere. It has come to fruition against a background of steadily growing literature on various aspects of the period, notably religion, political ideas and historiography. The first chapter serves several purposes: to survey some of that literature; to set the other chapters in context; and to indicate where further research is required. Those wishing an introduction to the politics of the reign might prefer to begin with Chapter 2.

Assistance with illustrations was kindly supplied by Ian Campbell, Hugh Cheape, Richard Emerson, Richard Fawcett, Miles Glendinning, David Henrie, E., N. and K. MacKechnie, Graeme MacMorran, Rosalind Marshall, Andrew Newby, Norman Reid, John Slorach, Michael Spearman, Margaret Stewart, Diane Watters, the staffs of Edinburgh University Library, the Royal Commission on the Ancient and Historical Monuments of Scotland, the National Monuments Record of Scotland, the National Library of Scotland, St Andrews University Library, the Scottish National Portrait Gallery, and the Stewartry Museum, Kirkcudbright. Thanks are also due to George Mudie for his drawing of the map of the Borders. We are grateful to our publishers, John and Val Tuckwell, for their consistent interest and encouragement.

Julian Goodare
Michael Lynch

Edinburgh, February 1999

ILLUSTRATIONS

PICTURE ACKNOWLEDGEMENTS

The cover illustration and no. 4 are reproduced by courtesy of the National Museums of Scotland. No. 2 is reproduced by courtesy of Hampshire Record Office. Nos. 3, 9 and 10 are reproduced by courtesy of the Trustees of the National Galleries of Scotland. No. 5 is reproduced by courtesy of the National Portrait Gallery. No. 6 is reproduced by courtesy of St Andrews University Library. No. 8 is reproduced by courtesy of the Stewartry Museum, Kirkcudbright, Dumfries and Galloway Museums Service. Nos. 11, 18, 20, 23, 24, 26, 29, 32, 33 and 34 are Crown copyright. Reproduced by courtesy of Historic Scotland. Nos. 13, 14 and 15 are reproduced by permission of Edinburgh University Library. Nos. 16, 25 and 30 are Crown copyright. Reproduced by permission of the Trustees of the National Library of Scotland. Nos. 17, 28 and 31 are Crown copyright. Reproduced by permission of the Royal Commission on the Ancient and Historical Monuments of Scotland.

CONVENTIONS AND ABBREVIATIONS

Money: All sums are in pounds (£s) Scots unless otherwise stated—except in Chapter 6, where they are in £s sterling unless otherwise stated. A merk was 13*s*. 4*d*., two-thirds of a £ Scots. In 1567 the English £ (sterling) was equal to about £4 10*s*. Scots at par, and the French crown to £1. 6*s*. 8*d*. Scots; by 1601 they were worth £12 Scots and £3. 6*s*. 8*d*. Scots respectively. The Scottish currency was pegged to the English in 1603, and from then until 1625 there were no major fluctuations in currency values.

Dates: These are given in old style (i.e. Julian calendar), but with the year beginning on 1 January.

The following abbreviations are used:

Add. MS	Additional MS (BL).
Adv. MS	Advocates' MS (NLS).
APS	*The Acts of the Parliaments of Scotland*, 12 vols., eds. T. Thomson and C. Innes (Edinburgh, 1814–75).
Ayr Accounts	*Ayr Burgh Accounts, 1534–1624*, ed. G.S. Pryde (SHS, 1937).
Balfour, *Practicks*	Sir James Balfour of Pittendreich, *Practicks*, 2 vols., ed. P.G.B. McNeill (Stair Society, 1962–3).
Balfour, *Works*	Sir James Balfour of Denmilne, *Historical Works*, 4 vols., ed. J. Haig (Edinburgh, 1824–5).
Birrel, 'Diary'	Robert Birrel, 'Diary, 1532–1605', in J.G. Dalyell (ed.), *Fragments of Scottish History* (Edinburgh, 1798).
BL	British Library, London.
BUK	*Booke of the Universall Kirk: Acts and Proceedings of the General Assembly of the Kirk of Scotland*, 3 vols., ed. T. Thomson (Bannatyne Club, 1839–45).
Calderwood, *History*	David Calderwood, *History of the Kirk of Scotland*, 8 vols., eds. T. Thomson and D. Laing (Wodrow Society, 1842–9).
CBP	*Calendar of Letters and Papers Relating to the Affairs of the Borders of England and Scotland, 1560–1603*, 2 vols., ed. J. Bain (London, 1894–6).

Colville, *Letters*	*Letters of Mr John Colville, 1582–1603*, ed. D. Laing (Bannatyne Club, 1858).
Courcelles Despatches	*Extracts from the Despatches of M. Courcelles, 1586–1587*, ed. R. Bell (Bannatyne Club, 1828).
CSP Scot.	*Calendar of State papers relating to Scotland and Mary, Queen of Scots, 1547–1603*, 13 vols., eds. J. Bain *et al.* (Edinburgh, 1898–1969).
CSP Spain	*Calendar of State Papers, Spanish*, 13 vols., eds. G. Bergenroth *et al.* (London, 1862–1954).
CSPF Eliz.	*Calendar of State Papers, Foreign, Elizabeth*, 23 vols., eds. J. Stevenson *et al.* (1863–1950).
DNB	*Dictionary of National Biography* (1885–1985).
Eccles. Letters	*Original Letters Relating to the Ecclesiastical Affairs of Scotland, 1603–1625*, 2 vols., ed. D. Laing (Bannatyne Club, 1851).
Edin. Recs.	*Extracts From the Records of the Burgh of Edinburgh*, 13 vols., eds. J.D. Marwick *et al.* (Scottish Burgh Records Society and Edinburgh, 1869–1967).
Elizabeth and James Letters	*Letters of Queen Elizabeth and King James VI of Scotland*, ed. J. Bruce (Camden Society, 1849).
ER	*The Exchequer Rolls of Scotland*, 23 vols., eds. J. Stuart *et al.* (Edinburgh, 1878–).
EUL	Edinburgh University Library.
Fowler, *Works*	William Fowler, *Works*, 3 vols., ed. H.W. Meikle (STS, 1914–40).
Gordon, *Sutherland*	Sir Robert Gordon, *A Genealogical History of the Earldom of Sutherland* (London, 1813).
Hist. KJVI	*The Historie and Life of King James the Sext*, ed. T. Thomson (Bannatyne Club, 1825).
HMC	Historical Manuscripts Commission.
HMC, *Mar & Kellie*	HMC, *Report on the Manuscripts of the Earl of Mar and Kellie*, 2 vols., ed. H. Paton (London, 1904–30).
HMC, *Salisbury*	HMC, *Calendar of the Manuscripts of the Marquis of Salisbury*, 24 vols., eds. S.R. Bird *et al.* (London, 1883–1976).
HP	*Highland Papers*, 4 vols., ed. J.R.N. Macphail (SHS, 1914–34).
James VI, *Basilicon Doron*	James VI, *Basilicon Doron*, 2 vols., ed. J. Craigie (STS, 1944–50).
James VI, *Letters*	*Letters of King James VI and I*, ed. G.P.V. Akrigg (Berkeley, Calif., 1984).

James VI, *Poems*	*The Poems of James VI of Scotland*, 2 vols., ed. J. Craigie (STS, 1955–8).
James I, *Political Works*	James I, *Political Works*, ed. C.H. McIlwain (New York, 1918).
James VI, *Prose Works*	*Minor Prose Works of King James VI and I*, ed. J. Craigie (STS, 1982).
James VI and I, *Political Writings*	James VI & I, *Political Writings*, ed. J.P. Sommerville (Cambridge, 1994).
LP James VI	*Letters and State Papers during the Reign of King James VI*, ed. J. Maidment (Abbotsford Club, 1838).
Melros Papers	*State Papers and Miscellaneous Correspondence of Thomas, Earl of Melros*, 2 vols., ed. J. Maidment (Abbotsford Club, 1837).
Melville, *Diary*	James Melville, *Autobiography and Diary*, ed. R. Pitcairn (Wodrow Society, 1843).
Melville, *Memoirs*	Sir James Melville of Halhill, *Memoirs of his Own Life*, ed. T. Thomson (Bannatyne Club, 1827).
Montgomerie, *Poems*	*The Poems of Alexander Montgomerie*, 2 vols., eds. J. Cranstoun and G. Stevenson (STS, 1887–1910).
Moysie, *Memoirs*	David Moysie, *Memoirs of the Affairs of Scotland, 1577–1603*, ed. J. Dennistoun (Maitland Club, 1830).
MWA	*Accounts of the Masters of Works*, 2 vols., eds. H.M. Paton *et al.* (Edinburgh, 1957–).
NAS	National Archives of Scotland (formerly Scottish Record Office), Edinburgh.
NLS	National Library of Scotland, Edinburgh.
Pitcairn, *Trials*	*Criminal Trials in Scotland, 1488–1624*, 3 vols., ed. R. Pitcairn (Edinburgh, 1833).
PRO	Public Record Office, London.
PSAS	*Proceedings of the Society of Antiquaries of Scotland.*
RMS	*Registrum Magni Sigilli Regum Scotorum* (*Register of the Great Seal of Scotland*), 11 vols., eds. J.M. Thomson *et al.* (Edinburgh, 1882–).
Row, *History*	John Row, *History of the Kirk of Scotland from the Year 1558 to August 1637*, ed. D. Laing (Wodrow Society, 1842).
RPC	*Register of the Privy Council of Scotland*, 38 vols., eds. J.H. Burton *et al.* (Edinburgh, 1877–).
RSCHS	*Records of the Scottish Church History Society.*

Scot, *Apologetical Narration*	William Scot, *An Apologetical Narration of the State and Government of the Kirk of Scotland since the Reformation* (Wodrow Society, 1846).
Scots Peerage	*The Scots Peerage*, 9 vols., ed. J. Balfour Paul (Edinburgh, 1904–14).
SHR	*Scottish Historical Review.*
SHS	Scottish History Society.
Spalding Misc.	*Miscellany of the Spalding Club*, 5 vols. (Spalding Club, 1844–52).
Spottiswoode, *History*	John Spottiswoode, *History of the Church of Scotland*, 3 vols., eds. M. Russell and M. Napier (Spottiswoode Society, 1847–51).
STS	Scottish Text Society.
TA	*Accounts of the (Lord High) Treasurer of Scotland*, 13 vols., eds. T. Dickson *et al*. (Edinburgh, 1877–).
TGSI	*Transactions of the Gaelic Society of Inverness.*
Warrender Papers	*The Warrender Papers*, 2 vols., ed. A.I. Cameron (SHS, 1931–2).
Winwood, *Memorials*	*Memorials of Affairs of State .. collected (chiefly) from the original papers of Sir R. Winwood*, 3 vols., ed. E. Sawyer (London, 1725).
Wodrow Misc.	*Miscellany of the Wodrow Society* (1844).

~ 1 ~

James VI: Universal King?

Julian Goodare and Michael Lynch

In June 1580, the young King James, just turned fourteen, went on progress through Fife and Angus. It had been planned that he would visit the royal burgh of Aberdeen, but his itinerary was unexpectedly changed. The provost, bailies and whole council of the burgh, on hearing the news, frantically rode south, through the night, to intercept him at Dunnottar. He would, they hoped in a long and elegant speech, prove as beneficent a king as King Robert of blessed memory—Robert Bruce, who had made extensive grants to Aberdeen 250 years earlier.[1] One more story of Aberdonians on the make is not likely to change the course of Scottish history, but this episode does illustrate the expectations that were heaped upon the young king after the earl of Morton's eight frustrating years in power. Aberdeen had recently escaped a £20,000 fine for having supported the wrong side in the civil wars of 1568-73. Were these expectations of the young king unrealistic? In a sense, they were bound to be. When Morton's Douglas kin and clients were thrown off the gravy train, there would be a large number of vacancies, but not enough to satisfy the pent-up thirst for good government which had built up during the 1570s. Good government, both nobles and Aberdonians would agree, meant place and preferment.

In another sense, these expectations were quite realistic. James, at fourteen, might well have been expected to begin his personal rule. The young James IV, when he had succeeded in 1488, had been sixteen, as had James V in 1528, when he escaped from Falkland to act out the familiar script of a Stewart king in a hurry. But the tour of the north-east in June 1580 was not the first but the third entry of the young James VI into politics, and it would not be the last. James had taken over the nominal reins of government on 12 March 1578, when the regency had come to an end with Morton's resignation.[2] In another view, his public entry into politics had come in October 1579, with a formal state entry into Edinburgh.[3]

1 *RPC*, iii, 294-5.
2 J. Goodare, 'Scottish politics in the reign of James VI', Chapter 2 below.
3 M. Lynch, 'Court ceremony and ritual during the personal reign of James VI', Chapter 4 below.

It is, however, difficult to be categorical about when his minority ended and personal rule began. In the accounts of many textbooks, the king entered politics in November 1585, with the overthrow of the earl of Arran. The king's apprenticeship had been seriously interrupted by his ten-month captivity by the Ruthven regime, which began in August 1582. The court, which had bustled with activity since the king's departure from his schoolroom in Stirling Castle and his formal entry into the capital in the autumn of 1579, was reported to be 'very quiet and small' during the Ruthven period. Yet the early months of 1582, prior to the coup, had seen a sharp increase in the appearances of James at meetings of the privy council.[1] When James escaped from his captors in June 1583, one might have expected him to emulate his grandfather in 1528 by also seizing the reins of power. Indeed the proclamation issued at Perth shortly after James's dramatic escape insisted that, having attained his seventeenth year, he intended to assume personal control of government and to rule impartially over all 'his nobilitie and gude subjectis'.[2] There were few other signs, however, of a 'king in a hurry'. The bird which had flown from its cage, to use the poet-king's own metaphor, continued to spend more time on the pleasures of the court than the business of government. Perhaps his most significant achievement up to 1585, as Rod Lyall suggests, was his debut as an author, for in 1584 he had published a small quarto volume, *Essays of a Prentise in the Diuine Arte of Poesie*.[3]

It is surprising that the criteria which have so clinically been applied by late medieval historians to debate the success and failure of previous Stewart kings have generally evaded the early career of James VI. Why did it take so long for him to enter politics? By November 1585 he was almost twenty years of age. What effect did this late entry into the political arena—for even James III had embarked on his personal reign by the time he was eighteen—have on Scottish politics? And how far do these considerations square with James VI's reputation as an immensely successful king of Scots by the time he acceded to the English throne? By 1603, James had been over seventeen years in power. Should historians not be entitled to *expect* a large measure of order and stability after such a long period? The equivalent point in the reign of James IV is 1513, when after fifteen years in power (as Norman Macdougall has argued) he had fully restored the confidence of the nobility in the crown. By 1542, just fourteen years into his personal reign, James V, despite sharply rising expenditure, had raised crown finances to a state of health not enjoyed by James VI before the 1610s. James would, arguably, have been a

1 *CSP Scot.*, vi, 322, 474; *RPC*, iii, 453, 459, 466, 474 (Feb.-April 1582).
2 *Warrender Papers*, i, 157-8; *RPC*, iii, 585-6.
3 R.J. Lyall, 'James VI and the sixteenth-century cultural crisis', Chapter 3 below.

striking failure—of the dimensions of Robert II—if he had *not* managed by 1603 to restore the status of the crown.[1]

I

Reigns, like centuries, are capricious things for historians. Dealing as we do in periods of time, we cannot do without them, but they can obstruct our understanding of historical developments more detached from high politics. We assume, often rightly, that a monarch's personal views and attitudes will have a political impact, but does this always justify tearing off a fragment from history's seamless robe and treating it as a tidy, complete and homogeneous entity—a 'reign'?

This book deals with topics for which the concept of a reign is relevant, because the king was involved in them personally. Sometimes he occupies centre stage, as with the chapters on the writings of this most literary of kings (Rod Lyall, Grant Simpson, Jenny Wormald). Sometimes the focus is on his political relationships—with the earl of Huntly (Ruth Grant), with his queen (Maureen Meikle), with the more distant and powerful English queen (Julian Goodare), with the general assembly of the church (Alan MacDonald), or with regions of his kingdom (Michael Lynch, Sharon Adams). Sometimes he is one figure among many, as in the chapter on court architecture (Aonghus MacKechnie). Clearly there could be no court architecture without a court, and no court without a king, but the *central* characters in this chapter are the royal masters of works; one of them, Sir Robert Drummond of Carnock, drew up plans for a new west quarter at Stirling Castle, overlooking formal parks and gardens, in the unlikely circumstances of the last weeks of the Ruthven regime in 1583.[2] These and other chapters provide a number of ways of looking at James's long reign, but the one thing they do not show is a 'reign' that was a tidy, complete and homogeneous entity. Rather it was something multifarious and sometimes ambiguous. This ambiguity is particularly clear from his early career: when is a personal reign not a personal reign?

We can thus treat his early career, from 1578 to 1585 or even 1587, as a kind of apprenticeship. After the downfall of the earl of Arran in 1585 there was no single predominant figure in the government *apart* from the king, but that is no evidence in itself that James had grasped the helm of the ship of state. There are different ways by which this might be measured. It has been pointed out that James regularly attended meetings of his privy council over the course of his personal reign: he averaged twenty-two sederunts a year between 1585 and 1603.[3] Yet this

1 N. Macdougall, *James IV* (Edinburgh, 1989), 303-10; S. Boardman, *The Early Stewart Kings: Robert II and Robert III, 1371-1406* (East Linton, 1996), 61-2, 171-3; J. Cameron, *James V: the Personal Rule, 1528-1542* (East Linton, 1998), 255-62.

2 A. MacKechnie, James VI's architects and their architecture', Chapter 9 below; *MWA*, i, 310.

3 M. Lee, *Great Britain's Solomon: James VI and I in his Three Kingdoms* (Urbana, Ill., 1990),

conceals as much as it reveals. James did not pay the same attention to the detail of council business in the second half of the 1580s as he did in the mid- and later 1590s; between late 1585 and the autumn of 1592 he attended seventy out of 160 meetings of the privy council—an average of ten a year. But between 1592 and 1603 his attendance record improved almost threefold: he turned up on 314 occasions—some thirty per year.[1] A comparison has been drawn between the personal reigns of James and his mother, to the latter's detriment. Yet James's attendance in the early years of his personal reign was not appreciably greater than Mary's; hard work and personal commitment to the detail of the business of governing was auspicious only in the years after James's prolonged visit to Denmark in 1589-90. The real difference in the period up to 1589 was the vastly greater amount of business transacted by the privy council—as much as a thirty-fold increase—rather than the attendance of the king.[2]

Probably it was at the very end of 1586 that James began to take distinctly personal initiatives in politics, with the crisis caused by his mother's imminent execution. He had to decide in December whether to threaten to break the recently-concluded English league if Mary were put to death; the fateful decision not to do so was taken under all sorts of pressures, but it was in a real sense his own.[3] After the axe had fallen, his reproachful letter to Queen Elizabeth was, as Grant Simpson shows, very much his own work.[4] James struck a more positive note in the spring of 1587. In March, the king, accompanied by the earl of Angus, headed a judicial raid to the south-west to counteract the conspiracies of the Catholic Lord Maxwell since his mother's death.

Two months later, James personally stage-managed a 'love-feast' for his feuding nobles in the streets of Edinburgh—later remembered as 'the gratest worke, and happiest game that the king had played in all his rainge heithertills'.[5] After what must have been an acrimonious convention of estates, he made feuding nobles walk hand in hand up the High Street of Edinburgh as a symbol of their reconciliation. It was the sixteenth-century equivalent of the political photo opportunity, and was reported as a 'triwmph' as far away as Easter Ross.[6] The love-feast forecast the end of noble feuding but did it signify King James's peace? In one sense, it did. The king had already acted promptly and firmly to quash a Maxwell rebellion in the south-west and would do so again in

137. Cf. J. Wormald, *Mary, Queen of Scots: a Study in Failure* (London, 1988), 117.

1 *RPC*, iv, p. xxviii; v, p. xx; vi, pp. xxi, xxxii; Wormald, *Mary*, 117.

2 Wormald, *Mary*, 117, 118.

3 R.S. Rait and A.I. Cameron (eds.), *King James's Secret: Negotiations between Elizabeth and James VI relating to the Execution of Mary, Queen of Scots* (London, 1927), 95-7, 101-2, 116-17.

4 G.G. Simpson, 'The personal letters of James VI', Chapter 8 below. For some of the pressures on him, see J. Goodare, 'James VI's English subsidy', Chapter 6 below.

5 Balfour, *Works*, i, 384-5; Calderwood, *History*, iv, 613-14. 'Heithertills' = hitherto.

6 *The Calendar of Fearn: Text and Additions, 1471-1667*, ed. R.J. Adam (SHS, 1991), 140.

1588.[1] When the north-eastern Catholic earls rose in rebellion in 1589, the king led an army to Aberdeenshire, forcing them to surrender at the Bridge of Dee. For contemporaries, it must have enhanced the image (however implausible with hindsight) of James as a warrior king.[2] Much of this, of course, reflected a king who was ever conscious of image and publicity. Yet his actions between late 1586 and 1589 placed James more clearly than before above the family-based factions that had dominated so much of his minority, and helped to make him what he had sought to become on his escape from the Ruthven Raiders in 1583—a 'universal king'.[3]

II

The balance sheet of success and failure during the personal reign has yet to be fully compiled. There are a surprisingly large number of black holes in it, in which even the basic configurations of politics remain unclear, and perhaps the largest of these is that between 1603 and 1625.[4] Two early examples of such holes are 1580-2 and 1582-3, when closer scrutiny begins to cast doubt on received notions of politics. The leading figure at court between early 1580 and August 1582 was the king's cousin Esmé Stewart, a convert from Catholicism; it was during the Esmé Stewart period that parliament set up a commission (1581) to improve ministers' stipends—a harbinger of the augmentation commissions of the 1590s and later—and it was in this period that the first covenant was subscribed, on its knees, by the whole court.[5] Yet the Esmé Stewart regime went down in the later, presbyterian canon of history as hostile to the kirk. It was replaced in August 1582 by the Ruthven regime, in a coup hailed by the general assembly as an 'act of reformation', yet that regime—which, as Gordon Donaldson pointed out, had a remarkable number of trimmers, timeservers and even ex-Marians within it—did little if anything for the kirk.[6]

Still, the Ruthven lords would have been unlikely to do what their successor, the earl of Arran, did in 1584 when he had parliament pass the confrontational 'Black Acts' against the 'new erected societie of ministers'—the thirteen model presbyteries set up by the general assembly in 1581.[7] This soon led to a crisis, not with the parliament itself or the formal, legal protests made by some ministers at the time, but in its

1 J. Goodare and M. Lynch, 'The Scottish state and its borderlands, 1567-1625', Chapter 11 below.
2 R. Grant, 'The Brig o' Dee affair, the sixth earl of Huntly and the politics of the Counter Reformation', Chapter 5 below.
3 *CSP Scot.*, vi, 523; cf. *RPC*, iii, 585-6.
4 With the exception of the pioneering work of M. Lee, *Government by Pen: Scotland under James VI and I* (Urbana, Ill., 1980).
5 Lynch, 'Court ceremony and ritual', Chapter 4 below.
6 G. Donaldson, *All the Queen's Men: Power and Politics in Mary Stewart's Scotland* (London, 1983), 140-4.
7 *Hist. KJVI*, 186-7.

aftermath—the enforced 'subscription' by individual clergy of a letter composed by Archbishop Adamson condemning the radical ministers who fled into exile in England. The exiles were few, about a score in all, encompassing university masters and students as well as ministers and generally drawn from Fife and Lothian; the protesters against subscription were many but, despite intellectual manoeuvrings such as agreeing to the Black Acts only in so far as they were 'agreeable to God's Word', the episode clearly demonstrated who had the whip hand in a crisis between church and state. The crown, it needs to be remembered, was the paymaster. For most clergy, and especially those north of the Tay, outside the hot-house areas of radical presbyterian strength, fear of loss of stipends was enough. For the more resolute who were called before the privy council, the threat of imprisonment or banishment to the 'dark corners of the land', such as Aberdeenshire or Inverness-shire, usually sufficed.[1] The experience of 1584-5 presaged the pressure which the crown would bring to bear on general assemblies in the period after 1606; and it also presaged the splits within the clergy which would afflict the church as a result.

The next generally acknowledged step in the history of James VI's relations with the church was the so-called 'Golden Act' of 1592, which granted presbyterianism a legal basis but also asserted the right of crown and parliament to intervene in the affairs of the church, as it had done in 1584-5; as time would show, the right extended to calling of meetings of general assemblies. Too much of the agenda for this part of the reign, however, is still dictated by the massive but highly selective compilations of the presbyterian party in the church—notably the extended party pamphlets of David Calderwood and James Melville—which might best be summed up as '1596 and all that'.[2] The issues here need to be separated out. Although it has been argued that James did not turn to the device of bishops to control the kirk until he was stripped of all other options—in 1600 rather than 1596 or 1597,[3] there is contemporary evidence, from as early as 1593, that James had already set his sights on restoring bishops.[4] Indeed, James had first tried (unsuccessfully) to persuade a leading churchman (Robert Pont) to become a bishop in

1 A.R. MacDonald, 'The subscription crisis and church-state relations, 1584-1586', *RSCHS*, xxv (1994); A.R. MacDonald, *The Jacobean Kirk, 1567-1625: Sovereignty, Polity and Liturgy* (Aldershot, 1998), 26-9; G. Donaldson, 'Scottish presbyterian exiles in England, 1584-8', RSCHS, xiv (1962); Calderwood, *History*, iv, 209-11; Melville, *Diary*, 200-18; *Spalding Misc.*, iv, 69-72; *Wodrow Misc.*, i, 413-37, 441.

2 Calderwood was in Edinburgh for much of the 1590s and after, until he finally took up his appointment as minister of Crailing, in Peebles presbytery, in 1601; thus his accounts partly reflect direct experience: A.R. MacDonald, 'David Calderwood: the not so hidden years, 1590-1604', *SHR*, lxxiv (1995).

3 M. Lee, 'James VI and the revival of episcopacy in Scotland, 1596-1600', *Church History*, xliii (1974).

4 D. Mullan, *Episcopacy in Scotland: the History of an Idea, 1560-1638* (Edinburgh, 1986), 87-91.

1587.[1] On the other hand, the notion, cultivated by successive generations of presbyterian historians since Calderwood, that the kirk was wrenched from its perfected status by damaging royal interference which began in 1596 has already been seriously questioned and no longer bears detailed scrutiny.[2] The 'Golden Act' of 1592 is another example of such a half-remembered history.

There can be little doubt, however, that the riot of 17 December 1596 did mark a turning-point in the relationship between king and church. For James, who had in 1590 tried to have the church agree to restrict itself to private rather than public criticism of the court or himself, the riot confirmed his existing suspicions of the subversive potential within presbyterianism and accelerated his self-appointed role as a new godly Constantine, presiding with a heavy hand over the kirk. The prominent ministers, who had been becoming uneasy since about 1592 about their increasingly difficult relationship with their godly prince, were suddenly confronted with a dilemma. Those who held to their principles, insisting on a strict separation of the 'two kingdoms', would increasingly find themselves labelled as subversives. Those who tried to adapt to the new, harder-line royal initiatives, which included active 'management' of general assemblies, would find themselves being dragged further into compromise than they could have imagined in 1597. They would also be vilified as trimmers by their radical colleagues. It is argued by Alan MacDonald that outright breakdown in this increasingly strained set of relationships did not come until after 1602 but was clearly visible by 1606, by which time no general assembly had met for four years.[3]

It is possible to mount a limited defence of James's religious policies. In 1590, immediately after his return from Denmark with his new bride, James addressed the general assembly, promising to give his full support to the 'sincerest church' in the world, weed out papistry and give the ministers a pay rise. The assembly erupted into fifteen minutes of rapturous applause. Despite generations of history thirled to the notion of a divide between the 'two kingdoms' of church and state, in practice the kirk was never so united as when it felt able to act in concert with the crown in pushing forward the goal of a godly society, particularly in the areas of clerical stipends, ecclesiastical discipline, provision for basic education and the pursuit of papistry—or so it must have seemed to most contemporaries up to about 1602. For the strength of the radical presbyterian element within the kirk ebbed and flowed, not least because it was divided within itself on major questions. On the issue of

1 *BUK*, ii, 696, 698.

2 Mullan, *Episcopacy*, 79-80; M. Lynch, 'Preaching to the converted? Perspectives on the Scottish Reformation', in A.A. MacDonald *et al.* (eds.), *The Renaissance in Scotland* (Leiden, 1994).

3 A.R. MacDonald, 'James VI and the general assembly', Chapter 10 below.

representation in parliament, there were sharp disputes; even Andrew Melville and his nephew James disagreed.[1] Such internal wranglings help explain why James was able to achieve—or to get away with—so much so long. Yet James, too, missed an opportunity. As is argued elsewhere in this volume, he achieved a working compromise with his fractious nobility in and after 1598.[2] There was no such compromise with the church. Here, as Alan MacDonald emphasises, James insisted that he wielded both swords, civil and ecclesiastical. It was an interpretation of the two kingdoms which was as radical and uncompromising as that of his most vocal critics within the ministry. It ultimately had the effect of creating a culture of opposition to the crown, intimately linked with a complex of Protestant fears. By the late 1610s and 1620s this operated on a number of different levels—including the threat posed to international Calvinism by a European war of religion as well as a suspected hidden, ecclesiastical agenda within James's notion of Great Britain.[3]

Amidst such complexities, it is tempting to turn to clashes of personality to shed light on them. The sound bite that most remember is the confrontation at Falkland in August 1596, when Andrew Melville tugged the king's sleeve to remind him that he was but 'God's sillie vassal'. A 'no surrender' view of the history of the kirk would later be built upon the phrase. But the real circumstances are forgotten. Andrew Melville broke in on a meeting the king was having with a group of leading ministers, the latest in a series of informal gatherings which had begun in 1594. These meetings would, James hoped, form the basis for an ecclesiastical council, which might act as a counter-balance to the 'privy conference' in which leading radicals had arranged the business of the general assembly since the late 1570s. Melville burst in so dramatically because he had not been invited.

The real Andrew Melville, one of the most shadowy figures in James's reign, has still to be fully identified—the defender of the integrity of the kirk; the Latin court poet of the 1590s writing sonnets to the king, plus 200 verses which he delivered at Queen Anna's coronation in 1590;[4] or the beleaguered rector of the university of St Andrews, armed with a white spear (his staff of office), besieged in his lair in St Mary's College in 1588, 1590 and 1593 by rival academics, students, lairds and the local crowd.[5] It is well known that St Andrews often does not like its principals

1 Lynch, 'Preaching to the converted?', 314-19.

2 Goodare, 'Scottish politics', Chapter 2 below.

3 J. Morrill, 'A British patriarchy? Ecclesiastical imperialism under the early Stuarts', in A. Fletcher and P. Roberts (eds.), *Religion, Culture and Society in Early Modern Britain* (Cambridge, 1994).

4 *Stephanisticon. Ad Scotiae Regum, habitum in Coronatione Reginae*, in P. Walker (ed.), *Documents relative to the Reception at Edinburgh of the Kings and Queens of Scotland, 1561-1650* (Edinburgh, 1822).

5 T. McCrie, *Andrew Melville* (Edinburgh, 1899), 154-5, 436-7.

but Melville took unpopularity to new depths. His own presbytery of St Andrews survived intact only by the device of creating a new body, at Cupar, as a refuge for his opponents. The standard Melvillian vote in the general assembly numbered little more than fifty-five.[1] As well as the systematic pressure exerted on general assemblies by James VI and his ministers, it is possible to argue that 'Melvillianism' collapsed in the first decade of the seventeenth century because of a failure of leadership—of Melville himself. The intransigence of the king was matched by Melville's high-profile and often histrionic stance. Both positions—of a king persuaded of his godliness and a preacher convinced of his own righteousness—were, ultimately, counter-productive. The result, visible by 1606, was a serious (and perhaps avoidable) fissure between the state and a significant part of the church. The presbyterian movement's recovery in the 1610s and 1620s was built on two sets of foundations—a mythology of loss and exile and the determined posture adopted by James himself.

III

Too many accounts of the reign have accepted—or reacted against—the view that 1596 saw the onset of hostilities between church and state, to the point where the struggle between the 'two kingdoms' has coloured almost all else. What should be the real agenda for the history of the 1590s? One item on it would be royal finance. In January 1596 the king had appointed the Octavians, eight exchequer commissioners, to reform his finances. The Edinburgh riot in December 1596 (when they were denounced as crypto-Catholics) and manoeuvres by courtiers (who disliked their cuts in royal spending) forced them to offer their resignation in January 1597. This may have been politically prudent, but it was financially disastrous. James's final years in Scotland degenerated into an embarrassing struggle to make ends meet, with court ceremony pruned drastically.[2] If finance were added to the criteria for assessing James's reign, would judgements of him be so favourable?[3]

It could well be argued that James blundered from one economic crisis to another, although rising exports were slowly leading the Scottish economy out of recession.[4] In 1582, his government privatised the collection of customs, handing the task over to the convention of royal burghs. The experiment was abandoned in 1587. Yet by then, burghs had been forced to resort to novel forms of direct taxation to compensate for a shortfall in revenue from customs. In Edinburgh, moneylenders and

1 Lynch, 'Preaching to the converted?', 315.

2 Lynch, 'Court ceremony and ritual', Chapter 4 below.

3 Finance has been a standard measure of Scottish kingship in other reigns: G. Donaldson, *Scotland: James V—James VII* (Edinburgh, 1965), 43-4, 56-8; Cameron, *James V*, 255-62, for James V; M. Lynch (ed.), *Mary Stewart: Queen in Three Kingdoms* (Oxford, 1988), 10-11.

4 P.G.B. McNeill and H.L. MacQueen (eds.), *Atlas of Scottish History to 1707* (Edinburgh, 1996), 241, 250-60.

younger sons of merchants were brought into the tax net for the first time, and craftsmen, now assessed individually rather than corporately, paid more. This widening of taxation continued for the rest of the reign. The government also turned—despite the warnings from history of the notorious 'black money' of James III and the unpopularity of Morton's profiteering from the mint in the late 1570s—to wholesale debasement of the coinage in 1583; by 1596 this had brought in some £100,000 worth of profits. It resorted to massive taxation in the 1590s, on a scale which far exceeded that of James V, despite warnings from that reign and the regency of Mary of Guise, heavily underlined by George Buchanan in his *History* published in 1582, about the political effects of high taxation.[1] So prices rose ever more steeply and the exchange rate tumbled, as a direct result of debasement of the coinage.[2] Thomas Craig, writing around 1603, warned that high taxation often led to rebellion. He cited the Dutch revolt, but he may have intended his message to apply closer to home.[3]

The political crisis of the reign may have been over by the end of 1594,[4] but the economic and fiscal crisis intensified throughout the 1590s. James's own finances were shored up by a humiliating English subsidy.[5] The nobility learned to accept an ever more demanding taxation system, as long as its effects were offset by patronage. Yet patronage required attendance at court. As a result, the 1590s were years when new figures began to haunt Scottish politics—the tax collector, credit broker[6] and political lobbyist.[7] We seem in the personal reign of James VI to be caught halfway—between traditional institutions of government and novel habits of governing.

Many of the black holes in our knowledge of the reign have been filled by black and white interpretations. These include the periods 1585-9 and

1 M. Lynch, 'Whatever happened to the medieval burgh?', *Scottish Economic and Social History*, iv (1984); J. Goodare, 'Parliamentary taxation in Scotland, 1560-1603', *SHR*, lxviii (1989); George Buchanan, *The History of Scotland*, ed. J. Aikman (Edinburgh, 1830), ii, 330-2.

2 In 1581, after the debasements by Morton, the silver content of the coinage stood at a quarter of what it had been in 1500; by 1601, it had fallen to a fifth. J.M. Gilbert, 'The usual money of Scotland and exchange rates against foreign coin', in D.M. Metcalf (ed.), *Coinage in Medieval Scotland, 1100-1600* (British Archaeological Reports, British series, xlv, Oxford, 1977), 141-53; A.J.S. Gibson and T.C. Smout, *Prices, Food and Wages in Scotland, 1550-1780* (Cambridge, 1995), 5-7.

3 Thomas Craig of Riccarton, *Jus Feudale*, 2 vols., ed. J.A. Clyde (Edinburgh, 1934), I.16.16.

4 K.M. Brown, 'In search of the godly magistrate in Reformation Scotland', *Journal of Ecclesiastical History*, xl (1989), 579.

5 Goodare, 'James VI's English subsidy', Chapter 6 below.

6 K.M. Brown, 'Noble indebtedness in Scotland between the Reformation and the Revolution', *Historical Research*, lxii (1989); J. Goodare, 'Thomas Foulis and the Scottish fiscal crisis of the 1590s', in W.M. Ormrod *et al.* (eds.), *Crises, Revolutions and Self-Sustained Growth: Essays in Fiscal History, 1130-1830* (Stamford, 1999, forthcoming).

7 M. Lynch, 'The crown and the burghs, 1500-1625', in M. Lynch (ed.), *The Early Modern Town in Scotland* (London, 1987), 73-5.

1593-6, which, in one view, represent the rise and reconfiguration of a Stewart absolutism that was initially master-minded by John Maitland of Thirlestane, James's influential chancellor from 1587. According to it, the 'eclipse' of Maitland, who became a 'political liability' in 1592, meant that it was the king who inherited his chancellor's 'system'.[1] Yet the very unpopularity of Maitland by 1592 made it unlikely that he would hand on an untainted inheritance. For much of the 1590s it is difficult to work on the premise that a single personality, even that of James VI, 'managed' politics. This was a period when each of the king's 'two bodies'—court and government—was taking on a multiple and often self-contradictory personality. These are years where it is still often difficult to describe how politics worked, what the balance between church and state was, or how much the king himself was at the controlling centre of politics. The standard measurements of late medieval kingship no longer give satisfactory answers. It is rather like leafing through the pages of *Basilicon Doron*; the impression that one gets on one page is confounded on the next. The adage of medieval historians that '*laissez-faire* monarchy' entails a king who regulates rather than rules no longer seems enough. Are there times in these periods when there is a king in office but not in power? Scottish society was in these years caught up in an erratic, bewildering process of change, made more difficult to comprehend because it was cast against the backcloth of a very real social crisis that deepened as the 1590s went on.

By the last decades of the sixteenth century, '*laissez-faire* monarchy' is no longer an appropriate term. It was coined to describe the political practice of the earlier Stewart kings: a combination of goodwill towards co-operative leading nobles, intense personal ferocity towards noble dissidence, and genial indifference to most of what the nobles got up to in their own localities.[2] A small indication of the breakdown of the model comes in the fact that James VI did not spend his time travelling round his kingdom in the manner of all his Stewart predecessors except James III. That king, who had shut himself away in Edinburgh, had suffered politically as a result. As late as the 1560s, Mary had virtually governed from the saddle, as she worked hard to make personal contact with local magnates from Inverness to Inveraray and Whithorn. But James VI did not need to; when in the saddle, he was not working but enjoying himself hunting. By 1591 he had already denuded the royal forests around Falkland of deer.[3] He governed less in person, and more through institutions. Through these institutions, the localities came to him, or (both before and after 1603) to his privy council in Edinburgh. They included,

1 M. Lee, *John Maitland of Thirlestane and the Foundation of the Stewart Despotism in Scotland* (Princeton, NJ, 1959); also his *Great Britain's Solomon*, 68, 70-1, 77, 105.

2 J. Wormald, *Court, Kirk and Community: Scotland, 1470-1625* (London, 1981), 9-20.

3 Lynch, 'Court ceremony and ritual', Chapter 4 below.

by 1610, both disaffected Border families[1] and previously troublesome Highland chiefs.[2]

As they did so, they produced a more active central government. James's parliaments passed far more legislation than ever before. The business of his privy council—a body that had not even existed before 1545—expanded hugely in the 1580s and 1590s. The college of justice, founded in 1532, likewise had more to do, and its judges were more involved in government. Lobbying judges or law officers became regular by the 1580s.[3] The permanent exchequer, a creation of the 1580s and 1590s, reorganised the royal finances. Justice ayres, however, which had brought criminal justice to the localities, died away, to be replaced by *ad hoc* commissions of justiciary, in which a journey to Edinburgh was necessary for each trial. As for the most crucial component of '*laissez-faire* monarchy'—an absence of taxation—it disappeared in the 1580s and 1590s, as taxes rocketed. The reign of James VI is decisively marked off from those of his predecessors by the growth of the state.

James was not indifferent to the localities; quite the reverse. But the policies of his government were recasting the relationship between them and the centre. James wanted to revoke, or at least undermine, the heritable jurisdictions that underpinned nobles' local power. He had lairds admitted to parliament in 1587 to inform him of local grievances. His preferred approach to the feuds of the nobility was not to aid those nobles who were his friends in their private wars, but to stamp out feuding altogether.

This brings us to the question of noble dissidence. The model of '*laissez-faire* monarchy' is one in which the crown faced occasional local revolts by dissatisfied magnates, but was usually able to crack down successfully, with the help of other magnates—thus showing that there was no conflict between crown and the nobles as a class. This pattern, common in the fifteenth century, was repeated as late as 1562 when the fourth earl of Huntly rebelled and was defeated at Corrichie. Only three years later, his son was restored to the earldom.

The political turbulence of the years 1578-85 largely follows this traditional model, but once James was no longer a child to be used as a political football, it ceased. The two prominent noble dissidents of the 1590s were Francis, fifth earl of Bothwell, and George, sixth earl of Huntly.[4] Bothwell, a Stewart in pursuit of what he probably saw as his

1 Goodare and Lynch, 'Borderlands', Chapter 11 below.

2 M. Lynch, 'James VI and the "Highland problem"', Chapter 12 below.

3 R.V. Agnew (ed.), *Correspondence of Sir Patrick Waus*, 2 vols. (Ayrshire and Galloway Archaeological Association, 1887), ii, 365-6, 476-7.

4 On Bothwell's career, see E.J. Cowan, 'The darker vision of the Scottish Renaissance: the Devil and Francis Stewart', in I.B. Cowan and D. Shaw (eds.), *The Renaissance and Reformation in Scotland* (Edinburgh, 1983); R.G. Macpherson, 'Francis Stewart, 5th Earl Bothwell, c.1562-1612: Lordship and Politics in Jacobean Scotland' (University of

rightful place in the sun, tried nostalgically to recreate the tradition of noble autonomy that had led to the hanging of James III's advisers by the nobles at Lauder in 1482. It is conventional to suggest that the king was stronger after 1603 because he could no longer be kidnapped. But the futility of kidnapping an adult monarch was proved by Bothwell as early as 1593: having got James in his power, he had to let him go again. After a disruptive but ultimately futile career as an outlaw, Bothwell was finally exiled in 1595.

Huntly's career as a dissident also fails to fit the traditional pattern. Both he and James, as Ruth Grant emphasises, often took up ambiguous stances.[1] Although a traditional magnate (and one of much greater power than Bothwell), Huntly was also right up to date in his political practice, for his international scheming resembled the populist machinations of the contemporary Catholic League in France—machinations that would soon lead to such a conspicuous noble reaction against the League and in favour of Henry IV. Catholicism was no longer a popular cause in Scotland outside Huntly's native north-east, but there we find him using the latest propaganda techniques in 1596 to bid for support for an anti-English policy.[2] However, Huntly too failed, and owed his survival less to his own power than to James's need to stand well with English Catholics in order to bolster his hopes of the succession to Elizabeth. Although James was indulgent of Huntly's Catholicism, for he was married to a close kinswoman of the king, his court was often as critical of Huntly as the general assembly was.[3]

Perhaps we should conclude that the much-criticised suggestion that James VI was 'the last and greatest exponent of the old style of Scottish kingship'[4] never rested on much more solid evidence than his personal friendship with Huntly. A different perspective on James's relations with the nobility is suggested by the career of another of his personal friends: John, second earl of Mar ('Jock o' the Slates'), with whom the king had been educated at Stirling. Mar was ruthlessly assertive in his youth, taking part in both the Ruthven Raid (1582) and the abortive Stirling Raid (1584). But although his reputation as a severe Protestant was as durable as Huntly's as a Catholic, Mar thereafter kept away from subversion, and in 1594 received the ultimate accolade of the king's trust:

Edinburgh Ph.D. thesis, 1998). On Huntly, see Grant, 'Brig o' Dee affair', Chapter 5 below.

1 Grant, 'Brig o' Dee affair', Chapter 5 below.

2 James Hudson to Anthony Bacon, 8 Nov. 1596, T. Birch, *Memorials of the Reign of Queen Elizabeth From the Year 1581 Until Her Death*, 2 vols. (London, 1754), ii, 196. See also Goodare, 'James VI's English subsidy', Chapter 6 below.

3 John Burel's play, *Pamphilus* (1590-1), contained lines with an obvious target in Huntly: 'Or can we call thame christians richt/ That seis the glorious glancing licht/ Syne to the mirke reteirs?'

4 J.M. Brown, 'Scottish politics, 1567-1625', in A.G.R. Smith (ed.), *The Reign of James VI and I* (London, 1973), 39.

the custody of the infant Prince Henry. As Maureen Meikle shows, Mar retained the prince even though the queen threw such political weight as she possessed behind every effort to shake his grip.[1] He was a union commissioner in 1604, although the Scottish parliament's trust in him was apparently less than the king's.[2] He was even prepared to become a bureaucrat, holding the post of treasurer from 1616 to 1630. Mar was not always happy at the direction of royal policy—he opposed the Act anent Feuding that curtailed private violence in 1598—but he knew how to obey. In him, unlike Huntly, we see a man who was a crown servant first and a regional magnate second.

IV

The royal court has been little considered in terms of its role in politics or of the relationship between the king's two 'bodies'—his household or chamber and his council. Courtly culture, by contrast, has received much attention. The monuments to history left by the work of the Castalian Band, with the young king cast as Apollo, patron of the arts, are well known.[3] Equally familiar, but only recently analysed, are the châteaux of the Scottish Renaissance, which demonstrate what is often difficult to prove by other means—both the 'trickle-down' effect of court style and the role of nobles, old and new, as cultural patrons. Formal dining rooms and elaborate gardens, as Aonghus MacKechnie shows, both testify to the spread of the cult of honour.[4]

Interpretations of the culture of the court often rest on received notions of how it operated as a political instrument. The internal dynamics of a volatile and highly competitive political forum, however, remain to be closely analysed. That culture, focused on recently elevated peers or members of the royal household as well as those who claimed to be the 'ancient blude' of the nobility, was more demanding of kingship and less tolerant of deviation from the norms of aristocratic courtliness. The stigmatisation of the Highlands as a barbarian culture has a provenance which goes back at least to the 1520s, and the work of John Mair, if not before.[5] It was a commonplace by the 1590s, when James VI wrote his well-known passage in *Basilicon Doron* about the lack of 'civilitie' of the Highlands and the Isles. The Edinburgh poet and dramatist, John Burel, in his *Passage of the Pilgremes* (1590-1), dedicated to the second duke of Lennox, depicted a Calvinist Pilgrim forced to wander among barbarous cannibals, who did not know God and whose behaviour, as a result,

1 M.M. Meikle, 'A meddlesome princess: Anna of Denmark and Scottish court politics, 1589-1603', Chapter 7 below.

2 *Calendar of State Papers ... in the Archives and Collections of Venice*, 38 vols., eds. R. Brown *et al.* (London, 1864-1940), x, 155.

3 Lyall, 'Cultural crisis', Chapter 3 below.

4 MacKechnie, 'James VI's architects', Chapter 9 below.

5 A.H. Williamson, 'Scots, Indians and empire: the Scottish politics of civilization, 1519-1609', *Past and Present*, 150 (Feb. 1996).

could partly be excused by 'blindness and ignorance'.[1] By contrast, the better-known jibe often ascribed, perhaps loosely, to the court poet, Alexander Montgomerie—'How the first Helandman of God was maid / Of ane horss turd, in Argyll, as is said'—may not be quite what it seems.[2] The meaning, or potential double meaning, depends on the unresolved date of its composition; it may have been directed specifically at the Campbells, with their characteristic dual pose as royal courtiers and west Highland patronage barons. During much of James's reign there was either a minor as head of the house of Argyll, or suspicion at court of Campbell aggrandizement.[3] The poet may have been satirising this, rather than Highland society as a whole.

The years that followed the king's second entry into politics in 1579 have acquired the reputation of a confused jumble of noble rivalries. They should also be seen as marking a serious attempt to establish a court and royal household, which had far-reaching implications for the future. A good deal of the cult of kingship which marked the 1590s can already be detected, especially in the eighteen months immediately following Morton's fall in December 1580. Montgomerie, in his poem *The Navigatioun*, not only hailed 'so sapient a ying and godly king', but a 'Solomon' who was 'the chosen vessel of the Lord'.[4] Here was Montgomerie, at an early stage in both the personal reign and his own career, bidding for the status of 'moral authority for the Scottish reader'.[5] Much of the familiar imagery from later in the reign first emerged at the entry of 1579.

The new royal court quickly proved to be outrageously expensive, enforcing a resort both to 'benevolences' and to higher levels of taxation.[6] Early in 1582, when wine suppliers to the royal household threatened to withhold supply because of unpaid bills, an official raid on the warehouses of merchants in east coast burghs was sanctioned; payment was promised, twelve months in arrears.[7] The setting up of the royal guard, even after it was halved in size in June 1581, was another sign of the times. By April 1582, most of its members were still unpaid, £2,000 being outstanding, and it took two further years of hapless trawling around

1 J. Reid Baxter, 'Poetry, politics and passion in the circle of James VI', in S. Mapstone and A.A. MacDonald (eds.), *A Palace in the Wild: Essays on Renaissance, Humanism and Vernacular Culture in Late Medieval and Early Modern Scotland* (forthcoming, 1999). We are grateful to Dr Baxter for a sight of this in advance of publication.

2 Montgomerie, *Poems*, i, 280-1.

3 E.J. Cowan, 'Clanship, kinship and the Campbell acquisition of Islay', *SHR*, lviii (1979); Lynch, 'James VI and the "Highland problem"', Chapter 12 below.

4 Montgomerie, *Poems*, i, no. XLVIII, ll.78-9, 82.

5 D. Parkinson, 'Authorship and Alexander Montgomerie', the introduction to *The Poems of Alexander Montgomerie*, 2 vols. (STS, forthcoming). We are grateful to Professor Parkinson for access to this work before its publication.

6 Goodare, 'Parliamentary taxation', 23, 49.

7 *RPC*, iii, 451-3.

the entrails of the king's finances to find satisfaction. An attempted permanent settlement of 1584 was never fully implemented. Between 1586 and 1590, most of the guard's funding may have come from the English subsidy.[1]

The hunt for payment became a familiar task for the king's servants as well as his creditors. Mounting debts and the unbridled expenditure of the new court produced a deficit of £45,000 by the spring of 1582, when the treasurer and the collector general of the thirds of benefices, in a desperate attempt to bridge the gap between expenditure and income, had their debts suspended. There were many motives involved in the Ruthven Raid in August 1582, when a group of the king's councillors seized the young king. They claimed to be acting in the same spirit as the Lords of the Congregation who had first pushed through the Reformation in 1559-60. And it has been argued that there are parallels between the Ruthven Raid and the Riccio murder of 1566: both were Protestant, Douglas-inspired protests against undesirable influences on the monarch.[2] Exasperation with a profligate royal household should be added to the manifold motives of the raiders. They included two key financial officials—the earl of Gowrie, treasurer, and Adam Erskine, commendator of Cambuskenneth, collector general of thirds.[3] There is another parallel here: with the Octavians' attempt, in 1596, to restrain the unbridled spending of king and household. For their pains, they were branded as papist conspirators. The point is that the Ruthven episode, like the Riccio murder and indeed the Octavians, concerned many issues besides religion. The Ruthven administration attempted to tighten up procedures in exchequer and council to control household expenditure. That effort barely survived its fall in June 1583.[4] By the 1590s, the royal household far exceeded that in previous reigns.

There were other pointers to the future shape of court politics. The unstable Lennox-Arran coalition had split by the end of 1581 into two factions, with different sections of the privy council meeting separately, at Holyrood and Dalkeith. The motives were mixed, the position complex and the split was patched up quickly, when Arran agreed to demit office as captain of the royal guard.[5] One of the key issues was access to the king, making this dispute a forerunner of the much more extensive

1 *RPC*, iii, 393, 465-6, 480, 686-7, 697, 708-9, 743-4; iv, 134; *APS*, iii, 298-9; K.M. Brown, *Bloodfeud in Scotland, 1573-1625* (Edinburgh, 1986), 126; Goodare, 'James VI's English subsidy', Chapter 6 below.

2 Donaldson, *Queen's Men*, 142-3.

3 *RPC*, iii, 340, 390, 458, 466; Donaldson, *Queen's Men*, 143-5. One of the purposes of a tax of £20,000 in Apr. 1583 was repayment of the crown's debts to Gowrie, and £100,000 was originally mooted: *APS*, iii, 328-30; *CSP Scot.*, vi, 398-9, 404-5.

4 *RPC*, iii, 562, 564, 626-7.

5 *RPC*, iii, pp. xxxiv, 431, 433, 435-6; Calderwood, *History*, iii, 593-4; viii, 212-14; Spottiswoode, *History*, ii, 315.

divide between chamber and council which would mark Maitland's years in power (1585-95). The king's relationship with Arran was never as close as that with Lennox. In a sense, the arrangement was a simple one: Lennox controlled the household whereas Arran's main sphere of influence was in the privy council. There were already in 1581-2 hints of a clash of cultures—of chamber and council. In October 1581, there was a violent dispute between Arran and Sir John Seton, who had recently been appointed master of horse, over precedence in the riding of parliament. Precedence would prove to be one of the most frequent sources of friction in James's reign—an inevitable reflection of the inflation of honours and the obsession of nobles, old and new, with status. Seton's office guaranteed riding at the king's left hand on state occasions, with the chamberlain (Lennox) on the king's right.[1] For Lennox and Seton, both with experience of other Renaissance courts, the issue was one of protocol; for Arran, a recently ennobled upstart, it was one of power. A further pointer to Arran's weakness came during the split at the end of 1581: Lennox was at Dalkeith with the king whereas Arran remained at Holyrood, closeted with future Ruthven conspirators.[2] Scottish kingship still remained intensely personal, but the nature of access to the king was changing, and disputes over access would dog the years until 1603.

Impressions of the years between 1585 and the arrival and coronation of James's queen, Anna of Denmark, in May 1590 are curiously mixed. It is a period conventionally seen in terms of the 'reassertion of kingship', one of warmer relations between the crown and the kirk, and the golden age of the Castalian Band. There is, at best, only a measure of truth in each of these generalisations. In 1585 James had promised a restoration of the old ways, with proper place being given to the 'old blood' of the nobility,[3] but there was recurrent discontent amongst his nobles. Rumours of changes at court reached a climax with the king's return from Denmark in 1590. A series of initiatives—involving the royal household, patronage and the general assembly—were taken shortly after the coronation and formal entry of Anna, in May. His intervention in the affairs of the church, it now seems clear, can be traced to this period—although many of the ministers found the prospect more palatable than they did later.[4] And James himself, 'prince of poets', was by 1588, as both Rod Lyall and Jenny Wormald emphasise, already shaping a new career in prose, with a particular focus in theology, demonology and political theory; it was in this year that he wrote his first biblical commentary, on Revelation.[5]

1 Calderwood, *History*, iii, 592; *Hist. KJVI*, 185-6. Cf. Brown, *Bloodfeud*, 114.
2 *RPC*, iii, 431, 433, 435-6.
3 *CSP Scot.*, viii, 161, 156, 160.
4 MacDonald, 'General assembly', Chapter 10 below.
5 Lyall, 'Cultural crisis', Chapter 3 below; J. Wormald, 'Tis true I am a cradle king: the view from the throne', Chapter 14 below.

If much of this suggests an accessible king, court ceremony indicates new refinements. From 1585, the 'riding' of parliament—its opening and closing procession—was increasingly formalised, culminating in the 'red' parliament of 1606. In 1587, parliament passed an act insisting that those who took part in the riding should do so 'on horseback decently with foot mantles'; new colours were assigned to each of the estates. The Honours of Scotland—the crown, sceptre and sword of state—were borne in the procession by the leading figures in the king's household and council, to signify the union of the king's 'two bodies'. At the end of the 1587 parliament, according to a French observer, all the nobility present knelt before the king, who had just reached his 'perfect age' of twenty-one, in an act of ritual obedience, followed by the other estates in turn.[1] A Scottish version of the devil of keeping state was emerging.[2]

This inflation of honours gathered pace, especially after 1598, which can be pinpointed as the vital turning-point for the king's relations with his nobles, when the signal was given that previous restrictions on patronage would be lifted.[3] It came during the crown's own period of financial crisis and retrenchment. In total, James created two dukes, two marquises, twenty-seven earls, six viscounts and twenty-nine lords during his reign; it was just as well that peerage titles were cheap. One effect of this new stress on ceremony was a vogue for family histories and elaborate armorials, such as the Seton Armorial of 1591 and Lindsay Secundus of *c.*1598, for both new and old nobility.[4] Another consequence was frequent disputes over precedence, protocol and access. Keeping state, however, was as much a part of this paradoxical personal reign as personal kingship. The mistake is to imagine that it was missing because it did not follow English practice.[5] New, formal images were being created for James and his nobles to set them apart, both from each other and from the other estates. Protocol was putting Renaissance-style kingship and aristocracy on pedestals. In turn, in their redesigned tower houses, nobles were distancing themselves from tenants and lesser kin;

1 *APS*, iii, 443; Moysie, *Memoirs*, 63-4; R.S. Rait, *The Parliaments of Scotland* (Glasgow, 1924), 529-31; C. Burnett, 'The Officers of Arms and Heraldic Art under King James VI and I, 1567-1625' (University of Edinburgh M.Litt. thesis, 1992), 23-4; *Courcelles Despatches*, 75-6; *RPC*, vi, 170-1.

2 Cf. D. Stevenson, 'The English devil of keeping state: élite manners and the downfall of Charles I in Scotland', in R. Mason and N. Macdougall (eds.), *People and Power in Scotland* (Edinburgh, 1992).

3 Goodare, 'Scottish politics', Chapter 2 below; see also J. Goodare, 'The nobility and the absolutist state in Scotland, 1584-1638', *History*, lxxviii (1993), 167, 169-70.

4 Burnett, 'Officers of Arms', 24, 28.

5 The question of increasing formality should be separated from that of access: see N. Cuddy, 'The revival of the entourage: the bedchamber of James I, 1603-1625', in D. Starkey (ed.), *The English Court: from the Wars of the Roses to the Civil War* (London, 1987), 178-80, who argues that the 'English court was designed for the preservation and manipulation of distance; the Scots for the management of relatively free and open access', in the French style.

formal galleries were built to display family memorabilia and mock battlements constructed, not for defence but as viewing terraces over their landed possessions.[1]

In the memoirs of a long-serving courtier, Sir James Melville of Halhill, there appears the fullest interpretation of the events of the personal reign in terms of the workings of the court. For Melville, much of the period between the king's return from Denmark in 1590 and the death of Chancellor Maitland in 1595 could be explained as a conflict between council and chamber.[2] Maitland's plans to run council and chamber through the exchequer fell foul of the king's cautious desire to have an all-inclusive council, which in turn alarmed his own chamber.[3] The Danish expedition and subsequent coronation brought to a head a number of issues here. As a result, the early 1590s saw a clash of expectations between the king and his nobles. They expected 'their auncient priveledges for their free accesse to the king's person', but the throng of suitors regularly induced the king to restrict access to his chamber and to limit the noble retinues at court. Such restrictions, even though they were mostly ineffectual, heightened the anxieties of the established nobility and frustrated the desire for status or display felt among others recently promoted in royal service. The scheme for a new royal guard in 1590 and the plans to limit earls and lords to six retainers and barons to a mere four in particular provoked fury amongst prominent courtiers; Bothwell, a kinsman ever conscious of his rights as a Stewart, and Lord Hamilton, James's potential successor until the birth of Prince Henry in 1594, took great offence when denied entry to the king's chamber. Hamilton spluttered angrily that 'this newe order wold offende all men'.[4] James and his privy council, on the other hand, became increasingly exasperated by the reluctance of such nobles to attend meetings of either parliament or privy council with any regularity. One solution to this dilemma was the quick fix of conventions, sub-parliamentary meetings consisting largely of the nobility and dealing with specific issues of vital concern to them as well as to the king's government; they were common in the 1590s, as never before or after.[5] The result was that governmental initiative lurched from one institution to another in this period.

Such was the prolixity of the royal propaganda machine that there are many images of James VI with which to conjure. Poets, dramatists,

1 D. Howard, *Scottish Architecture: Reformation to Restoration, 1560-1660* (Edinburgh, 1995), 51, 55, 83-4.

2 Melville, *Memoirs*, 375-6. The dispatches of the English correspondents, Robert Bowes, Roger Ashton and James Hudson, show the same preoccupation.

3 Melville, *Memoirs*, 372; *CSP Scot.*, x, 303, 306, 371, 416.

4 Melville, *Memoirs*, 373; *CSP Scot.*, x, 285, 297; *RPC*, vi, 207-8; Goodare, 'Nobility and the absolutist state', 166; Lynch, 'Court ceremony and ritual', Chapter 4 below.

5 Goodare, 'Nobility and the absolutist state', 167.

intellectuals and polemicists vied to capture the essence of the 'universal king' that James sought to be. The biblical images of the king, as young David and wise Solomon, were established early—in the royal entry of 1579.[1] They were enduring. A frieze depicting the judgement of Solomon can still be seen in Culross Palace, a laird entrepreneur's house built sometime between 1597 and 1611. More significantly, as Aonghus MacKechnie reveals, the building of a new Chapel Royal at Stirling, first used for the baptism of the king's first-born son and heir in 1594, provided an opportunity, on an unrivalled scale, to celebrate in stone 'Great Britain's Solomon'. Replete with Biblical and classical imagery, the chapel, he argues, was constructed to the same proportions as Solomon's Temple.[2] And it was here in 1594, set high on a hill above both the burgh and the surrounding landscape, that James, in his new Jerusalem, paraded as a Knight of Malta in the tournament which preceded the royal baptism—a surrogate St George, fit to cast out the infidel.[3] The conceit was both elaborate and breathtaking. Its impact, however, was probably greater on James himself than on the audience. His claims to divine right kingship, itemised in *The Trew Law of Free Monarchies* (1598), were already on display in symbolic form.

The image of a just king would not in itself induce the nobles to submit their rivalries and disputes to royal justice. The incidence of feuds showed little sign of slackening in the late 1580s, and that between Huntly and the 'bonnie earl' of Moray (1589-92) sometimes threatened to escalate into a full-scale civil war.[4] Part of the problem lay in the age structure of the greater nobility, teeming with hot-headed youths: in 1592, eight of the twenty-four earls were under twenty-one years of age and a further seven were under thirty-five.[5] The unburied corpses of Moray and the equally hotheaded Lord Maxwell (killed in battle with the Johnstones in December 1593), preserved for years by their families demanding royal justice against the killers, were awkward for a king who cultivated a reputation for justice.[6] The seriousness of the crisis which confronted James in the early 1590s should not be underestimated. This may have been the one point in Scottish history before the mid-1640s when a war of religion threatened. Yet James survived, and the scope of his government markedly increased during this same decade.

A number of the letters edited by Grant Simpson illustrate the achievements of a 'universal king'; some may also detect in them a fussy,

1 Lynch, 'Court ceremony and ritual', Chapter 4 below.
2 MacKechnie, 'James VI's architects', Chapter 9 below.
3 Lynch, 'Court ceremony and ritual', Chapter 4 below.
4 Brown, *Bloodfeud*, ch. 6.
5 Colville, *Letters*, 333-43.
6 Cf. G. Donaldson, 'James VI and vanishing frontiers', in G. Menzies (ed.), *The Scottish Nation* (London, 1972), 112-14.

intrusive personality.[1] With other images, however, there is less room for doubt. James certainly cultivated a style of monarchy that went beyond the personal kingship familiar in earlier Stewart reigns. For centuries, kings of Scots had been patrons of the church as well as exploiters of it; James aspired to be its 'nursing-father', a role that was more personal, less rapacious but also more proprietorial than that of his Stewart predecessors. He also cultivated an image of imperial monarchy which went considerably beyond the aspirations of kings of Scots since James III had affected the closed imperial crown on his coinage. James VI was just as keen on such traditional imagery, and after 1590, he could emulate his grandfather by having a real lion in residence.[2] James V had also cultivated the image of Hercules, with both club and lion.[3] But James VI had a more efficient stick with which to beat—or, more often, to prod—dissident nobles, unruly borderers and allegedly barbarous Highland chiefs. It was the state. Beyond the imagery—of the Christian emperor, Constantine, as well as Solomon—there lies a key point. The formation of the Scottish state belongs to the personal reign of James VI. It would be tested, and generally found to work, after 1603, when James became an absentee monarch.

V

James's Scottish reign after 1603 is conventionally described as a period of 'government by pen', picking up a phrase he used in 1607. This tends to give the impression that what is meant is the new system of royal government by correspondence from Westminster, rather than government by the king in person.[4] What James actually said—in a speech to the English parliament in praise of Scotland—was:

> This I must say for Scotland, and I may trewly vaunt it: here I sit and governe it with my pen, I write and it is done, and by a clearke of the councell I governe Scotland now, which others could not doe by the sword.[5]

1 Simpson, 'Personal letters', Chapter 8 below.

2 The lion was a gift from the king of Denmark, who had in turn been given it by the king of Poland, at the time of the marriage in 1590, although it probably did not arrive until *c.*1593. It was presumably the redundant lion of the baptismal banquet of 1594; it was not used lest it frighten the ladies of the court. In Aug. 1596 its keeper, William Freliche, who claimed not to have been paid during his three-year stay, petitioned for leave to return to Germany. W.D. Macray, 'Second report on the Royal Archives of Denmark, and Report on the Royal Library at Copenhagen', *46th Report of the Deputy Keeper of the Public Records* (London, 1886), app. II, no. 1, 35; J. Fergusson, *The White Hind and Other Discoveries* (London, 1963), 88-9; NAS, treasury precepts and receipts, E23/7/16. We are grateful to Dr Athol Murray for the latter reference.

3 H.M. Shire, 'The king in his house: three architectural artefacts belonging to the reign of James V', in J.H. Williams (ed.), *Stewart Style, 1513-1542: Essays on the Court of James V* (East Linton, 1996), 89-91, 95-6.

4 Lee, *Government by Pen*, pp. viii-ix and *passim*; R. Mitchison, *Lordship to Patronage: Scotland, 1603-1745* (London, 1983), ch. 1: 'Government by the king's pen'.

5 James VI & I, speech in parliament, 1607, in *Political Writings*, 173.

James, in his chosen role of peacemaker, was thus 'vaunting' that he had made the pen mightier than the sword. He was not referring to government *at a distance*, but government *by a bureaucracy*. And the work of creating this bureaucracy was done just as much before 1603 as after it. When James went south in 1603, he left behind a fully-functional government that did not need a king's daily attention to keep it running smoothly. The localities had already established links with his government in Edinburgh; these links continued and were strengthened. Only rarely did they come into direct contact with Westminster. The date 1603 is a useful dividing-line for some things, but it should not be used indiscriminately.

One of the reasons to be sceptical about 1603 as a turning-point is that James had been positioning himself as a future king of Britain even before then. Partly this was the inevitable consequence of his position as ruler of an English satellite state: he had to defer to Elizabeth's wishes, and ensure that Scottish domestic and foreign policies fitted with English interests.[1] But James did not just drift in Elizabeth's wake; while in Scotland, he deliberately shaped his course to converge with England, with an eye on the future. He included advice on ruling multiple kingdoms in *Basilicon Doron* (1598).[2] More tellingly, he was already grappling with English political theory, and developing his views of the English constitution. He argued that monarchs both in Scotland and in England owed their powers not to the people, but to a divinely-sanctioned right of conquest.[3] This helped to justify a common approach to ruling both kingdoms. While the union of crowns took place only in 1603, James for a long time before had been doing his best to act as if it was in force.

One difference that 1603 *did* make was in the field of state finance. James lived well beyond his means in the 1590s. Inflation eroded his traditional revenues, and his expenditure escalated with the need to impress both his own nobility and the English political establishment. The result was a series of desperate expedients, most notoriously the bankruptcy engineered for him in January 1598 by exploiting the goldsmith and financier Thomas Foulis. This left Foulis with unpaid debts of £160,522, and a worthless IOU from the crown.[4] There were also swarms of small debts, like the 2,000 merks James borrowed from the burgh of Aberdeen in 1589. James had been in Aberdeen with an army at the time, having just suppressed a rebellion raised by the earl of Huntly—always

1 Cf. Goodare, 'James VI's English subsidy', chapter 6 below.

2 James VI, *Basilicon Doron*, in *Political Writings*, 31-2.

3 R.A. Mason, 'James VI, George Buchanan, and *The True Lawe of Free Monarchies*', in his *Kingship and the Commonweal: Political Thought in Renaissance and Reformation Scotland* (East Linton, 1998), 230.

4 Goodare, 'Thomas Foulis'.

an expensive business.[1] At Chancellor Maitland's suggestion, the earl of Angus was persuaded to borrow 2,000 merks from the burgh on the king's behalf. Evidently the earl had a better credit rating than the king. However, the king's use of intermediaries like Angus or Foulis, together with his political power, enabled him to shelter from his creditors with impunity. The burgh spent the next twenty-three years trying to sue Angus and his heirs for repayment. As the king eventually admitted, 'they wer by severall warrantis under our hand and signet, inhibited and dischairged the prosequutioun of the same, under the payne of horneing, wee acknowledging by these warrantis the debt to be properlie dew by us ... and that therefore we oureselfis wold give order for satisfactioun thereof'. The 'order for satisfactioun' was finally issued in 1612. The court of session apparently ruled that the king and not Angus was the true debtor.[2]

Twenty-three years of unpaid debts seems a dismal return for the high expectations that Aberdeen had had of the young king in 1580. However, the point is that James did eventually pay his debts, or at least quite a few of them, once the cost of the court had been removed from the Scottish treasury. Many even of Foulis's creditors received payment during the years when James held court in England. This new-found fiscal stability was more important than 'absentee kingship' in changing the nature of politics after 1603.

Much is sometimes made of the idea of the royal court as a point of contact between governor and governed. It is possible to overlook the suggestion made below by Sharon Adams—that the localities were the primary places for such contact.[3] 'Localities' were no different from the 'centre' with which they are sometimes contrasted; all physical places, even Edinburgh, were localities. Rural localities were largely governed by nobles and lairds who were also the local landlords; towns were governed by burgh councils. Nobles and lairds had to have connections at the centre—the royal court and privy council, which were institutions rather than physical places. Some nobles and lairds were courtiers and councillors in their own right, while those who were not had links through family or clientage with those who were.

1 For the rebellion, see Grant, 'Brig o' Dee affair', Chapter 5 below.

2 W. Fraser, *The Douglas Book*, 4 vols. (Edinburgh, 1885), i, 374; iv, 375-6; 'Extracts from the accounts of the burgh of Aberdeen', *Spalding Club Miscellany*, v (1852), 116, 136; NLS, council to James, 31 Mar. 1612, Denmylne MSS, Adv. MS 33.1.1, vol. iv, no. 3; Aberdeen City Archives, William Kennedy's 'Alphabetical index to the first 67 volumes of the council register of the city of Aberdeen, 1398-1800', vol. i, p. 16. This loan was probably additional to the loan of £4,533 from Angus recorded in the comptroller's accounts in 1588-9: *ER*, xxii, 29.

3 S. Adams, 'James VI and the politics of south-west Scotland, 1603-1625', Chapter 13 below.

Centralisation, therefore, was not a process that took place at the centre—at least not if the 'centre' is thought of as being Edinburgh. Rather it was a process of reorientation of ruling elites all over the country. The nobility in particular were both 'central' *and* 'local'; they formed the link between central and local power. If they observed central standards, like current royal policy or statute law, in their own local courts, we can call this centralisation. If they did not, and this led to friction, this may appear as conflict between 'centre' and 'localities'—but such conflict only ever occurred with *some* localities. The concept of '*the* localities' is a treacherous one.

This subject is best pursued through an actual example. In Ayr, at the time when James VI and I was making his 'government by pen' speech, how did people experience being governed? Towns like Ayr were intensively governed by burgh councils composed largely of merchant oligarchies. Traditionally they were self-contained; but Ayr was now experiencing central government in a number of ways. One way was through the church. James VI's government was reimposing bishops on the Scottish church after two decades of presbyterianism—and radical presbyterians in Ayr were organizing resistance. The burgh's minister, John Welsh, a son-in-law of John Knox, was removed and exiled in 1606 in connection with this, but retained the support of the burgh council for some years; the council itself was purged by the crown in 1611.[1]

The state had military and administrative power that was more in evidence than before. In the summer of 1608, Ayr became the base for a military expedition to the Isles; the burgh council entertained the commanders and troops, while the burgesses had their ships requisitioned and their provisions subjected to compulsory purchase.[2] As for administration, 'government by pen' increasingly involved the courts and the legal profession. Compared with fifty years previously, the Ayr council's legal costs had increased about tenfold in real terms.[3] Still, central government also offered benefits. When plague broke out in the town in 1606, the magistrates received authority from the privy council to enforce quarantine regulations. In the aftermath of the 1608 expedition to the Isles, Ayr also tried to cash in on its strategic location, lobbying the privy council for a subsidy for harbour repairs. Unfortunately this failed, and the burgh had to pay.[4]

As well as the concept of 'centre and locality', it is worth noting the related concept of 'centre and periphery'.[5] The latter could be characterised as one in which the localities (or places) that were firmly

1 Adams, 'James VI and south-west Scotland', Chapter 13 below.
2 *RPC*, viii, 106, 521; *Ayr Accounts*, 236.
3 *Ayr Accounts*, 128, 235-7.
4 *RPC*, vii, 248; viii, 246-7, 255-6; *Ayr Accounts*, 240, 243-4.
5 Cf. Goodare and Lynch, 'Borderlands', Chapter 11 below.

connected to the centre are contrasted with the localities (or places) that were not prepared to acknowledge central authority. To a 'universal king' like James, the existence of such peripheries was intolerable and he determined to bring the outlying regions of his realm within his power. He may have preferred the power of the pen to that of the sword, but peripheries like the Western Isles tended to experience the sharp end of kingship.

Policies for the Isles always had a British context, because of the proximity of the southern Scottish islands to Ulster. This British context was not just '1603 and all that'; Scottish and English policies had already converged in the 1590s.[1] This was no doubt why, in early 1605, it must have seemed that the moment had come for a fully-integrated British effort to subdue the Isles. A proclamation was drafted in January:

> Finding in the North and West Iles of the North Iles [sic] of Britayne and the contynent next adjacent thereunto, although no rebellion, yet the inhabitants thereof neyther living under the feare of God in sincerity of religion, nor yealding to us those rentes and commodityes which were in auncient tymes a greate parte of the patrimonie of our croune of Scotland: and the fertility of these Iles and commodity of fishing which the greate oceane yealdes in those partes alluterlie neglected and left to be enjoyed by straungers, to the greate hurte of so many people within our dominions which might be sett a-worke there and have large boundes to dwell in, no less profitable then any parte of the continent which is civillie possessed.

The thought of these potential riches in the hands of uncivilised clansmen, continued the proclamation, had inspired the king to 'roote out of them all kind of barbarity'. All chiefs were to be summoned to produce their written titles to their land, to find surety for obedience to the law, and to pay royal rents. Those who failed to comply could expect 'the force of our wrath and discontentment, to the utter extermination of them and their posterity out of our dominions and nothing but merciles fyre and sworde'. The surviving copy of this draft has contemporary annotations listing proposed commissioners for the Isles. Four 'Englis commissioneris' were listed, including Sir Wilfred Lawson and Edward Gray of Morpeth, who at the same time were appointed to a joint Anglo-Scottish Border commission under the great seals of England and Scotland.[2] James apparently intended to give Englishmen responsibility for subduing the Isles, presumably feeling that the Scottish authorities could not achieve this on their own.

In the event, the proclamation was never issued. There was an expedition to the Isles in June, but it was a purely Scottish affair.[3] English involvement returned in a different form after 1607, when the flight of

1 Lynch, 'James VI and the "Highland problem"', Chapter 12 below.

2 NAS, 'Ane proclamatioun concerning the ylis of Scotland', 12 Jan. 1605, GD149/265, part 3, fos. 52r.-53v. For the Border commission see *RPC*, viii, 706-7.

3 *RPC*, vii, 59-60.

the earls of Tyrone and Tyrconnell from Ulster removed the pressure on the English garrisons there. They thus became available for military action in the Isles; the result was Lord Ochiltree's expedition of 1608, with support from English ships. Still, the expedition itself was under Scottish control.[1] Nor was the military traffic in one direction only. Shortly before Ochiltree's expedition, there had already been a Scottish force sent to Ulster in June 1608 to help suppress the uprising of Sir Cahir O'Dogherty there.[2]

Another remote region, Orkney and Shetland, experienced further aspects of government by pen. Unlike the Western Isles, the Northern Isles were not viewed with hostility by the Scottish establishment—they lacked the military power to rival the state. However, they were at first too remote for full integration into the Scottish polity, and retained their own Norse laws for a century and a half after they were first transferred from the Danish crown to Scotland (1468-9). Indeed, when the earldom of Orkney and lordship of Shetland were annexed to the crown in 1472, it had been enacted that they might form an apanage for a younger son of the king. In the later 1560s a private-enterprise apanage had been carved out by Robert Stewart, an illegitimate son of James V, who eventually became earl of Orkney.[3] Robert's son Patrick, the second earl, tried to consolidate his domains, but his grandiose and incompetent local despotism was no match for the state's increasing sophistication. He lost favour at court in the 1590s by associating with Queen Anna's intrigues against the earl of Mar. Enmeshed in debt and lawsuits, harassed by local opponents, Patrick found himself imprisoned for contempt of court in 1609. Goaded into promoting a rebellion, he was executed in 1615.[4]

One of the criticisms of the view of James as an old-style king is that it paid less attention to the period after 1603.[5] In the later part of his reign, James became even less conciliatory. After the destruction of the wayward earl of Orkney, James kept the rich earldom in crown hands and used the lease of Orkney as patronage—preferring to offer it to someone with 'noe relatione to onye great man'.[6] Patrick's brother and heir, though loyal, was fobbed off with a pension. And yet even this kind of aggression against traditional structures of local authority can be

1 J. Goodare, 'The Statutes of Iona in context', *SHR*, lxxvii (1998).

2 M. Perceval-Maxwell, *The Scottish Migration to Ulster in the Reign of James I* (London, 1973), 78-9. In the event the force was not needed, and was diverted to support Ochiltree.

3 *APS*, ii, 102; P.D. Anderson, *Robert Stewart, Earl of Orkney, Lord of Shetland, 1533-1593* (Edinburgh, 1982), ch. 5 and *passim*.

4 P.D. Anderson, *Black Patie: the Life and Times of Patrick Stewart, Earl of Orkney, Lord of Shetland* (Edinburgh, 1992), 24-5, 77-93. For the difficulties of Anna's supporters, see Meikle, 'Meddlesome princess', Chapter 7 below.

5 M. Lee, 'James VI and the aristocracy', *Scotia*, i (1977), 21.

6 Earl of Kellie to Mar, 22 Nov. 1621, HMC, *Mar & Kellie*, ii, 109-10. The lease usually brought the crown £25,000 per year: NAS, comptroller's accounts, 1619-20, E24/56.

paralleled in the 1590s, with the attempt to colonise the Isle of Lewis by the Fife Adventurers. There were also thoughts in 1598 of a parallel colony, by Lothian landowners, in Skye.[1]

The downfall of a regional magnate, not through bloodfeud but through indebtedness, was something new. It would soon be repeated, with the enforced exile of the earl of Caithness in 1623.[2] This was a period in which the ability to put cash on the table was beginning to count for more in politics than the capacity to resort to violence. Political violence was becoming a state monopoly.

Meanwhile, the state's administrative requirements were growing—even in its most remote regions. The machinery enforcing its orders mostly consisted of regular institutions, but there were also *ad hoc* commissioners for various purposes. In the case of Orkney, the initial campaign to collect the disgraced earl's rents for the crown in 1613 entailed the making of 2,400 copies of the official order and a nine-month tour of the islands by a sheriff depute.[3] Such commissions were usually obtained at the royal court through a system of aristocratic clientage which was characteristic of the early modern absolutist state.[4] The opening up of the Northern Isles to royal authority offered a fresh and enticing field to the projector; James Alexander obtained a patent concerning the islands in 1617. He may have been related to the courtier-poet Sir William Alexander of Menstrie, who had recently become master of requests. The patent empowered Alexander to enforce a new administrative order in the islands, and to collect the fines from offenders. This was an order obliging the inhabitants to clip their sheep rather than pulling the wool from them ('rooing'), as rooing was held to be cruel to the sheep. This is another illustration of the establishment's view of the islanders as ignorant yokels, who were somehow different from the menacing savages found in the *Gaidhealtachd*. The islanders complained that rooing was not cruel and was more effective for their breed of sheep; the patent, and the order against rooing, were cancelled in 1619.[5]

The authority of the state was now being exercised more actively over the church—much to the anger of those who objected to the episcopalian programme of the years after 1596. There had always been much *local* co-operation between religious and civil authorities, but disagreements were highlighted when people could not agree about the nature of authority. This is often discussed in terms of the 'two kingdoms' theory of religious authority—the separation (or alleged separation) of church and state. However, the theory was not just about this, but also about

1 Lynch, 'James VI and the "Highland problem"', Chapter 12 below.

2 Goodare and Lynch, 'Borderlands', Chapter 11 below.

3 Anderson, *Black Patie*, 100.

4 J. Goodare, *State and Society in Early Modern Scotland* (Oxford, 1999), ch. 3.

5 *RPC*, xii, 111-12. On rooing, which continued into the twentieth century, see A. Fenton, *The Northern Isles: Orkney and Shetland* (Edinburgh, 1978), 456-8.

the overall nature of authority. It was agreed that all authority was ultimately divine. The point at dispute was whether terrestrial authority *descended* from the king to the people or *ascended* from the people who conferred legitimacy on the king. The descending theory, in the form of the divine right of kings, was one of King James's favourite topics. The ascending theory, favoured by many of his opponents, could operate through either or both of two representative bodies: the general assembly of the church, or parliament. In the case of the former, it was facilitated by the commission of the general assembly, which until 1597 had been one of the main channels for conveying the kirk's opposition to royal policy. After 1597, however, James began to use it to convey *his* wishes to the kirk.[1] Increasingly, leading presbyterians appealed to parliamentary statutes. In 1606, for example, John Forbes listed:

> in the 1st parliament [of James VI], acts 1, 2, 3, 4, 5, 6, wherin at length is contained the substance of doctrine, and description of the trew kirk; in the 2d parl. act 2; and in the 3d parl. act 46, 47; in the 5th parl. act 1; in the 6th parl. act 1, 2; in the 7th parl. act 1; in the 11th parl. act 2; in the 12th parl. act 1; in the 13th parl. act 2; in the 14th parl. act 2; in the 15th parl. act 1.[2]

Silently omitted from this impressive-looking list were the Black Acts of 1584. It is true that some—those promoting episcopacy—had been repealed in 1592; but one of the most important—that establishing royal authority over the church—was still very much in force. Still, although Forbes objected to royal authority over the church, he clearly had no problem with *parliamentary* authority over the church. Possibly statutes always had a higher authority even than acts of the general assembly, even for devotees of the 'two kingdoms' theory. Whether or not he believed in two separate kingdoms, Forbes certainly believed in authority that arose from the people. But he was not in power: James's bishops were.

This is why James might be also credited with two achievements which are, on the face of it, unlikely. It was not the radical presbyterians who first went out to confront papistry in the dark corners of the land, the north-east and south-west; it was his bishops. They included William Cowper, bishop of Galloway, who claimed to have planted ministers and kirks when he took over the diocese in 1612; John Spottiswoode, archbishop of Glasgow, who conducted a visitation of the wilds of Annandale in 1609; Andrew Knox, bishop of the Isles, who constructed a Protestant agenda for the Highland chiefs in the form of the so-called Statutes of Iona in 1609; and Patrick Forbes, bishop of Aberdeen from 1618 to 1635, who confronted the Catholic threat head-on and pushed

1 MacDonald, 'General assembly', Chapter 10 below.

2 John Forbes, *Certaine Records Touching the Estate of the Church of Scotland*, ed. D. Laing (Wodrow Society, 1846), 346-7.

through a thorough reform of King's College, Aberdeen.[1] This concerted episcopal programme did not come from high-flying Anglican bishops. Most of them had in their younger years been radicals, and often pupils of Andrew Melville. They deserve a better press.[2]

What of the parish ministers themselves? Since 1560 the kirk had had to struggle ineffectively with inadequate stipends. The First Book of Discipline was acknowledged by the general assembly to be out of date by 1563. In 1578, the Second Book of Discipline, sometimes described as a comprehensive programme of church government,[3] shut its eyes to the problem of finance. The only solution, as the Melvillians knew but did not want to admit, lay with the state. James promised a solution in 1590, which explained his standing ovation. It was not achieved overnight and indeed, in 1590, could not have been. It took over forty years to implement fully, and was not complete by 1625. Yet James eventually kept his promise. The parliamentary augmentation commissioners in 1617-18, in particular, did more to raise the status of the parish ministry than all the posturings, protest votes and taking of notarial instruments by Melvillians. The result by the 1630s was not only an educated ministry but a reasonably well-paid one.[4] It would take a well-paid ministry to revolt against James's son in 1638.

'Government by pen' also meant correspondence, and this complemented public pronouncements as an area for royal image-making. The privy council wrote to James in 1611:

> Quhen we remark this ever-running current of your majesteis bountifull munificence to this haill kingdome, we hald ourselffis happilie born in this aige, whenas the regiment of this impyre [i.e. ruling of this realm] is managed be your excellent majestie, the lyvelie architip of all princelie graceis and accomplissit perfectionis, raising up such onlie to markis of hyest honnour, alsweele in the generall serviceis of the weele publict as in the advancement to privat credite about your majesteis sacred persone, in whome the caracteir of vertew hes maid most vive impressioun. In regaird whairof this commounwelth, being bot one body, participating of lyffe and lustre derivat frome your majestie, the sole head and essence of the same, and thairfra conveyed to all the memberis thairof, bot in more peculiar maner to this House and Colledge of Justice, whairof your sacred self is the fader and fortres, the florrisheing whairof is inseparablie tyed with most strait linkis to the weele of this kingdome ...[5]

1 Mullan, *Episcopacy*, 125, 136; Goodare and Lynch, 'Borderlands', Chapter 11 below; Lynch, 'James VI and the "Highland problem"', Chapter 12 below; D. Stevenson, *King's College, Aberdeen, 1560-1641* (Aberdeen, 1990), 61-93.

2 J. Wormald, 'No bishop, no king: the Scottish Jacobean episcopate, 1600-1625', *Bibliothèque de la Revue d'Histoire Ecclésiastique: Miscellanea Historiae Ecclesiasticae*, viii (1987).

3 *The Second Book of Discipline*, ed. J. Kirk (Edinburgh, 1980), 57.

4 W.R. Foster, *The Church before the Covenants, 1596-1638* (Edinburgh, 1975), 161-4; W.H. Makey, *The Church of the Covenant, 1637-1651: Revolution and Social Change in Scotland* (Edinburgh, 1979), 109-12.

5 Privy council to James, 24 Jan. 1611, *RPC*, ix, 593.

They certainly wrote elaborate thank-you letters in those days. This one was to thank James for nominating a judge to the court of session—a matter that one might have thought routine. But James's right to nominate the judges was not normally an absolute right of appointment, since his candidate had to be examined and confirmed by the existing judges.[1] An absolute king, who could override the due procedures, had to be thanked for following them.

James's own letters were often direct and to the point, though his later prose tended towards rambling prolixity.[2] The council's letter was evidently not written with concision in mind, but neither was it diffuse. It began with the kingdom as a whole, and then moved to the specifics of the court of session ('this House and Colledge of Justice'), outlining the king's relationship to both. A detailed exegesis of all its metaphors is impossible here, but elision of state and society is detectable in the presentation of the king as 'sole head and essence' of the commonwealth. Yet a distinction was also drawn between the 'weele publict' and 'privat credite about your majesteis sacred persone'. The whole luxuriant growth was watered by the 'ever-running current' of the king's 'bountifull munificence'—which implied a need to maximise the taxes and other revenues from which the bounty flowed.

So letters like this had a broad purpose, beyond the immediate business with which they dealt. They established standards for political discourse. Absolute monarchy was lubricated every time some institution (like the court of session) acknowledged the king as its 'fader and fortres' in the course of its routine business. By contrast, anyone who failed to echo this note could be marked as politically suspect. From this point of view, the council's letter was addressed less to the king himself than to his other ministers and courtiers—anyone around him who might read it, in fact. Even a 'universal king' could not deal personally with all his official correspondence. Still, James must have read at least some of the unctuous verbiage that came his way, and its effect on him should be pondered. It is said that flattery is all right, provided you don't inhale. James's abilities were considerable, but he surely did often inhale. This may even help to explain some of the insensitivities and miscalculations of his later years.[3]

Political discourse also provides a final window through which to view, not just James's reign, but the issue of what his 'reign' means. If the vocabulary of government was fashioned at the royal court, then the king himself could set the tone for it, as he did for the court as a whole. James advised his son to 'make all your reformations to beginne at your

1 R.K. Hannay, *The College of Justice* (1933: repr. Stair Society, 1990), 117-28.
2 Simpson, 'Personal letters', Chapter 8 below; Wormald, 'Cradle king', Chapter 14 below.
3 Goodare, 'Scottish politics', Chapter 2 below; Wormald, 'Cradle king', Chapter 14 below.

elbow, and so by degrees to flow to the extremities of the land'.[1] Not just 'reformations', but also degeneration, could arise in this way—as the later, scandal-ridden years of James's court showed only too clearly.[2] Charles did much to set a new moral standard at his court, but he did nothing to change the sycophantic tone of political discourse. Indeed he could hardly have done otherwise; it was by then an essential component of the structure of absolute monarchy, rather than something characterising a single 'reign'. Once James had become a 'universal king', presiding over the entire political nation rather than committing himself to a faction, he may in some ways have been *less* able to chart his own course. The political system of absolute monarchy was something more than the individual monarch; it had a momentum of its own that continued after 1625. Therein lies part—but an important part—of the reason why Charles faced serious opposition when he first visited his Scottish kingdom in 1633, and outright revolt by 1637-8.

1 James VI, *Basilicon Doron*, in *Political Writings*, 28.
2 Lee, *Great Britain's Solomon*, 143-58.

~ 2 ~

Scottish politics in the reign of James VI

Julian Goodare

The minority of King James VI ended on 12 March 1578. The regent, the earl of Morton, was forced to resign by a hostile aristocratic coalition, and James was declared to be of age. Morton had helped to lead the English-backed 'king's party' to victory in the civil wars of 1567-73 against the supporters of James's mother, the deposed Mary; he had governed as regent since 1572. Although he had done quite an efficient job, Morton had made many enemies, who now elbowed him aside.

But James was still far from being able to govern Scotland himself: he was not yet twelve years old, and remained at school in Stirling Castle, under the charge of Alexander Erskine, master of Mar. Six weeks after James's 'acceptatioun' of the government, Morton's faction staged a counter-coup (26 April) with the aid of Erskine's nephew, the young earl of Mar, who had been a schoolmate of the king and was now aged about seventeen. There was a fight in the great hall of the castle, with the terrified king looking on; several men were killed, including Erskine's son. A parliament was summoned to ratify the change of regime; it met on 15 July in the great hall. It was against tradition for parliament to meet inside a castle, and there were complaints that there was no free access for the subjects to give in their petitions. James was brought in to declare, prompted by Morton: 'Least any man sould judge this not to be a free parliament, I declare it to be free; and those that love me will thinke as I think.'[1]

I

This chapter is about patterns in the politics of James's reign in Scotland, and the part the king played in them. Politics is about seeking power, about winning power, and about using power. In order to act politically, people have to enter into associations. Although the monarch may be 'absolute'—James certainly said that he was—this still applied to him. He had to work with the people he agreed with and who would support him, in order to get what he wanted against the people who wanted something different.

So it is necessary to look for patterns of consensus between people who joined together to seek a common aim—such as the control of Stirling Castle. The pattern here was that nobles and their followers joined

1 Calderwood, *History*, iii, 414.

together against other nobles and *their* followers. Rivalries were horizontal ones, between nobles of roughly equal status, and the disputes did not have to be about different political programmes. No obvious principles linked the leaders of the anti-Morton faction in 1578, the earls of Atholl, Argyll and Montrose; indeed Atholl and Argyll had only recently ended a quarrel in order to join against Morton. They simply felt that they could get more power by displacing Morton than by co-operating with him. As for the dispute within the Erskine family, between Alexander Erskine and his nephew the earl of Mar, it was entirely about personalities. Disputes within families, however, were unusual, for one of the basic patterns of traditional politics was that families would stick together to seek advancement against rival families.

Consensus can be sought at a deeper level, by finding out what the rules of the game were. Both factions in a political struggle may recognise the same rules. This was certainly so on 26 April 1578: when Alexander Erskine was confronted by a group demanding the keys of the castle, his immediate reaction was to grab a halberd and attack them, while they were equally well prepared for a fight. Both sides knew that their political position depended on the force they could command. The demand for the keys did have some colour of legitimacy, based on the claim that Erskine's nephew, the earl of Mar, was the hereditary and rightful keeper of the castle. Erskine could have replied that it was a royal castle and that the keepership had been granted to him personally; but there were no authorities who could adjudicate this dispute peacefully.

Patterns of conflict also have to be identified. It is obvious enough that there were conflicts between rival nobles at the outset of the reign, and we can look at how nobles became enemies. There could be disputes over local spheres of influence: nobles and their families often sought to dominate a particular territory. Once a noble had asserted a claim to some property or other rights, the conventions of honour demanded that the claim be vindicated—by force if necessary—whether or not it was legally well-grounded. Not only had honour to be upheld, but insults to it had to be revenged; disputes thus led to bloodfeuds that were sometimes carried on for years or even generations.[1]

These feuds were often simply miniature private wars, fought out in the locality, with no reference to central authority. Sometimes the dispute did involve the crown, either directly or indirectly. Atholl's quarrel with Argyll arose over his office of royal lieutenant, giving him a jurisdiction over Argyll's lands that the latter resisted. But nobles' feuds were usually settled by resort to violence; royal justice, if involved at all, usually did no more than ratify the outcome. If Argyll had defeated Atholl, the crown would have had to help settle the feud by revoking

1 K.M. Brown, *Bloodfeud in Scotland, 1573-1625* (Edinburgh, 1986); J. Wormald, *Lords and Men in Scotland: Bonds of Manrent, 1442-1603* (Edinburgh, 1985).

the latter's lieutenancy: anything else would have been politically impossible. Settled, however, bloodfeuds always were, for as well as a readiness to fight, the Scottish nobles had traditions of negotiation, compromise, and compensation for injuries done. Historians used to deplore this pattern of politics as the 'turbulence' of a 'lawless' nobility; nowadays we are more likely to see it as a functional system of autonomous dispute-settlement. But if we take a benign, or at least neutral, view of the bloodfeud, James did not; when he grew up, hostility to it would become a cornerstone of his policies.

While most rivalries between nobles were purely local, those that were played out on the national stage constituted national politics. The normal pattern of politics in the 1570s was that of factionalism—as it had been for generations. A faction was a group within the government or ruling elite, usually headed by a leading noble. The faction sought more power for itself by elbowing aside its rivals. In a monarchical state like Scotland, this was done by a combination of persuasion and mild coercion directed at the king; the faction either persuaded the king of its value, or made itself indispensable, whereupon it could demand the removal of its opponents. Sometimes rival factions espoused different policies; thus the 'king's party' in the civil war had staunchly upheld the English alliance (on which they depended for support), while the 'queen's party' had sought French or Spanish aid. But that was an unusually deep political rift; the factions could not even agree who should be the monarch. Factions did not have to have policies. Often the rivalry was simply about who would have access to the king and to a share in royal power.

Factions were held together by personal ties between lords and followers. Traditionally, nobles recruited followers through kinship and land tenure: they had a network of lesser landed kinsmen in their territory. The follower might hold land directly from the lord, who was then his feudal superior, although that was not essential. This was what anthropologists call a gift-exchange relationship, not a contractual one: the lord gave free gifts (of land or other resources) to his followers, who in return recognised his overlordship and generosity, and served him freely out of gratitude. The system of lordship worked because it benefited both lord and follower.

This system could also use patronage. Here, a lord used his court influence to procure grants of *crown* land or government office for his followers, thus strengthening their faction's position. This was also a gift-exchange relationship, in which clients were grateful for the benevolence of their patrons. Although the follower held his grant from the crown, his primary loyalty was still to his patron. This was one of the reasons why a faction wanted to win favour: it could gain rewards for its members.

Lordship in the traditional sense was largely independent of the crown. Nobles in the 1570s wielded much the same kind of power whether in or out of favour. They used their locally-based client networks, with which they could offer to serve the crown (or not). As a result, there was a danger that factional crises could lead to noble revolts. If two factions came into such serious conflict that they could no longer tolerate one another's presence, each would try to get the other ejected from court, and this could lead to fighting. The king might wish to be served by both factions, but they would try to force him to choose between them.

By the 1570s, some broader principles had begun to make inroads into these traditional patterns of politics. Scotland had become an officially Protestant country in 1560; a few nobles were determined to reverse the Reformation if they could, while another group were committed to the maintenance and extension of Protestantism. For most, however, the religious status quo was broadly acceptable without arousing fervent passions. The nobles *would* have resisted any threat to their possession of secularised church property, but any such threat was at least as likely to come from radical Protestants (who sought a better-endowed church) as from Catholics.

A related question of principle was that of Scotland's international allegiance. The 'auld alliance' between France and Scotland, based on mutual hostility to England, had collapsed in 1560, and a Scottish regime sympathetic to England had been installed by English arms. This was bolstered both by direct intervention (English armies again entered Scotland in 1570 and 1573) and by the fostering of a pro-English party among the Scottish nobility. This was linked to religion, because England was Protestant, France Catholic; the Protestant party and the supporters of the so-called 'amity' with England tended to overlap. Others, however, resented Scotland's dependence on England; in the 1580s and 1590s, they turned increasingly to Spain, now the premier Catholic power.

As a result, these essentially *ideological* questions could form the basis for factions, or could at least influence factions. If ideology should come to be dominant it would produce a different pattern of politics. People would not take orders from their patrons as powerful protectors whom it was honourable to serve and dangerous to disobey; they would do so because they believed in the cause. This pattern emerged only gradually, but it will need further attention later on.

II

After James's 'acceptatioun' of the government in 1578, there were still seven more years before he finally emerged from tutelage. These were years of constant factional turmoil, with at least six palace coups, five of which were successful. In August 1582, a pro-English faction kidnapped the king in the so-called 'Ruthven Raid' and ruled for ten months against his will.

Political patterns sometimes stand out clearly in a snapshot of the political community in action, such as is provided by meetings of parliament. Scottish parliaments were gatherings of the entire political community, the 'three estates' of clergy, nobles and burgesses. They took, or at least ratified, most of the big, contentious political decisions. Parliaments also made new laws and imposed taxes, but these were not common until the later 1580s. Along with parliaments, the Scots also held 'conventions of estates', which were parliaments in almost all but name, and were particularly useful for taking political decisions.

Two examples will illustrate patterns of politics early in the reign. The first is the convention of estates of June 1578 that granted Morton the 'first rowme and place in counsale', setting the seal on his political comeback.[1] The convention was not ratifying a decision already made elsewhere, for there was actually a vote—a rare occurrence in this period; Morton's faction won by 25 votes to 23. The spiritual estate was made up of eight bishops and eight 'commendators' of monasteries.[2] The noble estate consisted of nine earls, eleven lords and two lords' sons. There were nine burgesses for the burgess estate. Most of those present—and almost all of the nobles, the group who really counted—were active members of one faction or the other, as can be seen by comparing the attendance and voting records with contemporary lists of 'malecontentes' (Atholl's group) and 'biencontentes' (Morton's).[3] The whole convention was a struggle between two factions for supremacy, in which there were few innocent bystanders. It failed to convince the defeated faction; next month, Atholl, Argyll and Montrose raised an army in an attempt to regain power, while Morton did the same in order to keep it. There was no fighting, and a new compromise was reached—without a convention this time;[4] the anti-Morton faction was eventually crippled by Atholl's death in April 1579, and Morton enjoyed another eighteen months in power.

A different kind of parliament was held towards the end of James's tutelage, in May 1584. The dominant man in the government was now James Stewart, earl of Arran, who had risen to power after the collapse of the Ruthven regime. Arran's parliament, much better attended than the 1578 convention, amounted to more than a meeting of two rival groups.[5] But factionalism was still apparent in the attendance. One

1 *APS*, iii, 120-1.

2 These were laymen, since the monasteries had been secularised at the Reformation.

3 *CSP Scot.*, v, 295-6. Cf. the vote in council on sending an ambassador to England, 18 June 1578, ibid., 301.

4 Articles between James and the lords, 13-14 Aug. 1578, *CSP Scot.*, v, 316.

5 *APS*, iii, 290-2. There were eight bishops and thirteen commendators; one duke, thirteen earls and fifteen lords; and twenty-three burgesses.

group was conspicuously absent—those among the Ruthven lords who had carried out the failed Stirling Raid the previous month; the parliament forfeited them. There were several former Ruthven Raiders, but they were mostly lesser figures. No Ruthven supporters were chosen to the lords of the articles, the key committee that managed parliamentary business. By contrast, four Catholic earls were at the parliament;[1] all were on the Articles, showing that the regime's centre of gravity was conservative. Arran, himself a Stewart, seems to have attempted to construct a Stewart connection: there were eleven Stewart nobles and commendators present.

The 1584 parliament was also significant for what it *did*. It did not just ratify Arran's possession of power; it enabled him to do new things with that power. The church, which had been organised independently of the state since the Reformation of 1560, had used that independence to back the Ruthven faction; it was now to be brought under government control. A series of statutes (dubbed the 'Black Acts' by critics) asserted royal supremacy over the church and ordered that it was to be governed by crown-appointed bishops, not by presbyteries.[2] There was to be a new royal guard, funded on a lavish scale from the revenues of the monasteries (which were largely in nobles' hands). Censorship was tightened by an act banning speeches contemptuous of the king or his council.[3]

Arran fell from power in November 1585, removed by a noble coalition backed by the English government and including a number of former Ruthven Raiders. The king, aged nineteen, was now in a position where he could begin to govern for himself. The transition was a smooth and gradual one. Arran's regime had based itself upon the monarchy and the institutions of the state, rather than manipulating them in the interests of specific families. This explains not only why Arran was overthrown so easily—his officials, like the secretary, John Maitland of Thirlestane, were primarily loyal to the crown and not to him—but also why the regime that succeeded him, now under the leadership of James himself, continued his policies: enhancement of state authority, particularly over the church, but also over the autonomous power of the nobility; and closer connection with England.[4]

1 Crawford, Eglinton, Huntly and Morton; the latter was the eighth Lord Maxwell, nephew and enemy of the late Regent Morton.

2 Presbyteries (committees of parish ministers) had begun to be set up in 1581, following a programme launched in 1578. They aimed to take over control of the church at local level. Since the Reformation, the church had been run by an *ad hoc* combination of bishops, superintendents, and temporary commissioners from the general assembly of the church. During the 1570s the ideas of presbyterianism and episcopalianism became more formalised, and it began to be realised that conflict between them was inevitable.

3 *APS*, iii, 292-312, cc. 1-6, 8, 13, 20, 22, 31.

4 Even the royal guard scheme continued: for its enforcement in Jan. 1587, see *RPC*, iv, 134.

From 1585 to 1589 there was a temporary political consensus—or perhaps simply a lull in the intensity of factional conflict. This facilitated some progress in the extension of state authority. James's leading adviser here was Maitland, who became chancellor in 1587. Arran had begun a new use of parliament, using statutes as weapons to coerce recalcitrant subjects into religious conformity. James and Maitland used parliament more intensively than ever before. Legislation was called for on many topics, since the law was now intended to settle disputes that formerly had been settled through feuds. Parliamentary taxation was extended, to support more intensive government. All this was achieved through parliaments that were broadly based, not simply the weapons of a faction. One change masterminded by Maitland was the admission of lairds to parliament in 1587, as shire commissioners. The obvious intention was to offset the power of the nobility by granting those below them an independent voice in central government. It was probably also hoped to create a wider political consensus for government decisions. Taxation would be hard to collect if the political community had not been seen to consent to it. This bolstered the regime, but it also stored up problems for the future.

The issue of international allegiance was settled, finally as it turned out, in 1586, when James signed a treaty with England and accepted a regular subsidy from Elizabeth. This was not universally popular, but it ended English destabilisation of the kind that had damaged Arran. The price was the acceptance of Scotland's status as a satellite state: although still independent, it had to defer to English wishes on important matters. This fitted with James's personal interests: he had a good claim to succeed Queen Elizabeth on the English throne, so he had to stay on good terms with her while she lived. If he occasionally negotiated with her enemies, this was largely a gesture to increase his value to her.

Apart from the English succession, James's main concern up to about 1598 was his authority over the nobility. He felt that he could not rule effectively if the nobles pursued their own disputes without reference to his authority. Factionalism at court, if he could not control it, posed the same problem. One of James's earliest declared intentions was to be a 'universal king'—to rule without being beholden to any one faction. He probably did not think he was innovating here; he merely aimed to establish himself as the respected and obeyed king of an orderly kingdom.

In fact, James *was* innovating. Past monarchs had always had to deal with nobles who were effectively autonomous, and who co-operated with the crown for what they could get out of it. Some monarchs—particularly James IV—had cultivated good relations with their nobles, and had reduced the problem of factionalism. But a state in which noble revolts were *impossible* would be a different kind of state from one in which king and leading nobles happened to be friends. All James's Stewart predecessors had faced noble revolts.[1]

James had no wish to get rid of the nobles; he was keen to have them as his courtiers and servants. This respect for an ideal of nobility, together with a dislike for much of what the nobles actually got up to, can make James's book, *Basilicon Doron*, seem contradictory. Nobles, he advised, were to be maintained at court and used in the 'greatest affaires', but there was a vagueness as to whether they were actually to be officers of state, running the government. Financial officers, at least, were to be 'meane, but responsall men'. He praised the severe justice of James V, but warned that too much contempt for the nobility (the same thing as his severe justice, in fact) 'brake the king my grand-fathers heart'.[2]

From 1589 until 1598, it sometimes seemed as if James was following in his grandfather's footsteps. Pressure on the nobility led to two active problems, and a third one in the background.

The active problems were two dissident earls: Huntly, a Catholic and anti-English schemer, and Bothwell, a Protestant and pro-English maverick. Both were hostile to Maitland, for whom it was fortunate that they were also hostile to one another. There was a factional crisis at court early in 1589, when Huntly attempted to eject Maitland from court, but failed and had to leave court himself. Thereafter he and two other Catholic earls intrigued with Spain—England's leading enemy—and used his great regional following in the north-east to lead several rebellions until his surrender to a royal army in 1594. Huntly was leniently treated; James, who himself had occasional contacts with Spain, felt that a well-established conservative magnate might be of service to him, though in the end Huntly proved incorrigible and was never trusted with governmental responsibility after his rehabilitation. As for Bothwell, who was no great magnate, he unluckily fell out with James in 1591; outlawed, he spent three years on the run, conducting daring raids on the royal palaces, before being forced into exile in 1595.

The background problem—the only one, indeed, that made the plottings of Huntly and the escapades of Bothwell serious—was the fact that most other nobles were disenchanted with the Maitland regime, which in the early 1590s was doing more to curb the nobility than *Basilicon Doron* (written in late 1598) might indicate. Lairds, as we have seen, had been officially admitted to parliament in 1587. The captaincy of the guard, Huntly's old job at court, was given to a laird in 1590. There was

1 Fewest revolts were faced by James IV, at least after the initial turbulent years of his reign. After 1495 there were no revolts in the Lowlands, although there was a small group of discontented nobles (supporters of the overthrown James III) in traitorous correspondence with England: N. Macdougall, *James IV* (Edinburgh, 1989), 127-9.

2 James VI, *Basilicon Doron*, in *Political Writings*, 29, 37, 24.

an effort to reduce nobles' role in the privy council and in parliamentary commissions; the exchequer—a largely noble-free institution—was given an expanded role in government. There was even an attempt to deny the nobles automatic access to the king's chamber. As a result, although few nobles joined Huntly or Bothwell, many sympathised with them. After Huntly's forfeiture in 1594, it was hard to find anyone who would go north and administer his estates; several nobles refused the task, and James had to appoint Huntly's brother-in-law, the duke of Lennox, who ensured that Huntly's interests were protected.[1] But, although nobody knew it at the time, Huntly's rebellion of 1594 was the last regional rebellion ever to take place in Scotland—except in the Highlands, which were not fully integrated into the state. To that extent, the regime of James and Maitland succeeded.

All this time, James had had fairly good relations with the church. After Arran's fall in 1585, Maitland discovered that it was possible to work with the radical presbyterians who had opposed him. This group had come to dominate the general assembly and had built a popular following in several key towns, including Edinburgh. They did not fit the traditional pattern of politics; the ties that linked them were based on ideology, not clientage. The presbyterians proved willing to co-operate with the government in return for the abandonment of bishops; without official support, the episcopal system shrivelled, and was formally abandoned in 1592. But the presbyterians were demanding partners. They wanted complete godliness from the king personally, from his queen, and from his government; exclusion of the ungodly, and especially any suspected Catholics, from royal service; and more generous funding—*much* more generous funding—for the parish ministry.

By 1594, the king's efforts to give the impression that he might be able to deliver all this were becoming increasingly strained; and after Huntly's surrender, the presbyterians were no longer so necessary as a counterweight to the Catholic earls. But it took them some time to realise this, and they were anyway too doctrinaire to be able to adjust to their new political position. Conflict was inevitable. The showdown came on 17 December 1596, when there was a religious riot in Edinburgh; the king fled, leaving the radicals apparently in control of the town. They appealed to godly noblemen such as Lord Hamilton to back their cause—no insurgent movement at that time could survive without noble leadership—but were unsuccessful;[2] within days the king was back in control, and the leading presbyterians had to flee from the royalist clampdown.

1 *Warrender Papers*, ii, 269-70; *APS*, iv, 99.

2 Cf. H.G. Koenigsberger, 'The organization of revolutionary parties in France and the Netherlands during the sixteenth century', in his *Estates and Revolutions* (London, 1971).

From then onwards, committed presbyterians were systematically excluded from the political consensus. At first, James merely insisted that his authority should be recognised, which isolated the radical leadership. But he soon served notice that he intended to reintroduce bishops. It was this on which he had most to say in *Basilicon Doron*, and on which he spent most of his efforts to restructure the church. The presbyterian principle of 'paritie' in the ministry was also relevant to the secular government, 'for if by the example thereof, once established in the ecclesiasticall government, the politicke and civill estate should be drawen to the like, the great confusion that thereupon would arise may easily be discerned'.[1] A better argument to detach the nobility from the presbyterians could scarcely have been devised; but episcopalianism had long since lost its universal acceptability and had become, like presbyterianism, a divisive and confrontational ideology.

In June 1598, James would finally bring his nobles to accept that their disputes would have to be submitted to royal justice—the most significant turning-point in his reign, and the culmination of a long process of pressure and negotiation. James himself put much effort into mediating between his feuding nobles, while the church preached against the code of morals that sustained the bloodfeud. But one thing that speaks louder than words is money.

To explain the role of money in ending the bloodfeud, we must glance at the royal finances. James's government was innovative in its gathering of revenue, even though the king himself took no interest in it—money, to him, was something to be spent. Maitland, however, saw money as a political tool. He had launched a revitalised organ of central government, the permanent exchequer, in 1590; it involved itself in politics as well as managing the royal finances more actively. Maitland's involvement in finance may have been overlooked by historians who have treated him simply as a politician.[2] The exchequer became still more important, and more political, after Maitland's death in 1595. Power fell in January 1596 to a committee of eight exchequer auditors who became known as the Octavians. They exercised full control over the revenues, and attempted to reduce expenditure on the royal court—and on handouts to the nobility. This triggered off a new pattern of political factionalism, in which discontented nobles and courtiers combined to try to shake the Octavians' control of the purse-strings. They succeeded at a convention of estates in June 1598, where a deal was struck between king and nobles. The permanent exchequer—the Octavians' power-base—was abolished. In return, the convention passed a measure that

1 James VI, *Basilicon Doron*, in *Political Writings*, 26.

2 He acted informally as a financial officer between 1589 and 1593, handling nearly £229,000 received from England and Denmark: BL, Maitland's accounts, 1589-93, Add. MS 22,958.

the king had long sought in vain: an act agreeing that feuds would be submitted to justice in the royal courts.

The writing had been on the wall for feuding nobles since 1594, if not before; the crown was now too strong to be coerced by a noble taking up arms, even a great magnate like Huntly with foreign backing and a large local network of supporters and allies. Feuding did not end overnight, but gradually the serious feuds were patched up, while few new ones started. By 1612-13, it was possible for two peers who had committed vengeance killings (Lords Sanquhar and Maxwell) to be executed for murder, which had never happened before. The ending of noble violence and the acceptance of state authority transformed the behaviour of the nobility; to the extent that they retained their networks of kinsmen and dependants, they would use them in the peaceful service of the crown. Here, the abolition of the permanent exchequer was compensation: it promised continued noble access to the king and royal patronage, with no administrative limits placed on royal giving. The only question—admittedly a big one—was whether the finances could afford the kind of royal spending spree that the deal envisaged.

III

The year 1598 marked a shift in the politics of the reign. After it, James and his government were as active as before, but the target had shifted. The nobility had been reconciled; the church, however, was more disaffected than usual. But since the collapse in 1596 of what he had deemed an insurrection, the king held the initiative on religious matters. Another issue, a hardy perennial, was money. Indeed, now that the Octavians' retrenchment policy had been jettisoned, it was far more of an issue than before.

Gradually, a new pattern of politics was stabilising. The courtiers who had ousted the Octavians emerged to take over the government; two gentlemen of the chamber, Sir David Home of Gospertie and Sir George Home of Spott, became respectively comptroller (1600) and treasurer (1601). They were soon ennobled as Lord Scone and earl of Dunbar. Several former Octavians joined the new regime, particularly Alexander Seton, lord president of the court of session, who became earl of Dunfermline. The watchword was consensus, not conflict; ministers co-operated with the king to advance policies agreed between them. Sometimes there were disputes, but they were minor. There was never again a faction crisis remotely as serious as the struggle of 1589 between Maitland and Huntly.

The major issue for the regime was financial. Despite the Octavians, James had been sinking into bankruptcy for some time, and had periodically defaulted on some of his debts. There was a particularly serious bankruptcy in January 1598, when the king's officials froze payments to the goldsmith and financier Thomas Foulis, who had taken on responsibility for most of the royal finances as the culmination of his years of lending to the crown. The Foulis debt hardly began to be paid off before 1606, and payments were still being made in 1625.[1] And yet this was a regime that had abandoned the Octavians' policy of controlling expenditure, because this had alienated the nobility. The only solution was a drive to raise more revenue.

This had begun under the Octavians; parliament in 1597 had voted a larger direct tax than ever before, and had also imposed general customs duties on imports for the first time. The new regime went further, debasing the coinage and searching desperately for new sources of cash. One scheme was for a sales tax on cattle and grain; the English agent, George Nicolson, thought it would lead to civil war, and it had to be dropped in March 1600.[2] A more important and sophisticated project was to revise the tax assessment system: the traditional assessments were too uneven to tap the country's wealth effectually. In 1599-1600, lengthy efforts were made to cajole a series of wary conventions of estates to agree to this. Provisional approval was given in April 1600, and the final decision was to be made in June. The result of the June convention of estates, however, was an outright defeat for the government; the atmosphere was so hostile that the proposal could not even be put to a vote. The king, who had argued passionately for the proposal, was publicly humiliated by the disaster. What had gone wrong?

One thing that had *not* gone wrong was James's newly-established rapport with the nobility, for most nobles backed his scheme. Instead, it was the shire commissioners and burgesses who destroyed it—and this is a vital clue to the newly-emerging pattern of politics. Of the few opposition nobles (most nursing personal grievances), the most significant was probably the earl of Gowrie, an enigmatic figure linked to the presbyterian party.[3] As on 17 December 1596, the opposition needed noble leadership, but the bulk of its support came from other groups more distanced from the court. This was probably what Nicolson had in mind when he reported in February 1600: 'Such is the malcontentment here as, if any should take [the leadership] upon them, the country I fear would all back them against this government, so much is it here repined at now.'[4]

1 J. Goodare, 'Thomas Foulis and the Scottish fiscal crisis of the 1590s', in W.M. Ormrod *et al.* (eds.), *Crises, Revolutions and Self-Sustained Growth: Essays in Fiscal History, 1130-1830* (Stamford, 1999, forthcoming).

2 Nicolson to Cecil, 6 Feb. 1600, *CSP Scot.*, xiii, II, 621; same to same, 9 Mar. 1600, HMC, *Salisbury*, x, 59-61.

3 Denis Campbell to Nicolson, July 1600, *CSP Scot.*, xiii, II, 670.

4 Nicolson to Cecil, 6 Feb. 1600, *CSP Scot.*, xiii, II, 621. Nicolson's use of the term 'country', which was then beginning to be a recognised term in English political life, may indicate that he saw parallels with England.

That the 'country' might be something distinct from the court and government was a new idea. The central concept of sixteenth-century political discourse had been the 'commonweal', an ideal in which the political nation was united under enlightened royal leadership by a shared common interest. The ideal of the 'commonweal' had made good sense when there had been strong vertical ties linking nobles with their followers, and when political divisions between noble factions had had such a low ideological content. Commentators thought that the nobles simply had to make friends with one another and with the king, and the 'commonweal'—the political nation—would become united and harmonious. By 1598, James had largely achieved this, as far as the nobles themselves were concerned—but it was beginning to be clear that he had not carried the rest of the political nation with him. The nobles had got their handouts, and their place at court, but the whole gravy train was funded by increased taxes on the country. Direct taxes had been few and small before the 1580s; now, the 'country' was a nation of taxpayers.

As for the presbyterians, they had to devise a mode of politics appropriate for the wilderness. Here, they had the advantage of giving their allegiance not to a court patron, but to an ideology. Presbyterianism provided an all-encompassing way of looking at the world, and issued a call to action. It looked in two directions. Backwards, in anger—to the alleged purity of the Scottish church before 1596, the sullying of which was so clearly the king's responsibility that it was difficult to avoid calling him a traitor to God. But also forwards, in hope—to the approaching millennium, the personal reign of Christ, to which the present political arrangements were a mere prologue. This could seem near at hand, particularly in the apocalyptic European wars of the 1620s. The presbyterians built links with the Continent, aided by the exile of several of their leaders; they agitated in those parishes they still controlled; and they hoped for better times.

The country opposition, which first began to emerge in the late 1590s, was a heterogeneous collection of politically-involved people who were sceptical about some of the directions taken by the current government. They were spread unevenly throughout Scotland; the court did not control the localities directly, so some areas were loyalist, others seedbeds of dissidence, as local patterns dictated. Their motives varied. For committed presbyterians, the desire to free the church from impurities was paramount, while more secular-minded folk were concerned about their tax bills, and the trading classes had further worries about monopolies and other government restrictions on commerce. But in parliament they all tended to vote the same way. Some may have had ideas of what *they* would do if in government; most just wanted the government to leave them alone. But with the government intervening in a wide range of areas, from religion to trade, those who were unhappy about one aspect began to see the links with other issues—as we shall see.

Meanwhile, the paramount duty of a courtier was to be happy about everything, and to serve the king loyally by implementing his government's agreed policies without question. The presbyterians, when at court in the early 1590s, had offered what they saw as outspoken but friendly criticism of the king; this was no longer tolerated. The new atmosphere was captured by Peter Blackburn, bishop of Aberdeen, writing to James to defend himself from 'hard information which your majestie received anent my cariage in the effeiris of the church and your majesties service', and declaring that 'at this present parliament I have not been deficient in any goode service'.[1] This was not a serious faction struggle, rather an example of the way in which loyal ministers vied with one another for the best means of serving the king.

As they did so, they began to recognise a novel distinction between themselves, as loyal servants, and the world outside. In 1598, Alexander Douglas (one of the general assembly commissioners, newly appointed by the king to help control the assembly) wrote to James complaining of a local injustice he had suffered: 'this I am informed is done to me becaus I am your majesties man'. Patrick Galloway urged the king to pay Peter Hewat's pension in 1607, 'to put difference betuix those that ar your majesties owne men and others'. To the government, the Perth general assembly in 1618 was divided into two groups: 'the opposites' and 'the weel affected'.[2] These terms did not need to be explained; such a duality was taken for granted. James himself endorsed the view that parties had arisen in the political system, telling his English parliament in 1604 that 'if Scotland should refuse' the proposed Anglo-Scottish union, 'he would compell theyr assents, having a stronger party there than the opposite party of the mutiners'.[3]

Apart from finance, the main concern for James and his government between about 1598 and 1610 was the drive to control the church through re-establishing bishops. It was an easy task at first, for the radical presbyterians were just one party in the church; after the riot of 1596, there was a rallying to the government, and the radicals lost their grip on the general assembly. In 1597 the assembly had to accept a set of 'commissioners', nominated in practice by the king; from 1600 bishops, answerable to the crown alone, were appointed; and in 1606 and 1610, the assembly was persuaded to grant these bishops authority over the

1 Blackburn to James, n.d. [1612?], 'Extracts from the manuscript collections of the Rev. Robert Wodrow, 1605-1697', *Spalding Misc.*, ii, 158-9.

2 Douglas to James, 22 June 1598, *Warrender Papers*, ii, 357; Galloway to James, 7 Apr. 1607, *Eccles. Letters*, i, 83; Lord Binning to James, 27 Aug. 1618, 'Extracts from the manuscript collections of the Rev. Robert Wodrow, 1605-1697', *Spalding Misc.*, ii, 159-62.

3 J. Bruce (ed.), *Report on the Union of England and Scotland*, 2 vols. (Edinburgh, 1799), ii, p. xxii.

church in their dioceses, while this was enforced in the localities by royal commissioners. Meanwhile, general assemblies met with declining frequency; James often got what he wanted from post-1597 assemblies, partly through gerrymandering, but he did not trust them and preferred to operate through the bishops.

As the government manipulated its way to the muzzling of the assembly and the restoration of episcopacy, and as the appalling reality of heavy taxation began to dawn, the presbyterians recovered their confidence in the first decade of the new century. They were not winning the battles, but they were consolidating their support. In 1606, many people were shocked by a rigged show-trial (for treason) of six presbyterian ministers who had helped to organise an unauthorised general assembly in Aberdeen. The presbyterians began to make links with the country opposition. The contemporary presbyterian historian and pamphleteer, David Calderwood, had much to say about the delinquencies of the new bishops—and one of his main complaints was their leading role in persuading parliaments to vote unpopular taxes. And while Calderwood was primarily concerned with religion, he was just as sceptical of James's Highland policy as he was of his religious policy.[1]

The re-establishment of bishops made Scotland more like England, and this was one of James's intentions. After he succeeded to the English throne in 1603, he wanted a closer union between his two kingdoms, a union of institutions that would be more than a dual monarchy. This would have been a real upheaval in politics; but it never happened. The English refused to countenance closer union, and the Scots never had to debate the scheme seriously. There was friction at court between Scottish and English courtiers yoked together unwillingly by their unionist king; in Scotland itself, however, the institutions of government continued unchanged. All Scottish politicians accepted the link with England, and a few courtiers could now hope for careers there; but they had accepted this link long before 1603, and it is hard to see much really changing in the structure of politics when the king went south. The realignment in Scotland's foreign allegiance had occurred in 1560, and the union of crowns merely confirmed it. James himself was rather less involved in the government—after all, he had England to govern as well—but policy was still made in the same way, by Scottish ministers supervised by their monarch. James had to take English interests into account, but this was hardly new; he had governed for years in Scotland with English ambassadors at his elbow. 1603 was not the political watershed it is sometimes made out to be. Its main result was to solve the fiscal crisis, for the departure of James's court to England lifted the heaviest burden from

1 Calderwood, *History*, vi, 247.

the Scottish treasury. Payments of pensions to nobles and courtiers could now expand comfortably.

Union also had an effect in the peripheral regions of Scotland—the Highlands and Borders. The latter were savagely and effectively subdued by a military force operating on both sides of the Border, ending the advantage that had been enjoyed by cross-Border families in the days of separate jurisdictions. International links were equally important in the Gaelic-speaking Highlands, which had connections with Ulster. Here, James exploited Elizabeth's victory in Ulster in the Nine Years' War (1594-1603); from the 1610s, expropriated Ulster lands were systematically settled with Englishmen and Lowland Scots. But union was not everything, even here. In Ireland, the English had half a century of experience with such plantations, while a smaller version had been tried also in Scotland when the island of Lewis was colonised in 1598 by a group of Lowland 'adventurers'. The Lewis experiment ultimately failed, the colonists falling victim to local resistance, and the island was granted in 1610 to a compliant clan chief, Kenneth Mackenzie of Kintail. Compliant clans were used on a larger scale in the south-west Highlands, where the MacDonald heartland of Kintyre (close to the Ulster MacDonnells) was taken over by Campbells, headed by the earl of Argyll. None of this was politically contentious, since the victims of the policy—the traditional governing elites of the Highlands—had never been incorporated into the Scottish political system.

The seal was placed on James's episcopal policy by the parliament of 1612, which ratified the decisions of the 1610 general assembly. There appears to have been no open opposition. The parliament did, however, see a major row about taxation; the tax voted was less than half what the government asked for. This was partly caused by a minor factional dispute between the bishops (led by John Spottiswoode, archbishop of Glasgow) and a group of nobles supporting Chancellor Dunfermline. The bishops, always ultra-royalists (for they owed their position to the crown alone), argued for a tax of £800,000, but parliament was 'so wilful and opposit as it was a labour of muche busines'. Dunfermline's supporters claimed (wrongly) that James had said he wanted only £120,000. Eventually parliament agreed on £240,000. This was a victory for the Dunfermline group, though they got into trouble with the king afterwards. But behind them we glimpse the country party, who did not just want a lower tax (£240,000 was, in fact, a similar rate to the last tax) but would have 'maid it nothing, it if had ben in thair power so to do'.[1]

Between 1612 and 1617 there were fewer contentious political issues. Maurice Lee, whose detailed account of the politics of this period is indispensable, attributes this to the moderating influence of Dunfermline, who

[1] The bishops to James, 25 Oct. 1612, W. Fraser, *Memoirs of the Maxwells of Pollok*, 2 vols. (Edinburgh, 1863), ii, 61-3.

as head of the privy council had a consensual style of government. By contrast, he explains the controversies of the years 1606-10 by reference to the abrasive personality of Treasurer Dunbar, who was allegedly dominant in politics until his death in 1611.[1] But other explanations of this new-found calm are possible, and indeed are surely necessary to explain the remarkable harmony among James's ministers throughout this whole period. After about 1601, hardly anyone in the government lost their job through faction struggle.[2] The point about 1606-10 was not Dunbar's personality, but the fact that newly-appointed bishops were being forced down the throats of local elites all over Scotland, sometimes meeting fierce resistance. As for the harmony of 1612-17, this was largely because there happened to be a relative lull in religious innovations, and because there were no parliaments to cause trouble.

Why this lull occurred, we shall see in a moment. But it is also worth observing that Dunfermline's ascendancy may have seemed quite confrontational from some points of view: it was just that the victims were politically marginal. There were national government campaigns against overcharging maltsters; against usurers taking more than the statutory 10 per cent interest; and against the outlawed MacGregor clan and their supporters in the eastern Highlands. There was the destruction of the last semi-independent earl of Orkney, executed in 1615. This was hardly consensual, but it did not generate the heat that religion or taxation were capable of doing.

Harmony ceased abruptly in 1617, when James visited his ancient kingdom for the first and only time since 1603. The visit itself was welcome, but he used the occasion to unveil a renewed programme of religious innovations. Having completed his episcopal programme, the king had now turned to the question of worship in churches. Indeed, he and the bishops had been at work on this for some years, drafting new forms of service;[3] the harmony of the Dunfermline years was thus due to the fact that the scheme only now became public. It was natural, thought James, that in a hierarchical church and society in which people revered their superiors, people should worship in a formal and ceremonial way. This upset the presbyterians, who favoured a plain church service focused on a lengthy sermon. Some proposed innovations (like

1 M. Lee, *Government by Pen: Scotland under James VI and I* (Urbana, Ill., 1980), ch. 3, 'Dunbar in Power: the Triumph of the Bishops'; ch. 4, 'The Dunfermline Administration'.

2 The master of Elphinstone was forced out of the treasurership in 1601 to make way for Dunbar. After this, there was only a half-hearted and abortive attempt by Spottiswoode to unseat Dunfermline in 1606. The secretary, Lord Balmerino, was disgraced in 1609, but this was less because of faction than because the king needed a scapegoat in a complicated dispute with the pope.

3 Work had been continuous since at least 1614: G. Donaldson, *The Making of the Scottish Prayer Book of 1637* (Edinburgh, 1954), 31-5. Cf. 'A Scottish liturgy of the reign of James VI', ed. G. Donaldson, *SHS Misc.*, x (1965).

confirmation by bishops or the celebration of Christmas) were denounced as unscriptural; others (like ministers wearing elaborate vestments) were condemned as too close to Catholic practice. The most contentious proposal, affecting every worshipper directly, was the requirement that communion should be received kneeling, rather than seated round a table in imitation of the Last Supper.

While in Scotland, James held a parliament. In order to avoid trouble, he had to withdraw a proposed statute that would have allowed him to introduce these innovations by royal edict. Later in the year, he had the proposals placed before the general assembly—and they were rejected. The king, furious, ordered another assembly, threatening that another rejection would have dire consequences for all concerned. The assembly, held in Perth in 1618, duly passed the proposals, which became known as the Five Articles of Perth.

Implementation of the Five Articles (particularly the requirement to kneel at communion) proved a nightmare. The presbyterians' years of struggle now paid off, and it became clear that they had solid local support in much of Lowland Scotland. Only in the remote north-east could the Articles be implemented properly. The key battles were fought in the east-central regions of Fife and Angus, and in Edinburgh, where a determined effort was made to force ministers to worship in the new way. There was some success, but at a heavy price: hostile congregations, bitter divisions and the emergence of an organised underground resistance network run by presbyterian diehards. Over most of the rest of southern Scotland, the authorities gave in, making little attempt to implement the Articles.[1]

In the parliament of 1621, the presbyterians rallied. Parliament was the one forum in which the opposition could still find a voice; although the crown had an inbuilt advantage in parliament, which had increased since the restoration of bishops, it never controlled that body automatically. The result was a titanic struggle over both the Five Articles and a new tax scheme. Opposition to both proposals came from the same group, in which a prominent role was played by Lord Balmerino and the earl of Rothes. The ratification of the Articles came close to defeat, which would have been catastrophic for the regime. The government majority came largely from bishops, nobles, courtiers and their clients, while most of the central belt of Scotland supported the opposition. James's policy was in tatters; it was clear that he had gone too far.

Nor was there any obvious way for him to retrieve his position. He seems never to have considered the unheroic option of cancelling the Five Articles, which would have left him little credibility. Indeed, in 1624 he was planning another campaign to enforce them.[2] But bishops and

1 P.H.R. Mackay, 'The reception given to the five articles of Perth', *RSCHS*, xix (1977).
2 Kellie to Mar, 26 Aug. 1624, HMC, *Mar & Kellie*, ii, 210.

privy council, exhausted by the effort, could do no more to overcome the mass resistance. By now, the Five Articles could be implemented only sporadically and in a token way. This was not a carefully-planned tactical withdrawal, as is sometimes said, but an outright defeat for the crown in the localities.

After 1621, the most significant political event of the last four years of James's reign was the one that did not happen. Defeat did not lead to a change of direction, or the disgrace of the ministers responsible—mainly Archbishop Spottiswoode, with his ally, the earl of Melrose, lord president and secretary. Spottiswoode was passed over for the chancellorship when Dunfermline died in 1622, but he did not lose favour, and there was no faction struggle at court. On the contrary, Melrose formed an alliance with the treasurer, the earl of Mar, who had opposed Spottiswoode in the 1612 parliament.[1] All three retained office well into the next reign. This was an unhealthy sign, because it meant that an important strand of opinion in the country was denied representation at court. Early modern monarchs could govern more effectively, and keep more of their options open, if their court represented a wide spectrum of political opinion. James had known this in the 1590s; he had tried to keep Huntly at court in order to keep the pro-Spanish option open, and to wean the pro-Spanish nobility away from open revolt. But where were the presbyterian nobles in the 1620s? None were at court, if the voting record of the 1621 parliament is anything to go by.[2] Surrounded by yes-men, James was unaware of the trouble brewing, or unable to change course to meet it.

IV

This polarisation of politics was not something that anyone intended. The opposition themselves hoped that a more consensual style of politics would return—if not in James's reign, then perhaps in the next one. The news of James's death reached Scotland on 31 March 1625.[3] On 14 April, the earl of Rothes (who had led the opposition in the 1621 parliament) wrote anxiously but with determined optimism to Sir Robert Kerr of Ancrum, a gentleman of the bedchamber, on a matter which 'may import the good or misery of our stat'. He sought 'sum notic from you of the disposition of our master [King Charles] touards such courses as uas intended in this countray, which you micht perseav did bread greit greif and miscontentment amongst the best both in plac and knawledg [Rothes and his friends]'. The grievances were: authoritarian practices in the privy council; 'the imposing of certain novations upon the Kirk, which bread such caus of miscontentment', in other words the Five

1 Melrose to Mar, 10 Apr. 1622, ed. M. Lee, *SHR*, lviii (1979); on Mar in 1612, see Viscount Fenton to Mar, 24 Oct. 1612, HMC, *Mar & Kellie*, ii, 43-4.

2 J. Goodare, 'The Scottish parliament of 1621', *Historical Journal*, xxxviii (1995), 43-5.

3 *RPC*, 2nd ser., i, 1-3. He died on 27 Mar.

Articles, and possibly also episcopacy; 'and the impairing of the libertys of the nobility, both in Counsell and Parliament'. Rothes continued that Kerr had told him that nothing could be done in James's reign, but Rothes

> did hop quhen itt suld pleas God to bring his majestie to his father's plac ther suld be a mitigatioun of thos extremitys.... Now the tym being precious befor the stamp of any bad impression which thos quho uar exalted and benificed be the former corruptiones uill preas to imprint,

he exhorted Kerr to work for a 'pacification of thos extremitys', offering the prospect of the 'good of the stat of this nation' and its affection to the new king.[1] In effect, he was trying to restore an older pattern of politics in which he would create a faction with a voice at court—a voice that would gain the sympathy of the king. By the 'libertys of the nobility', he probably meant the ancient right of the nobility to offer counsel to the monarch, and he certainly had in mind the restrictions on parliamentary debate that had been introduced to stifle opposition in 1621.

Rothes was to be sadly disappointed in King Charles, but at the time he had grounds for his optimism. Charles had gone against his father's foreign policy in 1624, and by pressing for war against Spain had even seemed to be courting the radical Protestants in England. He was known to be at odds with the old king's Scottish councillors, who had frustrated his plans as prince of Scotland in 1624.[2] Early in the new reign they were reduced in influence, though not removed. But the result was just another authoritarian regime from which the voice of the country was still excluded.[3] In general, Charles continued James's policies. He was just as keen on taxation. He also introduced a major revocation, following on from his father's revocation of 1587 but more far-reaching in practice, with the aim of restructuring landed property; this caused endless trouble. On the other hand, despite his well-advertised preference for ceremony in religion, he did surprisingly little to revive the Five Articles; probably he and his ministers preferred to focus on projects where they could hope to make more progress. For tactical reasons, the opposition under Charles sometimes referred selectively to the 'great wisdom' of James's rule—after all, the things that Charles was doing were things that James had never got around to doing, so it could be

1 Rothes to Ancram, 14 Apr. 1625, *Correspondence of Sir Robert Kerr, First Earl of Ancram, and his Son, William, Third Earl of Lothian, 1616-1649*, 2 vols., ed. D. Laing (Bannatyne Club, 1875), i, 35-8.

2 *RPC*, xiii, pp. lxiii-lxv, 559-63.

3 Essential reading here is M. Lee, *The Road to Revolution: Scotland under Charles I, 1625-1637* (Urbana, Ill., 1985), ch. 1: 'The end of the Jacobean system'. But whether the regime of Melrose, Mar and Chancellor Hay amounted to a distinctive 'system' is questionable.

argued that he had been *against* doing them.[1] But those who objected to Charles's own innovations (such as more elaborate vestments for ministers) objected equally to James's (such as episcopacy or the Five Articles).

This last point is important, since some historians make excuses for James's unpopular policies that they do not extend to his son's. Charles is convicted out of hand of political incompetence and allowed no remission of sentence. But James, we are told, stayed within the limits of what was possible. He *talked* about absolute monarchy, but acted consensually. He knew the Scottish nobles personally, and got along well with them. Now, the last point is relevant only for those who assume (as I do not) that all problems stemmed from noble disaffection; while the others are not true. The Five Articles were well beyond the limits of the possible, and were introduced with no significant consultation. Some of the consultation that did take place was just window-dressing: government business in the 1621 parliament was managed secretly by a hand-picked group, while the full council and nobility were ostentatiously summoned to discuss minor matters, to prevent them 'suspect[ing] that conclusions wer made by a few nomber, and they neglected'.[2] James's determination to push unpopular measures through parliament with a numerical majority—a new feature of the early seventeenth century, since previously voting had been rare—showed a reckless lack of concern for consensus.

During James's long reign, a long-term shift can be detected in the deep structure of Scottish politics. At the beginning, there was *factionalism*—horizontal disputes between regionally-based magnates and their followings. Political disputes at national level followed the same form as local feuds, usually concerning access to resources rather than ideology. At the end of the reign, a vertical division had opened up between *court and country*. The structures of politics were more linked to the court, rather than to local client networks; people with no significant local base could wield great power nationally. Some factional potential continued—competition among courtiers was part of the structure of absolute monarchy; on the whole, however, faction struggles after 1598 were subsumed in the unity of the court. The paradigm was not the feud spilling over into court politics, but court decisions impacting on the localities.

There was also a third pattern, driven by *ideology*. Traditional faction disputes were not about rival ideas; factional conflicts were structured by a chivalric code of honour, loyalty and vengeance which was shared by all participants. The concepts of court and country did involve rival

1 Supplication of 1634, in W.C. Dickinson *et al.* (eds.), *A Source Book of Scottish History*, 3 vols. (2nd edn., Edinburgh, 1961), iii, 79-82.

2 Melrose to James, 26 July 1621, *Melros Papers*, ii, 411-12.

ideas, with the 'country' placing local interests first and resenting interference from a court that it suspected of various forms of corruption.[1] But there were sharper and more sophisticated ideological systems. Presbyterianism was one, and we have seen how confrontational it could be. Its ideological bite was sharpened by adopting secular ideas of limited monarchy and the subjects' right of resistance, an example of the inseparability of religion and politics in early modern Europe. Meanwhile the presbyterians' opponents (headed, of course, by James himself) became equally confrontational. To their high-flying episcopalianism they added the divine right of kings—the secular ideology of European absolute monarchy.

Unlike the vertical court-country split, these were horizontal divisions between incipient parties. The term 'party' should not be taken to imply much in the way of formal organisation. The efficiency of the presbyterian underground movement should not be discounted, but on the whole we should be thinking of informal groupings of like-minded people. The rival ideological positions attracted committed supporters on both sides, within both the court and the country—except that the episcopalians controlled the court and did their best to exclude their opponents. The court-country split and the presbyterian-episcopalian split were different, both in their origins and their structure, but they tended to overlap.

Two contrasts may illustrate how far the regime had travelled. The first parliament of James's majority, that of 1578, had been the weapon of a faction, and had simply endorsed that faction's possession of power without enacting any significant policies; the last, that of 1621, was a forum for the whole political nation, but also the weapon of the court in forcing through two crucial measures against bitter opposition. The chancellor in 1578 had been the earl of Atholl, a regional magnate and faction leader; in 1625 it was Sir George Hay of Kinfauns, the second son of a minor Perthshire laird, who had risen in royal service, first as a gentleman of the bedchamber, then as clerk register (1616) and finally chancellor (1622). Some courtiers did have local links: Hay's patron, the marquis of Hamilton, lived in England but wielded influence through his extensive Lanarkshire estates (he could not, however, control the burgh of Lanark, which voted against the government in 1621). Such links cut across the court-country division to some extent, since clients in the localities recognised their connection to a courtier. But many courtiers had no significant local base, and some, like the earl of

1 The debate provoked by P. Zagorin, *The Court and the Country: the Beginnings of the English Revolution* (London, 1969), is reviewed by D.D. Brautigam, '*The Court and the Country* revisited', in B.Y. Kunze and D.D. Brautigam (eds.), *Court, Country and Culture* (Rochester, NY, 1992).

Nithsdale, were *unpopular* in their localities.[1] Further research may reveal more about clientage links to the court, but few of the dissident shire and burgh commissioners had such links in the 1621 parliament. Others, such as the magistrates of Edinburgh, had to co-operate with the court out of fear; but that does not reduce the significance of the court's unpopularity in Edinburgh, indeed it underlines it.

It has been argued that James's early experience of ruling Scotland gave him advantages as king of England after 1603, even if the English rarely appreciated the fact.[2] This review of Scottish political patterns suggests that other interpretations are possible. The main things that James learned from his experience of ruling Scotland were the need to stamp out dissidence and to unite the nobility in obedience to his government. In his last years in Scotland, he had a fair degree of success in this; but it is questionable if he ever realised that trouble might come from another direction. He built a powerful regime that not only ended magnate revolts but also recruited the nobles as docile, tax-subsidised courtiers—a remarkable achievement. But by allowing the formation of an excluded opposition group, drawn largely from those below the nobility, James left his son a malign legacy.

1 Lee, *Government by Pen*, 208-9.
2 J. Wormald, 'James VI and I: two kings or one?', *History*, lxviii (1983).

~ 3 ~

James VI and the Sixteenth-Century Cultural Crisis

Roderick J. Lyall

In the autumn of 1584, the eighteen-year-old King James VI published his *Essayes of a Prentise in the Diuine Arte of Poesie*.[1] Despite the self-conscious modesty of the title, the collection is an ambitious work, both in its reflection of the king's own literary aspirations and in its articulation of a programme which aims at radical change, little short of a cultural revolution, in Scotland. The principal vehicle of this enterprise is 'Some Reulis and Cautelis to be observit and eschewit in Scottis Poesie', a rhetorical treatise, modelled on French and English texts, which sets out the basis for a renewal of vernacular verse, incorporating stylistic principles already well established in Italy, France and Spain. In reformed Scotland, the poetics of 'Reulis and Cautelis' was indeed radical, for one cultural consequence of Protestantism was a reaction against overtly decorative rhetoric. Plainer styles—equally rhetorical, it should be noted, but employing a rhetoric of direct, largely unmetaphorical statement—are evident in such early reforming works as the *Gude and Godlie Ballatis* (some of which were probably first published in the 1540s) and were predominant through the middle decades of the sixteenth century.[2] While James did not personally bring about a reversion to more elaborate poetic language, the process does appear to have been somehow coincident with the emergence of his court around 1579-80;[3] and his 'Reulis and Cautelis' articulated an attitude towards poetry which had developed outside Scotland during the intervening period.

The poetic principles enunciated in the prose of the 'Reulis and Cautelis' are reinforced in verse by a 'Sonnet decifring the perfyte poete' which intervenes between the Preface and the treatise proper:

> Ane rype ingyne, ane quick and walkned witt,
> With sommair reasons, suddenlie applyit,

1 A fairly exact date is clear from the record in the Treasurer's Accounts, under October 1584, of a payment of £225 and 'ten crownis of drinksiluer' to Thomas Vautrollier 'for ye prenting of his maiesties buik' (NAS, E21/64, fo. 211v).

2 The relationship between Reformation ideology and the aesthetics of the plain style has not yet been discussed in detail in a Scottish context, although it is clearly of significance for an understanding of the work of such poets as Sir Richard Maitland, Alexander Arbuthnot and Robert Sempill; cf., in an English context, J.N. King, *English Reformation Literature: The Tudor Origins of the Protestant Tradition* (Princeton, NJ, 1982).

3 A striking sign of the change is *The Promine* by Patrick Hume of Polwarth, written in 1579 and published by John Ross for Henry Charteris the following year; cf. Alexander Hume, *Poems*, ed. A. Lawson (STS, 1902), 204-10.

For euery purpose vsing reasons fitt,
With skilfulnes, where learning may be spyit,
With pithie wordis, for to expres ȝow by it
His full intention in his proper leid,
The puritie quhairof, weill hes he tryit;
With memorie to keip quhat he dois reid,
With skilfulnes and figuris, quhilks proceid
From Rhetorique, with euerlasting fame,
With vthers woundring, preassing with all speid
For to atteine to merite sic a name.
All thir into the perfyte Poete be:
Goddis, grant I may obteine the Laurell trie.[1]

The self-absorption of the final line pervades the whole collection, and conforms pretty well to contemporary accounts of a thoughtful but somewhat egocentric youth. But that is not the main point of the sonnet, and the catalogue of desirable, indeed necessary, attributes for the aspiring poet which precedes it gives a very clear picture of the values which would characterise the movement which has often (on the basis of one of James's metaphors) been termed 'Castalian'. We should note, first of all, the pairing of the synonyms 'ingyne' and 'witt' in the opening line: although *ingenium* was a traditional feature of rhetorical texts, related to that quality of 'inventioun' which looms so large in the 'Reulis and Cautelis' themselves, it undoubtedly took on powerful new resonances in the sixteenth, and even more in the early seventeenth, centuries, when in its vernacular Italian and Spanish form *ingegno* it became the dominant concept in rhetorical treatises which provided the intellectual justification of such poetic phenomena as *marinismo* and *góngorismo*.

As Danilo Aguzzi-Barbagli has recently demonstrated, the main elements of this Baroque poetics, although it did not emerge, either in practice or in theory, until after the turn of the seventeenth century, began to be put together in sixteenth-century Italy, at least partly in a series of commentaries on the recently-rediscovered *Poetics* of Aristotle. Works such as Francesco Robortello's *In librum Aristotelis de arte poetica explicationes* (1548), the *In Aristotelis librum de poetica communes explicationes* of Bartolomeo Lombardi and Vincenzo Maggi (1550), and Alessandro Piccolomini's *Annotazioni nel libro della Poetica di Aristotile* (1575) all contributed to the development of a poetic theory which laid great emphasis on appropriate and striking use of metaphor, through which the poet demonstrates his *ingegno* (wit) and *acutezza* (sharpness of imagination).[2] The Scots *ingyne*, obviously, is both cognate with and a fairly precise synonym of the Latin *ingenium* and the Italian *ingegno*, and the opening line of the king's sonnet exactly catches the flavour of

1 James VI, *Poems*, i, 69.

2 D. Aguzzi-Barbagli, '*Ingegno, acutezza,* and *meraviglia* in the sixteenth century great commentaries to Aristotle's *Poetics*', in *Petrarch to Pirandello: Studies in Italian Literature in honour of Beatrice Corrigan* (Toronto, 1973), 73-93.

the Italian critics of the previous thirty-five years or so, with their repeated insistence upon the poetic importance of *'un acuto ingegno'*.[1] By foregrounding it so clearly here then, James is catching a late sixteenth-century wave, placing himself and his literary revolution in a contemporary movement of which he can in 1584 have been at most very dimly aware.

The following lines, moreover, spell out what in practice 'ingyne' implies: concise argument ('sommair reasons'), a certain abruptness ('suddenlie applyit'—unless 'applyit' means 'interpreted'), a display of 'learning', vigorous language ('pithie wordis'), and above all, a command of the figures of rhetoric. Nowhere, of course, are such values more appropriate than in the sonnet; and it is to the sonnet that James and his courtiers would most frequently turn in seeking to demonstrate their poetic 'skilfulnes'. Outside Britain, the sonnet had by 1580 become a dominant lyric form, but in England and Scotland, despite the earlier experiments of Wyatt and Surrey, it was only now beginning to become really fashionable. In this respect, too, James's liminary sonnet reflects the extent to which he was seeking to change the direction of Scots verse, taking it away from Reformation stylistic norms and bringing it closer to the cultural values of Continental (and overwhelmingly Catholic!) courts. The issues surely seemed to him to be aesthetic rather than ideological; but we can scarcely ignore the fact that there was, however unrecognised, an ideological subtext.

It must be acknowledged that despite the hints of an awareness of the latest developments in Italian literary theory, the 'Reulis and Cautelis' themselves are something of a disappointment. James does, it is true, lay some emphasis on the importance of originality, admitting in his Preface the limits within which his textbook can operate,

> for gif Nature be nocht the cheif worker in this airt, Reulis wilbe bot a band to Nature, and will mak ʒow within short space weary of the haill airt: quhair as, gif Nature be cheif, and bent to it, reulis will be ane help and staff to Nature.[2]

He reverts to this point within the treatise proper, praising 'Invention' asane of the cheif vertewis in a Poete' and remarking that 'ʒe can not haue the Inuentioun except it come of Nature'; and it is clear that there is a connection between this commitment to originality and his discussion of metaphor. Many of his detailed comments in this area are, however, frankly banal, and where he does verge on the territory in which the Italian theorists had been laying the groundwork for the

1 The particular phrase is Piccolomini's, quoted by Aguzzi-Barbagli, *'Ingegno'*, 88, but there are many variations in all the works he discusses.

2 James VI, *Poems*, i, 68.

meravigli of Baroque metaphorics, James shows himself to be something of a conservative:

> As for Comparisons, take heid that they be sa proper for the subiect that nather they be ouer bas, gif ȝour subiect be heich, for then sould ȝour subiect disgrace ȝour Comparisoun, nather ȝour Comparisoun be heich quhen ȝour subiect is basse, for then sall ȝour Comparisoun disgrace ȝour subiect. Bot let sic a mutuall correspondence and similitude be betwixt them, as it may appeare to be meit Comparisoun for sic a subiect, and sa sall they ilkane decore vther.[1]

This emphasis on decorum is the dominant motif of the whole treatise, and it leaves no room for the striking uses of poetic language which would soon make the verse of Marino, Góngora and Donne so revolutionary. Nor do we find much evidence of such stylistic radicalism in the practice of James and his Scottish contemporaries. But in a Scottish context, the poetic values embodied in 'Reulis and Cautelis' and in the poetry which it sought to justify and encourage was radical enough, and there can be little doubt that James himself was both an enthusiast for, and a practitioner of, a literary style which had predominated in the courts of the Continent for a generation and more, and which can best be described as 'mannerist'.[2] The term itself, borrowed from art history, remains a controversial one, but it will perhaps suffice for the present to offer a list of some of those poets whose work I am thinking of, and whose aesthetic values I believe to be parallelled in the 'Castalian' circle presided over by James: it certainly includes such Italians as Bernardino Rota, Bernardo Tasso and Luigi Tansillo; Spanish poets like Garcilaso de la Vega and Fernando de Herrera; and in France, such writers as Maurice Scève, the major figures of the Pléiade, and Philippe Desportes. In the half-century before 1580, the elegant, 'stylish' style of the sonnets, songs and other lyric poems of such men had come to dominate the polite literature of the (mainly Catholic) courts of Europe; and it was these aesthetic priorities which James and his courtiers now set about importing into Scots verse.

There is not space here to explore fully the relationship between this 'stylish' mannerism, so effectively discussed in John Shearman's classic 1967 study and many subsequent works, and the nervous, even anguished, forms of expression which are equally remarked upon by other

1 ibid., 77.

2 The best short introduction to this difficult topic remains J. Shearman, *Mannerism* (Harmondsworth, 1967). For a comprehensive review of the copious literature, see J.V. Mirollo, *Mannerism and Renaissance Poetry: Concept, Mode, Inner Design* (New Haven, NJ, 1984); for a strongly sceptical counter-view, see J.M. Steadman, *Redefining a Period Style: 'Renaissance', 'Mannerist' and 'Baroque' in Literature* (Pittsburg, 1990). While there have been some notable attempts to apply the term to specific English writers and texts, no adequate overall study, comparable with, for example, Marcel Raymond's *anthologie raisonnée La Poésie Francaise et le Manierisme, 1546-1610* (London, 1971), so far exists.

writers upon the arts of the sixteenth century. But the very contradiction, as it may appear to be, between the tortured wordplay of a Michelangelo sonnet and the more elegant, graceful lines of a poem by Bernardo Tasso or Tansillo is in reality an index of the tensions which existed within the culture of the period. Faced with a world in which religious belief was becoming increasingly polarised, in which the power of princes was being wielded with greater display and the uncertainties of the life of a courtier were more and more manifest, and in which even the very structures of the universe were under challenge, artists responded both by breaking up the symmetries and highly unified order of the Renaissance and by seeking forms of expression in which uncertainty was masked by verbal grandiloquence and the splendid elaboration of detail. The debate about whether mannerism is characterised by anguish or stylishness, then, seems to me to miss the point rather: the reality is that these two tendencies are manifestations of the same crisis of uncertainty which has its roots in the fundamental tensions of the age. By the beginning of the 1580s, mannerist techniques in art, music and literature were well established throughout the courts of Western Europe; and it is my view that James's 'Castalian' experiment needs to be understood against this wider European background of crisis and response.

In the five years preceding the publication of the *Essaies of a Prentise*, the Scottish court was a focus for considerable jostling for power, in literary as well as in political and religious terms. Although James was nominally free of tutelage after the termination of Morton's regency in March 1578, it was after his formal entry into Edinburgh in October 1579 that we can see clear signs of the development of a household, centred at Holyrood, which has the true characteristics of a Renaissance court. This should certainly be connected with the arrival, the month before the king's ritualised occupation of his capital, of his cousin Esmé Stewart, sieur d'Aubigny, who brought with him, along with an entourage with disturbingly Catholic sympathies, the manners and values of the French court. For James, who had been educated on earnestly Protestant lines in the comparatively austere surroundings of Stirling, the contrast must have been dramatic; and the cultural conflict implied by the difference can only have been exacerbated by the ten-month period in 1582-3 when he was the virtual prisoner of the earl of Gowrie and his fellow zealots in Ruthven Castle. It was Esmé Stewart, created earl of Lennox in March 1580 and duke in August 1581, and his entourage who were the principal targets of the militants, and they succeeded, not only in separating the king from his favourite, but in causing the latter to return to Paris, where he died in June 1583.

The abrupt separation of James, who was now sixteen, from the attractive, exotic Lennox seems to have been directly connected with the beginning of the king's literary career. That, at least, is the conclusion we can piece together from two pieces of manuscript evidence: the copy of the three stanzas beginning 'Since thought is free' in BL MS. Addit. 24195, a manuscript written in the early seventeenth century and in James's own family circle,[1] is entitled 'the first verses that euer the King made', while another copy, preserved among fragments which probably once belonged to the lawyer Thomas Hamilton (1563-1637), one of the so-called 'Octavians' whose early connections were interestingly on the Catholic side, states flatly that 'Thir maid in anno 1583, at ye duik of obiynnie his putting out of Scotland'.[2] Whatever public ambitions for his own verse and that of his courtiers may subsequently have developed, it was in the intensely private experience of his loss of Lennox that James found his vernacular poetic voice.

'Sen thocht is frie' (to put the poem back into its original Scots form) does not appear in *Essayes of a Prentise*, but another, much longer poem associated with the fall of Lennox certainly does. This is *Ane Metaphoricall Invention of a Tragedie called Phoenix*, an allegorical piece in rhyme royal stanzas, prefaced with a very intricate eighteen-line poem, which combines a double acrostic with a form of internal rhyme known to sixteenth-century French poets as *rime batellée*:

Elf Echo help, that both together we
(Since cause there be) may now lament with tearis
My murnefull yearis. Ye furies als with him,
Euen Pluto grim, who dwels in dark, that he,
Since cheif we se him to you all that bearis
The style men fearis of Dirae: I request
Eche greizlie ghest, that dwells beneth the se
With all yon thre, whose hairis ar snaiks full blew,
And all your crew, assist me in thir twa:
Repeit and sha my Tragedie full neir,
The chance fell heir ...[3]

The name of 'ESME STEWART DWIKE' is clearly inscribed both at the beginning and end of each line, making the poem a considerable formal achievement even without the recurrence of the rhyme in the middle of each following line. Not content with this, James also presents it as a shape-poem of a kind very fashionable in the sixteenth century, although, as James Craigie pointed out, James appears to have missed the point of the convention, which is that the syntax of the poem should correspond to the demands of the lineation, rather than the shape being created merely by an arbitrary arrangement of the words.

1 James VI, *Poems*, ii, p. xxiii.
2 NAS, RH 13/38. I am grateful to Dr Sally Mapstone for drawing my attention to this copy of James's poem.
3 James VI, *Poems*, i, 39-59, at 40-1; all references to *The Phoenix* are based on this edition.

It is, however, with *The Phoenix* itself that we really have to deal. Read biographically, the poem is a moving tribute to Lennox, who is also implicitly identified with the bird which is the poem's subject through the similarity of its name ('which doeth end in X'). In the exotic splendour of its appearance we see something of the impact which Lennox's Parisian fashions must have had upon the dour court of Scotland,

> this countrey cold,
> Which not but hills and darknes ay dois beare,
> (And for this cause was Scotia calld of old) ... (122-4)

The etymology is, of course, false; but the picture of a dark, benighted, sunless kingdom is an image which runs through the poem, reinforced by the Phoenix's Arabian origins and eventual immolation by a fire caused directly by the sun's rays. In the envious hatred of the drab carrion birds which attack this magnificent creature, 'the rauine, the stainchell & the gledd' (146), we can detect an allusion, at least in general terms, to the stern Protestants like the earl of Gowrie who led the Ruthven coup; it is a conscious irony that they recall the clerical birds who tear the now-virtuous Papyngo to pieces at the end of Sir David Lindsay's *Testament and Complaynt of Oure Soverane Lordis Papyngo* (1530), for James himself alludes to that work in ll. 22-28. But it may *not* be deliberately ironic that Lindsay's Papyngo starts out as a figure of the scandalously ambitious courtier whose mortal wound is the direct result of her own determination to climb too high: this is a sense, if he understood it, which James suppresses in his allusion to the earlier poem.

In literary terms, it must be conceded, *The Phoenix* is less convincing. It cannot be said that the poem lacks a strong subject, or that it is entirely without local strengths, both narratively and descriptively. The account of the report of the protagonist's messenger, for example, conveys very powerfully the anxiety and pain which the news of Lennox's death must surely have had upon James:

> Fra he returnd, then sone without delay
> I speared at him, (the certeantie to try)
> What word of *Phoenix* which was flowen away?
> And if through all the lands he could her spy,
> Where through he went, I bad him not deny,
> But tell the trueth, yea whither good or ill
> Was come of her, to wit it was my will.
>
> He tauld me then, how she flew bak againe,
> Where fra she came and als he did receit,
> How in *Panchaia* toun, she did remaine
> On *Phoebus* altar, there for to compleit
> With *Thus* and *Myrrh*, and other odours sweit
> Of flowers of dyuers kyndes, and of *Incens*
> Her nest. With that he left me in suspens,

Till that I charged him no wayes for to spair,
But presently to tell me out the rest ... (197-212)

And there is the description of Panchaia itself, mythically an island to the east of Arabia, but allegorically Paris, to which the Phoenix

homeward had returnde againe
Where she was bred, where storms dois neuer blow,
Nor bitter blasts, nor winter snows, nor raine,
Bot sommer still: that countrey doeth so staine
All realmes in fairnes. (184-8)

The detail is traditional; but it is evocatively done here, and in the overall pattern of climatological imagery in the poem it contrasts very strongly with the darkness which is repeatedly associated with the Scotland Lennox found, and which he has left behind him.

The problem posed by the poem really has to do with its structure. Although there is nominally a narrative line which binds the whole work together, and which provides the basis for the allegorical level of meaning which identifies the fate of the Phoenix with that of Lennox, it simply is not strong enough to support a poem of this length. It is as if James has taken the kind of image which might legitimately provide the central conceit for a sonnet, and extended it to a text of nearly 300 lines. The phoenix does, in fact, occur in many sixteenth-century sonnets, usually in a Petrarchan context, and there is every reason to suppose that it was in just such an application that James found his initial 'invention'.[1] But it is another thing entirely to build a long poem around a single such conceit; and it is difficult not to be struck here by the absence of those 'sommair reasons, suddenlie applyit' which are praised in the liminary sonnet to 'Reulis and Cautelis'.

Nor is the problem one which is confined to James and his *Phoenix*. Alexander Montgomerie, the acknowledged 'maister poete' of the Castalian group, was at this period at work upon his one extended poem, an allegorical dream-vision in the medieval fashion, which is quoted by the king in his 'Reulis and Cautelis' but which appears to have been abandoned unfinished, in the middle of a long psychological debate. It is, in fact, difficult to think of a wholly convincing example of an extended mannerist allegory anywhere in western Europe, with the notable exception of Spenser's *Faerie Queene*: the fact that Spenser took as the generic basis of his allegorical structure the supremely mannerist

[1] On the figure of the phoenix in French poetry of the period, e.g. Amadis Jamyn, see G. Mathieu-Castellani, *Les Thèmes Amoureux dans la poésie française, 1570-1600* (Strasbourg, 1975), 267-78; cf. the sonnet 'Alma Fenice, che dal sacro nido',printed in Domenichi's anthology *Rime diverse de molti eccellentissimi auttori* (Venice: Gabriel Giolito de Ferrari 1545) and frequently thereafter.

Italian form of the romance, in the style of Ariosto's *Orlando Furioso*, is no doubt the key to his achievement (which, after all, remained uncompleted), but neither James nor Montgomerie adopts such a bold narrative approach, and their attempts at allegorical ingenuity in consequence fall flat.

That the mannerism which is the essence of James's cultural revolution is most comfortable in the concentrated forms of the sonnet and the short stanzaic lyric is confirmed by the sequence of twelve sonnets with which the *Essayes of a Prentise* begin. While these poems reveal the young poet at his most self-regarding—the form of the sequence is an extended development of the ancient tradition of the invocation to the Muses—they also constitute a kind of poetic sampler, a demonstration of his command of a variety of subjects and styles. Addressed in turn to Jove, Phoebus Apollo, Neptune, Pluto and Proserpina, Mars, Pallas and Mercury, the sequence also includes a group of four sonnets, all nominally aimed at Phoebus, which describe the seasons, a neat variation on another familiar medieval topos. There are traces here of the descriptive norms of an earlier Scots poetry, as in the Henrysonian, Douglasesque echoes in the evocation of winter:

> But let them think, in verie deid they feill,
> When as I do the Winters stormes vnfolde,
> The bitter frosts, which waters dois congeill
> In Winter season, by a pearcing colde.
> And that they heare the whiddering Boreas bolde,
> With hiddeous hurling, rolling Rocks from hie.
> Or let them think, they see god Saturne olde,
> Whose hoarie haire owercouering earth, maks flie
> The lytle birds in flocks, fra tyme they see
> The earth and all with stormes of snow owercled:
> Yea, let them think, they heare the birds that die,
> Mak piteous mone, that Saturnes hairis are spred.[1]

This is really an amalgam of conventional details, with particular reference to Henryson's 'Preiching of the Swallow' and probably to *The Testament of Cresseid*, but it is also quite impressive of its kind. The skill lies in the organisation of the material in the small compass of a sonnet ('sommair reasons, suddenlie applyit'), and in the contribution this carefully-constructed segment makes to the overall pattern of the sequence.

The composite nature of the sonnet-sequence form is the fundamental basis of its attractiveness to the mannerist poet: John Shearman has noted the essentially fragmentary quality which is inherent in mannerism, and which was remarked upon by commentators even in the sixteenth

1 James VI, *Poems*, i, 9-14, at 11.

century.[1] Evoking the nature of each of the seasons, or describing the tumultuous, varied attributes of the sea, or conveying the violence of battle, James is engaged in the construction of a mosaic, each element of which is almost, but not quite, complete in itself, as the conjunctions which begin seven of the sonnets serve to emphasise. If this composite structure is one typically mannerist feature, the preoccupation with style, even with stylishness, is evidently another: the self-absorption we have already noted, then, is not merely a reflection of James's egocentrism, or of his sense of the creation of a new poetic, but is inherent in the project itself, the development of a poetry in which the way things are stated is at least as important, sometimes perhaps more important, than what is said.

James's appeal to the gods, however, has another important dimension. Over and over again, he stresses his ambition to break down or dissolve the boundary between art and reality:

O furious Mars, thow warlyke souldiour bold,
And hardy Pallas, goddess stout and graue:
Let Reidars think, quhen combats manyfold
I do descriue, they see two champions braue,
With armies huge approching to resaue
Thy will, with cloudds of dust into the air. (10: 1-6)

This, it is clear, is what James means by poetic perfection: a kind of verbal illusionism which conveys images so evocative that they persuade the reader that he/she is experiencing the thing described directly, rather than through the mediating power of language. This is a more sophisticated approach to metaphor than he demonstrates in his theoretical treatise; and this surely suggests that James had a better practical understanding of what he was about than a theoretical framework with which to describe it. The notion that language is capable, through metaphor, of dissolving the boundaries between physical and mental experience is an essentially mannerist one; it helps to provide a bridge between the mannerist aesthetics of the later Renaissance and the Baroque culture which it was beginning, even as James was producing his *Essayes of a Prentise*, to generate.

We have so far been preoccupied with those aspects of James's enterprise which can be associated with the stylish, mannerist poetics of Tansillo and Desportes. But the central position in the *Essayes* is assigned, both literally and metaphorically, to a rather different figure, the Protestant poet Saluste du Bartas, whose *Uranie* in James's Scots translation is strategically placed between the opening sonnet-sequence and the *Phoenix*. Du Bartas' importance for James was evidently very great indeed: the king's second poetic collection, *His Maiesties Poeticall*

1 Shearman, *Mannerism*, 140-51.

Exercises at vacant houres (1591), includes 'The furies', a translation of part of the French poet's *Seconde Septmaine*, published in 1584, and we also have a fragment of part of the second day of the *Premier Septmaine* as well. James also presided over the translation by Thomas Hudson of Du Bartas' *Judit*, one of the major works of the Castalian Renaissance. The attraction, no doubt, was du Bartas' combination of an impeccably Protestant ideology with a suitably grandiloquent style:

> O ye that wolde your browes with Laurel bind,
> What larger feild, I pray you, can you find,
> Then is his praise, who brydles heauens most cleare,
> Maks mountaines tremble, and howest hells to feare?
> That is a horne of plenty well repleat:
> That is a storehouse riche, a learning seat,
> An Ocean hudge, both lacking shore and ground,
> Of heauenly eloquence a spring profound.
> From subiects base, a base discours dois spring;
> A lofty subiect of it selfe doeth bring
> Graue words and weghtie, of it selfe diuine.[1]

It is, of course, appropriate to the concerns of the *Essayes* that du Bartas' *Uranie* is principally concerned with the nature of a Protestant poetics, and with the creation of a style which matches his Huguenot theology to the literary tastes of a mannerist age. But there are also traces in du Bartas of what Ian McFarlane aptly calls 'a *fin-de-siècle* awareness of the crumbling nature of the world',[2] and it is to this that James declares himself to be responding in his introduction to 'The furies',

> a uiue mirror of this last and most decreeped age. Heere shalt thou see clearlie, as in a glasse, the miseries of this wauering world: to wit, the cursed nature of mankinde, and the heauie plagues of God.[3]

This incipient pessimism is not strongly marked in James's writing; but its presence here is a reminder of the darker side of the mannerist consciousness, that brooding awareness of the transience of the material world and the ever-present threat of divine vengeance.

It is, perhaps, surprising that this note does not recur more strongly in the face of death itself, not even a death as traumatic as that of Sir Philip Sidney outside Zutphen in 1586. The sonnet which James composed in tribute to Sidney, published along with five Latin versions by the king himself and members of his circle in Alexander Neville's *Academiae Cantabrigiensis Lachrymae*, is elegantly Classicist in its lament for Sidney's 'inexpected fall', and may even echo some verses in praise of Sidney

1 James VI, *Poems*, i, 29-31.
2 I.D. McFarlane, *A Literary History of France: Renaissance France 1470-1589* (London, 1974), 389.
3 James VI, *Poems*, i, 99.

which were composed by Janus Dousa the Younger and published by his father in his *Odarum Britannicarum liber*:

O Sidnaeie, suas Pallas cui tradidit artes,
Eloquiumque Hermes, animos Mars, Carminis artem
Cynthius, & privam largita est Suada medullam,
Plutus opes, formam Cypris, Charitesque leporem ...

Thou mighty Mars, the Lord of souldiers brave,
And thou, Minerve, that dois in wit excell,
And thou, Apollo, who dois knowledge have
Of euery art that from Parnassus fell,
With all your Sisters that thaireon do dwell,
Lament for him, who duelie serv'd you all
Whome in you wisely all your arts did mell ...[1]

The device is, of course, a familiar one, and it would be rash to assume that James was alluding to Dousa's poem. But the context is strikingly close, and there is no doubt that such intertextuality formed an integral part of the literary world which James (and Sidney) inhabited. The idea of multiple translation in a memorial volume was itself a Continental tradition: the Netherlandish humanist Charles Utenhove, for example, had edited a collection in tribute to Henry II of France in 1560, to which Henry Keir (by 1579 a member of the Lennox circle) had contributed a Scots version of Utenhove's Latin original.[2]The little bundle of poems which the Scottish court added (late, apparently)[3] to Neville's *Lachrymae* was thus a thoroughly fashionable, European creation, and it is striking that the king's sonnet is the only vernacular element within it. Alexander Montgomerie, who might in other circumstances have been expected to contribute, was himself fighting in the Netherlands, where he almost certainly met Sidney;[4] and the other Scots poets of the court seem to have remained silent. It is the Latinity of the Castalian circle which here—unusually—finds its voice.

Nowhere is James's commitment to a mannerist aesthetics clearer than in the fragmentary masque he began to write, but presumably did not

1 For Dousa's poem, see J. van Dorsten, *Poets, Patrons and Professors* (Leiden, 1962), 181; for the contribution of James VI and his circle to the Sidney memorial volume, see Alexander Neville, *Academiae Cantabrigiensis Lachrymae Tumulo Nobilissimi Equitis, D. Philippi Sidneij Sacratae* (London: John Windet 1587), sig. k1-l2; there is a useful facsimile edition of the *Elegies for Sir Philip Sidney* (Delmar, NY, 1980). James's poem is also printed by Craigie: James VI, *Poems*, ii, 104.

2 *Epitaphium in Mortem Henrici Gallorum Regis Christianissimi ejus nomen Secundum* (Paris: Robert Estienne 1560); cf. L. Forster, 'Charles Utenhove and Germany', in *European Context: Studies in the History and Literature of the Netherlands presented to Theodore Weevers* (Cambridge, 1971), 60-80.

3 D. Baker-Smith, 'Great expectations: Sidney's death and the poets', in Jan van Dorsten *et al.* (eds.), *Sir Philip Sidney: 1586 and the Creation of a Legend* (Leiden, 1986), 92-5.

4 R.J. Lyall, 'Alexander Montgomerie and the Netherlands, 1586-1589', *Glasgow Review*, i (1993).

finish, for the marriage of his favourite, George Gordon, earl of Huntly, and Esmé Stuart's daughter Henrietta, in July 1588. The political context is in some ways astonishing: Huntly was already deeply involved in Catholic intrigue, and although he had 'turned Protestant for the occasion' of his wedding (in Maurice Lee's felicitous phrase),[1] his former ally Lord Maxwell was still awaiting trial for alleged plotting, in which Huntly may also have been involved, the previous year. At the very moment at which the marriage took place, moreover, the Armada was on its way northwards, with James still refusing to make clear his support for England until his political and financial demands were met.[2] That the king should have involved himself in the celebrations to the extent of even contemplating the writing of a masque, and perhaps performing in it himself, is therefore remarkable; and it is perhaps less surprising that, for whatever reasons, he apparently never finished it. He nevertheless included what he had written in his own holograph manuscript of his works, now MS. Bodley 165; and enough survives to give us a fairly clear idea of his intentions.

In composing an epithalamium, James was again in touch with contemporary Continental taste, as Leonard Forster's discussion of the Renaissance popularity of the form demonstrates.[3] In choosing the masque as a vehicle he was, moreover, placing his work within a tradition which had become extremely fashionable at the French court—perhaps the choice is to some degree a compliment to Henrietta Stuart's French up-bringing—and more recently in England.[4] As was very often the case, the masque is evidently a preliminary to a display of jousting; the same connection exists in the much less dramatically inventive *mascarade* with which Montgomerie had announced his presence to the court in 1580, and there are numerous parallels in Italy, France and England. The point is made explicit here by a chorus of Nimphes:

> We heir are sent by goddis aboue uith thir our brether deir,
> Quho are prepairid for gluife or ring, or any sporte uith speir;
> And ue haue brocht for uictoris pryce this yallou garlande rounde,
> Uouin of oure haire, uith pearlis thairat, quhiche ue in fisches founde.
> Then knichtis go to and make you for it; ue can no further say:
> Essay you, brethren, thoch I grant unusid at suche a play.[5] (47-52)

1 M. Lee Jr, *John Maitland of Thirlestane and the Foundation of the Stewart Despotism in Scotland* (Princeton, NJ, 1959), 170.

2 On the politics of this phase, see D.H. Willson, *King James VI and I* (2nd edn., London, 1963), 78-84.

3 L. Forster, *The Icy Fire: Five Studies in European Petrarchism* (Cambridge, 1969), 84-121.

4 On the significance of masques and related entertainments at the French court, see F. Yates, *The French Academies of the Sixteenth Century* (London, 1947), 236-74. There is a slight discussion of the English situation in E. Welsford, *The Court Masque* (Cambridge, 1927), 149-67.

5 James VI, *Poems*, ii, 134-45, at 138-9.

James may not have been sure where pearls came from, but he has a canny awareness of the comparative unfamiliarity of such celebrations at the Scottish court: there is a definite teasing note in the Nimphes' final line, although there is some evidence that the Scottish nobility were capable of holding their own at such chivalric sports with their Continental counterparts.

The characters who now appear are a somewhat mixed bunch: the three challengers who have, we are told, arrived from 'forrane vncouthe lands' are apparently a soldier, a 'landuart gentleman' and a 'uertuouse man', but their speeches are punctuated by interventions from a scholar, a passing woman whose chief function appears to be to conclude mistakenly that all the festivities are on her account rather than the bride's, and a 'zani', whose presence is clear evidence that James was aware, at least to some degree, of the conventions of the *commedia del arte*.[1] There are traces, indeed, of the *bragadoccio* role in the speeches of the soldier; and his praise of the bride is the most outrageously hypobolic of all:

> I quhom no bloodie battellis could afraye
> Ame nou become a simple uomanis praye.
> Bot quhat? Na uoman, bot a goddes bricht;
> Na schame to blindet be uith sicc a licht! (97-100)

But it is clear that James never really worked out what the action of his masque was going to be, and there is no meaningful exchange between any of the characters. It exists merely as a series of set speeches, the best of which do at least illustrate their author's rhetorical command.

It is easy to understand, even reading this fragmentary attempt at an *intermezzo*, why the form, even more than the sonnet-sequence, should be regarded as the quintessence of mannerist style. James's true interest, it would seem, is in formal variety, and despite a tendency to rely upon the fourteener, a characteristic of later sixteenth-century verse which any modern reader can only find regrettable, there is a good deal of 'grand' writing here. But the incompleteness of the text may well have an aesthetic as well as political explanation; and there are good reasons for supposing that James's poetic gifts were by 1588 beginning to become dormant. James Craigie has shown that his *Lepanto*, published in *Poeticall Exercises* in 1591, was probably composed as early as 1585; and while the

[1] It seems unlikely that James had direct knowledge of the Italian theatre, but *commedia del arte* exerted a considerable influence in France at this period; cf. A. Baschet, *Les comédiens italiens a la cour de France* (Paris, 1882), and M. Lazard, *Le Théatre en France au XVIe siècle* (Paris, 1930), 209-14. An earlier trace of an indirect influence of this tradition in Scotland can be found in the so-called 'Cupar Banns' composed to advertise Lindsay's *Thrie Estaitis* in 1552: see Sir David Lindsay, *Ane Satyre of the Thrie Estaitis*, ed. R.J. Lyall (Edinburgh, 1989), 165-75.

translation of 'The furies' may have been made as late as the summer of 1589, it too might well come from earlier in the decade.[1] There is, certainly, a flurry of poems associated with the king's journey to Scandinavia in 1589-90, but when in one of these he observes that

Now ar Castalias floods dried up in me
Like suddain shoures this time of yeere ye see[2]

there are reasonable grounds for supposing that he was not merely engaging in mannerist hyperbole: there *are*, certainly, surviving poems written between 1590 and 1603, and a few from the period after his accession to the English throne, but this output in no way rivals James's poetic achievement between 1582 and 1590. When Alexander Montgomerie, in exile from the court at an uncertain point in his life, reminds his fellow-courtier Robert Hudson that

ȝit ȝe have sene his Grace oft for me send,
Quhen he took plesure into poesie[3]

one possible interpretation is that he is looking back to an idyllic former age when James was still interested in poetry as a source of entertainment. Most of the king's literary endeavour after 1590 was devoted to works in prose: the *Basilicon Doron*, the *Daemonologie*, and various shorter pieces.

By the beginning of the 1590s, it is true, the Castalian project had effectively fallen apart. Its principal achievements—James's own collections, Fowler's *Tarantula of Love* and translations of Petrarch and Machiavelli, Thomas Hudson's *Historie of Judith*, Stewart of Baldynneis' *Roland Furious*—were largely complete by 1586-7. Baldynneis gave the presentation manuscript of his works to the king in 1586, and we have no evidence of subsequent work by him. Much of Montgomerie's best writing, so far as it can be dated, was produced before he returned to the Netherlands in the same year; although he evidently wrote a good deal in the ten years between his return and his death in 1598, much of it is dominated by his alienation from the court as a result of his failed attempt to hold on to the pension the king had granted him in happier times. Alexander Hume had by the end of the 1580s destroyed his earlier, secular verse and had turned to the writing of strongly Calvinist religious poetry which makes du Bartas seem positively hedonistic. While it is evident that some younger members of the court circle, such as William Alexander of Menstrie (later earl of Stirling) and Sir Robert Ayton, were still active during the later years of the Scottish reign, there

1 James VI, *Poems*, i, pp. xlvii-xlix.
2 James VI, *Poems*, ii, 70.
3 Montgomerie, *Poems*, i, 102.

does not seem to have been anything like the shared sense of an aesthetic programme which we can legitimately infer from the inter-related texts produced between 1584 and 1587.

In purely Scottish terms, this change of focus and apparent loss of purpose can perhaps be related to the shadow of the English accession, which undoubtedly lengthened across the Scottish court as Elizabeth I grew older. But this process, too, can be given a European perspective. Already by the time the first fruits of the mannerist Castalian Renaissance were being published, the mannerist tradition on the Continent was undergoing radical change. By the 1590s, the development of a new poetic was apparent everywhere: in the work of Marino in Italy, of Góngora in Spain, of d'Aubigné, de Sponde and others in France, of Donne in England. This represented less an abandonment of mannerist approaches to metaphoric language and to literary structure than a conversion of them to new purposes; the generation of the 1590s would transform the literary scene across Western Europe, not least at the court which James would soon be establishing at Westminster. Jacobean literature, as it is defined by historians of English literature, is unmistakably a variety of the Baroque, in which the tensions of mannerist art are given new expression, whether the novelty is seen in the butchery of Jacobean tragedy or the brilliant casuistry of a Donne poem.

There are, it can be argued, if not here, important traces of this Baroque sensibility in the poetry of Montgomerie; and one of the great unanswerable questions is how this very gifted poet might have reacted to the collision of English and Scottish court culture after 1603. But what is very striking is the absence of such a response in the later poetry of the king himself. Those few poems which can definitely be dated after 1603, such as his verses 'On the blazeing starr' (1618), 'On the death of Queene Anne' (1619) and the elegy beginning 'Ye women that doe London loue so well' (1622), show no awareness of Donne's innovations or, for that matter, of the work of Marino—though Drummond of Hawthornden, in his comparatively remote library near Dalkeith, read, admired and imitated the Italian poet. Writing in a polite, restrained style, James is closer to the urbanity of Ben Jonson than to the wit of Donne or the more extravagant language of Marino. If the 'Castalian moment' of 1584 reflects James's engagement with the European cultural crisis of the mid-sixteenth century, the more pragmatic calls of statecraft and the wider stage of a London court may have insulated him from the even more radical changes which European culture underwent later in his life.

~ 4 ~

Court Ceremony and Ritual during the Personal Reign of James VI

Michael Lynch

On Saturday 28 January 1581, the King's Confession, composed by the royal chaplain John Craig, was subscribed by the young James VI, his cousin Esmé Stewart, who had recently been created earl of Lennox, and the 'whole council and court'.[1] This calculated assault on papistry, which would later form the kernel of the National Covenant of 1638, has permitted a phalanx of historians, contemporary and modern, to trace from it the beginnings of covenant theology.[2] Far more attention has been devoted to the Confession's future symbolic status—it would become the first 'national' covenant—than to its contemporary provenance. A good deal is sometimes made of the godly camouflage which it allegedly provided for Esmé Stewart, suspected by some radical Protestants of being a papal agent. Little, by contrast, has been made of the role played by the royal court in the confused years which followed the young king's first appearance in politics in September 1579, when, having just entered his fourteenth year, he left the comparative security of Stirling Castle where he had been brought up and schooled. The Confession was an early mark of the godly status claimed, not only for the young king, but for his new court and government.

Most of the major political events in the period between 1579 and the capture of the king in August 1582 by the Ruthven raiders should be read in tandem with the emergence of a mature court, which also at times was itself one of the major issues at stake in magnatial politics.[3] Alongside the politics of place and profit, overlaid by the natural pull of kin and connection—which, together, have come to be understood as the way Scottish politics worked in the sixteenth century[4]—there needs, for a

1 Spottiswoode, *History*, ii, 268; Calderwood, *History*, iii, 501.

2 S.A. Burrell, 'The covenant idea as a revolutionary symbol: Scotland, 1597-1637', *Church History*, xxvii (1958); A.H. Williamson, *Scottish National Consciousness in the Age of James VI* (Edinburgh, 1979), 68-85; E.J. Cowan, 'The making of the National Covenant', in J. Morrill (ed.), *The Scottish National Covenant in its British Context, 1638-1651* (Edinburgh, 1990), 68-89.

3 This is briefly but usefully discussed in K.M. Brown, *Bloodfeud in Scotland, 1573-1625* (Edinburgh, 1986), 116-21.

4 See J. Goodare and M. Lynch, 'James VI: universal king', Chapter 1 above; also G. Donaldson, *All the Queen's Men: Power, and Politics in Mary Stewart's Scotland* (London, 1983); J. Wormald, *Lords and Men in Scotland: Bonds of Manrent, 1442-1603* (Edinburgh, 1985).

fuller understanding of the personal reign, to be inserted the dynamic but often enigmatic role of the court in politics. This study examines one important aspect of James's court—set-piece ceremonies and triumphs. It looks at the three main such events of the personal reign—the 'joyous entry' into his capital of the fourteen-year-old king in 1579; the entry of his new queen, Anna, in 1590; and the baptism of their first child, Prince Henry, at Stirling in 1594. Such an approach may help explain some of the ways in which religion, the cult of kingship, politics and ceremony increasingly intertwined during the reign. It also suggests why the day after the Confession was subscribed—a Sunday—was devoted to the conventional pleasures of the court, including jousting and running at the ring, alongside new forms of militant Protestantism.[1]

The attention of the court, which was in process of being reorganised in the months before and after Morton's fall in December 1580, had for the previous few days been firmly concentrated on celebrating the marriage of the eldest daughter of the godly Regent Moray (assassinated by a Hamilton in 1570), and James Stewart, a client of Captain James Stewart (soon to be made earl of Arran); he was an otherwise obscure courtier who would find future fame as the 'bonnie earl' of Moray.[2] Nothing was allowed to interfere with the festivities. Morton was removed, under heavy armed guard, to Dumbarton Castle, where his gaoler was the bridegroom's father; his friends and kinsmen were ordered out of Edinburgh and the town gates were barred at night; and another hundred hagbutters were raised, at the capital's expense, to guard the King during his stay at Holyrood.[3]

The festivities lasted almost two weeks. They included a good deal of the king's favourite pastime of running at the ring. They also involved masques, in which the king was probably a reluctant participant; William Hudson, an English court musician, had just been paid the remarkable sum of £100 for his 'extraordiner panis' in trying to teach James to dance. The festivities culminated in the unlikely setting of the Water of Leith in January, with a water tournament and a staged assault on a floating mock fort, dubbed the 'Pope's pallas', which was put to the torch.[4] *In 1566*, a fort representing the divinity of the Stewart monarchy had been erected outside Stirling Castle as part of the celebrations marking the baptism of the future Catholic King James

1 Calderwood, *History*, iii, 486-7; R. Chambers, *Domestic Annals of Scotland*, 3 vols. (Edinburgh, 1858-61), i, 142.

2 He was the son of Sir James Stewart of Doune, commendator of St Colm, future Lord Doune and brother of Archibald Stewart, provost of Edinburgh in 1578; he was also a distant cousin of both the king and Lennox: *Scots Peerage*, vi, 316-17; Brown, *Bloodfeud*, 145.

3 *CSP Scot.*, v, 611; A.J. Mill, *Mediaeval Plays in Scotland* (Edinburgh, 1927), 55; *Edin. Recs.*, iv, 192-3, 196; *RPC*, iii, 348-9; Calderwood, *History*, iii, 484-5.

4 Mill, *Mediaeval Plays, 109, 334-5; CSP Scot., v, 611.*

VI.[1] This water pageant, centring on the Castelo S. Angele in Rome, recalled the mock battle between Henry VIII's men and the Pope's cardinals staged on the Thames at Westminster in 1539. By the 1580s, amidst the religious wars in the Netherlands, the device of a fort and mock battle had again become a favourite with pageant dramatists to enact the triumph of Protestant heroes (such as the earl of Leicester) over papistry.[2] In Scotland, while Morton languished in the castle of Dumbarton, the young, supposedly godly prince—actually a foul-mouthed and pleasure-seeking adolescent—held court.

Little attention has been given to the wider context which underpinned the gradual establishment of a royal court in Scotland over the course of the period 1579-82. The Renaissance triumph by then could be a Protestant event as much as a celebration of kingship. The instruments of 'splendour at court' were being adapted to Protestant monarchy in Scotland as well as in England, although the different structure of the two courts, with Scottish kings being more personally accessible to their nobility, made the creation of a Protestant icon of the king of Scots both difficult and potentially controversial.[3] The late 1570s, in England, were marked by a sustained propaganda campaign, conducted in masques, triumphs and tournaments as well as in print, by the Sidney circle against the prospect of a match between Queen Elizabeth and the duke of Anjou. This spilled over into Scotland. It was the Sidney circle who persuaded George Buchanan, the young king's tutor, to publish his *Baptistes* in 1577 and *De Jure Regni* in 1579, in a flurry of print at the end of his career which would culminate in 1582 with his *History of Scotland*.[4] In England, against a background of the growing popularity of chivalric literature, the celebration of England's delivery from papist bondage was becoming ever more intimately connected to a godly queen, the date of whose accession (17 November) became a national holiday. The prospect of the Anjou match, however, provoked a radical Protestant backlash, also using the imagery of tournament and triumph, in which the shepherd or wandering knight became a saviour of Christendom from the new Antichrist, the 'papist wolf'.[5]

1 M. Lynch, 'Queen Mary's triumph: the baptismal celebrations at Stirling in December 1566', *SHR*, lxix (1990).

2 S. Anglo, *Spectacle, Pageantry and Early Tudor Policy* (Oxford, 1969), 269-70; A. Young, *Tudor and Jacobean Tournaments* (London, 1987), 157-8; D.M. Bergeron, *English Civic Pageantry, 1558-1642* (London, 1971), 25, 46, 49; R.C. Strong and J.A. van Dorsten, *Leicester's Triumph* (London, 1962), 1-19.

3 N. Cuddy, 'The revival of the entourage: the bedchamber of James I, 1603-1625', in D. Starkey (ed.), *The English Court: from the Wars of the Roses to the Civil War* (London, 1987).

4 I.D. Macfarlane, *Buchanan* (London, 1981), 385-7, 394-6, 409-10.

5 J.E. Neale, 'The seventeenth of November', in his *Essays in Elizabethan History* (London, 1958); Young, *Tournaments*, 35-6, 56, 128, 136, 157-8; R. Strong, *The Cult of Elizabeth: Elizabethan Portraiture and Pageantry* (London, 1977), 146-51; D. Cressy, *Bonfires and Bells: National Memory and the Protestant Calendar in Elizabethan and Stuart England* (Berkeley,

In Scotland, two patterns of court culture were being laid down. One, as has been seen, was a novel Protestant layer of interpretation, which was all the more determined because it had to carry within its embrace courtiers from a variety of religious persuasions. In March 1581, the Protestant confession of the king and his household was given a national dimension, with the issue of a royal instruction to all parish ministers to enforce subscription by all their parishioners; it was the first real example of the king as a young David, the godly prince of a Protestant people.[1] The other, more conventional pattern lay in the re-establishment of the chamber, with a renewed stress on court ceremony and protocol. As was often the case after a minority, the reassertion of kingship involved a tightening of ceremonial, where much attention was paid to past precedent. Here, analogies can be drawn with France, where Henry III had in 1574 tried to stamp his authority on his court, as well as with the reigns of previous kings of Scots.[2] In both cases, the emphasis remained, despite the changes, on personal kingship.

I

There were many aspects to the emergence of the young king from his schoolroom in Stirling Castle in the autumn of 1579. The initial focus of the re-established court was at Holyroodhouse, where substantial, if hurried repairs and refurbishment were carried out to the apartments of the king and key members of his household, including Mar and Lennox. Other necessities of kingship were not forgotten—the 'dansing hous' and the stables were repaired, although (as the English ambassador noted) the king had only three or four horses; a billiard table was re-covered, tennis balls were purchased, hawks and hounds were acquired for the hunt, and sand was laid in the Abbey Close for running at the ring. The royal chapel, neglected since its ransacking in 1567 after the deposition of Queen Mary, was refurbished for Protestant worship; it alone needed over 540 feet of glass, costing more than £72.[3]

The purpose of these preparations and repairs was the king's formal 'joyous entry' into his capital, which took place on 19 October 1579, four months into James's fourteenth year.[4] It was a set-piece pageant which

Calif., 1989), 50-7; J. Guy, *Tudor England* (Oxford, 1988), 431-2. This was a direct Protestant counterpart to Loyola's *miles Christi*; see A. Scaglione, *Knights at Court: Courtliness, Chivalry and Courtesy from Ottonian Germany to the Italian Renaissance* (Berkeley, Calif., 1991), 245.

1 See Calderwood, *History*, iii, 501-02; the subscribers included the prominent Catholics, George, fifth Lord Seton and his son, Alexander, future earl of Dunfermline. Cf. Donaldson, *Queen's Men*, 138.

2 V.E. Graham and W. McAllister Johnson, *The Parisian Entries of Charles IX and Elizabeth of Austria* (Toronto, 1974), 159.

3 Mill, *Mediaeval Plays*, 335; *CSP Scot.*, v, 307, 445 (a gift of great horses was made by Elizabeth); *TA*, xiii, 197-201, 210-11, 292, 304; *MWA*, i, 302-7.

4 For accounts of the 1579 entry, see Mill, *Mediaeval Plays*, [opposite] 80, 89-90, 192-4; *Hist. KJVI*, 178-9; Calderwood, *History*, iii, 458-9; Moysie, *Memoirs*, 25; P. Walker (ed.),

was designed to ensure attendance at the parliament held a few days later, which set in train a ruthless campaign against the network of Hamilton power; previous experience, not least in the reign of James II, had shown that the consensus of the political community was needed to guarantee the eclipse of a great noble family. Yet this was no brief rite of passage. James had arrived, in procession with 'two thowsand hors or thereby', from Stirling on 30 September; the first day of the parliament came over three weeks later, on 23 October. The interval, spent by the court in banqueting and other festivities, allowed time for 'the whole nobility and gentlemen', estimated at 3,000 men, to gather; the parliament was attended by eleven earls, thirteen major nobles, seventeen commendators and representatives from no less than thirty-three burghs. This was a potentially explosive gathering, and the burgh's offer to parade in armour (as it would do for the entry of James's queen in 1590) was quickly turned down; the 300 burgesses who greeted the king in his formal entry to his capital were soberly dressed in black silk and velvet, and members of the town council each carried a white staff, a conventional symbol of the end of a feud as well as of office.[1]

Most of the themes and imagery permeating the triumphal entry were familiar, both to Renaissance pageantry and to the capital itself. The route followed was the well-established one used by James's mother in 1561.[2] At the West Port, the king was met by a canopy of purple velvet, emblem of his divinity, carried by thirty-two prominent burgesses, under which he rode through the burgh. The first tableau, enacting the judgement of Solomon between the two mothers, was a prelude to his being presented with sword and sceptre. This was a standard theme, which had been used in Renaissance entries for a century or more: Charles VIII of France had been confronted by the same tableau on his entry into Paris in 1491.[3] At the Over Bow, at the head of the High Street, James was presented with the keys to the burgh by Cupid, a young boy, descending in a globe from the heavens. This was almost certainly the

Documents relative to the Reception at Edinburgh of the Kings and Queens of Scotland, 1561-1650 (Edinburgh, 1822), 11-31; NLS, Johnston's History of Scotland, Adv. MS 35.4.2, fo. 524; W. Maitland, *History of Edinburgh* (Edinburgh, 1753), 37-8; Chambers, *Domestic Annals*, i, 129-31; *Edin. Recs.*, iv, pp. lxxi-lxxii, 144-24. See also, in general, M.M. Bartley, 'A Preliminary Study of the Scottish Royal Entries of Mary Stuart and Anne of Denmark' (University of Michigan Ph.D. thesis, 1981).

1 *RPC*, iii, 223n; Calderwood, *History*, iii, 457; *CSP Scot.*, vi, 257; Donaldson, *Queen's Men*, 130-31; *Edin. Recs.*, iv, 122.

2 A.A. MacDonald, 'Mary Stewart's entry to Edinburgh: an ambiguous triumph', *Innes Review*, xlii (1991), 101-10. It is possible that in 1503 Margaret Tudor entered the capital by the Bristo Port rather than the West Port; otherwise, her route was also the same. I. Campbell, 'James IV and Edinburgh's first triumphal arches', in D. Mays (ed.), *The Architecture of Scottish Cities and Towns* (East Linton, 1997), 27, 33n.

3 L.M. Bryant, *The King and the City in the Parisian Royal Entry Ceremony* (Geneva, 1986), 182.

same mechanical device that had been used in 1561.[1] At the tolbooth, James was greeted by another familiar allegory: four 'young maidens' (who were probably boy pupils of the grammar school) representing Peace, Justice, Plenty and Policy, a Renaissance variant on the standard theme of the four cardinal virtues; each delivered an oration.[2] Nearby, at St Giles', Dame Religion issued an invitation to enter to hear a sermon by James Lawson, principal minister of the burgh, on the duties of kings and their subjects; it was followed by the singing of Psalm xxi, on the duty of kings. Outside again, presumably some considerable time later, James was greeted at the market cross by four trumpeters and the pagan deity of Bacchus, distributing wine from a hogshead to the crowd; the lively drinking song, *Nou let us sing,* which refers to Bacchus and a fountain running wine, probably commemorates the event.[3] At the Salt Tron, the king passed paintings representing the genealogy of kings of Scots going back to Fergus I; the precise form this took is unclear. A genealogical tree, symbolising the blessedness and antiquity of the royal line, was a familiar Renaissance image;[4] but the collection of well-known, iconic portraits of Stewart kings from James I to James V, which dates from this period, seems to have been designed to hang on a board rather than to have been framed.[5] If this group portrait was produced for the 1579 entry and mounted on the Salt Tron, its triumphal celebration of the past established a motif for the reign as a whole; part of the propaganda campaign waged in the 1590s to promote James's case for the English succession used the same visual imagery of past Stewart kings. The much more elaborate entry organised for Charles I in 1633 embellished the same image, with a portrait gallery of 107 kings of Scots.[6] The final image within the capital, at the Netherbow Port—a representation of the configuration of the planets at the time of the king's birth—had been used in Paris in 1558 during the celebrations of Mary's marriage to the Dauphin and was also used in 1633. One last tableau was performed

1 Bergeron, *English Civic Pageantry*, 24.

2 D. Gray, 'The royal entry in sixteenth-century Scotland', in S. Mapstone and J. Wood, *The Rose and the Thistle: Essays on the Culture of Late Medieval and Renaissance Scotland* (East Linton, 1998), 28, 30; the 1590 entry saw another, minor variant of the four virtues. See also Bryant, *King and City*, 17-19, for parallels in French ceremonies since the 1460s.

3 K. Elliot and F. Rimmer, *A History of Scottish Music* (1973), 35; D.J. Ross, *Musick Fyne: Robert Carver and the Art of Music in Sixteenth Century Scotland* (Edinburgh, 1993), 133-4; *MB* XV, 48.

4 Bryant, *King and City*, 184-5.

5 D. Thomson, *Painting in Scotland, 1570-1650* (Edinburgh, 1975), 20-1; J.L. Caw, 'Portraits of the first five Jameses', *SHR*, vii (1910), 113-18; I am particularly grateful to Rosalind Marshall for her advice and guidance here. The omission of Queen Mary from the group portrait may have been linked to the assault on the Hamiltons, the major concern of the parliament which followed.

6 See E. McGrath, 'Local heroes: the Scottish humanist Parnassus for Charles I', in E. Chaney and P. Mack (eds.), *England and the Continental Renaissance* (London, 1990), 257-70.

at the market cross of the neighbouring burgh of the Canongate. It was a 'brief fable', reminiscent of 1561, depicting the abolition of the pope and the mass.[1]

The 1579 triumph was an uneasy mixture of conventional royal entry imagery, standard didactic messages drawn from 'advice to princes' literature, and explicit Protestant sermonising. Mythological gods were juxtaposed with religious propaganda. Civic ceremony had largely fallen into disuse since the Reformation of 1560. Before the re-articulation of monarchical imagery in the 1590s, some of the point of the divinity of kingship signified by the canopy carried above the king would have been lost with the disappearance of the Corpus Christi procession on which it was originally based. Angels could no longer easily descend from the clouds with the emblems of kingship; Cupid had to do instead.[2] The four virtues, embodied by 'faire young maides' outside St Giles', were emphasised in the sermon within the church, but the gap between the image and the message illustrated some of the problems posed for Protestant festival.[3]

No royal entry in Scotland before 1633 has an official printed text.[4] Relying on fragmentary accounts and incidental details, it is difficult to be sure of the whole point of the pageantry. It is likely that the emphasis on the antiquity of the king's line was matched by a celebration of noble lineage: 'effigies of noble men and women' were depicted on tapestries, or paintings on boards hanging from houses along the High Street. All of this was general, conservative and unexceptionable. By the later sixteenth century, however, it was becoming more usual for Renaissance triumphs to carry specific political messages. Other than the crude anti-papist tableau in the Canongate, which probably reflected growing fears in 1579 of a Counter-Reformation mission, it is difficult to detect much other than conventional advice to princes. Two particular themes, however, probably underpinned the 1579 celebrations. The entry was an astrological pageant: at the tolbooth, the Wheel of Fortune was ritually burned and later, at the Netherbow, 'King' Ptolemy, as representative of astronomy, 'vivelie' explained the significance of the conjunction of the

1 Mill, *Mediaeval Plays*, 183-4, 194; cf. MacDonald, 'Mary Stewart's entry', 107.

2 B. Guenée and F. Lehoux, *Les Entrées Royales Françaises de 1328 à 1515* (Paris, 1968), 14-8; Bryant, *King and City*, 102, 154. Angels, however, featured in Anna's entry in 1590.

3 This difficulty would partly be resolved by a physical personification of the king by an actor during his queen's entry in 1590. Even for Anna's entry, however, there was little of the complex intertwining of classical and religious imagery which had marked the pageantry outside St Giles' in 1503, when the Annunciation and Marriage of the Virgin was juxtaposed against the Judgement of Paris: Gray, 'Royal entry', 18-20.

4 William Drummond of Hawthornden, *The Entertainment of the High and Mighty Monarch Charles ... into ... Edinburgh, the fifteenth of June, 1633* (Edinburgh, 1633). There is, however, a detailed account of Margaret Tudor's entry in 1503 by John Young, Somerset Herald: J. Leland, *Collectanea*, 6 vols. (2nd edn., London, 1774), iv, 265-300. See also Gray, 'Royal entry', 16, 25n.

planets at the time of the king's birth.[1] The young king was being invited into the 'magico-scientific world' of the northern Renaissance, which by the 1590s was prominent in the thoughts of intellectuals such as Robert Pont and John Napier of Merchiston.[2] Ptolemy was one of the conventional authorities in the widely accepted notion of the seven ages of man and their relationship to the seven planets: the king's passage, at fourteen years, from the second to the third age of man—from Mercury to Venus—was what lay behind the pageant of the four virtues and the burning of Fortune's wheel before his entry into St Giles'. The four figures displayed outside St Giles' celebrated the standard accomplishments of the king's four ages to come—Temperance, Prudence, Fortitude and Justice—after his present age of adolescence: these were, respectively, youth, manhood, old age and decrepitude.[3]

This was underpinned by another set of messages, celebrating the education of the boy king. At the West Port, James listened to an oration in Latin; the figures at the tolbooth addressed him in Greek, Latin and Scots; and Dame Religion, on the steps of St Giles', greeted him in Hebrew. James would have had no difficulty in understanding these messages which were, as convention dictated, designed for him alone: brought up on a diet of Greek before breakfast, he once complained that he had been forced to learn Latin before he could speak Scots.[4]

Godly ministers, poets, genealogists, mathematicians and astrologers joined in chorus to acclaim the boy king who would, all the portents foretold, fulfil his historic role. The significance of the moving wheel outside St Giles' was both astrological and religious. Here, according to Augustine, was the perfect age, when, as in the kingdom of the biblical David, the king, in the flower of his age, was poised enthroned and motionless at the top of what for others around him was a moving Wheel of Fortune or Life. The young David had already become Solomon.[5]

1 *Hist. KJVI*, 179. An multi-layered astrological pageant had also been laid on for Katherine of Aragon's entry into London in 1501: Anglo, *Spectacle*, 56-97. The influence was also common in poetry, seen in the fifteenth-century *Ratis Raving*, and David Lindsay's *Squire Meldrum*. Lindsay's works were printed in five separate editions 1568-82, including one each in 1580 and 1582. See also McGrath, 'Local heroes', 258-9, for Ptolemy in 1633.

2 A.H. Williamson, 'Numbers and national consciousness: the Edinburgh mathematicians and Scottish political culture at the union of the crowns', in R.A. Mason (ed.), *Scots and Britons: Scottish Political Thought and the Union of 1603* (Cambridge, 1994), 187-212.

3 Burrow, 197-8, 44. In 1587, when the king reached his 'perfect age', he passed from young manhood (the sun) to manhood itself (Mars). It is possible that the four parts in the drinking song, *Nou let us sing* (treble, counter, tenor and bass) corresponded to the four ages: Ross, *Musick Fyne*, 133-4.

4 Maitland, *History of Edinburgh*, 37-8. James was acclaimed by Alexander Montgomerie as 'In eviry language eloquent': Montgomerie, *Poems*, i, no. XLVIII, l.80.

5 M. Dove, *The Perfect Age of Man's Life* (Cambridge, 1986), 60, 70-76. Montgomerie's poem, 'The Navigatioun', hailed 'A Salomon for richt and judgiment': *MT*, XLVIII, l.79.

II

The entry was followed, during the first six months of 1580, by another rite of passage—an extensive royal progress, designed to take the young king to the major burghs of his realm and perhaps also to provide some relief for the hard-pressed treasury which, according to Lord Ruthven, the treasurer, was exhausted by the high cost of the king's entry.[1] Dundee was visited early in June, followed by Aberdeen, which had spent almost six weeks in elaborate arrangements including the staging of plays and 'histories', for which a hefty tax of £2,000 was specially raised on the burgh. At St Andrews, a play was also staged, in the New Abbey, in July.[2] By June, repairs were also under way at Doune Castle, which was intended as the venue for court 'pastimes', outdoors as well as inside.[3] In the autumn, a larger, more elaborate royal household was set up, consolidating the control already enjoyed by Mar and Lennox over the king's privy council and the chamber. Mar (the king's companion during most of his boyhood years at Stirling Castle) became chancellor. Lennox (his thirty-seven-year-old kinsman) was made chamberlain, and twenty-four ordinary gentlemen of the chamber were appointed.[4] Within three months—in December 1580—Morton was displaced and the re-establishment of the court took on a new urgency as factional struggles intensified.

In January 1581, with Morton safely locked up in Dumbarton, the marriage of the 'bonnie earl of Moray' set the scene for a redistribution of Morton's lands and revenues, an inflation of honours on a scale not seen since 1565, and an attempted consolidation of Stewart family power.[5] The course of the year deserves fuller attention than can be given here. In March, Arran, who had just been admitted to the privy council, was made captain of the recently established royal guard. His meteoric rise to influence was confirmed in April, when he was created an earl, but he was only one of a phalanx of Stewart beneficiaries of royal patronage. After the trial and execution of Morton in early June, Lennox was proclaimed a duke in August, prior to a six-week royal visit to Glasgow, in the heartland of Lennox territory.[6] The calling of

1 *Hist. KJVI*, 180.

2 Mill, *Mediaeval Plays*, 161; *RPC*, iii, 289, 294-5; Calderwood, *History*, iii, 462; Melville, *Diary*, 81-2.

3 Doune was the seat of another 'Stewart of our blood', the father of the future earl of Moray, created Lord Doune in November 1581: see n. 6, above; *APS*, iii, 234, 235; Donaldson, *Queen's Men*, 135; *Scots Peerage*, vi, 316-17; *MWA*, i, 307.

4 *RPC*, iii, 316, 322-3; *CSP Scot.*, v, 529, 531; Spottiswoode, *History*, ii, 268-9; Cuddy, 'Entourage', 178, 180; Brown, *Bloodfeud*, 117-18. The office of chamberlain had been vacant since 1569.

5 J. Goodare, 'Queen Mary's Catholic interlude', in M. Lynch (ed.), *Mary Stewart: Queen in Three Kingdoms* (Oxford, 1988), 154-70; Donaldson, *Queen's Men*, 134-5.

6 J. Ferguson, *The Man Behind Macbeth (London, 1969), 36; Donaldson, Queen's Men, 135-6; Moysie, Memoirs*, 34; *RPC*, iii, 412-14.

a parliament, in late October, was preceded by another set-piece occasion at Holyroodhouse where in the great hall, amidst wooden stands specially erected for the event, Lennox was formally invested, along with three earls and fifteen knights.[1] Two weeks later, the daughter of one of the new earls—Lord Ruthven, now earl of Gowrie—was married to the Master of Ogilvie, one of the gentlemen of the new chamber. The ceremony took place at the same royal palace amidst 'great triumphe' and fireworks, by now an essential ingredient of Renaissance festivals.[2]

It was important that the loyalty of Gowrie, outwith the Stewart nexus, be retained since it was his personal credit as treasurer which had financed much of the conspicuous consumption which accompanied the revival of the court after 1579; the deficit had risen from £36,000 to £45,000 in a matter of a few months of 1581.[3] Power politics and court ceremony were played out, side by side. The new cult of honour, which would prove to be a marked feature of James's personal reign, and the successful coup staged against Morton were jointly celebrated in physical form in the great hall of Balbegno Castle in Angus, probably late in 1581, where the armorial devices of sixteen earls—including those recently elevated—were carved in plaster.[4]

An essential ingredient of this quickening court culture was the emergence of a band of court poets. James's departure in state from Stirling Castle in September 1579 had been celebrated in verse by Patrick Hume of Polwarth. The flyting between Hume and Alexander Montgomerie, both beneficiaries of the redistribution of Douglas lands which followed Morton's execution, took place, according to Montgomerie's, 'probably' sometime in 1580, although its references to masques may suggest a slightly later date. The English poet, Thomas Churchyard, was a paid visitor at the court between June 1580 and June 1581.[5] Such vernacular poets would have been necessary to compose speeches for the court masques which make enigmatic appearances in the record from 1580 onwards—such as the 'strange mask' at Holyrood mentioned by the

1 C.J. Burnett, 'The Officers of Arms and Heraldic Art under King James VI and I, 1567-1625' (University of Edinburgh M.Litt. thesis, 1992), 22, citing NAS, treasurer's accounts, 1581-2, E21/62, fo. 167; Moysie, *Memoirs*, 34. The plan to have the parliament of Oct. 1581 declare Lennox heir to the throne was abandoned as too controversial: *CSP Scot.*, vi, 55, 59, 92.

2 Moysie, *Memoirs*, 34; *RPC*, iii, 427-8n.

3 *RPC*, iii, pp. xl, 390, 392. Gowrie had to wadset his lands to raise credit: NAS, treasurer's accounts, 1581-2, E21/62, fo. 67r.

4 J. Sutherland, 'The heraldic ceiling of Balbegno Castle', *Aberdeen University Review*, xlvi (1975-6), 270-1; Burnett, 'Officers of Arms', 70-1; N. Tranter, *The Fortified House in Scotland* (Edinburgh, 1977), iv, 149-50. There is one gap, where the arms were subsequently removed—probably after Gowrie's forfeiture in 1584.

5 Montgomerie, *Poems*, ii, pp. lv-lvi, 134, ll. 43-4; cf. *Longer Scottish Poems, Volume One, 1375-1650*, ed. P. Bawcutt and F. Riddy (Edinburgh, 1987), 279-81; H.M. Shire, *Song, Dance and Poetry of the Court of Scotland under King James VI* (Cambridge, 1969), 79, 80; G.R. Hewitt, *Scotland under Morton, 1572-80* (Edinburgh, 1982), 204.

English ambassador in Lent 1581, after the Moray marriage.[1] Robert Sempill was paid in September 1581 for the composing of a 'pastyme' for the king, probably performed during the six-week visit to Glasgow.[2] Such poetry was essentially public. Although Montgomerie's *The Navigatioun* and *A Cartell of the Three Ventrous Knichts* cannot be dated with precision, internal references—such as the invitation to the ball at the end of former and the running at the ring in the latter—make it likely that the date of their composition was 1581 (for an event such as Moray's marriage) or early 1582 (which was the point at which the number of appearances by the king sharply increased)[3] rather than the 'joyous entry' to Edinburgh of September 1579. The king had been given dancing lessons only at the end of 1580 and the dancing chamber was still in need of extensive repairs early in 1582.[4] It is intriguing that it was also in this period, 1580-82, that the works of Sir David Lindsay, dramatist, public poet and royal herald of James V, were twice republished in new editions.

The Ruthven raid brought this burgeoning court culture to an abrupt halt. Little activity in the court can detected during the ten months of the Ruthven regime, which fell in June 1583. Financial retrenchment was one of its hallmarks, and one of the few signs of conspicuous expenditure was an estimate for essential repairs to the royal palaces made in May 1583. With the king in semi-captivity, the court, as an English agent reported, was 'very quiet and small' and 'utterly unfurnished'.[5] It is hardly surprising that the demise of the Ruthven regime saw a burst of renewed activity: John Stewart of Baldynnies recalled a ceremony at court in 1583 to honour the king as a poet; and James was crowned poet-king at New Year of 1583-4 after writing his *Phoenix*.[6] The period 1584-5 saw a flurry of printed works, in verse and music, much of it reflecting the influence of the Pléiade poets, probably first introduced to the king by Lennox, and also the achievements of the Castalian Band before the Ruthven coup. The published works included James's own *Reulis and Cautelis* and *Essayes of a Prentise in The Divine Art of Poesie*, which included vernacular verse by five of the members of the Castalian Band, Thomas Hudson's translation of Du Bartas' *Judith*, and James Lauder's celebrated musical piece, *My Lorde of marche paven*, dedicated to the new earl of March (the former seventh earl of Lennox, uncle of Esmé Stewart).[7] If Montgomerie, a client of the court, felt himself to be

1 *CSP Scot.*, v, 619.

2 R.D.S. Jack, *The Italian Influence on Scottish Literature* (Edinburgh, 1972), 42; Mill, *Mediaeval Plays*, 192n.

3 *RPC*, iii, 453, 459, 466, 469, 474 (Feb.-Apr. 1582).

4 Mill, *Mediaeval Plays*, 334, 335.

5 *MWA*, i, 310-14; *CSP Scot.*, vi, 474, 322.

6 Shire, *Song, Dance and Poetry*, 101; see also R. Lyall, 'James VI and the sixteenth-century cultural crisis', Chapter 3 above.

7 Elliot and Rimmer, *Scottish Music*, 34; Ross, *Musick Fyne*, 131-2. See Fowler, *Works*, iii, pp.

at the zenith of Fortune's wheel,[1] the royal court had self-consciously cast for itself the role of a temple of the arts, with the young Apollo or Titan at its centre, as portrayed in the Uranie sonnets. This was a restoration of courtly kingship after the Ruthven interlude rather than a fresh establishment of it.

The mid- and later 1580s leave conflicting impressions. The public persona of James as poet was probably never more prominent than in July 1588, when he composed and appeared in a masque for the wedding of the earl of Huntly to Henrietta, daughter of his former mentor, Esmé Stewart. But the young Apollo also was trying to acquire *gravitas* and developed other personae after 1588, including those of theologian and political commentator.[2] It has been estimated that the king spent at least half of his time in England hunting or on progress.[3] It would be difficult to make the same calculation for his years in Scotland as much of the information about his favourite pastime comes in vague asides in diplomatic dispatches, but the proportion spent hunting was probably only a little less. By 1591, his enthusiasm had denuded his favourite hunting grounds around Falkland of male fallow deer and, after much impatient chiding from James, restocking from England was arranged by the English ambassador.[4] Banqueting took up only a little less of his time, although James took every opportunity to play the guest rather than the host. In May 1585, he was entertained by Arran at Dirleton Castle for twelve days.[5] It became common for the leading nobility in the court to throw banquets for the king, at their own expense, in private houses within Edinburgh, often of their merchants or bankers; many degenerated into drunken brawls or worse.[6] These houses were also, it is likely, a natural venue for the poets of the Castalian Band. Huntly seems often to have used the house of William Fowler, the poet, who after 1590 provided a discreet link with the queen as her secretary. It is also likely that the splendidly furnished house of Fowler's mother, the money-lender Janet Fockart, who had provided for Esmé Stewart at his first arrival in 1579, was a centre for both literary discourse and political intrigue.[7]

xviii-xxi.

1 R.D.S. Jack, *Alexander Montgomerie* (Edinburgh, 1985), 8.

2 James VI, *Poems*, ii, 134-45. See also J. Wormald, '"Tis true I am a cradle king": the view from the throne', Chapter 14 below.

3 Cuddy, 'Revival of the entourage', 193.

4 M. Lee, *Great Britain's Solomon: James VI and I in his Three Kingdoms* (Urbana, Ill., 1990), 111, 146-7; *CSP Scot.*, x, 458, 468, 505, 512, 519, 674.

5 Calderwood, *History*, iv, 366; Moysie, *Memoirs*, 52.

6 Moysie, *Memoirs*, 73 (March 1589).

7 Calderwood, *History*, v, 37; M.H.B. Sanderson, *Mary Stewart's People* (Edinburgh, 1987), 98-9. The exchequer also met in Fockart's house in 1593: *ER*, xxii, 309. See T. van Heijnsbergen, 'The interaction between literature and history in Queen Mary's Edinburgh: the Bannatyne Manuscript and its prosopographical context', in A.A.

This was government by gesture, although the timing of the gestures underlines their significance. In 1586, James insisted that the meeting at Berwick of the commissioners to conclude a league with England take place, with due 'solemnities', on his birthday.[1] In May 1587, on the last day of the meeting of a convention at Holyroodhouse at which James had harangued his nobles for the need for a 'perfect unioun and reconciliatioun', the king, at the end of a drunken banquet in the Palace, led his feuding nobles in procession, hand in hand, up the High Street to Edinburgh's market cross for a continuation of the festivities. This 'love feast' was a Renaissance triumph in miniature, demonstrating in public, at the historic centre of the king's capital, the alleged new-found harmony amongst the nobility. Debtors were released from prison, the gibbets at the cross were ritually destroyed, and musicians, trumpeters, fireworks and cannon firing from the Castle were all employed to foster a sense of what James himself would later term a 'universal king', who would rule justly and above faction.[2] Although this may have been what would now be called 'government by photo opportunity', it would be a mistake simply to dismiss it as ineffectual.[3] There was a clear link between this convention, another in early June (which met shortly after the king had warded Lord Yester for a feud), and the parliament which met on 29 July.[4] The point of the exercise was not to resolve issues but to provide a distraction from them. This was hardly a careful balancing of one faction against another, for too often events at or near the court threatened to cascade out of control, but it was treating politics as theatre.

III

In May 1590, after considerable delays, the king returned to Scotland with his new queen, Anna of Denmark. The events of the next five months—most of Anna's retinue stayed until September—encapsulated many of the strains of the rest of the personal reign. The original intention, that the queen be crowned in St Giles', had to be abandoned after objections from some of the leading ministers about the ceremony taking place on a Sunday and the anointing of the queen. The new venue, the Abbey Church at Holyrood, posed a number of difficulties: the queen had to wait five days in Leith while hurried refurbishment of the church took place. More significantly, coronation and royal entry to the capital

MacDonald *et al.* (eds.), *The Renaissance in Scotland* (Leiden, 1994), for literary circles in Edinburgh a generation earlier.

1 *CSP Scot.*, viii, 394, 423. For more on the league with England, see J. Goodare, 'James VI's English subsidy', Chapter 6 below.

2 *RPC*, iv, 164-9 and note; Moysie, *Memoirs*, 63; *Hist. KJVI*, 229; Calderwood, *History*, iv, 613-14. Birrel, 'Diary', misdates it. The cost was met by the burgh: *Edin. Recs.*, iv, p. lxx.

3 As is done by Brown, *Bloodfeud*, 216. Cf. M. Lee, *John Maitland of Thirlestane and the Foundation of the Stewart Despotism in Scotland* (Princeton, NJ, 1959), 117.

4 *RPC*, iv, 185-6 and note.

were now separated; the iconography of the marriage of a new queen to both kingdom and capital, which conventionally marked such occasions, became blurred.[1]

Scotland had not seen a combined coronation and royal entry of a queen since 1503. The magnificence of that entry—of Margaret, queen of James IV[2]—had underlined two points that were common to many formal entries of queens after a royal marriage elsewhere in Europe in the sixteenth century, and particularly in France: such an occasion was often more elaborate than the previous entry of the king himself and it was also usually more pointed in its political messages.[3] On 19 May, two days after her coronation, Anna made her entry into her capital alone, without James (as convention by then usually dictated).[4] Her retinue included eighteen Danish notables, at least as many Scottish nobles, and sixty halberdiers, paid for by the burgh. The mythological apparatus which greeted her was more elaborate than that in 1579, and the musical content was considerably greater; both doubtless reflected the influence of the Castalian Band. In outline, the set-piece tableaux and much of their content, as well as the route, seem similar to those in 1579 or before.[5] Anna was greeted at the West Port by a Latin oration and a globe, which opened to reveal a child, 'the angel of the town', who gave her the keys of the burgh, a bible and a psalter.[6] Although both the globe and the gift were reminiscent of the entry of Mary in 1561, the ceremony of 1590 was far less controversial. Anna was welcomed at the tolbooth by the same four figures as in 1579: Temperance, Prudence, Fortitude and Justice, the

1 For the coronation and entry, see *Papers relative to the Marriage of King James the Sixth of Scotland* (Bannatyne Club, 1828), *passim*; its appendices include the poetic description of the entry by John Burel and a contemporary list of the 180 members of the new royal households, set up in Feb. 1590. Another account was published in London: *The joyful receiving of Iames the Sext of that name king of Scotland ...* (London, 1590). Also, Moysie, *Memoirs*, 83-4; Birrel, 'Diary', 25; Calderwood, *History*, v, 94-8; Spottiswoode, *History*, ii, 406-08; Melville, *Diary*, 279-80; NLS, Johnston's History, Adv. MS 35.4.2, fo. 598; *CSP Scot.*, x, 295, 299-300; Walker (ed.), *Reception of the Kings and Queens of Scotland*, 34-45; *Edin. Recs., 1589-1603*, 19-21, 327-32; Mill, *Mediaeval Plays*, 110-11, 195-204; Chambers, *Domestic Annals*, i, 196-200; Bergeron, *English Civic Pageantry*, 67-9. The 'Danish Account' of the coronation and entry is reprinted and translated in D. Stevenson, *Scotland's Last Royal Wedding: the Marriage of James VI and Anne of Denmark* (Edinburgh, 1997), 100-22.

2 An entry into Edinburgh had been staged for Mary of Guise in July 1538, although there is no detailed account of it. One of its devisers was David Lindsay, poet and royal herald: C. Edington, *Court and Culture in Renaissance Scotland: Sir David Lindsay of the Mount* (Amherst, Mass., 1994), 108-10. Her coronation at Holyrood, however, did not take place until Feb. 1540. For 1503, see Leland, *Collectanea*, iv, 258-62; R.L. Mackie, *King James IV of Scotland* (Edinburgh, 1958), 105-12; Gray, 'Royal entry', 16-22.

3 Bryant, *King and City*, 95-8; Strong, *Splendour at Court*, 141-2.

4 Margaret Tudor, by contrast, had been accompanied by James IV in 1503; they had even shared the same horse: Leland, *Collectanea*, iv, 288-91. I am grateful to Theo van Heijnsbergen for this point.

5 Bergeron, *English Civic Pageantry*, 69, criticises the entry as 'bankrupt' of ideas; but this account relies on a limited number of sources.

6 'DanishAccount', 108, which gives the speech.

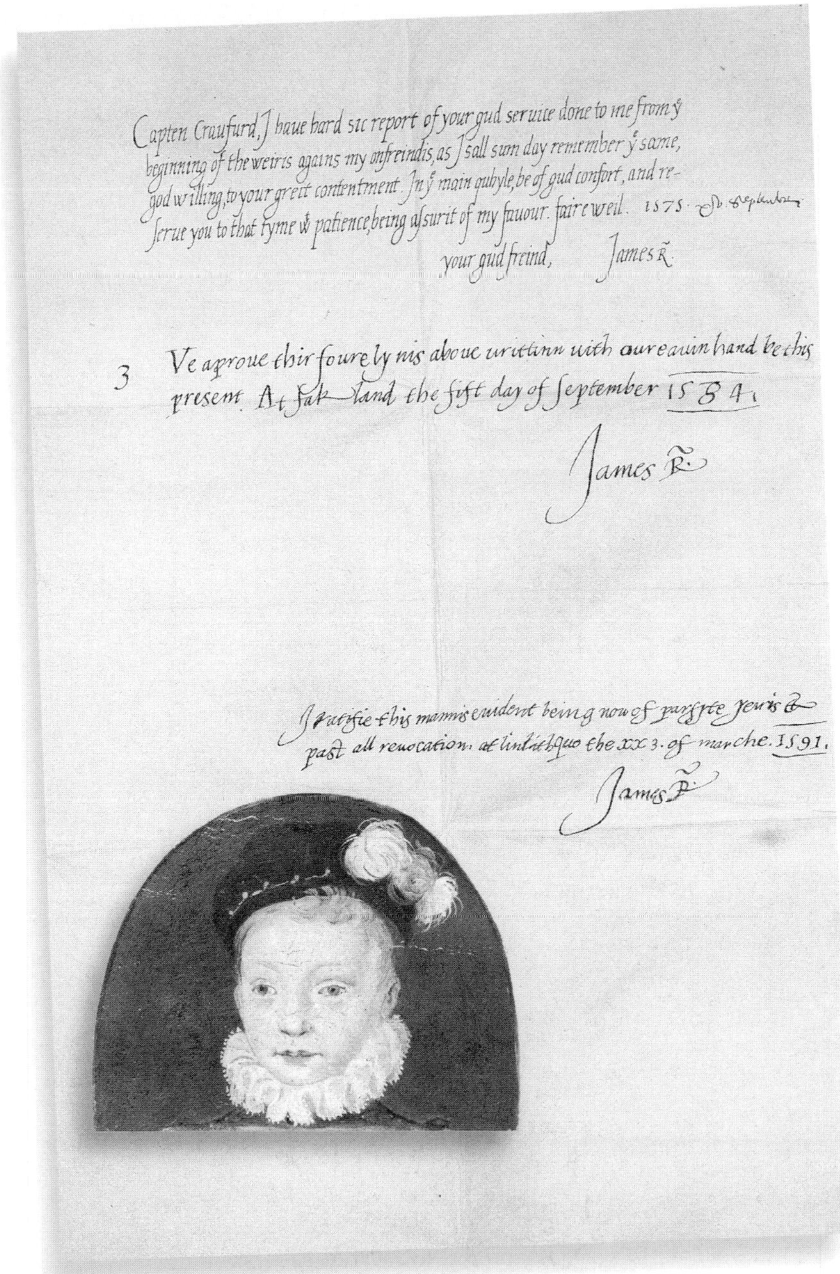

Capten Craufurd, I haue hard sic report of your gud seruice done to me from ye beginning of the weiris agains my onfreindis, as I sall sum day remember ye same, god willing, to your greit contentment. In ye main quhyle, be of gud confort, and reserue you to that tyme wt patience, being assurit of my fauour. faire weil. 1575. September

your gud freind, James R.

3 Ve aproue thir foure lynis aboue urittinn with oure awin hand be this present. At Falkland the fift day of September 1584.

James R.

I ratifie this mannis euident being now of parfyte yeiris & past all reuocation. at linlithquo the xx3. of marche. 1591.

James R.

1. Writ of James VI, dated 1575, promising to reward Captain Thomas Crawford. James renewed the promise in a more adult hand in 1584, and again in 1592. A royal post-dated cheque?

2 (*inset*). The young King James, from a genealogical portrait of kings and queens of England. After a portrait painted *c.* 1575.

3. Anna of Denmark, queen of James VI. Attrib. to Adrian Vanson, 1595.

4. The Biblical King David, panel in Dean House, Edinburgh, *c.* 1605. The image of David was first used in James VI's entry of 1579.

5. Queen Elizabeth I of England, paymaster of James VI from 1586 onwards. By Marcus Gheeraerts, *c.* 1590.

6. Andrew Melville (1545–1622), principal of St Mary's College and rector of St Andrews University, leading religious reformer and court poet manqué. He had a turbulent relationship with James and was exiled to Sedan in 1611. Eighteenth-century engraving after a Sedan portrait.

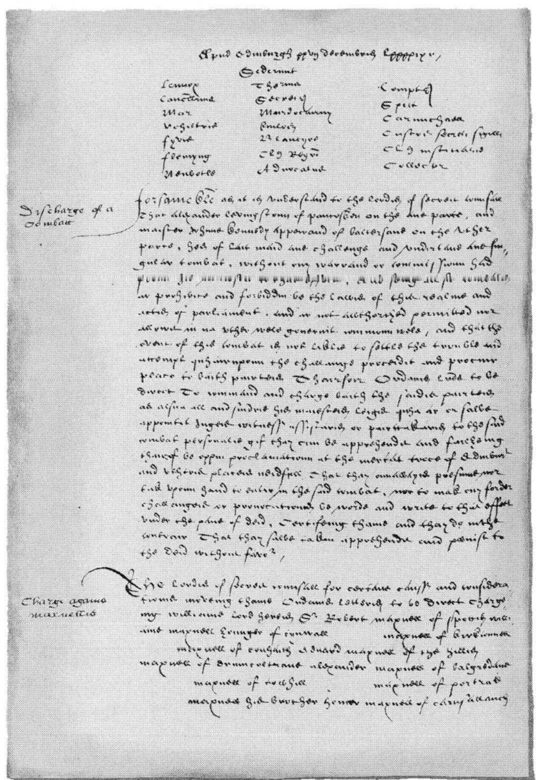

7. The register of the privy council, showing a list of councillors on 27 Dec. 1599. (See *RPC*, vi, 65.) There are few nobles, but many working administrators – including five of the six surviving former Octavians. Gentlemen of the chamber, who had ousted the Octavian regime in June 1598, are also prominent. Names to watch are 'Fyvie' (Alexander Seton, former Octavian, lord president and future earl of Dunfermline), 'Advocatus' (Thomas Hamilton of Drumcairn, former Octavian, lord advocate and future earl of Melrose and Haddington) and 'Spott' (Sir George Home of Spott, gentleman of the chamber, master of the wardrobe and future earl of Dunbar). As chancellor, secretary and treasurer respectively, they dominated much of James's reign after 1603.

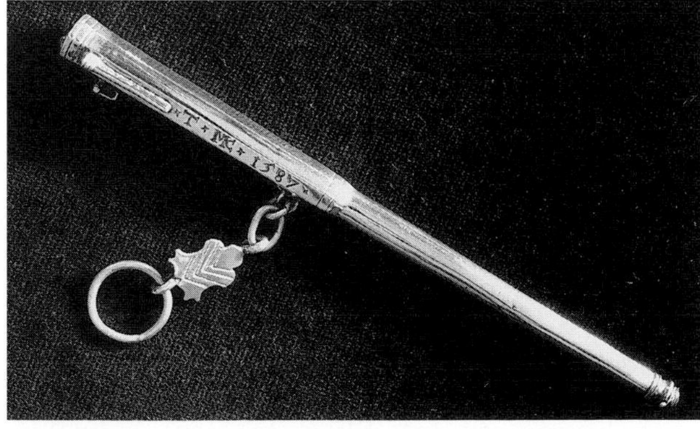

8. Silver gun, presented by James VI to the burgh council of Kirkcudbright as the prize for an annual shooting competition after his expedition against Lord Maxwell in 1587. It bears the initials of the burgh's provost, Thomas MacLellan.

9. George Gordon, 6th earl of Huntly (1562–1636), leading Catholic magnate and occasional dissident, created marquess of Huntly 1599, and his wife from 1588, Henrietta Stewart (1573–1642), cousin of James VI. Nineteenth-century drawing after George Jamesone.

10. John Erskine, 2nd earl of Mar (1562–1634), close friend of James VI since their schooling together in Stirling Castle in the 1570s. After an early radical career as a Ruthven raider (1582) and brief exile, he learned the benefits of being a loyal crown servant. Attrib. to Adam de Colone, 1626.

11. Huntly Castle, in Strathbogie, principal seat of the Gordon earls of Huntly; rebuilt from *c.* 1599 with grandeur and vigour.

12. An enormous sculptural panel, displaying the heraldry of the Gordon dynasty, above the main doorway of Huntly Castle. The armorial's elaborate Catholic symbolism, including the Five Wounds of Christ, was later removed by iconoclasts.

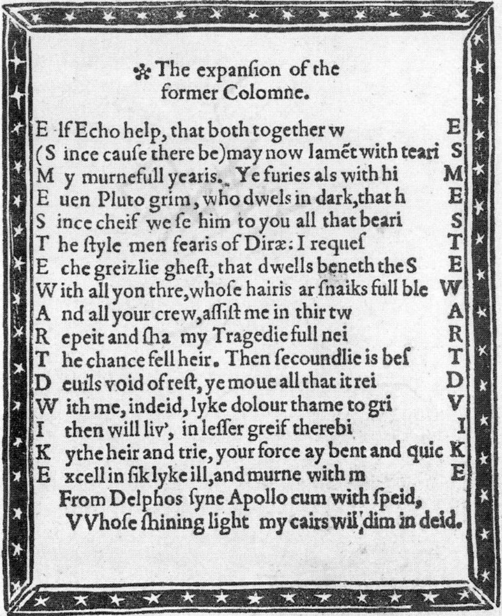

❦ The expanſion of the
former Colomne.

E lf Echo help, that both together w E
(S ince cauſe there be)may now lamēt with teari S
M y murnefull yearis. Ye furies als with hi M
E uen Pluto grim, who dwels in dark,that h E
S ince cheif we ſe him to you all that beari S
T he ſtyle men fearis of Diræ: I requeſ T
E che greizlie gheſt, that dwells beneth the S E
W ith all yon thre,whoſe hairis ar ſnaiks full ble W
A nd all your crew,aſſiſt me in thir tw A
R epeit and ſha my Tragedie full nei R
T he chance fell heir. Then ſecoundlie is beſ T
D euils void of reſt, ye moue all that it rei D
W ith me, indeid, lyke dolour thame to gri V
I then will liv', in leſſer greif therebi I
K ythe heir and trie, your force ay bent and quic K
E xcell in ſik lyke ill,and murne with m E
From Delphos ſyne Apollo cum with ſpeid,
VVhoſe ſhining light my cairs wil'dim in deid.

13. James's preface to his poem 'Phoenix' (1584), with an elaborate acrostic spelling out the name of his banished favourite 'ESME STEWART DWIKE' who had died in 1583.

THE REVLIS AND CAV-
TELIS TO BE OBSERVIT
and eſchewit in Scottis
Poeſie.

CAP. I.

FIRST, ze ſall keip iuſt cullouris, quhairof the cautelis are thir.

That ze ryme nocht twyſe in ane ſyllabe. As for exemple, that ze make not *proue* and *reproue* ryme together,nor *houe* for houeing on hors bak, and *behoue.*

That ze ryme ay to the hinmeſt lang ſyllabe,(with accent) in the lyne, ſuppoſe it be not the hinmeſt ſyllabe in the lyne, as *bakbyte zovv,* & *out flyte zovv,*It rymes in *byte* & *flyte,*becauſe of the lenth of the ſyllabe, & accent being there,and not in *zovv,* howbeit it be the hinmeſt ſyllabe of ather of the lynis. Or *queſtion* and *digeſtion,* It rymes in *ques* & *ges*, albeit they be bot the antepenult ſyllabis,and vther twa behind ilkane of thame.

Ze aucht alwayis to note,That as in thir foirſaidis, or the lyke wordis, it rymes in the hinmeſt lang ſyllabe in the lyne, althoucht there be vther ſhort ſyllabis behind it, Sa is the hinmeſt lang ſyllabe the hinmeſt fute, ſuppoſe there be vther ſhort ſyllabis behind it, quhilkis are eatin vp in the pronounceing, and na wayis comptit as fete.

L

14. First page of James's essay of 1584, laying down rules for Scots vernacular verse. In it he acted out the role of Apollo, patron of the arts and of his Muses, the 'Castalian band' of court poets.

15. The title page of James's *Complete Works* (1616), containing works ranging from biblical commentary to thoughts on demonology and tobacco. By 1588, James the author had moved from poetry to prose.

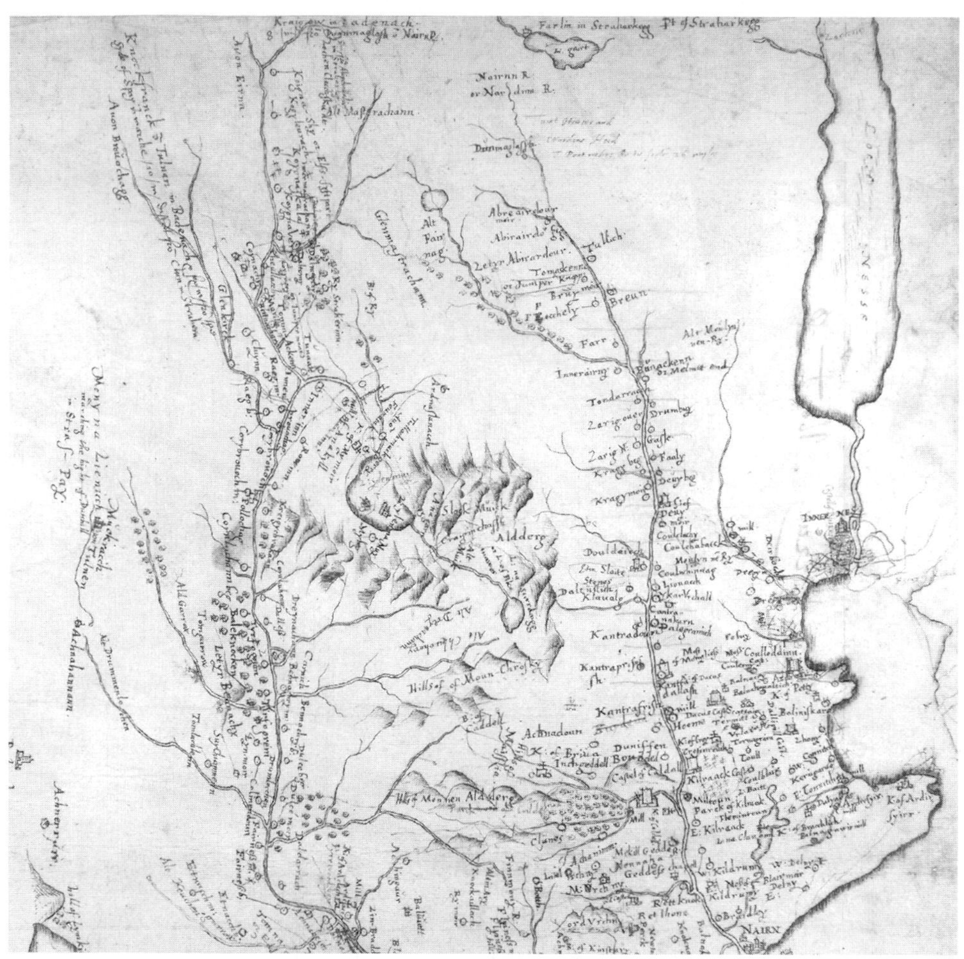

16. Map of Nairn and Moray, drawn by Timothy Pont, probably in the 1590s. North is to the right. Symbols of power and civilisation, representing burghs, tower houses and castles, are clustered between Nairn and Inverness. Beyond, around Loch Ness (*top right*), the 'barbarous' Highlands are a blank.

attributes of the four future ages of a fifteen-year-old queen. Here they were represented as the four daughters of Virtue and Piety.[1] She then entered St Giles' to hear a sermon and the singing of psalms. The market cross again had Bacchus distributing wine and the Netherbow witnessed another astrological pageant about the configuration of the planets.

There were, however, a number of differences between the entries of 1579 and 1590. Anna's entry struck a more even balance between learned display and popular festival. Most of the proceedings of 1590 were in Latin, because the queen's education, while adequate, hardly matched the precocity of her husband's and she, as yet, spoke no Scots.[2] The balance between religion and classical allusion, which had been the centrepiece of the parade of a godly prince in 1579, was different. In 1590, the Protestant symbolism was muted, being confined to the presentation of a bible and psalter at the West Port and an uncharacteristically short sermon, of a mere half hour, by the burgh's first minister, Robert Bruce; there was no final, crude anti-papist tableau in the Canongate, as in 1561 and 1579. The preparations as well as the content were more elaborate. The steeple of St Giles' was festooned with streamers and its interior bestrewn with flowers; there were not one but two tableaux with artificial globes, and large sums were spent on tapestries, paintings and other decorations, many of them depicting classical and mythological scenes. Predictably, Venus symbolised Love (as well as the queen's present age), Diana (whose nymphs supped nectar on a stage at the Butter Tron) represented Virginity and Dido (posing as sister of Anna) featured, but so did Ptolemy (as in 1579), Paris (representing wisdom and justice), Janus (emblem of memory and foresight) and others.[3] The actors and musicians were decidedly more numerous and more elaborately clothed than in 1579. The burgh, which paid most of the ceremony, spent £51 on a sword dance performed by 'Highland dansers', who, in reality, were probably pupils of the song school—a curious, early example of Scottish cultural *kitsch*. Prisoners were set free (a right extended for over a century by French kings to their queens at their first entries) and the poor were cleared from the streets.[4]

More of the burgh's inhabitants were actively involved than in 1579. Six leading burgesses carried the traditional purple canopy above the queen's head but the whole town burgh council was also involved, as were prominent craftsmen; ten members of the large hammermen guild joined the procession in formal attire. The queen's coach, brought from Denmark and drawn by eight horses, was preceded by sixty young men

1 ibid., 111-14.

2 See M. Meikle, 'A meddlesome princess: Anna of Denmark and Scottish court politics, 1589-1603', Chapter 7 below.

3 The details come from Burel's poem.

4 Bryant, *King and City*, 26, 93-8.

of the town, elaborately dressed as Moors. The allegory here was conventional and had been seen in 1561—the gold chains around their necks signified the links between loyal subjects and their queen—but there were also novelties, emphasising the entry as popular festival: the Moors also affected different gaits to keep the crowd amused and the street clear.[1] The precise meaning of some of the imagery can only be guessed at. The figure of Hercules armed with 'baton and rod' was familiar to the courts of both France and Scotland: it was one of the 'Stirling heads' devised for James V.[2] But in French pageantry it was ambiguous: it could be both a symbol of the achievement of France's kings in leading Celtic peoples to civilisation and an icon of the French king as a 'Hercules on earth', bringer of peace rather than war. [3]Both messages would have been appropriate to Scotland in 1590: James had quashed two rebellions in the past two years and he had in 1587 signalled his desire to inflict 'civilitie' on both Borders and Highlands.[4]

The other main feature of the entry was the emphasis on James's lineage and the succession, which the marriage would guarantee. The second globe (borrowed from Dundee) was placed at the Over Bow, at the head of the High Street; it was a globe of the world, and a boy representing the king himself, 'in the garb of an astronomer ... pretending to be a mathematician', delivered an oration. In one sense, this resembled the emphasis in 1579 on astrological learning. Yet it was also an allegorical personification of majesty which was fairly new to entry spectacle; it had, for example, been used in 1571 at the entry into Paris of Charles IX.[5] The oration recorded in the Danish account stressed the propitiousness of the royal union and it had clear overtones of the images of Peace and Plenty which abounded elsewhere.[6] They were the two extra figures who, with the four virtues, addressed the queen at the tolbooth; and Ceres, goddess of plenty, held court with Bacchus at the market cross. Outside the church, at the Salt Tron, an elaborate genealogical tree of Jesse depicted the blessedness of the line of kings of Scots since Bruce. This was also, according to the Danish account, juxtaposed against Anna's lineage, thereby tracing the consanguinity of the royal

1 MacDonald, 'Mary Stewart's entry', 104-5; 'Danish Account', 109.

2 *Edin. Recs., 1589-1603*, 332; H.M. Shire, 'The king in his house: three architectural artefacts belonging to the reign of James V', in J.H. Williams (ed.), *Stewart Style, 1513-1542: Essays on the Court of James V* (East Linton, 1996), 95.

3 L.M. Bryant, 'Politics, ceremonies and embodiments of majesty in Henry II's France', in H. Duckhart, R.A. Jackson and D. Sturdy (eds.), European Monarchy (Stuttgart, 1992), 127-54; Bryant, *King and City*, 130. Hercules had also appeared in the pageant for Elizabeth I at Kenilworth in 1575: Bergeron, *English Civic Pageantry*, 31.

4 See R. Grant, 'The Brig o' Dee affair: the sixth earl of Huntly and the politics of the Counter Reformation', Chapter 5 below, and J. Goodare and M. Lynch, 'The Scottish state and its borderlands, 1567-1625', Chapter 11 below.

5 Bryant, *King and City*, 187-8. 'Danish account', 109-19. Cf. Stevenson, *Royal Wedding*, 145.

6 'Danish Account', 110.

houses of Denmark and Scotland since the marriage of Margaret, daughter of Christian I, to James III in 1469. There were also stage effects; one of the kings arose, perhaps out of the painting itself, to address the queen.[1] The same device was probably used at the Netherbow, where—amidst a configuration of the seven planets—the marriage of a king and queen, surrounded by their loyal nobility, was depicted on a stage; a youth stepped out to describe the blessedness and propitiousness of the union. Here, Anna was depicted as Sheba—a fitting queen for a king who had already, in 1579, been hailed as Solomon.[2]

The political capital made out of the entry is hard to measure. James had clearly intended the coronation to mark yet another turning-point in his reign: the reform of his privy chamber was supposed to accompany the establishment of the queen's own household; access to his chamber was to be curtailed; and he addressed the general assembly three months later, in August 1590, promising a new, more fruitful relationship between church and crown.[3] Yet much of this was counter-productive: the coronation was surrounded by controversy, even before it took place. Although it was customary for a sizeable number of earls and knights to be created at such royal weddings (as in 1565), only a select few, including Chancellor Maitland and Alexander Lindsay, the vice-chamberlain, were favoured.[4] According to Sir James Melville of Halhill, a number of nobles had found the chaotic arrangements for the coronation so demeaning of their honour that they boycotted a convention of estates, held three weeks later.[5] Many nobles resented the new restrictions imposed on both access to the king and attendance at court: earls and lords were limited to a retinue of six and barons to a mere four. Like many proposed reforms of royal government in the reign, all this proved ineffectual. The privy council was still trying to restrict access to the chamber in 1601.[6] Part of the reason for the failure was the inadequacy of the royal guard to police access to the king; this, in turn, was directly related to the king's seeming inability to pay for his guard.

The coronation had come amidst an unnatural lull in court factionalism, in the aftermath of the Brig o' Dee affair. It did not last long. There was, however, a difference after 1590. Feud and factionalism took novel forms: often they fed on the increased tension between council and chamber; at other times, they drew on the sharp antipathy between the

1 ibid., 115-17.
2 The play's mention of Solomon and Sheba appears only in the 'Danish account', at 117.
3 *BUK*, ii, 771; Calderwood, *History*, v, 105-06.
4 Maitland was the only peer; in addition, 12 knights were created: *RPC*, iv, 481n; *Papers relative to Marriage*, 49, lists 15.
5 Melville, *Memoirs*, 376; *CSP Scot.*, x, 315, 322; *RPC*, iv, 490.
6 Melville, *Memoirs*, 373; *RPC*, vi, 207-08; Brown, *Bloodfeud*, 121; Cuddy, 'Entourage', 178-9; J. Goodare, 'The nobility and the absolutist state in Scotland, 1584-1638', *History*, lxxviii (1993), 166-7.

queen's household and the chancellor's faction. Disputes over ceremony and protocol multiplied. The queen's formal entry into Perth in June 1591 was marred by a brawl between the earls of Errol, constable of the realm, and Atholl, provost of the burgh.[1] The rapprochement between the king and the ministers was short-lived. By mid-1591 there were already strident demands from the general assembly for decisive action to be taken against the rebel, papist earls; and by the end of that year the kirk had become unhappy with the ungodly atmosphere in the royal household.[2] One particular set of images from the entry may have backfired—the emphasis on the succession. There was by 1592 already distinct disappointment with the queen's failure to produce an heir.

The coronation had also marked a sharp upsurge in spending on the household. By early 1592, there were rumours that the queen's household was out-spending the king's. New heights of both expenditure and taxation were reached after 1590. A convention of estates had already, in 1588, agreed to a tax of £100,000 to pay for the marriage and this was supplemented by a £20,000 loan from the burghs in August 1589.[3] Much of the expense of the coronation and entry fell on the burgh of Edinburgh, which had already also financed the fitting out of one of the ships which went to Denmark.[4]

IV

The details of the baptism of Prince Henry, at Stirling Castle, on 30 August 1594, a full six months after his birth, are better known than any of the other set-piece court ceremonies of the sixteenth century because of the existence of a pageant book, by the poet William Fowler.[5] It described a three-day festival, which began with a tilting tournament, with four sets of knights, each with their own shields bearing an *impresa*—Amazons, Turks, Moors (who failed to appear), and Knights of Malta (who included the king himself). A second day's tournament, which would have added exotic, fake animals to the proceedings, including a camel, elephant, dragon and unicorn, had to be abandoned because the workmen required to stage it were needed elsewhere. The formal banquet which followed the baptism, on the third day,

1 *CSP Scot.*, x, 540.

2 Calderwood, *History*, v, 139-40.

3 *CSP Scot.*, x, 611; *APS*, iii, 523; *RPC*, iv, 410-11; J. Goodare, 'Parliamentary taxation in Scotland, 1560-1603', *SHR*, lxviii (1989), 50.

4 *Edin. Recs.*, iv, 543-4.

5 *A True Reportaire of ... the Baptisme* (Edinburgh, n.d. [c.1594-5]): see Fowler, *Works*, ii, 169-95; iii, pp. xxvii-xviii. Fowler had been in England, in 1582-3, and in contact with Elizabeth's secretary of state, Francis Walsingham. Other accounts are to be found in *Warrender Papers*, ii, 42-3, 258-62; Calderwood, *History*, v, 342-6; *Hist. KJVI*, 335-8; Moysie, *Memoirs*, 118-19; *CSP Scot.*, xi, 411-13; Melville, *Memoirs*, 410-13. See also Mill, *Mediaeval Plays*, 50, 52, 53-4, 109, 335; J. Nichols, *The Progresses and Public Processions of Queen Elizabeth*, 4 vols. (London, 1788-1821), iii, 353ff; J. Ferguson, *The White Hind and Other Discoveries* (London, 1963), 84-96.

employed elaborate machinery, including a triumphal chariot drawn by a Moor; a 'ship of state', eighteen feet in length and crewed by Arion, Triton and Neptune; and six assorted goddesses (Ceres, Fecundity, Faith, Concord, Liberality and Perseverance).

Despite its exotic trappings, the tournament was a straightforward copy of what by the 1580s had become a regular spectacle in England, the Accession Day tilts, where a Protestant ethic was grafted on to a revived tradition of Burgundian chivalry. The tourney had given a prominent role to the queen and ladies of the court. Similarly, the banquet, at which female virtues were pre-eminent and ladies of the court were placed between each of the foreign visitors, was reminiscent of the court of Elizabeth of England.[1] It was hardly surprising that both meal and baptism were delayed to await the late arrival of the English ambassador. It was, in one vein, a triumph epitomising the Elizabethan succession; it drew, in unexceptionable terms, on the standard English-style chivalric festival of the 1580s—which usually included the dubbing of knights, the exercise of arms, and the conspicuous presence of ladies of the court, all overlaid by a combative Protestantism.[2] If it aimed to be a surrogate Elizabethan triumph, dedicated to the English queen as Henry's godmother, the Stirling baptism failed. The elaborate iconography of the banquet was virtually ignored in diplomatic dispatches sent to London; instead, some offensive allusions to a future king of Britain made in a poem by Andrew Melville and in the sermon by the bishop of Aberdeen were fully reported.[3] The festivities also provoked some offence at home, none more so than James's appearance in the tiltyard as a Knight of Malta. This was a further Protestant version of Loyola's Counter-Reformation recycling of the centuries-old image of *miles Christi* which had become a commonplace of English tourneys since the 1560s. Nonetheless, it was greatly disliked by some ministers of the kirk, to whom it was probably unfamiliar.[4]

This event seems out of place amidst the previous ceremonies which had marked the reign. Described by one historian as 'tiresome and elaborate pomp',[5] it was unusual in its apparent lack of political messages for the king's own nobility. James himself was extravagantly lauded, especially in the plethora of classical allusions and epigrams

1 Cf. Lee, *Great Britain's Solomon*, 142, which stresses the usual masculinity of James's court, 'a place for fun and relaxation with his male cronies'.

2 Young, *Tournaments*, 35-6; Strong and van Dorsten, *Leicester's Triumph*, 69-70; Guy, *Tudor England*, 427, 431. The Burgundian tradition would have been familiar: a tournament involving Burgundian knights had taken place at Stirling in 1449, before the marriage of James II to Mary of Guelders.

3 Cf. *CSP Scot.*, xi, 411-13 (before the baptism); 422, 431 (after it).

4 Young, *Tournaments*, 157; Scaglione, *Knights at Court*, 245, 284; Calderwood, *History*, v, 346.

5 Lee, *Maitland of Thirlestane*, 277.

composed by Fowler accompanying the 'ship of state', which was the climax to the formal banquet in the great Hall; but this was little reward for the large investment of time and money which had gone into the event. Much also seems to have gone wrong, despite the close attention paid by the king to the proceedings. The second day of the elaborately staged tournament had been abandoned and the original idea of having a lion 'pull' one of the machines at the banquet was dropped. Yet it is likely that the baptismal triumph was intended as a political coup which would have rivalled that of the king's own baptism at Stirling in 1566, when his mother had used the device of a Renaissance triumph to try to recover the initiative after a rebellion of nobles nine months before.[1] James's situation in the spring of 1594 was hardly less serious than Mary's in 1566. The six months between Henry's birth and the baptism were largely spent in avoiding the threat of a coup staged by the earl of Bothwell, while condemning Huntly and the other rebel northern earls and warding off pressure from their enemies and the general assembly to take decisive action against them. It is likely that the king had been trying to arrange a formal reconciliation with Huntly and the northern earls at the baptism itself. That was probably the real reason for James's insistence—against the advice of his privy council—that the ceremony be staged in the new Chapel Royal, which was still unfinished, rather than in the capital. The guard at the baptism, amounting to 100 armed men, was nevertheless paid by the burgh of Edinburgh.[2] If the baptism was planned as a spectacular political *coup de théâtre*, that also failed. Instead, a different, unexpected *rapprochement* took place, when Bothwell joined forces with the northern earls. It was to prove the undoing of them both, although James could not have known this as he donned his Maltese armour.

V

The baptism of 1594 was the last great set-piece ceremony before 1603. Its cost is difficult to establish. A convention of estates voted £100,000 for the purpose in January 1594, but this would have taken years to collect and may have proved inadequate to meet the expenditure which was far more than was anticipated, partly because of the delays in staging the ceremony.[3] Financial stringencies, combined with the bruising

1 Lynch, 'Queen Mary's triumph'.

2 *CSP Scot.*, xi, 417. See Lee, *Maitland of Thirlestane*, 270-83, for the background. It is possible that a similar manoeuvre involving Huntly had been planned in 1591, at the time of the queen's entry into Perth: *CSP Scot.*, x, 540, 541.

3 Goodare, 'Parliamentary taxation', 42, 50. The goldsmith and financier Thomas Foulis spent £14,598 on gold chains and silver work given by James to visiting ambassadors at the baptism; in exchange, Foulis was given two large gold drinking cups, gifts presented by the Dutch ambassadors, which later in the year he melted down into £5 pieces: *RPC*, v, 167; NAS, E30/14, fos. 3r., 29r.; E30/15/2; Melville, Memoirs, 413. The London financier, Baptist Hicks, was not so fortunate; he was still trying to collect old debts from James in 1606, including £1,500 sterling (*c.* £18,000 Scots) for the baptism: HMC, *Salisbury*,

experience of 1594, brought a less ambitious kind of ceremony into operation thereafter. Court festivities continued, notably at New Year and on birthdays, but they took the form of the masque rather than the tournament or set-piece triumph.[1] The births of four royal children between 1596 and 1602 saw muted celebrations.[2] The baptism of Princess Elizabeth, at Holyroodhouse on 28 November 1596, at the height of the Octavians' control of the exchequer, took place with 'litle or no triumphe' and without 'inviting of any strengeris', except the English ambassador; very few of the nobility were present. The Octavians' suggestion that it be combined with the queen's birthday celebrations, however, was resisted.[3] The ceremonial for Elizabeth's sister, Margaret, born in December 1598 and baptised in the following April, was more fulsome; Anna's brother, the hard-drinking duke of Holstein, was there, although none of the other foreign representatives was of consequence. A tournament was arranged, a number of knights were dubbed and Huntly and Hamilton were created marquises—a ceremony which provoked heated debate in the privy council.[4] The baptism of Charles, on 23 December 1600, by contrast, was a low-key affair; it took place only five weeks after the birth because of the sickliness of the child.[5] Robert, born in January 1602, was baptised in the following April; two days of celebrations were arranged, but only six knights were dubbed, including the representative of the Dutch states.[6]

In 1603, by contrast, the royal exit from Edinburgh recalled the extravagance of earlier years. Elizabeth died on 24 March. Four days after the formal proclamation in London of James as her successor, the ceremonies began at the market cross of the Scottish capital, the focal point of many previous festivities.[7] The governor of the Castle rendered up his staff of office and keys to the king and was formally reinvested in his office. On the 31st, James returned to the cross, where he was formally

xviii, 408-09; J. Goodare, 'Thomas Foulis and the Scottish fiscal crisis of the 1590s', in W.M. Ormrod *et al.* (eds.), *Crises, Revolutions and Self-Sustained Growth: Essays in Fiscal Growth, 1130-1830* (Stamford, 1999, forthcoming).

1 Shire, *Song, Dance and Poetry*, 180; Fowler's masques from this period, however, are mostly lost.

2 A.H. Dunbar, *Scottish Kings: a Revised Chronology of Scottish History, 1005-1625* (2nd edn., Edinburgh, 1906), 273-4.

3 Moysie, *Memoirs*, 127; *Hist. KJVI*, 373; Calderwood, *History*, v, 438-9; Birrel, 'Diary', 39; *CSP Scot.*, xii, 356, 358, 387; Bergeron, *Royal Family*, 59; Lee, *Great Britain's Solomon*, 135.

4 *RPC*, v, 542; *CSP Scot.*, xiii, I, 439, 444, 447, 450-51; also Calderwood, *History*, v, 728, 736 (but the account is confused). Margaret died in Aug. 1600.

5 Nichols, *Progresses*, iii, 23-4; this account was written by one of the heralds. Another account, in Folger Library, Washington D.C., N.a. 102, fos. 1-15. I owe this reference to Dr Maureen Meikle. See also *CSP Scot.*, xiii, II, 739, 748, 758; Spottiswoode, *History*, iii, 91; Birrel, 'Diary', 53; Calderwood, *History*, vi, 100; Chambers, *Domestic Annals*, i, 321.

6 Birrel, 'Diary', 56; Calderwood, *History*, vi, 143, 151; *CSP Scot.*, xiii, II, 967, 969, 977, 982; cf. E. Carleton Williams, *Anne of Denmark* (London, 1970), 66.

7 Guy, *Tudor England*, 453.

proclaimed in his new titles. Hundreds of bonfires were lit, with 'great feasting and merriment' through the night. The royal entourage set off the next day on a leisurely progress to James's new capital, which took thirty-seven days and saw the conferring of no fewer than 237 knighthoods. This inflation of honours was matched by the extravagance of the entertainments on the way. Clearly, news of James VI's taste for the symbolic and exotic had reached his new English subjects. At Berwick, the king was confronted by an 'enchanted castle', smothered in smoke which cleared to reveal the entrance to his new kingdom. At the house of the earl of Shrewsbury near Worksop, on the edge of Sherwood Forest, he was greeted by huntsmen all in green and a 'woodman's speech'. And at Stanford there was a fanciful pageant of men on stilts twelve feet high who were meant to resemble Patagonian Indians 'on the mayne of Brasil'. The pattern was set for a court suited to the 'royall and imperiall manner' in which the king entered his new capital. James had rediscovered his *métier*.[1]

[1] Nichols, *Progresses*, iii, 4-6, 7, 14, 16, 21.

~ 5 ~

The Brig o' Dee Affair, the Sixth Earl of Huntly and the Politics of the Counter-Reformation

Ruth Grant

Born in 1562, the year in which his grandfather died on the battlefield of Corrichie, George Gordon became the sixth earl of Huntly in 1576 when his father 'deceisset suddentlie ane ... eftir noune cumyn fra ye fuitbau'. He would be created the first marquess of Huntly in 1599. During his career, Huntly's official titles included Deputy Chamberlain, Captain of the Guard and Lieutenant and Justiciar of the North; unofficially, from 1589 onwards, Elizabethan officials also identified him as the leader of the Scottish Catholics and Counter-Reformation movement in Scotland.

It is in this latter capacity, as well as that of the king's favourite, that Huntly is most commonly identified by historians. Modern perceptions of him, however, have been coloured by the biases of his sixteenth-century contemporaries, who frequently cast him in the one-dimensional role of 'Catholic lord', scheming against kirk and king. By accepting this portrayal of Huntly, historians have merely applied a sixteenth-century Anglo-Protestant perspective to historiography. Although it is difficult to move away from such convenient labels, until historians do, they will fail to understand the role which Huntly played in the complex and shifting relationship between religion and politics during the personal reign of James VI. Yet, in laying these labels aside, it must be realised that the perceptions formed of Huntly by his contemporaries, accurate or otherwise, certainly influenced their actions towards him.[1]

The first of Huntly's rebellions came in 1589, five weeks after fleeing from Edinburgh to his power base in the north, amidst rumours of plotting against him at court. There, he joined other so-called 'Catholic lords', including Crawford and Errol, and the dissident but Protestant earl of Bothwell. When the king rode north to confront the rebels at the

1 *The Calendar of Fearn: Text and Additions, 1471-1667*, ed. R.J. Adam (SHS, 1991), 152. For contemporary accounts, see Calderwood, *History*; Spottiswoode, *History*; Row, *History*; Moysie, *Memoirs*; and *CSP Scot.*, *CBP*, etc.; for modern historians, M. Lee Jr., *John Maitland of Thirlestane and the Foundation of the Stewart Despotism in Scotland* (Princeton, NJ, 1959), esp. ch. 8; M. Lee Jr., *Great Britain's Solomon: James VI and I in his Three Kingdoms* (Urbana, Ill., 1990); G. Donaldson, *Scotland: James V—James VII* (Edinburgh, 1965), 188-90. K.M. Brown, *Bloodfeud in Scotland, 1573-1625* (Edinburgh, 1986), 144-9, is the most insightful account, yet within a Counter-Reformation context, with a strict Catholic-Protestant dichotomy.

Brig o' Dee, just outside Aberdeen, on 17 April, none of them took the field against him. Huntly surrendered a few days later. Within the space of a month, he was tried, found guilty of treason and imprisoned in Borthwick Castle. Like the two Catholic rebellions in the south-west orchestrated by Lord Maxwell in 1587 and 1588, the Brig o' Dee affair also quickly fizzled out, seemingly as a result of quick and decisive action taken by the king. In neither case did heavy-handed reprisals follow, but there was a distinct difference in the nature of the treatment meted out. On the face of it, Maxwell escaped lightly. He agreed to go into exile, but his full rehabilitation took some three years. Huntly, by contrast, faced a treason trial—yet, within four months, he was set free and restored to royal favour.

I

In June 1579 John Leslie, bishop of Ross, referred to Huntly as 'Rome's rising star' and expressed hope that he would 'restore the worship of God in Scotland ... one day'. Huntly's significance to European Catholics, however, extended beyond Scotland. According to Robert Parsons, a leading figure in the Jesuit mission to England, 'our chief hope is in Scotland, on which depends the conversion not of England only, but of all the north of Europe'.[1] The spirits of those directing the Counter-Reformation in the late 1570s and 1580s were high: young seminary priests embarked on evangelical missions, the Society of Jesus was flourishing and powerful men in Spain and France took an active interest in the movement. Yet, although tangible support was given by both the duke of Guise, as head of the Catholic League in France, and Philip II of Spain, their personal interests conflicted. The rivalry between France and Spain did little to further the cause of the Counter-Reformation. The domestic agendas of each dictated the extent of their involvement and mutual co-operation. Guise was fighting a rearguard action in France in promoting a monotheistic state and the French king was wary of Spain's imperialist intentions regarding England. Spain, on the other hand, was embroiled in an expensive and lengthy military campaign in the Netherlands attempting to subdue a Protestant, nationalist revolt—terminating English aid to the Dutch rebels would facilitate the Spanish war effort. Spain was also aware that France could prove an awkward obstacle to establishing Spanish control over England. So, although nominally on the same side and sharing personnel, as well as—to a limited extent—plans, Spain and France had little in common save the desire to return England and Scotland to the Catholic fold. Hence the distinctions recognised by contemporaries between French and Spanish sympathisers are important, especially when the relative power of each is considered.

[1] W. Forbes Leith (ed.), *Narratives of Scottish Catholics under Mary Stuart and James VI* (Edinburgh, 1885), 139, 166, 171-2; for Huntly's power base, Brown, *Bloodfeud*, 144, 145.

During the reigns of Philip II and Elizabeth Tudor, and especially after Elizabeth's excommunication by the pope in 1570, the militant profile of the Counter-Reformation increased markedly, overshadowing the equally important evangelical missions. Although the Counter-Reformation had an outwardly religious mandate, it was used periodically by France and Spain to legitimise their own political agendas. England, the largest and wealthiest Protestant country, became the key target in Counter-Reformation strategy for more than just religious purposes. Hence, the ultimate manifestation of the militant Counter-Reformation, the Spanish Armada, embodied both the religious and secular political elements of the movement. The Armada's legacy, despite its failure, however, was one which enabled Protestants to equate all Catholic missionary work or any relations with Spain as the forerunner of armed conflict.

Scotland was seen as a means of obtaining a foothold in England. Not only was James VI next in line to the English throne, but entry into Scotland was relatively simple and crossing the Anglo-Scottish border (especially the West March) was safer than entering through English ports. Thus, the leaders of the European Counter-Reformation pinned hope to the earl of Huntly for a variety of reasons. Huntly was the greatest and most influential landed magnate in the north. Besides his personal lands and far-reaching bonds of manrent, the jurisdiction of the Lieutenancy of the North stretched from the Mearns on the east coast to the west coast with its adjacent islands and included the whole of the northern hinterland. Huntly held this powerful position for most of his adult life. In addition to this, he also wielded considerable influence in the burgh of Aberdeen as well as on the Moray Firth, despite the presence of his rival, the earl of Moray. Both these locations had deep-water ports, making them ideal reception points outwith the reach of strong interference by either the central government or kirk.

Huntly's first documented contact with the Counter-Reformation, along with seven other nobles, was in October 1581 when a Welsh seminary priest, William Watts, was sent to Scotland by Bernardino de Mendoza (the Spanish ambassador in England) in order to discover the religious and political climate. Favourably received, Watts was followed by Fathers Robert Parsons and William Crichton, both Jesuits, in December.[1] In an audience arranged by Sir Thomas Kerr of Ferniehurst, they gave James the details of their mission. The king 'accepted it extremely well, and said that although for certain reasons it was advisable for him to appear publicly in favour of the French, he assured him that in his

1 Crichton, a Scot, was sent to Scotland again in 1584 with Fr James Gordon; their ship was captured by Dutch merchants and Crichton was sent to the Tower of London. Gordon was released due to fear of reprisals from his nephew, Huntly. Subsequently released, Crichton later wrote an account of the Scottish mission: see *Catholic Narratives*.

heart he would rather be Spanish.'[1] This is the first documented instance of James's involvement with either the Counter-Reformation or Spain and is the first firm indication of the king's future covert political course. James's foreign policy was built upon episodes such as this, covertly encouraging what he publicly condemned—in effect, relatively successfully pandering to two diametrically opposed elements.[2] Unlike Huntly, however, the King's role was more than tangential; James's well-chosen words fed the aspirations of the Counter-Reformers.

It is perhaps significant that Huntly was involved in the inception of the international movement in Scotland, but he was just a bystander until about 1586. He remained aloof from the politics of the Counter-Reformation and his contacts extended only to the evangelical side of the mission. Although the Counter-Reformation encompassed political, militant and evangelical objectives, distinctions were made by the agents directing the movement as well as by those participating in it. Many Scottish Catholics had little to do with the political or militant wings, concerned only with the fulfilment of their spiritual needs. The secular priests concentrated on this aspect, whereas the Jesuits, although directed to abstain from politicking, tended to be involved in the wider objectives of the mission. To many Protestants, however, there were no such distinctions: all Catholics embodied the political, militant and evangelical goals of the Counter-Reformation.

Outside the immediate circle of Catholic intriguers, Huntly was not readily identified as a potential agent of the Spanish-directed Counter-Reformation. Upon his return from France in July 1581, he was marked as a conservative, at most as a Francophile; two years later, he was described as 'in religion doubted and in affection Frenche' and it was during the intervening period from 1581 to 1583 that he began to be identified as a courtier and favourite of the king. The implications, however, had changed by August 1587 when a correspondent with England wrote that Huntly 'is indeid ane greit curteour and knawis mair of the Kingis secreittis nor ony man at this present doithe'. Although he was still consistently noted as being aligned with the 'French party', as opposed to the Anglophiles, until the end of 1588, by this point, his role as a courtier had become politicised: his intimacy with the king had begun to make the opposition apprehensive.[3] His marriage in July 1588

[1] *CSP Spain*, iii, 196, 234, 238; for further details regarding Parsons, P.J. Morris, 'Robert Parsons, S.J. (1546-1610), and the Counter-Reformation in England: a Study of his Actions within the Context of the Political' (University of Notre Dame Ph.D. dissertation, 1984).

[2] Not without suspicions and anxieties; for examples, *The Hamilton Papers*, 2 vols., ed. J. Bain (Edinburgh, 1892), ii, 677, 685, 694, 697, 702; *Courcelles Despatches*, 77-8.

[3] *CSP Scot.*, ix, 476; the first reference to him as a 'courtier' occurs in September 1581, *CSP Scot.*, vi, 52; for French associations, *Estimate of the Scottish Nobility During the Minority of James VI*, ed. C. Rogers (London, 1873), 31, 43, 44, 45-6, 51; *Hamilton Papers*, ii, 677; NAS, Leven and Melville Muniments, GD26/7/392/4, fos. 38-39; BL, Add. MS. 38,823, fo. 9;

to Henrietta Stewart, daughter of Lennox and a kinswoman of the king, may have particularly heightened these fears: James even paid for the wedding and composed a masque for the celebrations.[1]

The king did unquestionably play the Catholic card in trying to manipulate both domestic and foreign politics, but it must also be remembered that in James's experience it had consistently been the Anglo-Protestant faction which had threatened his security—the Ruthven Raid of August 1582 and the Stirling Raid of April 1584 being two potent examples. The Ruthven regime collapsed after James had been rescued by a coalition of Catholic, Marian and *politique* nobility and courtiers led by Huntly: thereafter, the distinction between Catholic and Protestant held little sway with James in decisions about politics or personal loyalties. It had been Protestant rather than Catholic zealots who had betrayed his trust, and had even undermined the basic premise of monarchy as well.[2] Confident in his faithfulness and zeal for service, James bestowed on Huntly something much more substantial than material wealth: he became a close, personal friend. This friendship and confidence in the earl's fidelity was consistently manifested throughout James's reign.

Huntly's association with the French party led to oblique references in 1586 to his Catholicism; possible connections with 'papist intriguers' in France and his reception of Jesuits also began to circulate. Resetting Jesuits, however, did not necessarily indicate political ties with the Counter-Reformation: Huntly's uncle, James Gordon, was the Jesuit superior in Scotland.[3] Despite his Francophile credentials, Huntly until roughly 1586 was a stabilising element in the central government, albeit a conservative one. In 1588 there were even reports of his conversion to Protestantism, but he was still perceived as promoting the interests of the Francophile faction. It was not until the summer of 1588, amidst trepidation concerning the Spanish Armada, that Huntly began to be sporadically linked to correspondence with the duke of Parma, usually within the context of the 'northern lords' or 'papistical faction'; it was only in January 1589 that Scottish Protestants and English diplomats began specifically to connect Huntly with the Counter-Reformation. Even in December 1588, Huntly, Bothwell and Crawford were said to 'seem rather French than English'.[4]

CSP Scot., ix, 169, 327, 406.

1 R.J. Lyall, 'James VI and the sixteenth-century cultural crisis', Chapter 3 above.

2 R.A. Mason, *Kingship and the Commonweal: Political Thought in Renaissance and Reformation Scotland* (East Linton, 1998), 187-214. James's own publications, *Basilikon Doron* and *The Trew Law of Free Monarchies*, provide further insights into his attitudes towards Protestant zealots (presbyterian or puritan). See, for example, James I, *Political Works*, 23, 24, 39, 60.

3 *CSP Scot.*, ix, 174, 175; *Courcelles Despatches*, 21.

4 For Huntly's conversion and political alignment, *CSP Scot.*, ix, 583, 638, 640, 642, 646, 649; miscellaneous entries in *CSP Scot.*, ix, Aug. 1588—Dec. 1588 for links with Spain. There

II

Huntly first entered into correspondence with Spain in May 1586; he, along with Lord Claud Hamilton and Lord Maxwell, did so on the advice of and by the means of the duke of Guise. Although Huntly was careful to clothe his missive to Philip II in the rhetoric of faith, aid was specifically asked for in order to remove James from 'the power of his enemies', thus releasing him from following the policies of Elizabeth, which 'are not popular even in her own country'.[1] The desire to restore Catholicism to Scotland was undoubtedly real; so was the political target of deposing certain members of the Scottish government. Even Mendoza partially recognised this, warning Philip II in 1586 that the Scottish messenger, although a Catholic, was also 'a politician'.[2] Huntly had finally entered the political spectrum of the Counter-Reformation; the English, though, failed to recognise this. They had qualms that his Catholic and French sympathies might adversely influence James, but they did not attribute an international agenda to Huntly himself.

During the 1580s Huntly was seen as a waverer by both mainstream Protestants and Catholics. In 1587, the Justice Clerk, Bellenden, wrote as 'to the Earle of Huntleys lyinge in his majestie chambre and preaces papistrie, truthe it is I thinke he be ane papiste, but not so precise as he had not rather lyie in a faire gentlewomans chambre then either in the Kinges or yet where he might have ane hundrethe messes'.[3] In 1589, Robert Bruce, a Scottish spy for Spain, described Huntly as having a 'a saull euer gude albeit he have nocht sic vigour to persevere and execut sic as is requisit in sa great ane enterpryser'.[4]

It appears that Huntly's motive was as much to break the influence of Chancellor Maitland as it was to support Catholicism in Britain. When placed within the context of the political factions of the mid to late 1580s, this becomes more apparent. Both Maitland and Huntly had been closely involved at the court since 1581.[5] After 1585, the two parties polarised.

is only one reference conjecturally linking Huntly with Spain before 1588: *Courcelles Despatches*, 35. Most comment regarding Spain during this period was reserved for Maxwell: K.M. Brown, 'The making of a *politique*: the Counter-Reformation and regional politics of John, eighth Lord Maxwell', *SHR*, lxvi (1987).

1 *CSP Spain*, iii, 580, 581; Philip II's response to Guise and Mendoza, ibid., 630-1; Parma's initial reaction, ibid., 665.

2 *CSP Spain*, iii, 681-3. Mendoza concluded that the friendship of these Scots was important for maintaining the balance of power with England, warranting financial aid. The Scottish Catholics were still to be held to their pledge to take up arms but *only* when directed to do so: *CSP Spain*, iv, 10, 28, 46, 58. Catholic activities, *CSP Spain*, iii, 580-691 and iv, *passim*; J.D. Mackie, 'Scotland and the Spanish Armada', *SHR*, xii (1914-15); T.G. Law, 'Robert Bruce, conspirator and spy', in P.H. Brown (ed.), *Collected Essays and Reviews of Thomas Graves Law* (Edinburgh, 1904).

3 *CSP Scot.*, ix, 491.

4 NAS, Warrender Papers, GD1/371/3, fos. 85v.-89v. (contemporary copy with marginal notations from a Catholic sympathiser); *CSP Scot.*, ix, 687.

5 *CBP*, i, 76.

The Anglo-Protestant party was focused on Maitland, who became secretary in 1584, vice-chancellor and keeper of the great seal in 1586 and chancellor in 1587; opposed to it was the conservative, generally Francophile party under Huntly. Each party had its roots in the combative politics of the Esmé Stewart period in the early 1580s, which had seen the restoring of a French interest in Scottish politics. The antipathy to Maitland was based on two points: firstly, that as chancellor he was perceived as eroding the privileges of the nobility and, secondly, for his steadfast Anglophile policies.[1]

James's persistent attempts to pander simultaneously to both Catholic and Protestant sentiments helped create this polarisation. James maintained a careful balance between these two seemingly irreconcilable parties: in February 1587 Maitland was granted Kelso Abbey and three months later Huntly received the commendatorship of Dunfermline Abbey. Because of this, Maitland and Huntly sought assistance from England and France respectively, rivals in the Counter-Reformation, in an attempt to swing the balance of power to their own domestic party. It was in the same month in 1586 when Huntly first entered into correspondence with Spain that Maitland was made keeper of the great seal and vice-chancellor. In the increasingly bellicose atmosphere following the defeat of the Spanish Armada, however, both Maitland's and Huntly's relative positions were perceived within the framework of the confessional politics of the period. This does not negate the fact that Huntly personally supported the religious aims of the Counter-Reformation but, in furthering the Catholic cause, he believed that he was also promoting the position of his own house and party. James's dual and incompatible policies, therefore, facilitated in popular perceptions the elevation of the Brig o' Dee affair from domestic factional fighting onto the stage of Counter-Reformation politics.

Huntly's party, however, was not entirely composed of Catholics; the factions were neither static nor drawn along strict religious lines. For example, in 1587-8, Protestants such as Rothes, Atholl, Montrose and Lord John Hamilton were described as being of Huntly's faction, which also included Lennox, Errol, Crawford, Seton, and Maxwell. Additionally, Huntly was not recognised as the head of the Scottish Catholics until well after the failure of the Armada. Kerr of Ferniehurst, Lords Seton and Maxwell were consistently acknowledged as the Catholic leaders, even after they had ceased to function as such. Additionally, although Maitland's and Huntly's factions differed on many points, neither was adverse to using the other in order to achieve a particular political end.

1 J. Goodare, 'The nobility and the absolutist state in Scotland, 1584-1638', *History*, lxxviii (1993).

Likewise, individuals such as the earl of Bothwell, the master of Glamis or the master of Gray would align with either party.[1]

It was not always in the king's interests to eradicate factions: in a decentralised state the ability to rule could be enhanced by factions which prevented the dominance of a single group. Divide and rule could sometimes be the best policy. In 1587, the French ambassador wrote that some suspected that the king promoted factions, 'to nourish them in pike on with an other; thinkinge, he shall beste maintaine him self in suretie with them, by this meanes, rather than by their union, which he hathe hindered as much as bene in him to doe'.[2] Through factions, James could also mollify Scottish, English and European Catholics while still toeing the Protestant line. James maintained the rivalry (and control) between Maitland and Huntly by consistently keeping both men at court 'by special command'. Although Huntly outwardly basked in the king's favour, Maitland's position and policies remained unaffected. Resentment between the parties increased, yet both were dependent on the king for the resolution of the conflict. As long as James maintained control over each faction, as demonstrated by his frequent demands that they become reconciled,[3] and thus preventing any serious escalations, each served a useful purpose: Maitland's faction pandered to Anglo-Protestant interests, Huntly's to the opposition, which included an international dimension—serving to keep England wary. Burghley, for example, wrote to Walsingham on 20 November 1587, 'It is to be considered whether Her Majesty may do the King of Scots more harm or he her.'[4]

Rumours of plots by Huntly's faction to oust Maitland abounded in the late 1580s. These plans, however, usually focused on persuasion rather than force. Invariably, the plots were founded on enticing James to Dunfermline. There, he would be convinced to change his government; force figured only to uphold the change *after* the king had given his consent.[5] Those hostile to Huntly, however, feared that he was planning a military coup followed by a Catholic settlement.[6] What is

1 Maitland using Huntly's faction: *CSP Scot.*, ix, 266, 480-81; *CSP Scot.*, x, 128. Glamis, Gray and Bothwell: *CSP Scot.*, ix, 327, 405-07, 486; *Letters and Papers Relating to Patrick, Master of Gray* (Bannatyne Club, 1835), 139, 145-7.

2 *Courcelles Despatches*, 35. In this particular case unity meant avenging the execution of Mary, 'and contrariwise by their disorder'.

3 Huntly's position at court: *CSP Scot.*, ix, 480-1, 649, 653, 655; *CBP*, i, 299, 321, 322; *CSPF Eliz., 1586-8*, 598; Melville, *Memoirs*, 321. Periodic reconciliations or separations: *CSP Scot.*, ix, 480-81, 536, 559, 603, 621, 624, 627, 628, 629, 638, 646.

4 *Calendar of State Papers, Domestic Series, 1581-90*, 438. Cf. Huntly's reply to a letter from Walsingham: *CSP Scot.*, ix, 577-8 (deteriorated). Donaldson, *James V—James VII*, 189.

5 *Letters and Papers, Master of Gray*, 146-7, and *CSP Scot.*, ix, 405-6, for the earliest recorded plot of this kind, Apr. 1587. Huntly and Lord Claud Hamilton brought 300 armed men into Edinburgh during that same month and conferred with James, causing little comment: *CBP*, i, 255-6.

6 *CSP Scot.*, ix, 536, 613, 614, 616, 622; *CBP*, i, 321, 333. Particularly worrying was Huntly's

important, however, is what was common to both the speculation and the concrete plans: each was placed firmly within a political context, the removal of Maitland. Religion was secondary.

III

From March 1586 to the end of 1588, the friction between the two factions was constant. In April 1588, Burghley commented that nobles opposed to England and drawn to a foreign course 'ar more moved with a particular dislyk of the Chancellor than with any comen cause'. During October and November, Huntly, Lord Seton and other prominent Catholics were removed from court and, although Huntly wrote numerous letters to the king promising to satisfy the kirk 'without epocrise', it was not until he had 'revealed to the King the plot to take away the Chancellor' that he was fully reconciled to James. The friction between the two factions, however, had not been resolved. According to Calderwood, Huntly spent that winter attempting to persuade James 'to remove from court the Chancellor, Treasurer, and other officers of estat, or ellis to change them'. Tension was still mounting by February 1589, when it was reported that 'the factions here growe jelious of another, and ... combine for there better strenght'.[1]

The defeat of the Spanish Armada in 1588 did not signal to the Protestant community the decline of Spanish power; rather, it was seen as a daunting manifestation of Spanish might and resources which would be mustered again. The English, with an unreliable alliance with France, increasing insolvency, and escalation of their involvement in the Spanish Netherlands, were aware of their vulnerable position. It was in this atmosphere of sustained animosity between Huntly's and Maitland's factions, heightened by the feeling of crisis still pervading the Anglophile party after the Armada, that Huntly's incriminating correspondence with Spain was discovered. The volatile state of domestic politics preceding and continuing after this discovery, however, has been overlooked. It was in such a climate that England intercepted Scottish letters to the duke of Parma and, consequently, for the first time, fully recognised Huntly as active in Counter-Reformation politics.

On 27 February 1589, the English ambassador presented James with deciphered copies of intercepted correspondence from Huntly, Errol, Crawford, Maxwell, Claud Hamilton and Robert Bruce to Parma; Bothwell was also fully implicated. The letters conveyed regret that Spain had not utilised Scotland in its attack on England; the situation, however,

command of the recently established royal guard: *CSP Scot.*, ix, 647, 653, 655; Calderwood, *History*, iv, 696.

1 *CSP Scot.*, ix, 327, 556, 601, 621, 627, 628, 629, 634, 637, 638, 662-3, 664, 677; *CSPF Eliz., 1586-8*, 554, 598; *CBP*, i, 298-9, 299, 322; *Letters and Papers, Master of Gray*, 139; Moysie, *Memoirs*, 65, 66; Calderwood, *History*, iv, 696; Melville, *Memoirs*, 361; NAS, GD1/371/3, fo. 260r. Lee, *Great Britain's Solomon*, 71-2, does discuss Brig o' Dee in a political light, albeit superficially.

could be salvaged if Spain would consider mounting a two-pronged attack from Scotland and Ireland. In an independent letter to Parma, Huntly excused himself for subscribing the Confession of Faith, claiming he had done so under heavy pressure from James, whilst lacking financial support from Spain. Huntly's missive was an attempt to reinstate himself with Parma in order to ensure future supplies of funds.[1]

English paranoia spread to Scottish Protestants, and it is their combined fears and objections to Huntly which have dominated the interpretation of ensuing events. Henceforth, English politicians and Scottish Protestants persistently viewed all of Huntly's actions as embodying the objectives of the Counter-Reformation. Contrary to Elizabeth's candid advice, James's reaction was decidedly mild—perhaps he was already aware that the correspondence existed. Indeed, there were not entirely unfounded allegations that James himself was corresponding with and perhaps receiving money from Spain.[2] After much persuasion, the king had Huntly warded in Edinburgh Castle, with free access given to his wife, friends and servants.[3] His confinement lasted little longer than a week.

James's personal reaction was revealed in a lengthy letter to Huntly in February 1589. His tone was that of an aggrieved friend, telling the earl that he had 'offendit twa personis in me, a particulare freind and a generall Christiane King'. The letter, though, did not dwell on the foreign correspondence; indeed there was only one direct reference to it. Instead, it concentrated on Huntly's past solicitations and attempts to remove Maitland from power. James stressed the 'innumerable tymes' that, at Huntly's request, he had smoothed matters over between Huntly and 'the particular men' about the king. James not only reminded the earl of his promise of friendship to these same men, but also reiterated his warning, given 'how many millioun of tymes', that Huntly could not 'baith trow me and thay bissie reportaris about yow, and ... that I could not be your freind gife ye trusted thais practizeris'. With regard to religion, it appears that James was personally grieved by Huntly's apostasy, rather than placing it within a political or Counter-Reformation context. James evaluated the situation within a domestic, factional context. He clearly saw Huntly's dabbling with Parma as an extension of the earl's personal rivalry with Maitland.[4] It is perhaps indicative of

1 Calderwood, *History*, v, 6, 7-8, copies of the letters, 8-35; Moysie, *Memoirs*, 72; Spottiswoode, *History*, ii, 390-1; *RPC*, iv, 361, 821-2; *CSP Scot.*, ix, 682-97 for copies of the letters and the English ambassador's instructions.

2 *CSP Scot.*, ix, 485, 505, 592, 642, 656; *CSP For., 1586-8*, 454; *CSPF Eliz., 1588*, 231; *CBP*, i, 310; *CSP Spain*, iv, 144-6, 159, 174-5, 230, 255, 351; *Courcelles Despatches*, 77-8; *Warrender Papers*, ii, 93-4; Scottish Catholic Archives, CA4/1/5; Lee, *Great Britain's Solomon*, 99.

3 *CSP Scot.*, ix, 701, 702, 703, 704.

4 *CSP Scot.*, ix, 699-700; James VI, *Letters*, 89-91.

the security of Maitland's position that his opponents could be driven to such extremes.

The most significant point regarding this Spanish correspondence, however, was the steady flow of money from Spain which helped to support the intimidatory posturings of Huntly's party, as demonstrated in the sizeable armed guard with which Huntly surrounded himself or the sudden large convocations of men appearing with Huntly, Errol or Crawford, jointly or severally.[1] Careful reading of the correspondence not only of the earls, but also of Bruce, Parma and Mendoza, shows that the Scots were consistently eliciting money from Spain. Aware that Spain was militarily over-extended, the Scots knew that their requests for troops were futile, hence the well-calculated solicitation for, 'at the very least', money to maintain their position. Philip II, wanting 'to keep them in hand', usually complied. One anonymous chronicler even described Huntly, Errol, Bothwell, Crawford and Montrose as 'having solemly swore by the crosse of the pistolett'.[2] This money was used to bolster their domestic position rather than furthering the Catholic mission *per se*. By extension, however, the earls believed that the defence of their political influence was indeed instrumental in furthering the Catholic cause as a whole.

One therefore cannot interpret Huntly's correspondence with Spain between 1586 and 1589 solely as Catholic idealism nor as a desire to be in the vanguard of the Counter-Reformation. Huntly's faith certainly was a significant factor, but his over-riding motivation was to shift the balance of power within domestic politics. This shift might have proven favourable to Catholicism; however, that was not at the top of the priorities set by Huntly's party. Contact with Spain was initiated soon after Maitland had consolidated his position. The objective of the Scots, as told to Philip II, was to restore James to his former liberty. In phraseology harking back to the Ruthven Raid and the botched Stirling Raid of 1584, this was a direct reference to the Maitland administration. So, although the fears of the English and Protestants were justifiable, it is erroneous to project *purely* Counter-Reformation ideology upon Huntly's correspondence and Brig o' Dee. Huntly was using the opportunities offered by the Counter-Reformation to further his party's domestic programme, which, by extension, may have promoted the Catholic cause as well.

1 *CSP Scot.*, ix, 536, 613, 614, 616, 622; *CBP*, i, 321, 333; *CSP Scot.*, ix, 647, 653, 655; Calderwood, *History*, iv, 696. Ordered to bring only 30 horse to court in 1588, Huntly refused, as 'he could not come without security': *CSP Spain*, iv, 228.

2 *CSP Spain*, iv, 197, 210, 224-5, 297, 351-2, 429-30, 456; BL, Royal MSS, 18A. xvi, 'An oulde Stoary of the Brigg of Dee', fo. 3v.

IV

During Huntly's eight-day confinement James visited him daily, lavishing great affection upon him. The night of his release, 7 March, Huntly slept in the king's bedchamber. Those interpreting events from an Anglo-Protestant perspective found the king's actions unfathomable. However, within the context of opposition to Maitland, James was neutralising Huntly, rather than further alienating him. This extraordinary favour shown to the man caught plotting against both kirk and state only heightened the insecurity felt by Maitland's party. Making concessions to Maitland, the king established an alternative guard to the one still under Huntly's captaincy, escalating an already volatile situation. Compelled to placate his chancellor, who vowed 'that one of them would be both discourted and disgarded', James finally discharged Huntly of the guard.[1] In an atmosphere of open hostility, Huntly left the court.

Before departing to the north, Huntly invited James to a banquet in Edinburgh on 13 March. While hunting together that morning, Huntly was advertised of a plot by Maitland's party planned for that afternoon. Supporting this are several reports of Edinburgh being in arms and, more specifically (according to Woddrington), Angus, Mar, Morton, Marischal, Maitland, the master of Glamis and their followers sent to the provost of Edinburgh to be ready in armour and with weapons and to slay Huntly upon his return. Huntly and James conferred together for two and a half hours, at the end of which James returned to the banquet, 'but his host durst not enter to entertain him'. Huntly rode to Dunfermline and the next day travelled via Perth to Strathbogie. James, however, remained in close contact with him, sending upon his return to Edinburgh, 'twoe of his owne servantes in all haist unto Huntley.... And every day sence, the kynge sendes to Huntleye.'[2] The seriousness with which James perceived the situation lends further credence to the reports of a plot against Huntly. Whether there actually was a plot or not, Huntly certainly perceived the situation as threatening. On 10 April, while passing through Perth, Huntly, Errol and Crawford captured the master of Glamis, having been forewarned that Atholl, Morton and Glamis 'haid conweneined forces, to intrap them within Sanct Jhonstown'. In a letter to James, Huntly emphasised that this action was taken 'to discouuer the secreit of our onfreindis mening touarts us' and 'praing your Maiestie for thir respectis to tak sic ane resolution as may not tend to the wrak of your nobilitie be the particular instigation of ane privat factioun'. Apologising that he was 'forsit to tak this forme of doinng for my auin

1 *CSP Spain*, ix, 701, 702, 703, 705, 706, 708, 709; x, 1-3, 3-4, 4-5, 7-8, 13.

2 *CSP Spain*, x, 1-3, 4-5, 6-7, 8; *CBP*, i, 335-6; Moysie, *Memoirs*, 73. Concerning Brig o' Dee and its aftermath: *CSP Scot.*, x, 1-142; Moysie, *Memoirs*, 73-5; Colville, *Letters*, 90-4; Spottiswoode, *History*, ii, 396-8; Calderwood, *History*, v, 1-93; *Hist. KJVI*, 224; *Letters and Papers, Master of Gray*, 155-8, 166, 168; BL, Royal MS. 18A. xvi, fos. 3r.-14v.; BL, Add. MS. 35,844; BL, Cott. Calig. D.I., 41, fo.153; NAS, GD1/371/3, fo. 260r.

securitie', the earl solicited James's advice, 'quhon without schame, and hurt of my frendschipe, I may best content your hienes'.[1]

The political rivalry between Huntly and Maitland dominated the period from Huntly's release from ward to his return to the north as much as it had coloured James's reaction to the Spanish correspondence. The nobility's perceived alienation from Maitland's government in 1590 supports this point: '[i]t was said in May 1590 that if opposition to the "Bridge of Dee" confederates ... were to start organising again, many nobles would now join them while even more would "stand at gaze".'[2] It seems unlikely that such sentiments could have been mooted if Brig o' Dee had been anything other than a demonstration against the government. There is little or no evidence that Huntly's prominence at court was connected with anything more *concrete* than the possible eclipse of Maitland and his policies; but such a political coup would have done little or nothing to bring nearer Scotland's return to the Catholic fold.

When Huntly, Errol, Crawford and Bothwell raised their troops in April 1589, it was hailed as the first move of the 'Catholic lords' in fulfilment of Spanish expectations. Some historians have attributed this to the Counter-Reformation. However, in doing so, they fail to recognise that the Catholic schemes had ceased to be the over-riding issue and that the Catholic party was not homogeneous. The 'Catholic lords', despite the persistent demands of the kirk and England, had not been prosecuted for either their religion or politics. Huntly, as demonstrated by the ample correspondence which passed between him and James, the continuing presence of some of Huntly's men within the king's chamber and the excuses made by James to the English ambassador, was still securely within the king's favour. They had not by any means been placed in the position where there was no alternative to rebellion. It is a surprising turn of events, but to label it as an exclusively Catholic rebellion, spontaneous or otherwise, is to mistake the context.

The terms in which the position of the earls was couched in April 1589 drew heavily, yet again, on the rivalry between Maitland's party and Huntly's. The latter maintained that arms were raised wholly in self-defence against the chancellor: their primary objective was to remove Maitland from power. It was almost as an aside that freedom of conscience was added to the agenda, perhaps to ensure the continued flow of money from Spain or to take advantage of the proffered opportunity. It must be noted, however, that Spain had not instigated the rebellion. Parma had directed Mendoza in November to inform the Scots that military aid in the near future would be impossible and no action should be taken in the interim. When Mendoza wrote to Philip II in July about

1 BL, Add. MS 19,401, fos. 166-7; *CSP Scot.*, x, 44; Colville, *Letters*, 90. For Glamis: *CSP Scot.*, x, 68, 93, 102; *Letters and Papers, Master of Gray*, 157-8, 166.

2 Goodare, 'The nobility and the absolutist state', 166-7.

Brig o' Dee, he too placed it within a political context, mentioning only that Huntly's surrender would cause the dissipation of the Catholic party.[1] Furthermore, the refusal of the earls to face James on the field at Brig o' Dee emphasises that their complaint was against the chancellor, not the king.

V

Having determined that there was no causal connection between Counter-Reformation politics and the armed rising in April 1589, and having placed it within its proper context, full sense is yet to be made of the affair. It is still puzzling as to why such a drastic step as raising troops was taken. The accounts of participants and observers conflict. The events prior to Brig o' Dee did not precipitate rebellion, especially if Maitland's version that there was no plot against Huntly is believed. What, however, did Huntly, or the circle around him, believe? James himself would later try to persuade Huntly that the 'alarumis' which he had heard 'so confidently' reported to him were without substance.[2] It is difficult conclusively to prove the claim made by Bothwell that the affair was 'not without the privity of the King'.[3] An additional factor to consider, nevertheless, is the king's role in the affair, real or perceived. Adversaries of Huntly must have wondered why James allowed Huntly to return to his northern stronghold, seemingly outwith direct royal control. What is certainly evident, however, is that the king had sent mixed signals to both factions and that this served only to escalate the situation. Although publicly supporting the chancellor and dismissing Huntly from the guard, James continued to surround himself with men who supported Huntly. When informed of troops being raised, he was initially reluctant to act and his anger was directed primarily against Bothwell. This did little to dampen the hostility on either side. Instead of compelling Maitland and Huntly to reconcile as he had done in the past, the king appears to have tried to play one card too many and effectively lost control of the situation.

James's unwillingness to break Huntly stemmed from more than the close friendship between the two men: he knew that it would create a vacuum in the north and destroy the balance of power in the central government. The latter is illustrated by the alliance of the Protestant master of Glamis, known to have been increasingly at odds with Maitland before Brig o' Dee, with Huntly's faction after April 1589. There was, however, a further, growing complication in the already complex world of court politics, which probably alarmed Maitland and Huntly in equal measure and would have concerned James if he was trying to maintain an implicit balance of power between rival factions: the

1 *CSP Spain*, iv, 479, 528, 548.
2 *Spalding Misc.*, iii, 215.
3 *CBP*, i, 337.

developing Stewart faction that the earl of Bothwell was cultivating in order to build his own position at court. Bothwell bore as much antipathy to Maitland as Huntly did, yet he also posed at least a potential threat to Huntly. The Stewarts, unlike the Gordons, were not an especially cohesive kin network with close affinities. Particularly after 1590, the faction recruited by Bothwell was dominated by men who had clashed with Huntly in the north-east: the earls of Moray, Atholl and Caithness.

James's stance—whether genuinely ambivalent or calculatedly ambiguous—was perhaps the key factor in the rapid escalation of the situation. In playing off both Catholic and Protestant sympathies, the king overlooked the fact that in an era of confessional politics there was, at moments of crisis, when events threatened to veer out of control, no room for anything other than unambiguous loyalty to the crown. Was it therefore James who created the underlying problem which sparked Brig o' Dee? Although he correctly perceived the affair as a manifestation of factional politics, did James not realise that others, and not only the kirk, were unable to separate political factionalism from confessional politics? His unwillingness to break either faction and deal effectively with the issues raised by Huntly's Spanish correspondence enabled Huntly's opponents to interpret the sequence of events within a purely religious framework—subsequently increasing the stakes.

There is much to be said for the argument that James, after having initially lost control of the situation, rapidly turned the aftermath of April 1589 to his own advantage. The propaganda value of Brig o' Dee was exploited, as had been done in the case of Maxwell's two revolts, to reinforce the king's position and to provide a potent illustration to Protestants, Catholics and the English. James used it to demonstrate not only his own might as a 'general Christian King' but also the damage which could be provoked by the 'Catholic lords'. Adroitly playing upon the paranoid fears of both English and Scottish Protestants and on the rivalry between Maitland and Huntly, James carefully cultivated his own image and importance. It was his own strength, it was claimed, that kept opposition at bay and maintained his chancellor's policies. This was image-making *extraordinaire*. It was meant to underline his importance to English security. Utilising English apprehensions regarding the Counter-Reformation and their reliance upon Maitland, Brig o' Dee may have been partly used as a bid to reinforce Scotland's strategic position to Elizabeth, demonstrating that without her proper support, respect and commitment, Scottish policy could easily change.[1] To Scottish Catholics, it was an oft repeated demonstration that, although disloyalty was intolerable, justice was applied equally across the

1 *CSP Scot.*, ix, 665-6; x, 16.

religious spectrum. Loyalty, rather than religion, was the issue. The message was equally relevant to Catholics outwith Scotland's borders.

Was Huntly leniently treated because he was the king's favourite? He certainly received more favourable treatment than Bothwell, a Stewart kinsman of the king, did in the early 1590s. Huntly was undoubtedly a favourite of the king's, but this favouritism must be understood within the context of James's general treatment of all Catholics. If compared to that received by other prominent Catholics, especially the fifth Lord Seton (*c.*1531-86), who played a pivotal role in the Scottish Counter-Reformation, or even Maxwell, who staged two rebellions in the space of ten months in 1587-8, it does not seem so unusual. Men such as Huntly and Seton were trustworthy, reliable and capable; so, up to a point, was Maxwell, who was restored to the privy council in 1591.[1] One would hesitate, however, to apply such adjectives to Bothwell. Simply put, albeit a Protestant, James felt seriously threatened by Bothwell but not by the mightiest Catholic noble in his realm.[2] This was especially apparent from 1591 onwards. Following his escape from ward in Edinburgh Castle during the North Berwick witch trials in which he was a suspect, Bothwell's position declined markedly. James interpreted Bothwell's erratic attempts to gain control of his person as a direct personal threat and he became increasingly obsessed with breaking the earl. Bothwell ultimately spent the last years of his life in exile, still plotting, and dependent on the charity of the Spanish king. Conversely, during the same period, Huntly grew in both stature and power—despite the discovery of further Spanish correspondence in 1592, a seriously escalating bloodfeud with the earl of Moray and a set-piece battle (which he won) against the king's lieutenant at Glenlivet in 1594. For his transgressions, Huntly spent less than a year in exile, while James ensured that the earl's livings, lands and powerbase remained intact. In 1599, Huntly was elevated to a marquisate. Although his political influence declined after 1603, his close relationship with James remained unaltered—so much so that the king requested that the son of his trusted friend be sent to London as a companion to Prince Charles.

In analysing the course of events leading from the interception of the Scottish correspondence with Parma in February 1589 to the armed rising in April, it is clear that the periods immediately before and after the Brig o' Dee were dominated by the political rivalry between Maitland and Huntly. So, although Brig o' Dee may have had a deliberate hint of a Catholic flavour to it, it was by no means a reflection of militant Catholic politics. Although Huntly was involved in the Counter-

1 See Brown, 'Making of a *politique*', 171-2, for his 'phoenix-like recovery'.

2 Lee briefly touches upon Huntly as a favourite: *Great Britain's Solomon*, 241; he stresses the comparison between Huntly and Bothwell, attributing James's reactions to a like or dislike of each man.

Reformation and had a devout personal faith, it must be concluded that Brig o' Dee did not represent his means of expression of militant Catholicism. James must also share the responsibility for the escalation of the event since his decidedly equivocal stance did not discourage a rebellion couched in traditional terms against Maitland, who was perceived as responsible for implementing unpopular policy. Huntly's subsequent career was speckled with events such as this, when he bore the burden of the king's propaganda or covert schemes. Huntly's fidelity was proved by deeds, as well as by his correspondence. Perhaps more importantly, however, was James's interpretation of the earl's career: before 1625, he was summoned to London where James presented him to Charles as 'the most faithful servant that ever served a prince, assuring Charles that so long as he would cherish and keep Huntly on his side, he needed not be very apprehensive of seditious or turbulent heads in Scotland'.[1]

1 *James VI Papers*, 145-6, 183, 189-90, note, 123; J.M. Bulloch, *History of the Gordons*, 3 vols. (New Spalding Club, 1907), ii, 129.

~ 6 ~

James VI's English Subsidy

Julian Goodare[1]

> Considering that God hath endewed ws with a crown that yeildeth more yerly profeit to us, than we understand yours doth to youe, by reason of the dissipation and evill governement therof of long tyme before your birth, we have latelie sent to youe a portion meete for your awin privat use; thogh not so large as our mynd wold yeld, but yet such as the tyme at this present permitteth us to do.
>
> *Elizabeth to James, 1586.*[2]

> We can not bot find strange that, seing our sa freindlye careing our self and luffing dispositioun, we have not bein so respected as we both merited and expected, and albeit we have in deid at dyvers tymes ... veary tymouslye resaved such soomes as hes advanced our affaires, yet not in that sort nor quantitye as was promised.
>
> *James to Elizabeth, 1590.*[3]

> Between Scotland and the queen all things are well, for he sends for his gratuity.
>
> *Sir Robert Cecil to Sir Henry Neville, 1599.*[4]

It is no secret that James VI was subsidised by Queen Elizabeth. But what did this mean for Anglo-Scottish relations? Did it, for instance, allow Elizabeth to influence James's policies? Did English gold make much practical difference to James's finances? How did he spend the money? And in an age where diplomacy was so full of religious issues, did mere cash have much impact?

Answers to some of these questions will emerge gradually in the course of this paper, but it is necessary to begin with a firm affirmative answer to the last one. Money was vital to kingship, for a king without it was a toothless lion, as James knew better than most. Chronically short

1 Sums of money in this chapter are given in £s sterling—the English currency, which had a fairly constant value in this period—unless otherwise stated. £1 sterling was worth £9 Scots from 1586 to 1594, and £10 Scots thereafter. A further devaluation of the £ Scots—£12 to £1 sterling—was carried out in 1601, but this was not reflected in the official accounts recording the subsidy. I am grateful to Ms Ruth Grant for discussions on Scottish foreign relations.

2 NLS, Elizabeth to James, 2 June 1586, Denmylne MSS, Adv. MS 33.1.7, vol. xxi, no. 3. Another copy at no. 20. Another version of this letter, entirely in Scottish orthography, was registered in the privy council books on 14 Nov. 1596: *RPC*, v, 324-5. The letter is calendared in *CSP Scot.*, viii, 414-15.

3 Instructions for Sir John Carmichael, ambassador from James VI, 10 June 1590, *CSP Scot.*, x, 318.

4 Cecil to Neville, ambassador in Paris, 18 Sept. 1599, Winwood, *Memorials*, i, 105.

of cash in the 1580s and 1590s, he was rightly envious of the Elizabethan regime, which so conspicuously maintained its financial stability while fighting a successful war—and subsidising its allies. As ally or as enemy, England always played the predominant role in shaping the international relations of its smaller northern neighbour. In James VI's personal reign in Scotland up to 1603, his relations with England were dominated by the subsidy. In his dealings with Elizabeth, James was of course mainly concerned to succeed her on the English throne; but while she lived there was nothing that interested him so much as her money.

I

If the subsidy symbolises a close Anglo-Scottish relationship, the road leading to it had been a long and winding one. England's attitude towards Scotland in the fifteenth century was one of ungracious coexistence, the legacy of failed attempts at outright conquest. There was regular friction and periodic small-scale warfare, but no more; even the Flodden campaign of 1513 was thought of by both sides as a large-scale Border raid, and the English did not think of following up their unexpected victory by carrying warfare into Scotland.

This changed completely in 1540-1, and English governments began to seek ways of exerting a controlling influence on Scottish policy. After a brief Anglo-Scottish war, the tempting vista of Scotland as an obedient English client state was opened up by the treaty of Greenwich in 1543, to be based on a marriage between the infant Queen Mary and Henry's son Edward. When the Scots repudiated this agreement, the English responded with seven years of aggression and attempted conquest. This war, unlike the wars of the past two centuries, had far-reaching aims—to revive either the marriage treaty of 1543, or the feudal suzerainty of 1292. In response, the Scots invited in a French army in 1548, and the English were defeated. This, however, led to a French occupation of Scotland which became increasingly unpopular in the 1550s; more Scots began to favour the English option, and (with the assistance of English arms) the pro-English party triumphed in 1560. In the process Scotland became officially Protestant. The English army then left, but there was no return to the old ways, for the English were determined to maintain their new-found and fragile 'amity' with Scotland.

One of the pillars of the 'amity' was the position of Queen Mary, and later James, in the English succession. Their hopes for official recognition as heir presumptive to Elizabeth (or, occasionally, their fears that she might recognise someone else) gave them a personal reason for staying friendly with her. This gave the English a diplomatic weapon that cost nothing in itself, but in practice needed to be backed up in Scotland by a group of pro-English nobles and courtiers who actually *wanted* the English succession. To fortify this group in power, money was needed. It was quite cheap to subsidise them—both to remind them of the value of the 'amity', and to enable them to act in its support. From about 1569 to 1586, a good deal of cash found its way into the pockets of reliable Scottish nobles.[1] But it was always difficult for the English to tell whether they were getting value for money, and such clientage became harder to sustain as James VI emerged from his minority and began to govern directly in the mid-1580s, since more nobles tended to follow his lead. So a more straightforward option emerged. James needed money. Why not subsidise him directly?

II

A regular subsidy to James was first suggested in late 1579, when the pro-English party had a project for a royal guard of 50 men, a resident council, and better pay for the Border wardens. The cost was estimated at £3,000 per year, to be paid by Elizabeth. Next year a loan to pay the king's debts was under discussion.[2] But between 1580 and 1582 the ascendancy of the French-connected duke of Lennox put an end to these schemes, and there were rumours that James would receive a subsidy from France.[3] The pro-English Ruthven regime (1582-3) received a loan of £1,000 to pay the guard, and in May 1583 a regular subsidy of 10,000 crowns (£3,000) was decided—but never paid because the Ruthven regime collapsed in the following month.[4]

After the assassination of William of Orange, the Dutch resistance leader, in June 1584, it began to seem likely that England would intervene militarily to prevent the breakaway Dutch provinces being reconquered by Spain. As England prepared for war, it needed all the friends it could get. The dominant figure at the Scottish court was the earl of Arran, not actually anti-English but an enemy of England's most reliable friends; this did not stop an Anglo-Scottish league being discussed. After his downfall (in an English-backed coup, November 1585), it was easy to negotiate a treaty in early 1586.

The treaty itself did not mention money.[5] The subsidy was discussed in parallel with the league but was formally separate. It is usually said that Elizabeth promised to pay James £4,000 per year: this is incorrect,

1 K.M. Brown, 'The price of friendship: the "well affected" and English economic clientage in Scotland before 1603', in R.A. Mason (ed.), *Scotland and England, 1286-1815* (Edinburgh, 1987). Complete figures are lacking for these subsidies.

2 Memorial of the present estate of Scotland, 31 Dec. 1579, HMC, *Salisbury*, ii, 284; Sir Francis Walsingham to earl of Shrewsbury, 27 Nov. 1580, ibid., 353.

3 James Beaton, archbishop of Glasgow, to [a correspondent in Rome], 31 Oct. 1581, and Robert Bowes to Lord Burghley and Walsingham, 11 Jan. 1581, *CSP Scot.*, v, 533, 581. For an unsubstantiated report that 6,000 crowns had actually been paid by the duke of Guise, see M. Fontenay (secretary of Mary's council) to Mary, Jan. 1583, *CSP Scot.*, vi, 283. French influence in Scotland worried the English, but it was not as bad as Spanish influence—England was, after all, allied to France.

4 Bowes to Walsingham, 7 Feb. 1583, BL, Cotton MSS, Caligula, C.VII, fos. 128r.-129r.; same to same, 12 Feb. 1583, *CSP Scot.*, vi, 295; Walsingham to Bowes, 29 May 1583, ibid., 472.

5 For the text of the treaty see T. Rymer (ed.), *Foedera*, xv (London, 1713), 803-7. It can be summarised as a Protestant alliance for mutual defence.

and the truth is a good deal more complicated. During the negotiations, Elizabeth seems to have had a figure of £5,000 per year in mind as a maximum; but her secretary of state, Sir Francis Walsingham, and her ambassadors, were so keen to get the alliance that they even mentioned the figure of £6,000 to James.[1] In fact Elizabeth reduced the first instalment to £4,000, commenting that this was all she could then afford.[2] But she never said that the normal figure was £4,000; indeed, until 1601 she conspicuously avoided any commitment to a fixed annual sum of any kind. James had merely a verbal assurance that he would be paid unspecified amounts from time to time.[3] The list of payments up to 1601 shows that the subsidy was indeed irregular and unpredictable, both in the times of payment and in the amounts paid. This vagueness on Elizabeth's part was surely deliberate, since it suited her aims well: James could count on nothing, and had to earn every instalment.[4]

The subsidy was always called the 'gratuity' by the English, while the Scots called it the 'annuity'. The difference between these terms encapsulates the differing views of the arrangement. James often claimed that he had been promised regular and assured payments, but the promises were never in writing or authorised by Elizabeth.[5] James asked for an English dukedom, suggesting that of Cornwall, so that the subsidy could

1 Walsingham to Edward Wotton, 1 June 1585, *CSP Scot.*, vii, 656, writing of 20,000 (French) crowns. Taking this as £6,000 assumes that Walsingham regarded the crown as worth 6*s*. sterling, the only rate that makes sense of all the figures. Exchange rates are complex, and officials did not necessarily use the same rates as merchants. In Apr. 1586 the crown was quoted at 6*s*. 7*d*. (HMC, *Salisbury*, xiii, 293), which would have made 20,000 crowns equal to £6,583. But Walsingham was clearly working in round figures of sterling, since the queen had mentioned a figure of £1,000 less than his.

2 Walsingham to Randolph, 19 Mar. 1586, *CSP Scot.*, viii, 254.

3 Elizabeth sometimes suggested that it was intended to be commensurate with the allowance she had received in her father's will. James was told this had been £5,000, but Elizabeth said truthfully that it had been £3,000: Burghley to Bowes, 12 Jan. 1593, and Bowes to Elizabeth, 21 Jan. 1593, *CSP Scot.*, xi, 19-20, 27; J.E. Neale, *Queen Elizabeth I* (Pelican edn., Harmondsworth, 1960), 28. But she had received *lands* to that value, whereas James was receiving only a discretionary payment. Elizabeth always insisted (and indeed demonstrated) that she could reduce the allowance at will, as when she initially offered only £2,000 in 1593: Melville to Burghley, 19 July 1593, *CSP Scot.*, xi, 125. Her attitude for most of the 1590s was that £3,000 was a rough norm, though there was no commitment to it: Elizabeth's instructions to George Nicolson, c. Mar. 1598, and Cecil to Nicolson, 27 Apr. 1598, *CSP Scot.*, xiii, I, 183, 196-7.

4 Subsidy payments were authorised by Elizabeth personally, and the decision was never a routine one. The £3,000 paid in Sept. 1589 came initially from Burghley, who pledged his own credit—'I must in honesty paye the same, which I will doo, though I leave not my self a spoone of silver.' He hoped to shame Elizabeth into reimbursing him by procuring a thank-you letter to her from James: Burghley to William Asheby, 12 Oct. & 30 Oct. 1589, *CSP Scot.*, x, 170, 182-3. £3,000 was issued from the exchequer in Dec., so presumably Burghley was able to keep his silver spoons: *CSP Scot.*, xi, 115-16.

5 English diplomats, unlike the queen, sometimes thought there might be some truth in Scottish claims that a specific figure had been agreed, though they were unsure what the figure should be. Even Burghley had to seek advice on this: Burghley to Thomas Mills, 29 July 1593, *CSP Scot.*, xi, 133-4.

be paid as the revenue from this; but this was exactly what Elizabeth had no intention of giving, any more than she would give him any assurance over the succession.[1]

James had a claim to some English lands through his grandmother, Margaret Douglas, countess of Lennox. Archbishop Spottiswoode, who was first involved in diplomatic affairs in 1601, wrote that the subsidy was 'a gift of annuity answerable to the lands possessed by the Lady Lennox in her time, which the king by divers ambassadors had formerly required as due to him'.[2] James may have liked to have it thought that this was so, but Elizabeth made sure that he never received title to the lands. She even refused James's request for an 'instrument' guaranteeing the subsidy: 'Must so great doubt be made of free good will, and gift be so mistrusted ...? Who should doubt performance of king's offer?'[3] Who indeed.

III

From 1586 to 1603, the subsidy payments fluctuated with James's fluctuating value to Elizabeth. There were four periods of relative generosity—broadly 1588-90, 1594-5, 1598 and 1601-2—and four when less was paid—1587, 1591-3, 1596-7 and 1599-1600. The level of payments reached a high point in 1589 and tended to fall thereafter, though there was a large jump in 1602. Some of these variations can be explained simply in terms of bilateral Anglo-Scottish relations, while at other times England's wider interests came into account. The absence of payments in 1587 is easily explained by the execution of James's mother in February. Elizabeth did not offer anything that year, nor did James ask for it; it would have looked too much like blood-money. This did not stop later Scottish critics of the subsidy linking it with Mary's fate, as we shall see.

The Anglo-Spanish war entered an acute phase in 1588, and Scottish friendship was vital. With the Armada in the Channel, a frightened English ambassador offered James the coveted dukedom, a regular £5,000 per year, and various other rewards—only to be reprimanded for

1 Wotton to Walsingham, 22 July 1585, *CSP Scot.*, viii, 35. Elizabeth refused the suggestion firmly: Walsingham to Wotton, 28 July 1585, *CSP Scot.*, viii, 41. The duchy of Cornwall was a traditional appurtenance of the heir to the English throne, and James had additional reasons for wanting to obtain lands in England. He foresaw objections to his title to the English succession because he was an alien under English common law; if he could have established title to a landed estate, that would have neutralised this. Also, however, a dukedom was a matter of honour—a point to which we shall return.

2 Spottiswoode, *History*, ii, 349.

3 Elizabeth to James, c. Mar. 1586, *Elizabeth and James Letters*, 30-1. H.G. Stafford, *James VI of Scotland and the Throne of England* (New York, 1940), 10, states that Elizabeth did sign an 'instrument', but this does not appear to be borne out by the evidence; the 'instrument' exists only in unsigned Scottish drafts. Had the Scots possessed a signed 'instrument' in 1596, it would have been registered in place of Elizabeth's financially-vague letter of 2 June 1586: see p. 110, note 2 above.

ENGLISH PAYMENTS TO JAMES VI, 1586-1602

Date; Amount **£ sterling** (£ Scots)	Scottish agent(s) receiving the money
12 May 1586: **£4,000** (£36,000)	Roger Ashton (English servant of James); William Home (brother of Sir James Home of Coldenknowes, lieutenant of the guard)
8 July 1588: **£2,000** (£18,000)	John Carmichael of that Ilk (later captain of the guard)
10 September 1588: **£3,000** (£27,000)	Carmichael
May 1589: **£3,000** (£27,000)	James Colville of Easter Wemyss (soldier, diplomat)
September 1589: **£3,000** (£27,000)	Mr John Colville (tax collector, diplomat)
21 June 1590: **£500** (£3,600)	Carmichael
2 July 1590: **£3,000** (£27,000)	Carmichael
31 May 1591: **£3,000** (£27,000)	James Hudson (English merchant, James's agent); Thomas Foulis (goldsmith, crown financier); Robert Jowsie (merchant, Foulis' partner)
18 July 1592: **£2,000** (£18,000)	Hudson; Thomas Foulis; Jowsie
18-20 July 1593: **£4,000** (£36,000)	Sir Robert Melville of Murdochcairny (treasurer depute)
1 July 1594: **£3,000** (£30,000)	Mr David Foulis (brother of Thomas, clerk of the chamber)
6 November 1594: **£2,000** (£20,000)	Sir Richard Cockburn younger of Clerkington (secretary)
11 August 1595: **£3,000** (£30,000)	David Foulis
29 September 1596: **£3,000** (£30,000)	David Foulis
30 May 1598: **£3,000** (£30,000)	Mr Edward Bruce (commendator of Kinloss, councillor); Jowsie
19 December 1598: **£3,000** (£30,000)	David Foulis
18 February 1600: **£3,000** (£30,000)	Mr James Sempill of Beltrees (courtier); Jowsie; Archibald Johnstone (merchant); George Heriot younger (goldsmith)
26 October 1601: **£2,000** (£20,000)	David Foulis; Johnstone; Mr James Hamilton (James's agent in London)
27 January 1602: **£3,000** (£30,000)	David Foulis; Ashton
24 June 1602: **£2,500** (£25,000)	Ashton
25 December 1602: **£2,500** (£25,000)	Ashton

Sources: various, but see *CSP Scot.* around the dates given. Of the contemporary lists of payments, the least inaccurate are *CSP Scot.*, xi, 471, and *CSP Scot.*, xiii, II, 742-3. Dates shown are when money came into Scottish hands, which are not always the same as the dates in the lists; the Sept. 1589 payment, for example, was not issued from the exchequer until Dec., the money having been advanced by Burghley. Several lists (e.g. *CSP Scot.*, x, 37-8, and PRO, SP12/266, fo. 121r.) include payments not for James. Amounts are given in **£ sterling** (£ Scots in brackets).

exceeding his authority once the crisis was past.[1] But James did get £5,000 in cash. After the Armada's defeat, the war intensified and spread to France, so payments stayed high. They declined in 1591-2, perhaps because of English suspicions (understandable at the time, although seeming exaggerated in retrospect) at James's favour to the Catholic earls led by Huntly. But fears that Scotland might slip out of the English orbit could lead to increased payments as well as reduced ones. We can pinpoint the reason for the decision to pay a generous £4,000 in May 1594: Elizabeth received news that a barque had arrived at Montrose bearing Spanish gold for the Catholic earls. She decided that gold had to be fought with gold.[2]

By 1596, the French war was winding down, but war at sea and in the Netherlands continued; probably Elizabeth was paying less because she felt that Scotland's allegiance was more secure. Huntly had submitted in 1594. The 'amity', though never rock-solid, had been tested and shown to be working. *Two* instalments of £3,000 were paid in 1598; perhaps the first represented arrears (nothing had been paid in 1597), while the second was when Essex's expedition to Ireland was in preparation. Scotland was important here, because the heartland of Irish resistance to England was Ulster, where the Irish leadership could obtain supplies from their friends in the west of Scotland—if James let them.

It was undoubtedly the Irish war that led to the subsidy being increased, and put on a more permanent basis, in May 1601. Lord Mountjoy had just begun the crucial campaign which would lead later in the year to the landing of a Spanish army and the battle of Kinsale. After so many defeats in the later 1590s, this was a campaign that the English could not afford to lose. Elizabeth 'was content to add to the annuity formerly paid the summe of two thousand pounds yearly, as long as he kept fast and held one course with her'.[3] Not only that, but she at last specified fixed times and amounts of payment: £5,000 per year, to be paid half-yearly in June and December.[4] These payments continued until the subsidy was brought to an end by Elizabeth's death on 24 March 1603.

IV

Between May 1586 and December 1602 James received a total of £58,500 from Elizabeth, an average of £3,441 per year over seventeen years. The average over the first fifteen years, when the amount to be paid was in

1 NLS, Denmilne MSS, Adv. MS 33.1.7, vol. 21, no. 21 (copy); Asheby to Walsingham, 3 Aug. & 12 Aug. 1588, *CSP Scot.*, ix, 589-90, 596. For the Scots' belief in his offers, see Richard Douglas to Archibald Douglas, 14 Aug. 1588, HMC, *Salisbury*, iii, 350.

2 Bowes to Burghley, 10 May 1594, and Cecil to Bowes, 17 May 1594 (2 letters of that date, the second written after Elizabeth received Bowes's letter and changed her mind), *CSP Scot.*, xi, 329-35.

3 Spottiswoode, *History*, iii, 94-5.

4 Elizabeth to James, 11 May 1601, *CSP Scot.*, xiii, II, 822.

dispute, was £3,233. What did James do with the money?[1] In the view of his paymasters, he had several choices. One option was to buy goods in London with it (or to pay his debts there). If the money came to Scotland, the question in English eyes was whether he would give it away, or spend it on an approved purpose—a royal guard, for instance, or (in the early 1590s) military action against the Catholic earls. The subsidy payments do not appear in any extant Scottish accounts before May 1589, but the cash all reached Scotland, being paid from Berwick. Officers of the guard were involved in its collection, and probably a good deal was spent on the guard.[2] The English welcomed this, since they felt that a professional guard was necessary to strengthen royal authority in Scotland. The other thing that James did with his early instalments of English money was to give it away:

> He geves to every one that axes what they desyer, even to vayne youthes and prowd foles the very landes of his crowne ... Ye[a], what he gettes from Ingland, if it were a myllion, they wold get it from him, so careles is he of any welth if he may enjoy his plesure in huntynge.[3]

Such comments have provoked many historians to denounce James's unthriftiness, but his view of money—that it existed to be spent—was common enough at the time; it was Elizabeth, so determined to maintain her credit and balance her books, who was unusual. There were clamorous pressures on James to spend; the royal court was expected to be a fountain of patronage, and one of his constant difficulties was that he had so little.

John Maitland of Thirlestane had been James's leading minister and chancellor since 1587; in 1589 he also took over for a time as his leading financial manager. He gained control of the May 1589 instalment, claiming that the last (September 1588) had been squandered: 'manie gatt fleses out of [it], and litle imployed as was most requisite'.[4] James Colville of Easter Wemyss collected the money, hoping that 'his majestie may think it cummis be my procurment'.[5] But he had to hand most of it (£21,753. 6*s*. 8*d*. Scots, equivalent to £2,417 sterling) over to Maitland, who spent £15,616. 13*s*. 4*d*. on the king's marriage, £4,500 on horsemen to suppress the Bridge of Dee rebellion, and £2,000 for general crown

1 We will never know about the distribution of much of the money. Most did not pass through the hands of the major financial officers, the treasurer and comptroller, and thus did not appear in their accounts. If a trusted royal agent brought the cash to court, where James himself gave it away or bought things with it, there was no need for it to be accounted for at all. But enough accounts and other indicators survive to give an outline of what happened to the money.

2 There are no extant accounts for the guard.

3 Thomas Fowler to Walsingham, 18 Dec. 1588, *CSP Scot.*, ix, 650.

4 Asheby to Burghley, 11 May 1589, *CSP Scot.*, x, 70-1.

5 *CSP Scot.*, x, 73-4.

expenses.[1] It was the remaining £5,246. 13*s*. 4*d*. Scots (£583 sterling) that explained the choice of Colville to collect the money. He used it to recruit a small Scottish army, under his command, to fight in France under English pay—a striking instance of the Anglo-Scottish 'amity' in action.[2]

Maitland again gained control of the July 1590 instalment. The disbursements were miscellaneous, some apparently being debt repayments (or perhaps gifts); £260 went to Sir James Sandilands 'to be play silver to his majestie'. The most significant items were £4,000 to Robert Jowsie, merchant of Edinburgh, and £2,666. 13*s*. 4*d*. to Thomas Foulis, goldsmith, 'for certane chenyeis of gold'.[3] Jowsie and Foulis were the king's suppliers respectively of clothes and jewellery, both in heavy demand at the time of James's marriage. Their purchases in London meant that the subsidy began to be paid there, instead of English agents bringing it to Berwick. By April 1591, Maitland was restive at the financial burden placed on him. He was £15,299 Scots superexpended, and wanted James to repay him from the next subsidy instalment.[4] Asking for one's superexpenses to be refunded was not the way to continue as one of James VI's financial officers, and after 1590 Maitland did not handle the subsidy again.

In 1591, control of the subsidy passed to the financier Thomas Foulis; he or his colleagues (Robert Jowsie, and his brother David Foulis) collected seven of the nine instalments up to 1598, and it seems clear that the money was administered from his office. It certainly was in 1594 and

1 BL, Add. MS 22,958, Sir John Maitland of Thirlestane's accounts, 1589-94, fos. 4r.-4v. The discharge exceeds the charge. Only the last £2,000 went through the regular accounts of treasurer and comptroller (£1,000 each): *ER*, xxii, 29, and NAS, E21/67, treasurer's accounts, 1588-90, fo. 92r. On Bridge of Dee, see R. Grant, 'The Brig o' Dee affair, the sixth earl of Huntly and the politics of the Counter-Reformation', Chapter 5 above.

2 In the spring of 1589 an envoy had come to Scotland 'fra the king of Navare, desyring to have thrie thousand waidged men; the laird of Wemyis past in Ingland for the gold to tak thame up with, and wes appoynted generall'. Later that year, Colville 'tuik up xv[c] waidged men for the king of Novar, now allegit king of France': Moysie, *Memoirs*, 73, 78. See also Henry of Navarre to James, c. Mar. 1589, *Warrender Papers*, ii, 101-2; Colville to Walsingham, 14 June 1589, *CSP Scot.*, x, 101; Colville to Paul Choart, sieur de Buzanval, 13 July 1589, ibid., 117-18. By the time the troops arrived in Dieppe they were under English pay: F. Michel, *Les Ecossais en France, les Français en Ecosse*, 2 vols. (London, 1862), ii, 122-3. Colville received an English reward in the form of a licence to export 1,000 cloths or kerseys from England custom-free: warrant, 2 May 1589, HMC, *Salisbury*, iii, 409.

3 BL, Add. MS 22,958, Sir John Maitland of Thirlestane's accounts, 1589-94, fos. 21r.-23r. Maitland was superexpended on this account too. Jowsie's accounts (formally in the name of Sir George Home of Spott, master of the wardrobe) show this £4,000 as having been received from the treasurer, but if this is correct the treasurer must himself have received it from Maitland: NAS, E35/13, apparel accounts, 1590-2, fo. 2r. Sir James Balfour later noted that Jowsie accounted for £4,000 Scots received from the subsidy in Aug. 1590: NLS, Denmilne MSS, Adv. MS 33.1.7, vol. 21, no. 45.

4 Sir John Carmichael, captain of the guard and warden of the west march, also wanted money from it, no doubt to reimburse him for military action in one capacity or the other: Bowes to Burghley, 3 Apr. 1591, *CSP Scot.*, x, 491-4. For Maitland's superexpenses, see BL, Add. MS 22,958, Maitland's accounts, 1589-94, fo. 13r.

1595, when his accounts survive.[1] Foulis and Jowsie had begun by making purchases for the king in London, but the credit they extended to him, and the credit they themselves obtained from English suppliers, meant that they could exert pressure for later subsidies to pass through their hands.[2] Most of the money went on jewellery, with some on military action and diplomacy, and miscellaneous expenses of the court.[3] James in effect used Foulis as a banker, paying the subsidy and other income into his account and drawing on it as needed.

The Octavians, an exchequer commission of eight reforming administrators, formed a new fiscal regime in January 1596. They sidelined Foulis and closed the king's account with him—it was then overdrawn by £51,881 Scots—but they failed to prise control of the subsidy away from him.[4] After the Octavian regime, Foulis returned to manage the royal finances, but he was bankrupted in January 1598 by James's contrived failure to meet obligations to him. Only then did the subsidy come for the first time into the hands of the crown's main financial officers.[5] This, however, was less a carefully-planned reform than a desperate expedient to meet a financial crisis. The subsidy was tossed in the storm, promised first to the comptroller, and then to the treasurer. The former's loss of the money, which would have been 'ane grite help' to him, led to his bankruptcy in February 1599.[6] After that the money went through the treasurer's accounts. James, who could no longer afford to pay his debts, was reluctant to let creditors get any of it, and to the very end he spent much of it in London.[7]

1 NAS, E30/14, accounts of Thomas Foulis, 1594-5. As well as the English subsidy, Foulis also managed revenues from the mint, the royal mines (which he leased), and later the customs. For his career see J. Goodare, 'Thomas Foulis and the Scottish fiscal crisis of the 1590s', in W.M. Ormrod *et al.* (eds.), *Crises, Revolutions and Self-Sustained Growth: Essays in Fiscal History, 1130-1830* (Stamford, 1999, forthcoming).

2 They had debts in England, for which Elizabeth earmarked £2,000 of the £4,000 paid in July 1593. In fact they received £3,000—and this was one of the instalments that did *not* go through Foulis's hands, because the envoy who collected it, Sir Robert Melville, was also treasurer depute. Melville to Burghley, 19 July & 24 July 1593, *CSP Scot.*, xi, 125, 131; NAS, E21/69, treasurer's accounts, 1592-3, fos. 225r.-225v. Foulis also borrowed on the expectation of receiving the subsidy, and had great 'adoues' when it was delayed: Ashton to Hudson, 30 May 1594, *CSP Scot.*, xi, 348.

3 Their London purchases filled 'four tronks and four pakkis' in 1593: Melville to Burghley, 24 July 1593, *CSP Scot.*, xi, 131.

4 They got James to agree in Jan. 1596 'that the ressaver of the annuitie of Ingland be appoyntit be advyse and consent of the saidis lordis, and that na pairt thairof be disponit unto [sc. until] his majesteis howse be first servit, and the residue be disponit be thair consent in his majesties maist necessar effaires, and that the said sowme be brocht hame in usuall money, aither Inglis or Scottis': *RPC*, v, 758. But when the next instalment was paid in Sept., it was collected by David Foulis in London, and did not pass through the hands of the main financial officers. £810 went to Jowsie (NAS, E35/13, apparel accounts), and the rest probably went through Thomas Foulis's accounts, now missing.

5 For the details of this, see Goodare, 'Thomas Foulis'.

6 *RPC*, v, 521, 525-6, 529.

7 Nicolson to Cecil, 27 Nov. 1599, *CSP Scot.*, xiii, I, 579; NAS, E21/76, treasurer's accounts,

V

It has been said that 'The Anglo-Scottish treaty of 1586 amounted to a tacit pledge of nonintervention on Elizabeth's part'.[1] This is true in the sense that Elizabeth had achieved her diplomatic aims in 1585-6 and no longer needed to resort to *destabilising* unsympathetic Scottish regimes (like that of 1580-2) by promoting a pro-English party.[2] But the treaty certainly did not mean that Elizabeth would no longer seek a voice in Scottish counsels—on the contrary. One only has to look at the subsidy negotiations of 1594, when the English demanded that James take military action against the Catholic earls, and that he change his councillors.[3] James, goaded by the pressure, threatened to 'kick up hell'[4] if Elizabeth would not see things his way. Later in the year, he needed money both for an army to deal with the Catholic earls and for the baptism of Prince Henry—but he mentioned only the army to Elizabeth, knowing that it alone would impress her.[5]

The threat from the Catholic earls faded after 1594, and the English ceased trying to dictate how the subsidy should be spent; but discussions on it were still linked with intervention in Scottish internal policy. In February 1596, not only did Burghley make demands over Border matters, or Scottish aid given to the earl of Tyrone in Ireland, but he also expected to influence the dispute over custody of the prince, the treatment of the Catholic earls, and the choice of candidates for the vacant Scottish chancellorship.[6] Intervention—perhaps it might even be called supervision—had reached a new level of detailed involvement. When Elizabeth loosened her purse-strings at last in 1601, the strings attached to the money were drawn tighter. The master of Gray wrote that the queen 'hes only grantit 2000 l. in augmentatioun of his pension, and that vith many cautiouns, and efter this if the king chainge not course, sche hes protestit sche will not continou the augmentation'.[7]

The £3,000-odd (eventually £5,000-odd) sterling, equivalent to about £30,000 Scots per year, was a good deal of money to James. His annual income from all other sources in the mid-1580s was about £150,000 Scots,

1601-4, fos. 226r.-227v.

1 M. Lee, *James I and Henri IV: An Essay in English Foreign Policy, 1603-1610* (Urbana, Ill., 1970), 5. Cf. M. Lee, *Great Britain's Solomon: James VI and I in his Three Kingdoms* (Urbana, Ill., 1990), 64.

2 Although when doubts appeared about the solidity of the 'amity' in 1592-4, the English were as ruthless as ever in inciting the earl of Bothwell to attack the king.

3 Answer to Lord Zouche, 1 Apr. 1594, *CSP Scot.*, xi, 303.

4 An idiomatic translation of James's '... constraining me to say with Virgil *flectere si nequeo superos Acheronta movebo*', James to Elizabeth, 13 Apr. 1594, James VI, *Letters*, 127-30. Elizabeth responded angrily, and James had trouble explaining the phrase away: same to same, 5 June 1594, ibid., 132-3.

5 Bowes to Burghley, 28 July 1594, *CSP Scot.*, xi, 392.

6 *CSP Scot.*, xii, 137-42.

7 Master of Gray to Lord Balmerino, n.d. [1601], HMC, *Sixth Report*, Appendix, MSS of earl of Moray, 663.

rising to about £200,000 Scots by 1603.[1] Elizabeth thus increased his income by about one-sixth. The hand-to-mouth handling of so many of the payments shows not only that the money was important to the king, but that he was suffering financial hardship. An occasional substantial payment in gold crowns could be a 'legion of angels' to him;[2] it was the only time he ever had so much disposable cash in hand.

But how much was £3,000 to Elizabeth? Did she refuse to make it £5,000 because she was at the limits of her resources, or does this just show that James was low on her scale of priorities? To answer this, we need to examine other comparable burdens on the English treasury. One is the loans made to Henry IV of France, which over a decade totalled £401,735 (£40,000 per year).[3] The purpose of the payments was a little different: Elizabeth was certain of Henry's allegiance in the struggle against Spain, and the money was spent on the war. She subsidised the United Netherlands from 1585, even more heavily; by 1598 they owed her £800,000 (£57,000 per year).[4] James received only a small fraction of these sums; his money was not to fight a war (though Elizabeth recruited Scottish troops), but to reward him for his friendly neutrality.

Another comparison may be made, nearer home. The Dublin government of Ireland required a subsidy which averaged, even in normal times (before the wars of the late 1590s), over £30,000 per year.[5] Of course, England claimed sovereignty over Ireland—but in reality, before 1602 at least, it exercised scarcely more control over most of Ireland than over Scotland. Moreover, from a hard-headed English point of view, both Ireland and Scotland were the same, being merely remote and uncivilised nuisances; controlling them could bring no possible positive benefit. Policy towards them could hope to do no more than to neutralise them—to keep them at the level of *potential* nuisances, preventing England's enemies from exploiting them.[6] With Scotland, this was achieved

1 The basis for these figures is complex; they are not intended as precise, merely as estimates. Almost all of the increase over the period would have been wiped out by inflation.

2 Asheby to Walsingham, 12 Sept. 1588, *CSP Scot.*, ix, 614.

3 'Memoire des sommes de deniers que la Reyne d'Angleterre a prestez ou deboursez pour le Roy Treschrestien', c. 1599, lists the payments between 1587 and 1596: Winwood, *Memorials*, i, 29. Much had been spent on English armies in France. These were *loans*, but their repayment was unlikely and did not in fact take place: Lee, *James I and Henri IV*, *passim*. 150,000 crowns (£45,000) was deducted in 1604, set off against a French subsidy to the United Netherlands: ibid., 51.

4 Guy, *Tudor England*, 348.

5 A. Sheehan, 'Irish revenues and English subventions, 1559-1622', *Proceedings of the Royal Irish Academy*, xc, section C, no. 2 (1990), table 2. £30,000 is the average of the first 36 years in the table, up to 1594-5.

6 The English crown also benefited from direct control over a certain amount of patronage in the Irish administration, so the parallel is inexact. But that administration did not control the country. For the argument that the Tudors' 'British' policy was a security-driven foreign policy, both in Scotland and in Ireland, see H. Morgan, 'British policies before the British state', in B. Bradshaw and J. Morrill (eds.), *The British Problem, c.1534-1707*

at something like a tenth of the cost of Ireland. And Elizabeth also had to pay for a long war of conquest in Ireland: if the 1601-2 payments (£10,000) were entirely intended to cover the English flank in Ireland, they were still not much compared with the cost of the war itself, £1,924,000.[1]

VI

The subsidy payments were gifts, not loans. Why? Did Elizabeth think that James would be unlikely to repay a loan because he was poor? But she had given the Regent Moray a loan in 1569.[2] And Henry IV was at least as unlikely to repay his loans—not because he was poor, but because he became rich and powerful. No: there is another reason why the subsidy was a gift, one that holds the key to understanding it. Loans are (or can be claimed to be) purely business transactions; gifts, however, are about status and honour at least as much as about money.[3] The giver demonstrated her high status, partly by displaying her wealth, but also by having her gift accepted with the requisite obsequious genuflexions. By contrast, the recipient had to *make* the obsequious genuflexions, not only displaying his poverty but also abasing himself in status. To obtain each irregularly-paid instalment, James had to deploy a characteristic combination of profuse affection and importunate demand, reminiscent of nothing so much as a pet cat that thinks it is, or ought to be, feeding time.

Compare James's position as an English pensioner with that of the Scots nobles discussed by Keith Brown.[4] They had no need to compete for status with a queen. They were *flattered* by an English subsidy, showing that they were important enough for Elizabeth to notice them. And of course it was the pro-English party that was subsidised: they believed that promoting the English cause (and being paid for it) was also loyal service to James. Several Scots nobles served other monarchs: there was nothing undignified or dishonourable about taking foreign money, so long as they were not serving an enemy of Scotland.[5]

With James, however, it was different. He was keenly aware that his formal status, as an independent prince equal to Elizabeth, meant that

(London, 1996).

1 R.B. Outhwaite, 'Dearth, the English crown and the "crisis of the 1590s"', in P. Clark (ed.), *The European Crisis of the 1590s* (London, 1985), 25. This paper gives some more figures for Elizabeth's expenditure: £1,420,000 to fight the war in the Netherlands; £161,000 to defeat the Armada; £575,000 on other naval costs; and £424,000 for fighting in France.

2 Melville, *Memoirs*, 214; *CSP Scot.*, ii, 603, 626.

3 For an anthropological perspective, see M. Mauss, *The Gift: The Form and Reason for Exchange in Archaic Societies*, trans. W.D. Halls (London, 1990); for an economist's view, A. Offer, 'Between the gift and the market: the economy of regard', *Economic History Review*, l (1997).

4 Brown, 'The price of friendship'.

5 E.g. the 7th earl of Argyll, who served Spain: although embarrassing to James, after the peace of 1604 this was legitimate.

he was not supposed to serve anyone. In 1585, he himself unwittingly expressed what would later be the common attitude to his position as Elizabeth's pensioner. Sir James Melville, trying to persuade him of the importance of Denmark, mentioned that France was

> paying yearly to the K. of Denmark a gret sowm of gold, to the valow of 16 or 20 thowsand crownis. His majeste said, the mair schame was his. I said, rather to the K. of France, wha mon bye his kyndnes.[1]

Melville's view might have been correct if it had been a question of 'kyndnes', kin-based relationships of unequal status in which there were chiefs and followers. But when it came to relations between formal equals, James was right and Melville wrong: the subsidy was shameful to the recipient, not the giver. That was why James searched constantly for ways of dressing up the subsidy as something which he could appear to claim of right—an 'honorable annuitie', as he put it, or better still, the revenue from an English estate—instead of waiting anxiously each time to discover how much or how little the queen was willing to dole out. Elizabeth, meanwhile, was willing enough to let him have money, but she was most careful not to give the payments any kind of honourable figleaf. So no dukedom, no English lands, no regular times of payment (before 1601), and not even any regular amounts—she went out of her way to show that she could reduce the payments (only £2,000 in 1592) or increase them (£4,000 in 1593) at will. Whatever crumbs she let fall, James knew that he had to accept them gratefully.

And in case he ever forgot the sacrifice he was making of his honour, there were always courtiers ready to remind him that the English had given him 'a puer pencyon to make your majesty theyr pencioner to your mare disgrace and shame to al prynces that knowes it'.[2] As soon as the 1586 treaty was concluded, courtiers were saying that James should now take care to follow an independent course in seeking a wife.[3] Some of the subsidy's critics may have been pro-Spanish, seeking merely to replace one foreign master with another, but some—including the Octavians—may have wished for a return to a genuinely independent status for the king of Scots. It was not to be. There were too many reasons for James to cultivate England.

In the view of many Scots, however, there were strong reasons for James to be *hostile* to England, and it is a measure of the success of the subsidy that this hostility was never allowed to dictate policy. Some of these reasons went back centuries, to the tradition of Anglo-Scottish wars. Others were new. The execution of Mary, in February 1587, came

1 Melville, *Memoirs*, 341.
2 Fowler to Walsingham, 8 Mar. 1589, *CSP Scot.*, ix, 707.
3 Instructions of Archibald Douglas, ambassador to England, 14 Aug. 1586, HMC, *Salisbury*, xiii, 299-305.

just seven months after the league with England was concluded, and opened up potentially seismic cracks in it. James's position thereafter was doubly undignified; from his subjects' point of view, not only had he become a pensioner of the traditional enemy, but he had done so at the time of his mother's execution which he ought to have avenged. Consider these proceedings in parliament in August 1587:

> My lord chancellour befoir the parliament endit said oppenlie that he had sumquhat moir to speik, to wit, concernyng the revenge of his majesteis motheris deithe. Then presentlie thairefter the haill lordis of parliament sitting on thair knees vowit that thay wald revenge the same to the uttermaist.[1]

Next month, the king was alleged to have promised action, with engines and scaling-ladders being collected to surprise Berwick.[2] Nothing came of it, but the issue refused to go away. Melville told himself that the king intended to 'abyd his tym to be revengit'.[3] In 1596, the 'Spaniards' in Scotland made a large number of ensigns depicting Mary's execution and calling for revenge from heaven and earth.[4] To the anonymous author of the *Historie of King James the Sext*, writing in the 1590s, the link between the subsidy and the queen's death cut deeply:

> Thus all memorie of Queyne Mareis murthor was bureit. The King ressavit thair ambassador, as I have sayd, and be his persuasioun, is becum thair yeirlie pensioner. What honestie the commonweill ressavis heirby, I think the posteritie sall better knaw than that this tyme can judge; for mair just occasion of weare [i.e. war] had never prince on this earth nor this had, and yit he hes bayth neglectit the thing that maist of all became him, and the thing that sould have bene a perpetuall honor to his commonweill ... [thus] we conqueis unto our selfis perpetuall shayme and ignominie.[5]

People like this could have caused a lot of damage to English interests if they had gained power. That they never did is attributable to many causes, but the knowledge that a break with England would slash James's income was surely one of the most important—both to the king himself, and to those at his court who depended on royal patronage. To that extent, Elizabeth's £3,000-odd per year was well spent.

This chapter began by mentioning that James's subsidy was not news. Nor is it news that he was particularly short of ready cash in the 1580s and 1590s, just when Elizabeth showed herself willing to pay him some.

1 News from Scotland, 13 Aug. 1587, *CSP Scot.*, ix, 476. Cf. Melville, *Memoirs*, 356-7. Catholics urged James to 'joyne with the Spaniard, the king of France and the bishope of Rome' to seek revenge: EUL, Laing MSS, III.203, Patrick Anderson's 'History of Scotland', vol. ii, fos. 215v.-216r.

2 Henry Withrington to Lord Hunsdon, 11 Sept. 1587, HMC, *Salisbury*, xiii, 280.

3 Melville, *Memoirs*, 360.

4 Hudson to Anthony Bacon, 8 Nov. 1596, T. Birch, *Memorials of the Reign of Queen Elizabeth From the Year 1581 Until Her Death*, 2 vols. (London, 1754), ii, 196.

5 *Hist. KJVI*, 236-7.

But if these two ideas are combined, they show how his poverty affected his relations with England: it meant that Elizabeth was able to buy him cheap.

~ 7 ~

A Meddlesome Princess: Anna of Denmark and Scottish Court Politics, 1589-1603

Maureen M. Meikle

To the Danes she was always Anna and this was her usual signature on all correspondence, whether it was in French, Scots or English.[1] The Scots sometimes called their young queen Annie, whilst the English knew her only as Anne. These three names for the queen consort of James VI symbolise her progression from Denmark to Scotland in 1590 and finally to England in 1603. Anna's Danish childhood and her years as queen of Scotland have received little attention from historians. More has been written on her reign as queen consort of Great Britain after 1603, but there has been an overall lack of interest in Anna. Her important role as queen-consort and royal mother has often been overlooked in favour of trivial issues such as her love of jewellery and dancing.

Anna's Scottish coronation took place on 17 May 1590 at Holyrood Abbey.[2] She was queen of Scotland for nearly thirteen years before becoming the first queen of Great Britain in 1603. However, historians who have recognised the importance of Scottish history before the union of the crowns can be dismissive of Anna as well. Maurice Lee commented in 1959: 'She was not an interesting woman. She had no particular distinction of mind or spirit. She showed occasional neurotic tendencies, she enjoyed intrigue, she was stupid, and she bore grudges'.[3] E.N. Williams gives Anna all of two lines in his dictionary summary of James VI and I, noting that 'She was blonde and graceful but shallow and frivolous'. D.H. Willson called her 'frivolous to the last' in his once standard text on James VI and I.[4] In 1980 Maurice Ashley noted Anna as a 'dumb blonde' who 'had neither the brains nor the education to satisfy the Scottish Solomon'. Anna merited ten pages in the *Dictionary of National Biography*, where the author of her article, A.W. Ward, made rather chauvinistic comments, yet unlike others of his generation

1 In 1590 she was 'Anna Royne decosse', and thereafter signed herself 'Anna R': Folger Shakespeare Library, Washington D.C., V.a. 325, fo. 3.

2 *Papers Relative to the Marriage of King James the Sixth of Scotland with the Princess Anna of Denmark, A.D. 1589, and the Form and Manner of Her Majesty's Coronation at Holyroodhouse, 1590*, ed. J.T. Gibson-Craig (Bannatyne Club, 1828).

3 M. Lee, Jr., *John Maitland of Thirlestane and the Foundation of the Stewart Despotism in Scotland* (Princeton, NJ, 1959), 204.

4 E.N. Williams, *The Penguin Dictionary of English and European History, 1485-1789* (Harmondsworth, 1980), 235; D.H. Willson, *King James VI and I* (London, 1956), 403. The index to Willson's book lists the queen as 'Anne, Queen of England'.

summarised her life as 'a virtuous wife, an affectionate mother, and a faithful friend; she was both generous and compassionate as becomes a queen and a woman; she had the courage of her race as well as its quick temper; and in the midst of her mostly frivolous existence she would seem to have cherished a desire if not to have possessed a capacity for higher things'.[1] Ethel Carleton Williams's 1970 biography was not flattering as she tended to highlight trivial moments in Anna's life, giving her an unjustifiable silliness and ignoring much of her political power. These negative images of Anna persist. In 1991, Michael Lynch referred to Anna as a 'largely anonymous figure' who 'made little impact on the very masculine Scottish court'.[2] So far, only Thomas Riis, Leeds Barroll and David Bergeron have come to Anna's rescue by highlighting her more important role in the Scottish court before the union of 1603.[3]

In reality, Anna was far from frivolous or anonymous. Like other neglected queens of fifteenth- and sixteenth-century Scotland, she carved out a distinctive role for herself in the Scottish court.[4] There had not been a resident queen since Mary, queen of Scots. Although she could not speak any Scots, Anna had learned French before her marriage and commanded respect from French-speaking courtiers as soon as she arrived in Scotland. The presence of a female royal household after many years undoubtedly curbed some of the excesses of male courtiers and made James VI keep his privy chamber 'more private than before'.[5] During 1591 Anna started to use her influence with James to gain favours and from 1592 she began deliberately to meddle in court politics. Inexperienced attempts to help her husband soon emerged as independent moves in the game of court faction. Rather than being manipulated, it was often Anna who did the manipulating. When the Scottish court moved south in 1603, Anna lost her carefully built-up command structure. She was never able to manipulate court politics to the same extent in England, and this is perhaps why historians who concentrate on her years in England have produced such negative images of her.

I

Anna's first real contact with a Scottish courtier was with the Earl Marischal, who was sent to Denmark on 17 June 1589 to negotiate the marriage contract and stand proxy for James VI at the ceremony.[6] As

1 *DNB*; M. Ashley, *The House of Stuart: its Rise and Fall* (London, 1980), 116.

2 M. Lynch, *Scotland: a New History* (London, 1991), 233.

3 T. Riis, *Should Auld Acquaintance Be Forgot: Scottish-Danish Relations, c.1450-1707*, 2 vols. (Odense, 1988), i, 269-82; L. Barroll, 'The court of the first Stuart Queen', in L.L. Peck (ed.), *The Mental World of the Jacobean Court* (Cambridge, 1991), 192-9; D. Bergeron, *Royal Family, Royal Lovers: King James of England and Scotland* (Columbia, Mo., 1991), 48-62.

4 L.O. Fradenburg (ed.), *Women and Sovereignty* (Edinburgh, 1992), 7, 78-100.

5 The first letter sent to Anna from Elizabeth I was in French, as she had written to Elizabeth in this language: *CSP Scot.*, x, 115, 272, 298.

6 *CSP Scot.*, x, 81, 103-5, 108, 126-7.

main rival to the chancellor, John Maitland of Thirlestane, Marischal probably informed the curious young queen of their rivalry at court.[1] Anna was therefore destined to become involved in court faction before she even met her real husband. The stormy seas that forced the Danish ships back to the Norwegian coast on two occasions made Anna wary of sea travel for the rest of her life and dashed hopes of a speedy second ceremony in Scotland. James 'was very impatient and sorowfull for hir lang delay' as he had fallen in love with Anna from studying her portrait.[2] He had not previously considered 'the company of any woman, not so much as in any dalliance', but his letters to Anna in their mutual French language are romantic. They contradict reports that 'the King is but a cold wooer'. The same correspondent later referred to the king, 'passionate as true lovers be', or 'distracte with a wourld of passionate cogitacions' and frequently 'sighing'.[3] Anna was reported to be very much 'in love with him that it were death to her to have it broken off'. In late October, the impatient James set sail for Norway to rendezvous with his bride and arrived in Norwegian waters on the 29th with no reported seasickness.[4]

Anna first met James on 19 November and although her first impressions are not recorded, the differences between him and his handsome proxy would have been apparent. The meeting, however, was noted as 'joyfull... on all sydis', and it led to the second marriage at Oslo four days later, conducted in French by the king's minister, Mr David Lindsay.[5] James heeded the advice of Danish counsellors not to return to Scotland during the stormy winter months, and was 'easily induced' to visit his new Danish relations.[6]

Anna and James proceeded to Elsinore in January 1590, and they remained in Denmark until the spring to attend the marriage of Anna's older sister with the duke of Brunswick.[7] Apart from feasting and being fêted, the royal newly-weds spent their time improving Scottish-Danish relations. They arrived back in Scotland on 1 May 1590, with a magnificent entourage.

Financially there was no real comparison between Scotland and Denmark. Even before the marriage, Thomas Fowler could 'see not how a queen can be here maintained, for there is not enough to maintain the King'.[8] The Danish embassy that accompanied Anna back to Scotland in

1 Melville, *Memoirs*, 372-3.

2 HMC, *Salisbury*, iii, 934; *CSP Scot.*, x, 150, 155, 157, 164, 166-8; Melville, *Memoirs*, 369.

3 *CSP Scot.*, ix, 655; x, 115, 122, 163, 164-6; *Warrender Papers*, ii, 109-10.

4 *CSP Scot.*, x, 129-30, 170, 174-5, 177, 187-8.

5 *CSP Scot.*, x, 187-8; D. Stevenson, *Scotland's Last Royal Wedding: the Marriage of James VI and Anne of Denmark* (Edinburgh, 1997), ch. 4.

6 *CSP Scot.*, x, 221; Spottiswoode, *History*, ii, 404.

7 *CSP Scot.*, x, 252, 287, 863-5; Stevenson, *Royal Wedding*, ch. 6.

8 *CSP Scot.*, x, 11.

1590 was instructed to make sure that there was satisfactory compensation for her dowry. They were aware that the elaborate reception for the new queen and the celebrations that followed her coronation were not typical of the impoverished Scottish court. Anna was used to opulent surroundings and, according to one report, 'Scotland was never in wourse state to receave a Quene ... for there is nether house in repaire but most ruinous and want furniture'.[1] Despite the lengthy delay in her arrival, the royal palaces were not ready. Just to entertain all the guests James had to beg and even threaten the landed men of Scotland to supply victuals or furnishing.[2] Elizabeth I sent £2,000 sterling worth of plate as a wedding gift, and warned that she would not send any more.[3] This was not a good start to a marriage, though Anna eventually established her own household at Dunfermline Abbey, which was substantially rebuilt and furnished with lavish items from her trousseau.

II

The first years of the marriage were fairly uneventful. There were many rumours that she was pregnant, but they were mostly without foundation and reflect the scrutiny that no royal woman, past or present, can avoid after marriage. The lack of an heir by September 1591 was even thought to be destabilising the country, but the author was exaggerating.[4] Anna passed her time hunting with James, learning Scots and observing her new court and country. Her ladies and gentlemen were supposedly chosen by James to give her 'gud and discret company' and assimilate her into Scottish ways, although there were several Danes in her first household who had been ordered by Queen Sophia of Denmark 'to attend upon her daughter the Queen of Scots, till she might be acquainted with this country and language'. William Van der Vaus (master of household) was called home in October 1590 to report to Queen Sophia and the Danish Council. Johannes Calixtus (secretary) and Hans Drier (cook) probably did not stay long, yet Anna Roos, a gentlewoman who had accompanied Anna from Denmark, would remain in the queen's household until her death in 1619. The queen was led to believe that Sir James Melville of Halhill was a keeper appointed by her husband and thus rejected his presence until he pointed out her lineage and that she was 'sa weill brocht up, that sche nedit ne keper'. Anna apologised, pleading that 'she was yet yngnorant of every mans qualities' and accepted him as a counsellor for several years thereafter.[5] She sensibly kept her distance from the various witchcraft trials that alleged

1 *CSP Scot.*, x, 137, 150, 293, 295-6, 299.

2 Requests made to the laird of Barnbarroch for beef, mutton (on foot), wildfowl and venison are in *Maitland Misc.*, i, II, 278-9. Another request for a hackney carriage is in *Selections From the Family Papers Preserved at Caldwell*, ed. W. Mure (Maitland Club, 1854), 83-4.

3 *CSP Scot.*, x, 144, 160-2; cf. J. Goodare, 'James VI's English subsidy', Chapter 6 above.

4 *CSP Scot.*, x, 252, 276, 325, 574, 591.

5 *CSP Scot.*, x, 371, 406; Melville, *Memoirs*, 393-4.

black magic as the cause of the storms which beset her initial voyage to Scotland.[1]

At court Anna relied on the Danish diplomats to argue for her property rights, but this led to friction with Chancellor Maitland as both wanted possession of Dunfermline Abbey's lordship of Musselburgh. This would develop into a full-scale feud with court faction building up on either side, so it was ironic that Maitland was initially charged with looking after Anna's interests at court by no less a person than Sophia of Denmark. Maitland had been granted the lordship of Musselburgh in 1587, and in the face of Danish competition he provocatively renewed his charter in 1591 and started to sell off some of its lands. Anna and the Danish ambassadors were furious at his double-dealing, so her refusal of Maitland's hospitality in April 1591 may have been intended as a slight. She remained at Dalkeith whilst James went on to his house alone. The queen had also discovered Maitland's 'gret hindrance to the Kingis mariage' as he had wanted James to marry the 'wyese stayd woman' Catherine of Navarre and not the Danish 'childe'. Anna was only fourteen at the time of her marriage to the twenty-three year old James, but he preferred her youth (and dowry) to Catherine's mature twenty-eight years.[2] Anna's growing animosity towards Maitland is contrasted by an interesting friendship between her and the rebellious earl of Bothwell. It was well enough established by July 1591 to make her plead with James on Bothwell's behalf. On this occasion 'she let it fall, with his [James's] good contentment', probably as this was her first attempt at manipulation. She may have failed to appreciate the dangers this maverick earl posed to James.[3]

At seventeen she still had much to learn about the full workings of court faction and patronage, though her decision to stand up for a friend in trouble does her credit. Bothwell was one of the Scottish courtiers who could converse with her in French, and they shared a love of Renaissance architecture that perhaps enabled her to ignore many accusations made against him. Some members of her household were also sympathetic to Bothwell and correspondingly antagonistic to Maitland, which left a lasting impression on the young queen. The Earl Marischal turned to her for help in August 1591. James let him out of ward before Anna arrived, but it is notable that she had been 'an earnest suitor for him'.[4] Anna also ventured into the field of international diplomacy in November 1591, to intercede on behalf of a fellow-Dane who had been the victim of English

1 For further details see R. Chambers, *Domestic Annals of Scotland*, 3 vols. (2nd edn., Edinburgh, 1861), i, 211-19; C. Larner, *Enemies of God: the Witch-hunt in Scotland* (London, 1981), 83; H. Stafford, 'Notes on Scottish witchcraft cases, 1590-1591', in N. Downes (ed.), *Essays in Honor of Conyers Read* (Chicago, 1953), 96-118; and Pitcairn, *Trials*, i, 216-23.

2 NLS, MS 13500, fos. 7r.-8r.; *CSP Scot.*, x, 82; Melville, *Memoirs*, 363, 403.

3 *CSP Scot.*, x, 543; Melville, *Memoirs*, 399-401.

4 *CSP Scot.*, x, 560.

piracy. James wrote to Elizabeth telling her that 'we have at hir desyre taikin occasioun to recommend this mater to your courrtesie and gracious favour'. She also tried to pacify the bloodfeud between the Kerrs of Cessford and Kerrs of Ancram, for which Robert Bowes, the English ambassador, thought 'she worthily deserves great thanks'. Anna was able to overcome her hatred for Maitland in this case—Cessford was married to his niece. In December, after hearing pleas from Lady Ferniehirst, Anna extracted a licence from James to allow her disgraced brother, Sir Walter Scott of Buccleuch, to return to Scotland.[1] These interventions hardly amount to frivolity.

Anna had learned how to gain James's attention and was demonstrating a good understanding of the country's political problems. This did not in any way undermine her deference to James as her husband. She often acted to protect his interests, and he defended her honour. Melville described her method in 1592, after she had spoken up for his brother Sir Robert, the treasurer-depute: 'The Quenis Majestie, according to hir custome, whenever sche understandis that his Majestie be wrang information, is sterit up against any honest sarvant or subject, sche uses gret deligence to get sure knawledge of the verite, that sche may the baldlyer speak in ther favour.'[2]

III

By January 1592 Anna must have gained a working knowledge of Scots, although she continued to write in French until 1593.[3] Her aptitude for languages was underestimated by Maitland's wife, who was indiscreet about the queen's friendship with Bothwell within her earshot.[4] Maitland's reputation suffered as a result of his wife's rudeness and it did little to repair the fragile relationship between him and Anna. This particular incident was not settled for many months as Anna felt that her honour had been damaged. When it was pointed out that her 'dryness' towards Maitland was hurting 'the King's service' she appointed a mediator, but was soon offended by the chancellor again for a different reason.[5] More evidence of Anna's trying to exert influence over James occurred in February 1592 when she tried to prevent the execution of a conspirator, but was talked out of it when it was explained that he had intended to kill her husband. However, she kept up her efforts at persuasion by urging James to 'hearken unto the cries of the people and advice of the best counsellors' and punish those who opposed him.

1 *CSP Scot.*, x, 587, 589, 610, 814; xi, 126. Anna also helped Buccleuch return in 1592.

2 Melville, *Memoirs*, 403-4.

3 Anna wrote to Elizabeth I in French during June 1593, but her reply of Dec. 1593 was in English and by Sept. 1594 Anna was writing to her in English. BL, Cotton, Caligula D.II, fo. 87r.; EUL, Special Collections DE.1.12/9; *CSP Scot.*, xi, 96, 126, 244, 436.

4 *CSP Scot.*, x, 626-7.

5 *CSP Scot.*, x, 687, 755; Melville, *Memoirs*, 405.

James duly sought the advice of his council after visiting Anna, which cannot have been mere coincidence.[1]

When rumours spread that William Stewart of Pittenweem had been writing in Anna's name without her permission, she was displeased and defended her old friend against his detractors. Anna expected loyalty and trusted those who gave her good service, especially those who had served her late father in Denmark. This defence was partly motivated by feelings of homesickness for Denmark after conflicting signals from James. During one of James's absences, she entertained the earl and countess of Atholl at Falkland Palace and received an invitation to visit them at Dunkeld. James sanctioned the visit, but then, just as Anna was leaving, another message arrived forbidding it. As an obedient wife she complied, but must have been confused by his contradictory orders. It is not surprising that she then 'fallethe into teares wishinge hirselfe ether with hir mother in Denmark, or els that she might se and speake with hir majestie [Elizabeth I]'. She would not have been the first bride to seek out a female relative to discuss marital problems. That she now regarded Elizabeth as a maternal figure is interesting, for Elizabeth had never been married. Anna asked Elizabeth to send some English court servants to her household and letters between them showed Elizabeth to be supportive.[2] Perhaps Anna wished that Elizabeth could reprimand James on her behalf by threatening to suspend his subsidy.[3] However, it appears that the tiff was soon over and they carried on as the same loving couple they had been beforehand.

James may have been aware that his wife was beginning to exploit factions within the court during 1592. A letter from Anna to Robert Murray of Abercairny, dated 7 March 1592, is a unique survival of her first dabbling in faction. She asked him to help with the reorganisation of the government to satisfy the nobility and people, but most of all to protect her beloved husband the king from the chancellor.[4] Anna clearly wanted Maitland removed from court with the assistance of her friends amongst the nobility. James may not have seen this secret correspondence, but he ordered Maitland to leave the court at the end of March and did not allow his return until October 1593.[5] The concept of honour within marriage had been upheld and in December 1592 it was reported that James would not ask Maitland back without having 'obtained the Queen's favour' first.[6] The situation was beneficial to them both: James wanted to prove that he could run the country without a chancellor and Anna wanted her honour defended. Other enemies of the chancellor

1 *CSP Scot.*, x, 631, 645, 649.
2 NLS, Adv. MS 33.1.11/8; *CSP Scot.*, x, 272, 308-9, 624-5, 720, 722, 765.
3 Cf. Goodare, 'James VI's English subsidy', Chapter 6 above.
4 NAS, GD24/5/59/1.
5 Cf. Lee, *Maitland*, 245-67.
6 *CSP Scot.*, x, 757, 788, 793, 824.

were delighted by this, but there is no question of Anna being led unwittingly into this faction-fighting as some historians have suggested. Maitland's exile was her triumph.

In 1593, Anna defied James's orders for the first time. In June, when there were signs of a genuine pregnancy, Anna determined to ignore her condition and travel during inclement weather. When James grasped that his wife was defying him he sent for his favourite minister, Robert Bruce, to intercede—even though this tactic had previously failed to reconcile her to Maitland. This was hardly the action of an assertive husband, although he blamed the June incident on her pregnant state making 'her the maire wilful'.[1] It cannot be mere coincidence, however, that at this precise moment Maitland agreed to hand over Musselburgh to Anna on a liferent basis to try and facilitate his return to court.[2] This was a high price for him, but Anna would settle for nothing less; two ambassadors were despatched from Denmark to make sure that she was properly infefted. Anna rode to Musselburgh on 20 July, to hold a court and secure her title to the lands.[3] Anna was prepared to forgive the murderer of one of her guards, but not those who offended her honour. Elizabeth I intervened in this feud to try to bring it to a successful conclusion. At an earlier point in the feud Anna had asked Elizabeth to ban Maitland from England, should he ask to retreat there. Elizabeth complied with this request as a mark of their growing friendship.[4] Anna was victorious, but the ever-scheming Maitland would not give up easily. His once-powerful position had been irreparably damaged by the feud and he refused to accept that James was able to cope without him. Most of all, he resented the influence of a young wife on a monarch whom he had become accustomed to dominating. When Anna reluctantly accepted Maitland back at court in late 1593, it was said that she still 'cannot hitherto well brook his wife'.[5]

The queen's position was less secure upon Maitland's official return to court than during his absence. She could not have predicted the final fall from grace of the earl of Bothwell in the autumn of 1593. This led to unjust accusations by the Maitland camp that she had helped Bothwell gain access to James at a critical moment in July. It had been Lady Atholl who let Bothwell into James's chamber and the bedroom farce that accompanied this escapade lent itself to dramatisation by Robert McLellan in *Jamie the Saxt* with a half-naked James emerging from his toilet to confront the earl. James fled to Anna's locked chamber door shouting 'Annie! Annie! Open the door! Let me in! Annie!' with the realisation

1 NAS, GD1/240/5; *CSP Scot.*, xi, 77-8, 80; James VI, *Letters*, 126-7.
2 *APS*, iv, 24-7, cc. 28-9; 150, c. 58; *CSP Scot.*, xi, 101-2; *RMS*, v, 1305, 1982, 2352; vi, 73, 75.
3 *CSP Scot.*, xi, 94, 100-1, 119-21, 127.
4 *CSP Scot.*, x, 803, 810-11, 829; xi, 88-90.
5 *CSP Scot.*, xi, 180, 228, 230-1, 233-4.

that he could not escape the earl—who did not intend to harm him anyway.[1] Only Calderwood recorded that James fled to Anna's door. Others probably felt it embarrassing enough that James had just been in his privy! In a time when only women were thought to be capable of hysteria, James's behaviour came close to it. Bothwell was nonetheless banished from the kingdom, so it was perhaps fortunate that Anna had her first full-term pregnancy to distract attention from her friendship with the disgraced earl. Nevertheless she remained sympathetic to Bothwell's plight and continued to send him letters of support.[2]

In December she was busy looking for a nurse and other requisites for her baby. James announced that he would not tolerate any words uttered against his wife and he 'gave to the Queen the greatest part of his jewels', in return for her assurances that she would concur with all his actions. Stirling had to be repaired for her confinement, so £50,000 was sought in taxation—but refused by a convention of estates—to pay for this and other expenses at the time of the birth.[3] James was delighted at the prospect of an heir and was quick to tell his Danish relations that the new baby looked like his late father-in-law, Frederick II, though James had never met him.[4]

IV

On 19 February 1594 the birth of Prince Henry at Stirling Castle should have strengthened the royal marriage. Instead, it led to the first serious split between Anna and James, over custody of the baby. A mother's right to the custody of her children is more easily understood today than in the sixteenth century. Anna's outrage when she realised that she could not keep her baby was misunderstood by contemporaries, and historians have not remedied this. Part of the problem lay with the differing ways in which Anna and James had been brought up. Anna had been surrounded by a close-knit family who showered love on her. James, on the other hand, had had a truly miserable childhood 'alone, without father or mother, brother or sister'.[5] His guardians, the earl and countess of Mar, had been strict and made sure that he was well educated by stern Protestant tutors. There would appear to have been little love in his formative years, whilst Anna knew nothing else. James insisted that his new-born son be placed in the Mar household for his own protection.[6]

1 *CSP Scot.*, xi, 318-19; Birrel, 'Diary', 30-1; Calderwood, *History*, 256; Melville, *Memoirs*, 414-16; Moysie, *Memoirs*, 102-3; *Hist. KJVI*, 271; R. McLellan, *Jamie the Saxt*, eds. I. Campbell and R.D.S. Jack (London, 1970), 47-8.

2 PRO, SP59/29, fos. 299r.-304r.; *CBP*, i, 482-3, 490-1, 540; *CSP Scot.*, xi, 147, 166, 196, 224; Winwood, *Memorials*, i, 326.

3 J. Goodare, 'Parliamentary taxation in Scotland, 1560-1603', *SHR*, lxviii (1989), 50-1.

4 *CSP Scot.*, xi, 237, 245-6, 248; *RPC*, v, 116; Moysie, *Memoirs*, 112; J.O. Halliwell (ed.), *Letters of the Kings of England*, 2 vols. (London, 1846), ii, 85-6.

5 *CSP Scot.*, x, 174; Moysie, *Memoirs*, 113.

6 *CSP Scot.*, xi, 280; HMC, *Mar & Kellie*, i, 39-41.

Anna never really accepted this enforced separation from her first child. The troubled history of the Stewart monarchy meant nothing to her. She wanted to bring up her son in the same fashion as in Denmark, where the threat of factional division made the royal family stay together. In Scotland this same threat had the opposite reaction. Fearing kidnap or even assassination, James insisted that his son should not be kept in the same household as himself. That Henry's great-great-grandfather James IV had been brought up by a Danish mother was conveniently forgotten, though his great-grandfather James V's custody had proved a battleground between his mother and the duke of Albany.[1]

Thomas Riis suggests that Anna chose to breastfeed this baby herself, contrary to the more usual practice of wet nursing. It is difficult to reconcile this theory with Anna's movements after Henry's birth. For instance, in July 1594 she travelled between Edinburgh and Falkland, whilst Henry would not have been allowed to leave Stirling. Gossip about another pregnancy in November would rather imply that she was not breastfeeding. A probable wetnurse, 'Margaret Maistertoun, maistres nureis to the Prince', was discharged in January 1595 after Henry had been weaned.[2] Anna pleaded with James, speaking 'plenlyar then befor', to allow Henry to be with her at Edinburgh Castle, but to no avail. James told her that if he died he would still leave Henry in Mar's care, to which she replied, 'rather the devil kept him then those that haue him'. He resorted to his tactic of using favourite ministers to make Anna obey him.[3] Anna continued to grieve, and worried that a change of nurse 'has done him great hurt'. She became sick and suffered a miscarriage.[4] This almost forced James into a change of heart, but politics intervened. The issue of Henry's custody was creating a powerful faction behind his wife and against Mar, so James issued an order in July 1595 that no one, including Anna, was to remove his son from Stirling Castle unless he sanctioned it or Henry attained the age of eighteen.[5] It was a horrid situation that has received little sympathy. Roger Ashton summed up Anna's dilemma:

> The Qune is nott mynded, so far as I can se, to moue or do any thing thatt maye offend the King, although I knoo her affeccion is withdrane in apartt from the houes of Mar, and wold be contentt to haue her son outt of there handes; yett, consedering the Kingis

1 Cf. Lynch, *Scotland*, 162, and Riis, *Auld Acquaintance*, i, 278; W. Seton, 'The early years of Henry Frederick, prince of Wales, and Charles, duke of Albany, 1593-1605', *SHR*, xiii (1916).

2 *CSP Scot.*, xi, 280, 377, 472; *RPC*, v, 200.

3 PRO, SP59/30, fos. 81r.-82r.; *CBP*, ii, 28, 38; *CSP Scot.*, xi, 545, 588, 599-600; *RPC*, v, 230-1n; Colville, *Letters*, 278-9, 282; HMC, *Mar & Kellie*, i, 43-4.

4 PRO, SP59/30, fos. 75r.-76v.; *CSP Scot.*, xi, 588, 601, 603-4, 607, 610, 626; cf. Seton, 'Early years of Henry Frederick and Charles', 377.

5 NAS, GD124/10/70/1; *CBP*, ii, 40; *CSP Scot.*, xi, 602-3, 607-8, 631, 637, 638-42; James VI, *Letters*, 141-2; Colville, *Letters*, 279.

> resolution in that poyntt, she is contentt rather to obey his wil then her one afeccion, tel some other ocasion entervene.[1]

Henry's guardian, the dowager countess of Mar, intimidated Anna as she had been a surrogate mother to James. Anna found her unbearable and refused to accept her counsel. To avoid conflict, 'Old Lady Mar' was asked to leave Stirling Castle when Anna visited her son in April 1595.[2] In September 1595, Anna refused to visit Stirling as she feared attack by Henry's guardians. By December she was reluctant to go there even with James.[3] Anna was aware of how upsetting a visit to Henry would be, but she may also have been trying to dissipate the court faction that was building around the prince, to help her husband. She blamed Maitland and Mar for her woes instead of him, and their marriage continued on loving terms, with occasional tears and sermons on wifely duties.[4]

Anna never forgot her son, however, and the custody battle culminated in a dreadful scene in 1603, just after James departed southwards. Henry wrote to his mother in a perturbed state:

> And seing by his Majesties departing I will lose that benefite quhilk I had by his frequent visitation, I mon humblie request your majesty to supplie that inlack be your presence, quhilk I have more just causse to crave, that I have wanted it so lang to my great greif and displeasure.[5]

Anna reacted to this letter as any normal mother would. She hurried to Stirling Castle to liberate her unhappy son, accompanied by the visible force of the anti-Mar camp—Hamilton, Glencairn, Linlithgow and the master of Elphinstone. On being refused entry, she collapsed in great distress and lost the child she was carrying. Her life was endangered by this incident and when the emotional significance of this dawned on James he sent angry letters north demanding to know what had happened.[6] He then sent the duke of Lennox north to request that the countess of Mar hand over the prince. James reminded Anna that as 'God is my witness I ever preferred you to all my bairns, much more than to any subject'. Regaining Henry's custody had cost Anna the loss of two unborn children, but she now had the sympathy of her husband and ultimate revenge on the Mar household. The nobility who accompanied her were forgiven, by Anna's intercession, and she eventually made her peace with Mar in England to appease James.[7]

1 Colville, *Letters*, 278.
2 *CSP Scot.*, xi, 531, 566; xii, 33.
3 *CSP Scot.*, xii, 18, 74, 77, 88.
4 *CSP Scot.*, xi, 662-3, 678, 681; xii, 43-5, 46-7.
5 BL, Harleian MS 7,007, fo. 16r.-16v.
6 *RPC*, vi, 571-2n; Calderwood, *History*, vi, 230-1; *LP James VI*, 48-58.
7 *Melros Papers*, i, 3-4; James VI, *Letters*, 214; *LP James VI*, 48-51, 53-5; HMC, *Mar & Kellie*, i, 50-2; *RPC*, vi, 571, 577-8. I am grateful to Professor Maurice Lee for clarifying the situation

Maitland's hand could be detected in some of the rumours that there were treasonous plots in existence to liberate Henry. Maitland was still smarting from his exile and tried to use Anna in his feud with Mar, but she saw through this and reportedly 'burned things she had signed for his benefit'.[1] The Danish ambassador realised the dangers this posed for Anna and warned her to be as neutral as possible.[2] Thanks to her councillors' information and advice she managed to keep up with the intricacies of court faction amidst all her emotional turmoil and avoided most pitfalls by keeping Maitland's scheming at arm's length.

James appointed a council for the queen in July 1593, consisting of Walter Stewart, commendator of Blantyre, Alexander Seton, commendator of Pluscarden, Mr Thomas Hamilton and Mr James Elphinstone, to sort out her business affairs.[3] James should really have been looking to his own affairs, for by 1594 he had used up all Anna's dowry to pay his debts.[4] Some of the debt was attributable to his son's magnificent baptism, but most of it was due to his living well beyond his means.[5] Anna's councillors formed the nucleus of a group later known as the Octavians. They were so successful at sorting out her affairs that she recommended them to the spendthrift James. At New Year, 1596, when the royal family traditionally gave and received gifts, Anna paraded £1,000 in gold pieces given to her by her councillors. She gave £600 to James and challenged him to use her councillors' talents to sort out his financial affairs. James duly appointed them but his finances were in a more desperate state.[6] James was bad at handling money and even had to pawn Anna's jewels which caused much royal embarrassment. In 1599 he ordered the treasurer to 'prefer his payment to all others for the relief of our said dearest bedfellow's jewels engaged, and our honour and promise cause'.[7]

Childbirth did not prevent Anna from continuing her royal duties such as soliciting pardons for landed men in trouble, or their servants.[8] She was still involved with court faction, and her feud with Maitland ended only with his death in 1595. Even before he died she was trying to place one of her councillors in his position as chancellor. This was a typical action of court politics, associated more with male courtiers than women. Anna was turning Maitland's scheming against himself and

of the prince at Stirling.

1 *CSP Scot.*, xi, 386-7, 416, 466, 476, 498, 529-31, 539, 550, 553, 559, 579-80, 610, 624.

2 Cf. Riis, *Auld Acquaintance*, i, 278-9.

3 *CSP Scot.*, xi, 119-20, 343, 420, 472, 537.

4 *CSP Scot.*, xi, 321; A. Montgomerie, 'King James VI's tocher gude and a local authorities loan of 1590', *SHR*, xxxvii (1958).

5 *CSP Scot.*, xi, 411, 421-3; Fowler, *Works*, ii, 169-95. Anna did not attend the baptism, though she received the various ambassadors and their gifts for the prince.

6 *CSP Scot.*, xii, 84-5, 89, 102, 104; cf. Lynch, *Scotland*, 234-5; A.L. Murray, 'Sir John Skene and the exchequer, 1594-1612', *Stair Society Miscellany*, i (1971), 127-9.

7 NAS, GD421/1/3/2; cf. Halliwell (ed.), *Letters*, ii, 96-7.

8 *CSP Scot.*, xi, 446, 451-2, 524-5, 548; xii, 10.

remained 'stiff at her mark' against him to the end. Relations between Anna and James noticeably improved after his death.[1] With Maitland gone, Anna chose to champion the cause of Mar's opponents, though John Colville was exaggerating when he stated that 'the Queen will rule all and I fear Mar go down'. Even Elizabeth warned Anna not to endanger her husband over the matter of Mar's guardianship of the prince. But, as had happened with the Bothwell fiasco in 1593, pregnancy intervened to inhibit her involvement in faction-fighting.[2] Princess Elizabeth was born at Dunfermline on 15 August 1596. She was baptised on 28 November at Holyrood, to the delight of the town council of Edinburgh who promised her a dowry of 10,000 merks.[3] As with Henry, this child was named to flatter Elizabeth I. The chief gossip was Anna's closest friend and confidante in Scotland, the countess of Huntly, who would attend all the royal births in Scotland. This friendship led Anna to plead the cause of the disgraced earl of Huntly to James within days of giving birth.[4]

The queen's friendship with the Huntlys was linked to their shared Catholicism. Anna was secretly converted to Catholicism in 1593, so when the guardianship of Princess Elizabeth was awarded to the Catholic household of Lord Livingstone, Anna did not object.[5] Lord Livingstone was a court rival of Mar, and as Lady Livingstone was attached to her own household, Anna was able to visit Elizabeth as often as she liked without having to confront people she feared. There was talk of the youngest royal daughter going to the Catholic Seton household in 1599 but Margaret, who was born on 24 December 1598, joined her older sister in the Livingstone household until her death in 1600. Anna's support for the Catholic nobility in Scotland from 1596 onwards was a problem for the government and the kirk, but it gave James VI some useful bargaining power. With his wife as the intermediary, he could play the Catholic faction along without committing himself to them and risking antagonising ministers and England alike. The kirk, however, demanded access to the queen to discuss her religion and remained suspicious of her friends and courtiers.[6]

1 *CSP Scot.*, xii, 25, 28-9, 33, 46-7.

2 *CSP Scot.*, xii, 51-2, 54, 57, 88, 90, 92-3, 95, 100-1, 119, 135, 137-8, 140-1, 149-51, 212-13, 294.

3 *CSP Scot.*, xii, 306, 387-8; *APS*, iv, 101; Moysie, *Memoirs*, 127.

4 *CSP Scot.*, xii, 313, 317-18, 326; xiii, I, 353; *CBP*, ii, 185, 226; *RPC*, v, 328-30.

5 *CSP Scot.*, xii, 326, 336, 388; xiii, I, 81, 405, 497; xiii, II, 691; *RPC*, v, 343.

6 *CSP Scot.*, xii, 493; xiii, I, 162, 257; *RPC*, v, 558; Calderwood, *History*, v, 459-60. Cf. F. de Borja Medina, 'Intrigues of a Scottish Jesuit at the Spanish court: unpublished letters of William Crichton to Claudio Acquaviva (Madrid 1590-1592)', in T.M. McCoog (ed.), *The Reckoned Expense: Edmund Campion and the Early English Jesuits* (London 1996), 231, 244-5.

V

By 1598 the battle lines of court faction had become blurred. Anna managed to confuse the English agent George Nicolson as to her allegiances at court, and James became more devious in his politicking as well. Neither were taking the advice of their councillors and they cast off the financial stringency of the Octavians.[1] As the visit of Anna's brother Ulric, duke of Holstein, cost £4,000 sterling, this was not a prudent move. The comment that 'always the Queen knows all that is thought' confirms that Anna was still very much in touch with the intricacies of court faction.[2] During their last years in Scotland, Anna publicly disagreed with James on more than one occasion, usually about factions. James apparently promised to bring Prince Henry to see his mother in 1600 and 1602 to patch up their relationship, but the visits never materialised.[3]

Royal bickering created real problems during the alleged 'Gowrie Conspiracy' of August 1600. There has been much speculation and exaggeration about Anna's role in this affair. As with the other crises during her Scottish years, Anna had another pregnancy to divert attention from her maintenance of the sisters of the disgraced earl of Gowrie in her household.[4] After the supposed plot to murder James was foiled and the earl and his brother killed, the family were forfeited and the sisters banished from court. Whilst this was an unpopular move, Anna was forced to comply. She had to pacify James and persuade him that, contrary to allegations, she had not been behind the plot. This episode demonstrates the risks of Anna's involvement with faction. That she was involved in the supposed plot is unlikely, for killing James would not have liberated Henry from Mar under the terms of his guardianship, and it would also have deprived her of the status of queen.

This did not stop the Mar camp from making accusations, however, and it led to a nasty scene at the royal dining tables: James accused Anna of being mad when she provoked him about the Gowrie affair. She replied that she was 'neither mad nor beside herself'.[5] James blamed the scene on the advanced stage of Anna's pregnancy, yet his support for her amazed the Mar faction. The loss of their year-old daughter Margaret, and the birth of their new son Charles on 19 November, seem to have reconciled the couple and blotted out the factional struggles that were raging around them. Charles was not given into Mar's care, but remained at Anna's house at Dunfermline with Seton (now Lord Fyvie)

1 *CSP Scot.*, xiii, I, 133, 162, 189, 206-7, 215, 238-9.
2 *CSP Scot.*, xiii, I, 217, 261, 264, 362-3.
3 *CSP Scot.*, xiii, II, 624, 640-1, 644, 658, 661, 667, 1008, 1028; HMC, *Salisbury*, xii, 124, 141.
4 *CSP Scot.*, xiii, I, 326; xiii, II, 644, 678, 1049, 1092; *RPC*, vi, 145-6, 510-12. She helped the Ruthven family in 1602.
5 *CBP*, ii, 678, 689, 698-9; HMC, *Salisbury*, x, 389; *CSP Scot.*, xiii, II, 679, 682, 714, 721, 723, 731.

and his wife as guardians.[1] Also, a veiled threat from Anna that she would ask her powerful brother Christian IV to visit and sort out those factions who opposed her may have added to her influence in 1600.

Anna believed that no opposition in the Scottish court was insurmountable, with the exception of Mar's control of Prince Henry. She was now a mature twenty-five year old mother, who had conquered the harsh realities of her adopted court and country. Dunfermline was increasingly her 'ordinarie place of residence ... and of thair Majesteis bairnis' (except Henry). Anna enjoyed having her children within the Dunfermline household and in January 1602 she gave birth to Robert there, although he died at four months leaving the royal couple devastated.[2] In June 1603 Anna left Scotland, accompanied by Henry and Elizabeth, to become the first queen consort of Great Britain. The sickly Charles was left at Dunfermline as he was thought too weak to travel.[3]

VI

Anna's involvement with Scottish court faction from 1590 to 1603 was inevitable. No one at court could ignore the dashing earl of Bothwell, the mounting opposition to Maitland as chancellor, or Mar's strength as guardian of Prince Henry. Those who supported Anna against the Mar faction were the progenitors of the rival court of Prince Henry that dominated the headlines at the post-union British court until Henry's early death in 1612. The Gowrie conspiracy was probably the most dangerous moment for Anna, although she survived it relatively unscathed.

This queen-consort, who was once dismissed as being frivolous, was involved in political intrigues at the highest level. She was quite capable of independent action, yet could yield to pressure on occasion if it was jeopardising her husband's position. Her willingness to defend those closest to her, even if this brought her into conflict with other courtiers, was honourable and reflects her deep-rooted sense of loyalty. Anna was a major player amongst the elite. She was not necessarily involved with every faction that arose in late sixteenth-century Scotland; but nor was James himself. By looking at the important role his wife played at court, some of the turmoil can be better understood.

1 *CBP*, ii, 712-13; *CSP Scot.*, xiii, II, 691, 719, 735, 737, 749; *RPC*, vi, 175n; Calderwood, *History*, v, 728.
2 HMC, *Salisbury*, xii, 124; *RPC*, vi, 361-2; Calderwood, *History*, vi, 143, 151.
3 *CSP Scot.*, xiii, II, 748, 762, 782, 788, 802, 841; *RPC*, vi, 578n; *LP James VI*, 55.

~ 8~

The Personal Letters of James VI: a Short Commentary

Grant G. Simpson

Clerk of Register
Because the Chancellor is occupied in his despatches, I must address my complaint to you. I have been Friday, Saturday and this day waiting upon the direction of my affairs and never even one man is coming. Those of the Exchequer who were ordered to take the accounts—never one awaits. The tasks of the household should have been settled this day—no man comes down. I sent for the Advocate on both Friday and Saturday—neither meeting nor answer. Similarly for the bailies of this town, for the matter of the tocher—the like answer. I ordered, as you heard, a certain number to make proposals for reforming the Session—no such thing is contemplated. I ordered the Treasurer to have charges made about the horners—I have heard nothing of that as yet. In short, no appointment or meeting is kept. What is spoken late tonight is forgotten in the morning. In the morning I see nothing spoken of but to girn about; seeing none of the work done, while I am earnestly waiting upon it. And when I am compelled to rest myself, then to lay the blame upon me: a pretty trick. Man cannot be always lively. Therefore let this writ be a witness for my part, whenever it is called in question. I protest I may do no more than I can. If I were then busy so long, I cannot be blamed. Farewell. Show this letter to the Chancellor and as many of our folks as you meet withal.

The above is a modern translation of a letter sent by James VI to Alexander Hay, his Clerk Register, probably in December 1591.[1] It is short, direct and very angry indeed. Comment will follow below on its context, content and style. But it serves to lead at the outset to the fact that here is a monarch of firm character, who can put pen to paper effectively. And historians of James's reign not only possess immense masses of official record, plus the king's own published works on a wide range of topics[2]—they can turn also to letters produced by the man himself. Official letters created by government clerks, with his signature attached, exist in thousands. James may have had a hand in drafting some of these, but we cannot be sure of that in detail. By the term 'personal letters' we mean those surviving in holograph, visibly in his

1 For a full edition of the text of this letter, see below, appendix 1. For editorial assistance with that, and the text in appendix 2, I have been greatly indebted to the expertise of Dr Athol L. Murray, whom I wish to thank most warmly.

2 On James as an author, see G.P.V. Akrigg, 'The literary achievement of King James I', *University of Toronto Quarterly*, xliv (1975), 116-29, and K. Sharpe, 'The king's writ: royal authors and royal authority in early modern England', in K. Sharpe and P. Lake (eds.), *Culture and Politics in Early Stuart England* (London, 1994), 123-31, which includes useful discussion of James's much-neglected biblical commentaries.

own distinctive script, or whose texts, although copies, can be proved to have originated from his pen.[1]

The first point to emphasise is that the corpus of his personal letters is strikingly large. About 650 are in print and others could certainly be added through further researches.[2] James has left to us far more letters of this kind than any other monarch of Scotland: those of his mother, for example, are fewer and much less interesting.[3] In an unkind phrase James has been described as 'an inveterate scribbler'.[4] He was in fact a man to whom writing came naturally and historians should be grateful that this extensive body of material is available for investigation.

We have to be thankful too that a modern edition of the letters has been produced. In 1984 Professor Emeritus Philip Akrigg, of the University of British Columbia, published the results of a major research project designed to track down James's letters and to edit a large selection of them. He has printed 227 texts in full and added a finding-list giving basic details for many others.[5] His volume contains a full introduction and appropriate critical apparatus for his texts, and it represents a notable step forward in the process of studying James from these vital primary sources. It is a pity that Akrigg decided to present his text in modernised spelling. He does retain some distinctively Scots words, which he inserts within quotation marks and explains in a glossary. This is an awkward procedure and Scottish historians are bound to regret a process which removes the true flavour from those texts which are in Scots. Yet it remains possible to sympathise with those many readers to whom an 'old spelling' edition, as the editor calls it, would have been a barrier to understanding. Altogether, Akrigg's production is of great benefit to scholars of the period and is a considerable achievement.

I

What value do these letters have for us? It is tempting to say that they enable us to penetrate into James's mind. To some degree, that must be so: virtually all of them are certainly composed by him.[6] But correspondence

1 In adult life James wrote in a distinctive but rather unlovely italic hand, which he described in a letter to Queen Elizabeth in 1600 as 'my raggit scribling' (*Elizabeth and James Letters*, 133).

2 Even published letters may be ignored: that in appendix 2, below, for example, although printed in 1715 and 1859, seems to have escaped the notice of all modern scholars except Akrigg.

3 See A. Labanoff (ed.), *Lettres et Mémoires de Marie Stuart, Reine d'Ecosse*, 7 vols. (London, 1852), and J.B.A.T. Teulet (ed.), *Lettres Inédites de Marie Stuart* (Paris, 1859).

4 Akrigg, 'The literary achievement', 126.

5 James VI, *Letters*. He includes a small number of texts which are formal, and not personal, letters. For a detailed and thoughtful review of his edition, see J. Wormald in *English Historical Review*, cviii (1988), 420-3.

6 The diplomat Sir James Melville recorded that in 1583, on the arrival of a letter from Queen Elizabeth, 'his Maieste commandit me to minut ane answer in his hyenes name, that he mycht wret it ouer again with his awen hand, samekle of it as he suld find meit' (Melville, *Memoirs*, 297). Even the existence of a holograph letter by James is not absolute

of any kind has pitfalls for the historian. There can easily occur in a letter some passing reference which made perfect sense to the recipient, but which is entirely obscure to us today, as perhaps it would have been also to some readers at the time. When James mentions in a letter to the earl of Huntly their conversation 'that nycht in the cabbinet' (the king's private apartment), we can have no idea of what is being referred to.[1] And letters produced by eminent persons, such as James, can range from those intended to be strictly private to those apparently private but actually meant for wider consumption. Even nowadays some letters of public figures clearly fall into the latter category. And if James's letters do reveal his mind, they also show us at once what a very complex mind that was. 'A prince can never without secrecie do great things', he said.[2] And James was capable of wrapping his meaning, if he chose, in the layered onion-skins of language. Yet, as we have already seen, he could also be brutally blunt. His character has had many wide-ranging epithets applied to it. Akrigg's comment that 'he was one of the most complicated neurotics ever to sit on either the English or the Scottish throne' is harsh, but has a glint of truth about it.[3] One key to understanding his personality may lie in the fact that he was an intellectual. Indeed, he was one of only two intellectuals among the ranks of the monarchs of Scotland, the other being his fifteenth-century namesake, James I. The 'hothouse' style of education imposed upon James as a child was certainly intended to develop his intellect, and it did so, mainly to his benefit. His letters do take us into James's thoughts, but it is too simple to expect that they will entirely explain him to us. Emanating as they do from such an intricate thinker, though sometimes a rather narrow one, they will tell us helpful things about him only when we analyse them and look closely into their subject-matter, style, structure and context.

The variety of topics on which he writes is enormous. They range from minutiae of daily administration, to family and personal issues, to principles of government policy.[4] As in many of his published works, he enjoys picking up subjects on which he can function as 'the great schoolmaster of the realm', often with a degree of pompous moralising. His high seriousness naturally emerges strongly in his diplomatic correspondence over many years with Queen Elizabeth. The letters exchanged by these two monarchs deserve far more detailed study than they have ever been given by scholars. Though many have been in print for nearly 150 years, they remain to be fully analysed as the productions

proof that he was the author of every word of it.

1 *CSP Scot.*, ix, 699; James VI, *Letters*, 90.

2 *Basilikon Doron*, in James I, *Political Works*, 42.

3 James VI, *Letters*, 3.

4 See, for example, an unusually extensive and elaborate letter of 1601 to two ambassadors in England about how to conduct negotiations there with a view to ensuring his accession to the throne: James VI, *Letters*, 173-7.

of a pair of acute, highly-educated and sometimes none too scrupulous political sparring-partners.[1]

At the other extreme, James's constant involvement in the details of Scottish government is well illustrated by the letter to the Clerk Register, quoted in full above. In one short letter James refers to no less than six matters of current administration with which he is closely concerned and on which he demands action. Linked to this particular evidence of his stimulus in governmental matters we must notice too the method which he here employs in order to impress himself on his bureaucrats: government by 'girning', one might call it. Elizabeth would no doubt have viewed it as undignified. But James's manner of ruling was often intensely personal, as was much of Scottish government in his time. There is every reason to think that thrusts of this kind quite often reached their mark. One English historian has described the last sentence of the letter—'Show this letter to the Chancellor and as many of our folks as you meet withal'—as a 'rather feeble injunction'.[2] Surely not so. It is not hard to imagine Alexander Hay encountering his colleagues on the High Street of Edinburgh, waving the paper at them and exclaiming, 'He's in a rage *again*! Get something *done*!' Such letters from James to his own civil servants are sadly few in number.[3] The reason is plain: a great deal of the running of the country was carried through by direct personal contact and by word of mouth, not by written communication.

II

The question of style in the letters raises at once the topic of language. James was able to write either in Scots or in English. Letters to close Scottish friends and to government officers are in rich and racy Scots. Those to Elizabeth, on the other hand, are in English, with an occasional Scots term here and there.[4] His *Basilicon Doron*, of which the holograph MS survives, was written in Scots. For publication it was translated into English, though not necessarily by the king himself.[5] James was an expert linguist: he had Latin, Greek and French, and a reasonable knowledge of Italian, plus a little Spanish.[6] But it is even more striking to find in him

1 *Elizabeth and James Letters*, published in 1849, contains 62 letters by Elizabeth and 32 by James.

2 J. Kenyon, review of James VI, *Letters* (Akrigg edn.), in *Times Literary Supplement*, 3 May 1985.

3 For one example, see a long and pungent letter to John Maitland, the chancellor, in 1591: *CSP Scot.*, x, 508-10, James VI, *Letters*, 112-15; another is the letter to the privy council in appendix 2, below.

4 James VI, *Letters*, 31.

5 James VI, *Basilicon Doron*, ii, 88-92, 105-6. Although Craigie's edition of the work is extensive and detailed, more study is needed of the numerous alterations and corrections in the MS, which can help to reveal James's methods of composition. At times it is possible to see him 'thinking on to the paper'.

6 C. Bingham, *The Making of a King: the Early Years of King James VI and I* (London, 1968), 96-7.

the ability to 'change mode' between two closely related languages, as Scots and English were.[1]

His overall command of style is remarkable. He can produce, for example, impressively elaborate rhetorical passages, especially in his letters to Elizabeth, and occasionally constructs deliberately inverted sentences, designed to attract the reader's attention.[2] He also knows how to use pace and contrast in writing. Even in the enraged epistle quoted above and amid its 'strong flavour of violent fury', as Jenny Wormald has called it,[3] his grip on style does not desert him. He outlines each matter on which his servants are failing and drives his points home with a sharp phrase at the end of each sentence: 'no man comes down', 'neither meeting nor answer', 'no such thing is contemplated'. Only towards the end of the letter does his anger get the better of him and his composition degenerates: one can almost hear his pen scratching through the paper. As this letter demonstrates, James, when he chose, was a master of the pithy phrase; and many examples could be quoted. In a letter of 1623 to Prince Charles, absent in Spain engaged in tortuous negotiations for a royal bride, James advises him to think 'as well upon the business of Christendom as upon the codpiece point'. He could at times be distinctly crude.[4] Though often vain and self-centred in manner, he could also speak with realism and modesty. In a letter of 1591 to John Maitland, his chancellor, touching on his poverty and perpetual crisis of finance, he remarks, 'Suppose we be not wealthy, let us be proud poor bodies'.[5]

Style, of course, has much to do with the fitness of language for its purpose, and the variety of style which James is capable of employing reveals a writer who is highly conscious of the person whom he is addressing, and of the effect he wants to achieve. His letters to Elizabeth, for example, contain some elements of deliberate teasing: pieces of bait to which she frequently rose, usually with irritation. He accomplishes this indirectly in a letter of November 1586, written to one of this agents in London in the early stages of the diplomatic effort to prevent the execution of Mary, queen of Scots. He instructs that the letter is to be shown to Elizabeth, even although (and indeed because) it contains a reference to Henry VIII's habit of 'beheading of his bedfellow(s)'.[6] The phrase was no accident, and Elizabeth's rage at the slur upon her father was very real.[7] By contrast, in an apparently secret letter of 1597 to his

1 For an example see p. 148, n. 1 below.
2 The first sentence of his address to Prince Henry, at the beginning of *Basilicon Doron*, is a good example of this device (James I, *Political Works*, 3).
3 A.G.R. Smith (ed.), *The Reign of James VI and I* (London, 1973), 229.
4 James VI, *Letters*, 420; for another example see ibid., 440-1.
5 James VI, *Letters*, 114.
6 James VI, *Letters*, 74-5.
7 *King James's Secret*, eds. R.S. Rait and A.I. Cameron (London, 1927), 64-70.

friend, the Catholic earl of Huntly, James commented on the zealots in the kirk who caused him so much trouble: 'I profess before God in extremity I love the religion they outwardly profess and hates their presumptuous and seditious behaviour'.[1] Huntly must have welcomed the remark, pressurised as he was by the kirk. Andrew Melville and his supporters would have greeted it with howls of fury—but the letter was not written for them.

Linked to stylistic ability is the matter of literary construction; and here again there are many letters which deserve commendation. It is true that he could produce slack and rambling texts at times, and much of his personal correspondence in his last years, especially to Prince Charles and the beloved Buckingham, is poor stuff, pathetic in every sense. But it would be unfair to judge him too harshly in his dotage. At his best his powers of composition are more than merely fair. Good structure, of course, is evident in many of his published works, notably *Basilicon Doron*. But clarity of arrangement adds to the interest and value of many of the letters as well. Amazingly, even the 'monarch in a huff' letter already quoted is made more powerful by its firmness of structure. He begins with a statement of the general topic: failure of action is a problem. He proceeds to list the various items which require attention but are not receiving it. He then summarises: 'In short no appointment or meeting is kept'—before erupting in wrath, and then finally ordering an intelligent procedure: 'Show this letter to the Chancellor ...' The text has a beginning, a middle and an end: modern students writing essays might do well to take some of James's works as their models.

By no means all the letters are of high quality. But amid the quantity and the variety which we meet as we read them, there is enough to warrant sincere praise. This is a writer of ability, and a man who possesses sharpness of mind and who displays involvement in his job.

III

To illustrate more fully these features of James's character, it is worthwhile finally to quote in full two further letters, both written against backgrounds of strong personal emotion.

We have met James using anger, but James in sarcastic mode can also be impressive. Following the execution of Mary, queen of Scots, on 8 February 1587, Elizabeth wrote to him personally, to explain in a patently feeble manner that his mother's death had been a sad but terrible mistake, a 'miserable accident'.[2] James's response was bound to be one of the most important letters he ever wrote. He rose to the occasion, in a text whose bitter irony leaps from the page.[3]

1 James VI, *Letters*, 148.
2 *King James's Secret*, 194-5.
3 Printed ibid., 200-1, here corrected from facsimile in James VI, *Letters*, 28 (plate ii). This holograph is clearly a draft, with numerous interlineations and corrections.

> Madame and dearest sister, quhairas by youre lettir and bearare, Robert Carey youre seruand and ambasadoure, ye purge youre self of yone unhappy fact. As, on the one pairt, considdering your ranke and sexe, consanguinitie and longe professed goode will to the defunct, together with youre many and solemne attestationis of youre innocentie [sic], I darr not wronge you so farre as not to iudge honorablie of youre unspotted pairt thairin, so, on the other syde, I uishe that youre honorable behauioure in all tymes heirafter may fully persuaide the quhole uorlde of the same. And, as for my pairt, I looke that ye will geue me at this tyme such a full satisfaction, in all respectis, as sall be a meane to strenthin and unite this yle, establishe and maintaine the treu religion, and obleis me to be, as befoire I was, youre most louing.
>
> [James R.]
>
> This bearare hath sumquhat to informe you of in my name, quhom I neid not desyre you to credit, for ye know I loue him.[1]

The construction is balanced, the wording is crisp. The descriptions of the execution as 'yone unhappy fact',[2] and of his mother as 'the defunct' are intentionally distant. Only in the postscript is a slightly warmer tone employed. On the surface he agrees that he is bound to accept the queen's protestations of personal innocence. But in the reality of politics there were many at the time who felt in their hearts that Mary dead was preferable to Mary alive: Queen Elizabeth, her councillors, the extremists in the Scottish kirk—and even in some ways James himself. His letter is based on the fundamentals of the situation; and written between its lines in invisible ink are the words: 'Madam, you are a liar; and in return for swallowing this insult I want rewards from you in the future'. As composition, the letter is splendid; as diplomacy, it is masterly.[3]

On a happier occasion, we find James in paternal style. When in 1603 he had just succeeded to the English throne, and was about to travel south to take over his long-desired inheritance, he wrote to his nine-year-old son and heir, Prince Henry, who was to stay in Scotland for some weeks longer. The letter displays the king's customary personal pride and his habitual sententiousness. Yet his shrewdness breaks through in the warning to Henry that a king of two kingdoms will have even greater worries and problems. James's language fits the occasion and an intelligent sense of concern for his son's welfare and behaviour shines from the text.[4]

1 The bearer was Sir Robert Carey, Elizabeth's own ambassador (*King James's Secret*, 201).

2 The word 'fact' could mean either simply a deed, an action, or a wicked, criminal act; and James certainly intended to make use here of the dubiety of meaning attached to the word.

3 Even so it has to be noted that, although James succeeded here in reminding Elizabeth of her weakened political situation, he did not achieve in the longer run what he was specifically demanding from her: acceptance that he was her legitimate heir, the grant of an English dukedom and lands, and an admission that the guilty verdict against Mary would not damage him (*King James's Secret*, 201-6).

4 Printed in H. Ellis (ed.), *Original Letters Illustrative of English History*, 1st ser., 3 vols (London, 1824), iii, 78-9; in James VI, *Letters*, 211-12; and elsewhere. The text above is from

My Sonne, that I see you not before my pairting impute it to this great occasion quhairin tyme is sa preciouse; but that shall by Goddis grace shortlie be recompencid by youre cumming to me shortlie,[1] and continuall residence uith me euer after. Lett not this[2] newis make you proude, or insolent; for a Kings sonne and heire uas ye before, and na maire are ye yett. The augmentation that is heirby lyke to fall unto you, is but in caires and heauie burthens. Be thairfor merrie, but not insolent; keepe a greatnes, but *sine fastu*;[3] be resolute but not willfull; keepe your kyndnes,[4] but in honorable sorte; choose nane to be youre play fellowis but thame that are well borne; and aboue all things giue neuer goode countenance to any but according as ye shall be informed that thay are in æstimation with me. Looke upon all Englishe men that shall cum to uisie[5] you as upon youre louing subjectis, not uith that ceremonie as touardis straingeris, and yett with such hartlines as at this tyme thay deserue. This gentleman quhom this bearare accumpanies is uorthie, and of guide ranke, and nou my familiare seruitoure; use him thairfore in a maire hamelie louing sorte nor otheris. I sende you hereuith my booke latelie prentid.[6] Studdie and profite in it as ye uolde deserue my blessing; and as thaire can na thing happen unto you quhairof ye will not finde the generall grounde thairin, if not the uerrie particulaire pointe touched, sa man[7] ye leuell everie mannis opinions or aduyces unto you as ye finde thaime agree or discorde uith the reulis thaire sett doun, allouing and follouing thaire aduyces that agrees with the same, mistrusting and frouning upon thaime that aduyses you to the contraire. Be diligent and earnist in youre studdies, that at youre meiting with me, I maye praise you for youre progresse in learning. Be obedient to youre maister, for youre awin ueill, and to procure my thankis; for in reuerencing him ye obeye me, and honoure youre selfe. Fairuell.

Youre louing Father
James R.

Appendix 1

Letter of King James VI to Alexander Hay, Clerk Register, about the failure of various officials to carry out administrative tasks, expressing anger that he is working harder than his servants do. (Probably December 1591)

Clerk of register[8]
becaus the chancellaire is occupied in his dispaches I man drese my complent to yow. I haue bene fryday, settirday and this day uathing upon the directioun of my effairis and neuir man command. thame

the holograph MS in BL, Harleian MS 6986, fo. 65.

1 *Sic*; the word is here repeated, in error.
2 MS *thir* (Scots, = *this*) has been altered by James to (English) *this*.
3 'Without haughtiness'.
4 To 'keep kindness' (related to 'kin') meant 'to maintain favour or mutual friendship'.
5 'to visit or inspect'.
6 *Basilikon Doron*, produced in its first London edition in Mar. 1603.
7 'must'.
8 The full title of this state official was Clerk of Register, Council and Rolls, later Lord Clerk Register. He was responsible for framing and custody of the principal series of public registers and records. Alexander Hay of Easter Kennet, who is addressed here, held the office from 1579 to 1594.

of the chaiker that wes ordanit to tak the comptis, uaitis neuer on. the turnis of the hous sould haue bene endit this day, na man comms doun. I sent for the aduocat baith fryday and satterday, nather meat nor anssuer. siclik efter the baillies of this toun for the matter of the tocher,[1] the lyk ansuere. I ordanit as ye harde a certane number to mak ouuertures for reforming of the sessioun,[2] na sic thing meditat.[a] I ordanit the theshaurar to garr mak chairgis about the horneris:[3] I haue hard na thing of that as yitt. in [s]chort[b] na trayst nor dayet is keipt. quhat is spokin this nicht lait is foryett the morne. in the morning I see na t[h]ingis[c] mennid bot to gurne.[d] neane[e] of this wark behalding of, als lang as I am earnestlie vaiting on. and quhen I am compellid to rest myselff then to laye the uyt vpoun abon[f] yek.[g4] man[h] cannot be allwayis ueue.[i] thairfor lett this writ be a witnes for my part, quhen evir it beis callid in questioun, I protest I may do na mair nor I may. gif I war thaine vaik[ing][j] on als lang I can not be wyted. fairw[e]ill.
Shau[k] this letter to the chancellar and als money of our folkis as ye meit withall.

Source: NLS, Adv. MS. 34.2.17, fo. 148r.; copy, in contemporary business hand.

Textual Notes

[In the above transcript punctuation has been modernised, the forms u/v and i/j have been retained, and abbreviations have been extended; but capitalisation has been left as in the text, since the meaning of some passages is possibly doubtful.]

[a] *MS.* me[]idat: *one letter lost at edge of sheet.*
[b] *MS.* chort.
[c] *MS.* natingis.
[d] *MS. sic; followed by* venrie *deleted.*
[e] *MS.* uearie.
[f] *MS. sic.*
[g] *MS. sic.*
[h] *MS.* nan.
[i] *MS.* vene.
[j] *Last 3 letters lost at edge of sheet.*
[k] *MS.* Suau.

1 The reference is to the tocher or marriage portion of Queen Anna (see 'Comment', below).
2 Plans for administrative reforms touching the Court of Session are mentioned in a document listing proposed acts for the parliament of June 1592 (NAS, PA 7/1/42). (I owe this reference to Dr Julian Goodare.) An act was passed in that parliament concerning the qualifications of lords of session (*APS*, iii, 569).
3 Persons who have been technically outlawed, often as part of routine debt-collection procedure.
4 Suggested emendation of this passage is as follows: *to laye the uyt upoun [me]: a bon[y] [g]ek.* (In translation: *to lay the blame upon me: a pretty trick.*) The word *gek* means a derisive gesture or scornful trick. The king's angry haste has evidently produced problems for the copyist. The phrase as amended may display a characteristically Jamesian tone of irony.

Glossary (in order as in text)

man: must
drese: address
chaiker: exchequer
ordanit: ordered
comptis: accounts
turnis: duties, tasks
hous: (royal) household
meat: meeting
siclik: similarly
tocher: dowry
Session: Court of Session
ouuertures: proposals, recommendations
sic: such
garr: cause (to)
horneris: outlaws, persons 'put to the horn'
trayst: tryst, appointment
dayet: diet, meeting
foryett: forgotten
mennid: spoken of
gurne, girn: snarl in rage
neane: none
uyt, wyte: blame
ueue, uiue: lively
beis: is
nor: than
gif: if
vaiking: busy
withall: as well

Comment

It is probable that this text should be dated to December 1591. D. Murray Rose, who printed it in 1897 (see below), suggests that date and refers to various related documents and events, but unfortunately does not supply source references for them. By a contract made in July 1590, the king had forced eleven of the principal burghs to receive loans of portions of the queen's tocher of £100,000 Scots and to pay interest to the crown at 10 per cent per annum: A. Montgomerie, 'King James VI's tocher gude and a local authorities loan of 1590', *SHR*, xxxvii (1958), 13. This matter was of current concern to the bailies of Edinburgh in November 1591: there is reference to a contract about the queen's tocher in their Town Council minutes on 17 November 1591: *Edin. Recs., 1589-1603*, 51.

Printed

(i) Sir William Purves, *Revenue of the Scottish Crown, 1681*, ed. D. Murray Rose (Edinburgh, 1897), pp. xxxvii-viii (with errors); (ii) James VI, *Letters*, no. 45 (modernised text).

Appendix 2

Letter of King James VI to his privy councillors, demanding that they continue to keep good order in Scotland during his absence in Denmark and giving instructions about the arrangements for his return, along with his new wife, and their reception on arrival. Kronborg Castle [Elsinore, Denmark], 19 February 1589/90.

[My][a] lordis of consale. That this generall letter of myne man serue as [weill to yow all] as to euery one of you in perticular, lay the blame I pray you upon the [hast and] fascheousnes of the dispatche and nocht upon my sweirnes, althoughe I can [not denye] that to write with myne owne hand I am both slawe and sweir aneuche. I [doubt not] then ye will take this in als[b] good part as if I wrote a through of pa[per to] euery one of you. Ye may nowe knaw by the season of the yere that my [comming] hame Godwilling drawes neire. I am suirelie trated here with all the h[onor and] hartelines that this contrie people can imagine. I thinck we should [be not] unthanckfull when theire[c] commes in our boundis [a king].[d] A king of Scotland with [a newe] maried wife will not come hame euery daye. For Godis sake respect not [only my] honour in this but the honour of our wholle nacion and speidelie of your sel[ues for my] part wilbe leist in it. It is knowne that I am absent and all the [world] knowes that when the gudeman is awaie he can not be wyted of th[e mis]orders in the house, but what may he thinck then of his servantis [and factors] he hes left therein. Now my lords sence this is onelie the great[est][e] pr[oof of] your deligence without my presence or assistance that euer I am able [for to] haue of you, let me knawe now what remembrance ye haue of me [during] my absence by deligent remembring and performing suche directions as the bea[rer] hereof the maister of work[1] hes in chardge of me to deliuer unto you. Reme[mber] spedely upon the ending out of thabbay[2] as yet lieing in dead thraw w[ithout the] which we can not be lodged at our landing, and in gude faith it is not the [manner] of this contrie to lye therout[f] for greatnes of the frostis. And for a token [that ye] have not forgotten us ye may send 2. or 3. shipps here to shew vs the [way] home, but lett na great men or gentlemen come in them but man[y] marinellis for I am alreadie ouerchardgable to these folkis here, besides that [every] one of you will haue ennoughe to do in the turnes I have

1 The Master of Works was a royal official responsible for building operations. At this date the post was held by William Schaw, on whose highly significant career as an architect see D. Howard, *Scottish Architecture: Reformation to Restoration, 1560-1660* (Edinburgh, 1995), 25-35, 211-12.

2 The reference is to Holyrood Abbey, which since the fifteenth century had been a royal palace as well as a monastery, and where much building had been undertaken by James IV and James V. King James is demanding completion of building or refurbishment work which has come to a stop. His instructions are evidently linked to the return to Scotland of the Master of Works, who was the bearer of this letter. The elision of *e* from the definite article and its attachment to a following word commencing with a vowel (*thabbey*) was an English scribal practice; this is further evidence that the copyist of this text was an English clerk.

imploied y[ou in][g] at hame. For Godis sake in ane thing respect my honour that all disco[rds and] vanities and quarrellis may be supercedit at this tyme, for giff I tooke sic [straite] order for that the last yere when I looked for my wifes comming hame, and a [certaine] companie of strangers with her, how mickle mare sould it be this yere when [we are] baith to come hame, and twise as great a nomber of strangers, and specially sen I [have] seene so gude an example in this countrie. In dede I haue gude cause to thanck y[ou all] of the gude quietnes that ye haue alreadie keped as I perceiued by your last letters. Rememb[er] likewise that na great man or counsellour presume to be at our landing, but sic [as] the bearer hereof will in a roll deliuer vnto you ut omnia fiant decenter [et] cum ordine.[1] Faile nocht to be carefull to prouide gude cheare for us for we hau[e here] aboundance of gude meit and part[2] of drinck. To the particulers of this I rem[it to your] directions as of all other things likewise. To conclude I both praye you and [commaund] you sleuth na tyme and for my part[h] sake do at this tyme evin mair [nor] possible for ye knaw I will neuer eitt[i] nor drinck a faire wynde.[3] [Farewell.] [From the Castle of Croneburghe] the 19th of February [one thousand fyve hundred eighty nine].[j]

[James R]

Endorsement

King [Jam]es letters to the lords of the Counsell. Castle of Croneburghe 19th February 1589. Preparations for his home coming and receivings. 1. litem

Source

BL, MS Cotton Caligula D.I, fo. 435; copy, in contemporary English secretary hand; MS damaged at edges as a result of fire in the Cottonian Library in 1731.

Textual Notes

[In the above transcript punctuation and capitalisation have been modernised, the forms u/v and i/j have been retained and abbreviations have been extended.]

1 'So that everything may be done decently and in order' (I Corinthians 14:40). The roll of instructions survives: see *Papers Relative to the Marriage of James VI of Scotland* (Bannatyne Club, 1828), 29-34.

2 In the sense of 'some drink'. The remark is presumably a joke, implying a modest quantity of drink. In fact, heavy drinking was a noted feature of the visit: James Melville recorded that James in Denmark 'made guid cheir, and drank stoutlie till the spring tyme' (Melville, *Diary*, 277). See also James VI, *Letters*, 103.

3 Presumably a proverb, meaning that good intentions will not provide the necessities of life.

[a] *Unless otherwise indicated, all words and letters in square brackets are editorially supplied from the text in Rymer (see below), which was printed in 1715 before the occurrence of fire damage.*
[b] *MS.* all.
[c] *MS.* theires.
[d] *Copyist appears to have omitted these two words in error, being misled because the same phrase occurs as start of the next sentence.*
[e] *MS.* great.
[f] *MS. sic.*
[g] *Printed text omits* in.
[h] *MS. sic.*
[i] *MS.* sitt.
[j] *sic printed text. But James invariably wrote year-dates in arabic numerals.*

Glossary (in order as in text)

man: must
fascheousness: troublesomeness
sweirnes: reluctance
through: sheet (of paper)
hartelines: heartiness, sincerity
gudeman: husband, head of household
wyted: blamed
factor: business agent
ending: completing
dead thraw: death-throe
marinellis: mariners
turnes: duties, tasks
mickle: much
sleuth, slouth: waste (by sloth)

Comment

The date and place of writing, as given in the printed text and in the endorsement, are confirmed by the similarity of language in a letter by James, of the same date and place, to the Rev. Robert Bruce, one of the ministers of Edinburgh, who had been appointed by James to give advice in the running of government during the king's absence abroad (James VI, *Letters*, 103-5).

Printed

(i) Thomas Rymer (ed.), *Foedera, Conventiones*, etc., 20 vols. (London, 1704-32), xvi, 41-2; (ii) James Taylor, *The Pictorial History of Scotland*, 2 vols. (London, 1852-9), ii, 337-8 (with errors); (iii) James VI, *Letters*, 472-3 (brief summary, misdated).

~ 9 ~

James VI's Architects and their Architecture

Aonghus MacKechnie

Watch towers and thundr'ng walls vain fences prove,
No guards to monarchs like their people's love.
Jacobus VI Rex, Anna Regina, 1606.[1]

Documentation casts little light upon James VI's thoughts on architecture, possibly because his cultural interests were mainly literary and philosophical. But important architectural investments were made both during his minority, and in his adulthood, when palace-building was revived (albeit not on the scale of some of his predecessors). James recognised architecture's propagandist potential, utilising it to broadcast his image of Stewart majesty. Consideration, though, of his architecture is hampered: mostly visual, fragmentary, primary or analogous evidence has to be pieced together, because iconoclasts savaged his chapels, Holyrood was rebuilt, and the other palaces spoiled through destruction, inappropriate usage or neglect.

The royal works contained a developed organisational structure, but it has not been clear who was responsible for architectural design. The following discussion stems partly from a seeming contradiction in past interpretations: that in the 1590s, the king's master of works designed royal palaces, while by the 1610s, this responsibility is said to have lain with the king's master mason.[2] Reconsideration of available evidence suggests that, by our period, it was the former of these whose role was central in palace design. Masters of works also became important as disseminators, through architecture, of royal propaganda, so some ways in which architecture related to James's kingship are also suggested. Because the masters of works are still hardly known, yet seem now to be crucial in formulation of architecture in this period, it seems worthwhile to highlight their names and something of their careers. But first, some contextualisation is required.

I

Edinburgh's developing role as 'capital' increasingly associated aristocracy and government with the burgh. Satellite houses for lairds were

1 Inscription, James VI statue, Netherbow Port, Edinburgh; quoted (translated from Latin) in J. Grant, *Old and New Edinburgh*, 3 vols. (London, n.d.), i, 218.

2 R. Fawcett, *The Abbey and Palace of Dunfermline* (Historic Scotland, 1990), 15, 26; D. Pringle, *Linlithgow Palace* (Historic Scotland, n.d.), 19. The uncertainty is noted by I. MacIvor, *Edinburgh Castle* (London, 1993), 72.

built round about, while the royal palaces were also in the east-central region. All this encouraged a distinction between court (and courtier) architecture, centred in these parts, and derivative regional variations where local schools of mason-architects operated.[1] These are most evident in the west and north-east—a pattern still visible in the early twentieth century, though by then any sense in the west of derivativeness was gone.

James inherited a brilliant—arguably, sometimes, precocious—series of royal palaces, the legacy essentially of James I and his successors until James V.[2] Mary had refitted interiors at Holyrood, but built no great new palaces. During James's earlier years, palaces were sometimes neglected. A major palace-building programme was unnecessary, and little royal building was done until the 1590s, when Dunfermline was rebuilt for Queen Anna. But others—including the Regents Mar and Morton—were to build, sometimes on a large scale.

James's birth-date, 1566, is inscribed over the rusticated entrance to the apartment in Edinburgh's royal palace in which he was born. The reconstruction presumably related to this event, and thus a consideration of the architecture of James's time might commence here.[3] James, of course, had no influence on architecture for some years to come. Yet the element of continuity in architecture was as marked as in music or literature; consideration of the architecture of a given period requires appreciation of the context from which it derived. As in other areas of culture, reference was made to the national, the classical and the Biblical past to inform and to legitimise the present.

Continuity has to be set against a constant programme of innovation, as new ideas were devised or imported. Any important new building had to be innovative. The Marian court—which used imagery from the two most culturally progressive European centres of the age, France and Italy—might have been cosmopolitan, but in many respects it was essentially modelled upon that of France. By James VI's time, politics had lessened the direct French link, validating a readier interest in and interchange with Protestant northern Europe, notably England and Denmark, while a growing emphasis upon classical scholarship was reflected in the young king's own outlook. Classicism was also to serve

1 Spectacular exceptions exist, such as Carnasserie: court architecture in rural Argyll.

2 M. Glendinning, R. MacInnes and A. MacKechnie, *A History of Scottish Architecture from the Renaissance to the Present Day* (Edinburgh, 1996), chapters 1 & 2; I. Campbell, 'A Romanesque revival and the early Renaissance in Scotland, *c*.1380-1513', *Journal of the Society of Architectural Historians*, liv (1995); I. Campbell, 'Linlithgow's "Princely Palace" and its influence in Europe', *Architectural Heritage*, v (1995).

3 Sometimes said to date from 1615-17, with retrospective datestone. But the monogram commemorates Mary and Henry, while the architecture differs from that of the identified 1615-17 work. The calligraphic evidence also indicates a sixteenth-century date.

as a model for the post-1603 'British' Stuart monarchy. Perhaps this was an extension of the imperial symbolism seen in the architecture of James IV, for a vastly-enhanced new 'empire'.

The dismantling of Mary's court, iconoclasm and diminution of ecclesiastical patronage of the visual arts represented a cultural reversal. It was perhaps counterbalanced by a new stress upon intellectualism and more developed interest in classicism, that was to manifest itself in architecture, which already had a tendency towards unadorned monumentality.[1] James's reign witnessed consolidation of the process begun after 1542 (and completed post-1689) when rural aristocratic houses became the touchstone of fashion, supplanting the role held formerly by the church and the royal palaces. Church architecture also broadcast messages: the classicism of Burntisland (1589), related to contemporary Dutch presbyterian plans, while the pseudo-antique neo-Gothic of Archbishop Spottiswoode's Dairsie (1621) asserted the antiquity of episcopalianism.[2]

The earlier decades of James's reign saw a vastly increased volume of building, funded primarily through secularisation of church property. This developed the existing aesthetic of externally plain, dignified, stone-built or harled massiveness, but now with a balanced asymmetry. By 1600, another new courtly fashion existed: a surer classicism combining symmetrical elevations and outline plans. From about 1620 fashion again changed, introducing more extensive applied decoration—a fashion whose spectacular swan-song was Glasgow College, on the point of becoming artistically old-fashioned when completed *c.*1660, albeit forward-looking in terms of promoting tenemental street architecture. Attempting to identify the mainstream at any point is not straightforward. It was a web of overlapping tendencies, survivals, revivals and innovations. The verticality and monumentality exemplified by Drochil may have remained dominant throughout our period, but the horizontalising seen at Falkland also reappeared, for instance at Pinkie (1613). Maitland's Lethington (renamed Thirlestane; *c.*1590) represents something of a hybrid, with the vertically divided façade exemplified by Falkland, but set on a massive, vertically-emphatic structure.

This was the architectural context into which James was born, and which he left behind at his death: a mainstream European tradition, yet distinctive and unique, constantly seeking modernisation.

1 M. Lynch, 'Scottish culture in its historical perspective', in P.H. Scott (ed.), *Scotland: a Concise Cultural History* (Edinburgh, 1993), 17-18.

2 Revived Gothic was similarly promoted at Wurzburg in 1573-1617 by Bishop Julius Echter von Mespelbrunn for comparable, symbolic reasons, as part of his Counter-Reformation activities: E. Hempel, *Baroque Art and Architecture* (Harmondsworth, 1965), 13.

II

Who, then, was responsible for palace design? Was it (as has been suggested in the case of Dunfermline) the master of works, or was it (as suggested at Linlithgow) the master mason?

Today, the term 'architect' applies to one trained to design buildings and to supervise their erection. In Renaissance thought, the concept of an architect had been set out by Vitruvius, in the first century BC. An architect not only created buildings for clients, but was the Renaissance ideal, the 'universal' individual, whose studies embraced literature, drawing, geometry, arithmetic, philosophy, music, medicine, law and astronomy.[1] The balance of available evidence suggests that this Vitruvian concept of an architect applied in appointment of royal masters of works. James Murray, for instance, as royal master gunner, presumably required surveying skills (including geometry and arithmetic) necessary for architects.[2] Masters of works had expertise in structural technicalities: Murray made official reports on bridges, such as Lasswade.[3] In preparation for an abortive visit by Charles in 1630, he was commissioned to 'assist ... with his advice ... anent the preparatiouns requisite to be made and perfytted within ... [St Giles'] ... kirk towards his Majesteis coronatioun.'[4] King Charles referred to Murray and to his partner, Anthony Alexander, by the term 'surveyor' ('generall surveyaris and principal maisteris of all his hienes werkis and buildinges')—the English equivalent both in terminology and—in Charles's perception—in post.[5] Alexander studied architecture abroad to qualify him for the mastership.[6] Just as Inigo Jones designed royal buildings for James in England, so at least one of his Scottish counterparts (Murray) is documented as having done likewise. The term 'architect[us]' was used of royal masters of works.[7] In the context of an intellectually based court culture where education centred upon the humanities, the word, surely, was understood in its Vitruvian sense.

William Schaw was a personal friend of royalty, and his being one of two people chosen in 1585 by Sir James Melville of Halhill to negotiate with a Danish delegation demonstrates a special regard. Yet this did not set Schaw apart from the artisan or tradesman. At Doune, in 1581, Robert Drummond was 'his majesties maister of wark, agrear with all the warkmen', duties subsequently performed by Schaw and Murray.[8] The

1 Vitruvius, *The Ten Books on Architecture*, trans. H. Morgan (Dover, NY, 1960).
2 R.S. Mylne, 'Notices of the king's master gunners of Scotland', *PSAS*, xxxiii (1898-9).
3 *RPC*, xii, 710.
4 *RPC*, 2nd ser., iii, 498.
5 R.S. Mylne, 'Masters of work to the crown of Scotland', *PSAS*, xxx (1895-6), 57.
6 *The Earl of Stirling's Register of Royal letters, 1615-1635*, 2 vols., ed. C. Rogers (Edinburgh, 1885), i, 69, 319.
7 E.g. *RMS*, vii, 689.
8 R.S. Mylne, *The Master Masons to the Crown of Scotland* (Edinburgh, 1893), 60; *MWA*, i, p.

king's master of works is seen—indeed, in his professional capacity, is only ever seen—operating between the patron, on the one hand, and the operative, or artisan, on the other. This was crucial for the Vitruvian role to be fulfilled. Although only for James Murray is there powerful documentary evidence to suggest an architect in the Vitruvian sense, the argument might tentatively be extended to include other masters of works. So who were they?

III

The first master of works in James's reign was sir William MacDowell (or MacDougall), who in 1536 was overseer at Salisbury quarry. Subsequently (from 1554 at least) master of works, he was probably dead when replaced in 1579, for the post was usually given for life.[1] A cleric, he had the vicarages of Dalmeny, Inch and Leswalt in Galloway.[2] In 1548 he had presentation of a Magdalene chapel at Whitehill, near Musselburgh.[3] His works included James's gallery of 1576-7, comprising the northern 'pile' of the Holyrood north quarter,[4] but he was busier at Edinburgh Castle, where his interventions included the 1566 palace reconstruction for Mary, notable for the above-mentioned doorway and innovative, long, scale staircase within.[5] He was engaged in the post-siege reconstruction from 1573—'bigging and reparing of the castell of Edinburgh'.[6] This included the Half-moon Battery and 'bigging of the inner yett within the castell' (the Portcullis Gateway). Its unorthodox main opening contrasted with its 'correct' overdoor aedicule, a formula almost suggestive of Michelangelo's Porta Pia (1562).[7]

This reconstruction was done for the Regent Morton, for whom Drochil was built and Aberdour enlarged, raising the possibility of MacDowell having been involved with either or both these houses. The Portcullis Gateway arch-springer detailing is similar to that at Mar's Wark (dated 1570 and 1572), the Regent Mar's Stirling town house. Each also has an understated overdoor pediment (reduced at Edinburgh to a plinth), and armorial over. Mar and Morton, like Governor Arran at Kinneil in the 1550s, were well-placed to exploit the services of the best architects and craftsmen. The distinctive shafted detailing seen at these two buildings matched that at Carnasserie, begun in the later 1560s for John Carswell, bishop of the Isles. Carswell was also linked with the

xxviii.

1 *MWA*, i, p. xxvii.

2 C.H. Haws (ed.), *Scottish Parish Clergy at the Reformation* (SRS, 1972), 59, 108, 160.

3 *MWA*, i, p. xxvii. Whitehill was later owned by a successor in post, James Smith (*c.*1645-1731).

4 *TA*, xiii, 150-1. The interior was painted by Walter Binning, 1577: ibid., 166. This gallery was rebuilt by Bruce and Mylne in the 1670s, possibly incorporating much 1570s work not now visible. MacDowell also built a gallery within the abbey kirk: ibid., 187.

5 *MWA*, i, p. xxvii, citing *TA*, xii, 514.

6 *TA*, xiii, 33.

7 *TA*, xiii, 187. Also known as the Regent Morton Gateway.

court, having been chancellor of the Chapel Royal from perhaps 1558 until his death in 1572.[1] Similarities of detail exist at Carnasserie and Torwood (1566). This small group of buildings can be associated with one another and, mostly, with the court. The possibility exists of the same architect influencing some or all of these. Might this be MacDowell?

IV

On 6 April 1579, MacDowell's successor, Sir Robert Drummond of Carnock, was appointed 'maister of all ... [James's] ... werkis and places, biggit and to be biggit'.[2] He held office until 1583. A seventeenth-century family history tells that he died in 1592, aged 74, and that he was 'Master and surveyor of all the King's works to King James'. He was grandfather of William Drummond of Hawthornden.[3] Alexander Montgomerie's epitaph is illuminating:

> All buildings brave bids DRUMMOND nou adeu;
> Quhais lyf furthsheu he lude thame by the laiv.
> Quhair sall we craiv sik policie to haiv?
> Quha with him straiv to polish, build, or plante?
> These giftis, I grant, God lent him by the laiv.[4]

God-given gifts of architectural and landscaping skills were his 'by the laiv'—in abundance. This could have applied only to an operative (which Drummond, an aristocrat, was not) or else to a designer or architect. It could hardly have been said of a lay administrator or accountant.

In May 1583, still during the period in power of the Ruthven regime, Drummond submitted an estimate of 'Outlays for Repair of Royal Palaces'. In it, he addressed past neglect and proposed ambitious new ideas. He had a sensitive eye—for instance, at Stirling, the 'westqwarter' was to be dismantled and rebuilt

> in the maist plesand maner that can be dewyssit; quhilk qwarter off the said paleys is the best and maist plesand sitwatione off ony of his hienes palayes be ressone it will have the maist plesand sycht of all the foure airthis, in speciall perk and gairdin, deir thairin, up the rawerais of Forthe, Teyth, Allone, and Gwddy to Lochlomwnd, ane sycht round about in all pairtis and downe the rewear of Forthe quhair thair standis many greit stane howssis provyding thair be ane fair gallery beildit on the ane syd of the said work, and this forsaid gallerie and tarras to be beildit and bigit upone the heich pairtis off the foirsaid work.[5]

1 D.E.R. Watt (ed.), *Fasti Ecclesiae Scoticanae Medii Aevi* (SRS, 1969), 338.
2 Mylne, 'Masters of work', 54.
3 W. Drummond, *The Genealogie of the Most Noble and Ancient House of Drummond* (Edinburgh, 1831), 71, 250, 267.
4 Alexander Montgomerie, *Poems*, ed. J. Cranstoun (STS, 1887), 221.
5 *MWA*, i, 310.

Drummond envisaged a substantial superstructure, its purpose being enjoyment of the view in all directions, like the *altana* of Italian Renaissance architecture.[1] This fitted into a pre-existing formula associated with Stewart monarchy, for at Linlithgow, the north-west tower is topped by a single viewing room, reportedly used by Queen Margaret as a lookout while awaiting news of James IV's English campaign of 1513. That such an arrangement threw out the symmetry was evidently unimportant: in Rome, for instance, the Palazzo Venezia had a viewing tower at one end, as had Peruzzi's Villa Farnesina, commissioned in 1508.[2] Drummond's ideas and epitaph are important in demonstrating the link in perception between landscape, both natural and man-made, and architecture. The view from Stirling was of James's kingdom—in the same way as, later, Louis XIV's great vista at Versailles was upon nothing specific: but upon France. The 'Scottish Historical Landscape' identified by Margaret Stewart[3]—the intentional visual exploitation of national history within a landscape, exemplified by the huge formal garden at Alloa planned by the earl of Mar *c*.1701—is perhaps illustrated here in embryo, for many of the great stone houses to be viewed from Drummond's high gallery were ancient, while nearby (and overlooked from the palace south front and terrace) lay Bannockburn, site of the military triumph still then central to royal and national propaganda. Such viewing platforms remained a feature of the royal works until the platforming of the towers at Charles II's Holyrood.[4]

Drummond's report was submitted to the lords of exchequer a month before the Ruthven regime ended in June 1583. Was it commissioned by that regime? Or was it prepared by Drummond as an action list for his successor? Although Drummond's appointment had been for life, a new master of works was created some six months after the fall of the Ruthven regime. Perhaps Drummond had become politically inappropriate, for after the Ruthven regime ended, 'certane of the Kingis seruandis, officiaris and utheris seruandis, fauoreris of the erle of Mar, war dischargit court; as namly Dounypace and Carnock maister

1 Cf. V. Vesey, 'Una nuova attribuzione a Martino Longhi il Vecchio: la villa Carafa, oggi Grazioli, di Grottaferrata', *Opus*, v (1996).

2 Other roof-top or high-level viewing structures of the general period include both internal spaces (e.g. the oriel-windowed topmost room at Maybole) and external platforms (e.g. Craigievar).

3 M.C.H. Stewart, 'Lord Mar's Plans, 1700-1732', (University of Glasgow M. Litt. thesis, 1988), 66; Glendinning *et al.*, *History of Scottish Architecture*, 104-5.

4 Conceivably, the 'over gallerie' referred to in 1628 represents that particular proposal by Drummond fulfilled: *MWA*, ii, 240. The same document also proposed (among much else) a two-storey dwelling for the captain of the castle over the 'new yett' at Edinburgh, to protect the portcullis mechanism from rain (a scheme carried out by William Schaw in 1584: MacIvor, *Edinburgh Castle*, 7) and rebuilding of the Chapel Royal. MacDowall assembled materials 'to mak the new galry in the castell of Striviling' in 1576: *TA*, xiii, 149.

steblaris'.[1] Patrick Drummond, younger of Carnock, held this post. By August 1584 he had been convicted of treason.[2] Drummond the elder possibly shared this unpopularity.[3]

Drummond's own Carnock is long gone, insufficiently recorded. Bannockburn House, which he also owned, was rebuilt in the seventeenth century, and his Stirling town house is unidentified.[4] Both in his own time, and in the seventeenth century, he was a highly-regarded contributor to architectural and to landscape design, but not enough survives to characterise this contribution.

V

On 20 December 1583 William Schaw was appointed 'grit maister of all and sindrie his hines palaceis, biggingis and reparationis, and grit oversear, directour and commandar of quhatsumevir palice devyset or to be devyset for our soverane lordis behuif and pleasure'.[5] He held office until his death in 1602. A modern account of Schaw's career exists so little is said here.[6] Of the Sauchie family, Schaw found favour with King James, and then Queen Anna, to whom he was chamberlain and for whom he rebuilt Dunfermline Palace, her dower house. He has been associated with the reconstruction of the Chapel Royal at Stirling.[7] In 1589, when James left for Norway and Denmark to fetch his bride, Schaw accompanied him, returning ahead of the royal party in March 1590 to prepare for the homecoming.[8] Schaw's epitaph, by his 'true-hearted friend', Alexander Seton (the future Chancellor Dunfermline), related that 'in his eagerness to improve his mind he travelled through France and many other kingdoms. Accomplished in every liberal art, he excelled in

1 D. Stevenson, *The Origins of Freemasonry* (Cambridge, 1988), 28; Moysie, *Memoirs*, 45-6. Cf. *RPC*, iii, 648.

2 *Registrum Secreti Sigilli Regum Scotorum (Register of the Privy Seal of Scotland)*, viii, 883, 2359. Another son, John (father of Hawthornden), was also suspect for a time in 1584: *RPC*, iii, 664. He was restored to favour, and by 1587 was 'ane of the yshearis of his majesteis chalmer': *RPC*, iv, 199.

3 An armorial from Gowrie House, now in the Scottish National Portrait Gallery, is dated 1582. If Carnock was turned out of his post, perhaps Montgomerie's friendship with him impeded his re-admittance to the court. While in prison after the regime ended, the earl of Gowrie wrote, 'What a pitie it were to take me from my parks and policie', and at Ruthven he had a gallery 'newly built and decored with Pictures': D. Pringle, *Huntingtower* (Historic Scotland, 1996), 7. Did any of this work involve the subsequently displaced Drummond?

4 *RPC*, iv, 229. Carnock is described in D. MacGibbon and T. Ross, *Castellated and Domestic Architecture of Scotland*, 5 vols. (Edinburgh, 1887-92), ii, 490-6. Similarities to other work may be significant: for instance, the ground plan had a latitudinal corridor fronting three rooms out of the four, as at Carnasserie. At first floor the hall was central, with a room either side, as at Melgund and (in its pre-1581 form) Airth. A staircase was set forward at either side of the entrance front, as at Carnasserie and Melgund. But evidence that Drummond worked at Carnock is lacking.

5 Stevenson, *Freemasonry*, 26; *MWA*, i, p. xxviii.

6 Stevenson, *Freemasonry*, 26-32.

7 Stevenson, *Freemasonry*, 93.

8 Moysie, *Memoirs*, 82.

architecture. Princes in particular esteemed him for his conspicuous gifts'.[1] An English complaint described him as 'praefectum architecturae'.[2] The 'Dunvegan Armorial', compiled in 1582-4, had been his.

During Schaw's term of office emerged the new fashion of houses symmetrical both in plan and elevation. Examples included Barnes (*c.*1594), Duntarvie (1589; western angle later infilled), Thirlestane, Fyvie (*c.*1596), Scone (post-1600) and Boyne. Perhaps Burntisland Kirk (1589) and the Chapel Royal (1594) should also be seen in this context. Might this be due to the classicism of James's court and to Schaw's influence upon architectural fashion, and even to his foreign travels to 'many kingdoms', as his epitaph claimed?[3]

Little survives of Dunfermline Palace. Slezer's seventeenth-century views suggest its scale and magnificence, showing a giant eastern quarter, long gone without proper record. But parts of the south quarter, including many of the cross-windows, and the three symmetrical western bays (an addition to pre-existing work) seem likely to be by Schaw.[4]

Schaw served on a committee for rebuilding Perth Bridge, and he built the classical north-east quarter at Seton.[5] Fyvie, built for Alexander Seton, was conceived as a symmetrical corner-towered quadrangle, its turreted castellation reminiscent of James IV's triumphalism, but perhaps also to be regarded in the context of James's 1590s chivalric phase, which found elaborate expression in the baptismal ceremonies for Prince Henry in 1594.[6] The entrance tower has a high-level arch between paired turrets. This could be interpreted as a giant Roman or triumphal arch like that within the portico of the Pantheon in Rome, and, in the Renaissance period, at, for instance, Alberti's S. Andrea in Mantua; while in Naples, the centre area of the arch of Alfonso (1452), is (like Fyvie) sculptural and in a contrasting material. Were Fyvie's arch a product of Seton's Italian travels, it would be tempting to suggest a covert allusion to Catholicism. It was reproduced at nearby Craigston (1607), and had been used previously at Saltcoats (1592). Did Seton use Schaw as his architect?

Direct Italian inspiration, noted in contemporary courtly literature,[7] is well-known from Crichton's north quarter (1581x1591), built for the fifth

1 Translation in *Inventory of Fife*, 112; repr. Stevenson, *Freemasonry*, 26-7.

2 Stevenson, *Freemasonry*, 28.

3 Schaw left for France in 1584 in the company of Lord Seton, whose son, Alexander, might well also have travelled with them: Stevenson, *Freemasonry*, 28-9.

4 John Slezer, *Theatrum Scotiae* (London, 1693), plates 45-6.

5 *RPC*, v, 532; Stevenson, *Freemasonry*, 29. Schaw—possibly in the role of James's Vitruvian architect—was also commissioned to demolish the 'place and fortalice' of Strathbogie in 1594: *RPC*, v, 186.

6 Scottish National Portrait Gallery, *Treasures of Fyvie* (exhibition catalogue, 1985), fig. 3; M. Lynch, 'Court ceremony and ritual during the personal reign of James VI', Chapter 4 above.

7 R.J. Lyall, 'The literature of Lowland Scotland, 1350-1700', in Scott (ed.), *Cultural History*, 94.

earl of Bothwell after his return from Italy. Other near-contemporary examples of Italianising include Newark (1597) on the Clyde, with its Michelangelesque pediments derived from the Porta Pia, and possibly the Chapel Royal, Stirling (1594); while, after Schaw's time, Culross Abbey House (1608) may be a third.[1]

The Chapel Royal was built hastily for Prince Henry's baptism, and must have involved Schaw. It was already anticipated that Henry might become king of a united Britain, so a great Renaissance festival was held, with foreign ambassadors present. Despite the crow-steps, at a glance the building looks Florentine, with paired round-arched windows set in round-arched frames (on the tympanum of each the ghost of a painted roundel). The doorway is a triumphal arch, which was originally more complex, with a superstructure, but sufficiently intact to denote it as Scotland's first known building based upon formal 'correct' use of classical Orders.[2]

However, might we expect William Schaw, re-creator of freemasonry, to be associated with more complex propagandist ideas, for an event otherwise crammed with allusions? James had many personae: the chapel proclaimed him as Solomon. As described in I Kings 6, Solomon's Temple had three components: the porch (*'ulam*) at one end, the Great Chamber (*hekhal* or *cella*) and, beyond, the Holy of Holies (*devir*), producing a total length : breadth ratio of 3.5:1. The height of the *cella* was 1.5 times the width, providing (although the Temple's end components were taller) an overall proportion of 1:3.5:1.5; as used also on Constantine's Old St Peter's, Rome.[3] These are also the proportions of the Chapel Royal.[4]

1 The near identical, console-bracketed Newark and Spedlins chimney piecess are likewise Italianate, possibly derived from Sebastiano Serlio, *Architettura et Prospettiva* (Venice, 1619; repr. Farnborough, 1964).

2 There was a 'pirament at the chaippell dore' (*MWA*, ii, 239), and a reference to 'the foir entrie of the chaippill with the pillaris and haill ordour thairof with the armes housingis crownellis [pediments] and siferis with tua new tafrellis [decorative panels?] to the housing' (ibid., 256). Is the pyramid an allusion to the pinnacle of Solomon's temple which featured in the Temptation of Christ? Cf. Luke 4:9.

3 T.C. Bannister, 'The Constantinian Basilica of Saint Peter at Rome', *Journal of the Society of Architectural Historians*, xxvii (1968).

4 Interior measurements of 31.685 x 9.030m give a ratio of 1:3.5 (9.030 x 3.5 = 31.605; a discrepancy of 0.08m; alternatively, 31.685/ 3.5 = 9.0528; a discrepancy of 0.0228). I am grateful to Graeme McMorran of Historic Scotland for providing such precise dimensions. The distance between floor and underside of tie-beam is 0.75 that of the width and half the overall height, giving a width : full-height ratio of 1:1.5. David Stevenson argues that seventeenth-century masonic lodges represented a notional re-creation of Solomon's Temple: D. Stevenson, *The First Freemasons* (Aberdeen, 1988), 7. Perhaps the partition at the east end of the chapel created a square, alluding to James and the great dignitaries occupying a notional 'Holy of Holies'. A dedication (1500) to James IV at King's College Aberdeen—with its imperial crown spire—stated the commencement date as 2 Apr., which was computed as the commencement date of Solomon's Temple: Stevenson, *Freemasonry*, 24. The King's College plan appears likewise

Moreover, the centre door is flanked on each side by three windows, containing six apertures—totalling twelve lights plus a door.[1] This one plus twelve formula represented Christ and his apostles. When this image was visually expressed, Christ was typically placed exactly central, the apostles in sixes, flanking, as in Leonardo da Vinci's *Last Supper* (1495-8). The formula was later used by James VII at his Thistle Chapel (1688), and by Louis XIV in his pavilion disposition at Marly (1679). Round-arched windows of the type used at Stirling had been illustrated, also in groups of three, in sixteenth-century religious commentaries, in connection with Ezekiel's visionary replacement of the first temple.[2] Not only—the architecture asserted—had James the God-given virtues of Solomon, and the semi-divine status his philosophical tracts claimed, but also Biblical legitimacy for his theology. And there were also, no doubt, allusions to Henry's status.[3] The Ezekiel allusions, if intentional, would show the new prince as symbolic almost of the new Messiah, of a new Jerusalem, and a new Solomon in a new Temple.[4]

James loved and used symbolism. For him, rapid completion of the chapel was so important that not only had he 'the supply of the greatest number of artificers in the whole country, convened there of all craftes for that service', but he personally undertook the function of 'dayly overseer, with large and liberall payment'.[5] The interior was lavish, with cloth of gold and tapestries; the sense of drama was heightened by partitioning, and James's throne at the north-east end. The ceremony was delayed until the English ambassadors arrived. It was important that they witnessed the regal grandeur and scholarly sophistication of this event and heard a recitation of royal pedigrees, in which the closeness of the Scottish and English dynasties was emphasised, and Patrick Galloway's sermon on Genesis 21; possibly to verse 13, or more especially, verse 18: 'Arise, lift up the lad, and hold him in thine hand; for I

to use proportions derived from the Temple. The 1:3.5 ratio relates to internal breadth : length from doorway to steps beyond founder's tomb (which area, significantly, is divided into double-square nave—square choir—half-square, beyond); the ratio may also apply externally, to overall breath : length). Plan in F. Eeles, *King's College Chapel Aberdeen* (Edinburgh, 1956), 271.

1 Did the columns represent the four evangelists? Had the doorway royal symbolism? Compare John 10:9, 'I am the door: by me if any man enter in, he shall be saved'.

2 Ezekiel 40-1; H. Rosenau, *Vision of the Temple* (London, 1979), 59 and *passim*. I am grateful to Ian Campbell for drawing my attention to these illustrations.

3 For example, Christ was brought as an infant to the Temple, 'to present him to the Lord': Luke 2:22, 27. He was aged twelve when he went missing, and was found in learned discussion with the theologians in the Temple: Luke 2:42-9.

4 The dimensions of Solomon's Temple were 70 x 20 cubits. At Stirling, this would result in a cubit length of about 0.45m (17.7 inches)—within the known range of ancient cubit measurements, between 17 and 21 inches: *Cambridge Companion to the Bible* (Cambridge, 1997), 147.

5 'A true reportaire of the baptisme of the Prince of Scotland', in H.W. Meikle (ed.), *The Works of William Fowler*, 2 vols. (STS, 1936), ii, 171.

will make him a great nation'. The allusion to anticipated regnal union, made before a select, international audience, can hardly have been blunter or louder. This sophisticated, classical and Biblically-inspired building was the venue in which James could impress the world, and legitimately and publicly stake his dynastic claim. Stewart architectural patronage and iconographically-laden classicism were now wedded. Clearly, Shaw's sophisticated design made the chapel a paradigmatic work of the Scottish Renaissance, important both for James's kingship and the history of freemasonry. Schaw himself may have been an important disseminator of classicism and architectural intellectualism throughout Britain.

VI

Sir David Cunningham of Robertland, master of works between 1602 and 1607, was the son and namesake of a man who fled to Denmark after his part in the murder of the earl of Eglinton in 1586. Cunningham the elder was received at the Danish royal court, was pardoned when King James visited Denmark, and returned to Scotland. He became one of the royal stablers.[1] Here again is a Danish link, and it is tempting to wonder whether Danish court architecture might have been studied by the younger Cunningham.

No Scottish buildings have a documented association with Cunningham, though a single pediment at Robertland, bearing the monogram of James and Anna and evidently from the long-demolished house, may date from his time. He presumably worked on William Schaw's monument in Dunfermline (*c.*1605), for it was raised at Anna's instruction. The monument bears an extraordinary number of mason's marks, all (except on the monogram stone) of one design. An identical mason's mark is seen on the Glencairn monument at Kilmaurs, together with the inscription 'WROCHT BE DAVID SCWGAL MASSON BURGES IN CAREL [Crail] 1600'. There can be little doubt that Scougal was responsible for both monuments, and perhaps he also worked on a similar monument at Ballantrae to Kennedy of Bargany. Is it significant that of these three related designs, one was a royal work, presumably involving the master of works, while the other two monuments are in Cunningham's native Ayrshire?

Cunningham went to England with his king, indicating that James required an architect familiar with the royal agenda. In June 1603 he was given the post equivalent to that of master of works in England, that of Surveyor, which he held until April 1606.[2] His contribution there has yet to be properly assessed.[3] In 1606, his new year gift to King James was 'a

1 *Hist. KJVI*, 239-40.
2 H. Colvin (ed.), *The History of the King's Works*, 6 vols. (London, 1963-82), iv, 105.
3 M. Girouard, 'Designs for a lodge at Ampthill', in H. Colvin and J. Harris (eds.), *The Country Seat* (Harmondsworth, 1970), 15, and *King's Works*, iii, 105-6, both dismiss him.

platt of an upright' (an architectural drawing), indicating the ability to make architectural compositions.[1] The term 'architectus' was used of him, posthumously, in 1614.[2]

Tantalisingly little is known of Cunningham, but perhaps he was talented. Two English designs are associated with him in his capacity as Surveyor: the Banqueting House at Whitehall (predecessor of Jones's better-known survivor) and a hunting lodge at Ampthill. In England, both designs are considered unusually forward-looking: the latter described as 'for 1603 [?*recte* 1605] a remarkably classical conception', the former as 'a rather advanced plan'.[3] This might be consistent with an architect coming from a land whose associations with classicism differed from those of England. Ultimately though, we pass Cunningham by, uncertain yet as to his architectural contribution. A reappraisal of his career is required.

VII

James VI's last master of works was Sir James Murray of Kilbaberton, who held the post between 1607 and 1634. He was of the Falahill family. His father and namesake (d. 1615), a master wright, was in royal service from at least 1575, and in 1601 was appointed master overseer.[4] Murray the younger is first on record in the royal works in 1594, as a wright, but by 1597 he was engaged in first of a series of special duties for the crown, 'transporting of xxviii deir' to Falkland.[5] Friends of Murray included Sir William Dick, the wealthiest of Edinburgh's merchants, and Sir Henry Wardlaw of Pitreavie, receiver of crown rents (Murray was godfather to a Wardlaw child). To Sir Gideon Murray of Elibank, he was (albeit not necessarily a blood relation) 'nevoy' (nephew). In December 1607 he was appointed 'principall master of all his majesties warkis and buildingis'; he held this post until his death in 1634.[6] In 1628, he was conjoined in post with Sir Anthony Alexander, son of Sir William, one-time poet friend of James, subsequently Charles's secretary for Scotland.

The orthodox view that William Wallace (d. 1631), king's master mason, was the outstanding royal architect of this period, now seems doubtful. Reappraisal of the evidence produces nothing to substantiate that reputation; he was probably a skilled designer, but as regards the *royal* works, Wallace is found only in the role of operative, being paid

1 J. Nichols, *The Progresses, Processions and Magnificent Festivities of James I...*, 4 vols. (London, 1828), i, 596.

2 *RMS*, vii, 986.

3 *King's Works*, iv, 46; J. Harris and G. Higgot (eds.), *Inigo Jones: Complete Architectural Drawings* (New York, 1989), 108.

4 This was given in succession to the late sir William MacDowell, suggesting that the post may have been dormant since his time: *TA*, xiii, 81; *MWA*, i, p. xxxvii.

5 *Edin. Recs.*, v, 113; *Letters to King James The Sixth* (Maitland Club, 1835), p. lxxiii.

6 *MWA*, i, p. xxix.

for specific tasks.[1] Where, in the royal works, he is given a further designation, it is that of 'carver'—again, hardly suggestive of the role of architect.[2] Murray, who recommended Wallace for the post of master mason, is on the other hand seen only in the role of supervisor, having supreme authority over works, and generally fulfilling the role of architect. He is known to have designed two major buildings: the earl of Dunbar's colossal, though long-gone house in Berwick (work abandoned 1611), and Parliament House, designed in 1632.[3] He was regarded by the captain of Berwick as potentially suitable for building a new stone bridge there, where technical complexities suggested the work to be beyond local expertise.[4] Perhaps he had an input to other great courtier houses, such as Culross Abbey House and Pinkie.

Murray's royal works included preparation of the palaces for the 1617 royal visit, notably reconstruction of Edinburgh (1615-17), where Wallace was engaged as master mason and carver, and Holyrood, where (presumably as a preamble to what became the Five Articles of Perth) the royal chapel was set up for what seemed to many to be Anglican-style worship, with English craftsmen employed. At Edinburgh Castle, symmetry was impossible because it incorporated the pre-existing palace, including James's birth-room, which was given an elaborate commemorative painted decoration by James Anderson, underlining its role as historical artefact; but the additions were given the same restrained classicism introduced at the Chapel Royal and the aedicule-windowed Culross Abbey House. Murray's eastern façade, set in the only spot overlooking the High Street, had square bartizans like those at Pinkie and Parliament House. Also like Parliament House, the roof was flat and leaded (as Culross appears to have been) as a viewing platform. Fronting the courtyard and on the north end flank were half-projecting polygonal stair turrets, each containing a main entrance: an arrangement seen previously at royal palaces elsewhere, such as Kronborg and, more famously, Blois.

Linlithgow's north quarter collapsed in 1607, through official neglect. James, who did not visit there in 1617, instructed that it should be rebuilt. Murray began work in 1618. The courtyard façade is symmetrical, dropped down from end towers, a central stair turret of the kind noted at Edinburgh set between smaller openings—an arrangement paralleled

1 E.g. for making a horn for the unicorn of an armorial: *MWA*, ii, 81. Wallace had to transport his 'warklumes', indicating his need to do manual labour: ibid., 134. In 1625, Wallace had two days 'attending' at Ravelston quarry because 'nyne great stanes for the kingis badges [were] to be wrocht in for the rigging of the great hall' at Stirling—where a carver had a particular interest in overseeing: ibid., 170.

2 *MWA*, i, p. xxxv.

3 *King's Works*, iv, 771; *Edin. Recs.*, vii, 119.

4 *King's Works*, iv, 771.

on the flanks of Heriot's Hospital, begun in 1628.[1] The different floors are essentially uniform, enabled by stacked apartments in near-symmetrical disposition, a formula important in the genesis of tenement design. At first floor level, a north-facing gallery, with sophisticated classical chimney-pieces, extended near-full length. Fenestration would have emphasised its presence externally before the palace was burnt.

Despite the losses, something of the fine quality of interior ornament of James's palaces is known from fragments of paintwork, plaster, timber and stonework, and from similar decoration in non-royal architecture. At Edinburgh in 1617, 'paper and floore' were supplied to the painters, presumably wallpaper; John Anderson was also paid for 'furneisching of all sortis of cullouris and warkmanschip with marble dures and chinnayes' (paint marbling of doors and chimneys).[2] The new work at Linlithgow involved

> Johne Binning and James Warkman painteris ... for furnisching all sortis of cullouris and gold ... and lykwayes ... for painting and laying over with oyle cullour and for gilting with gold the haill foir face of the new wark with the timber windowis and window brodis staine windowis and crownellis.[3]

These palaces must have been astonishingly beautiful.

The 1620s saw development of the new style, exemplified by Heriot's (1628), while both Parliament House and the Moray House gatepiers (mid-1620s) introduced hints of an 'antique' Roman monumentality. Influenced by North European Mannerism, some English references are also identifiable: Winton's parapet, for instance, is a version of that at Haddon Hall. Murray's own house, Kilbaberton (with 1622 and 1623 datestones), survives, its flank aligned upon Edinburgh Castle: another illustration of the Scottish Historical Landscape. A symmetrical U-plan, it is compellingly similar to Wardlaw's Pitreavie and to the apparently very dissimilar (because of the return to the ideas of asymmetry and of unequal sized end towers) Winton. All share a repertoire of ornament.[4] Visual links confirm, or extend, the documentary possibilities.

James died during Murray's term in office. But the fashions of his reign continued to develop, with new ideas and responses to new situations—for instance, at Glasgow College. With Alexander's death in 1637, and political strife thereafter, the mastership of works, despite being temporarily revived from 1671 as a 'surveyorship' for Bruce and Smith, was

1 This was also paralleled in vernacular form at Lamb's House, Leith, and in half-width at Caerlaverock (1634) and Gladstone's Land, Edinburgh.

2 *MWA*, ii, 79, 81.

3 *MWA*, ii, 269.

4 The chimney piece at Kilbaberton is evidently a stripped version of that at Winton; the chimney-pieces of the Linlithgow gallery were reproduced in variant form in the Argyll Lodging chamber; the pediment sculpture of the palace within Edinburgh Castle is near-identical to pediments at Pitreavie, Parliament House and Kilbaberton.

headed towards irrelevance, becoming a sinecure. The court, especially after 1689, would never again be resident, and the permanent post of royal architect to supervise 'palice [work] devyset or to be devyset' was hardly necessary.

VIII

Architectural commissions for the crown served far more than the private requirements of James or Anna. Each work spread propaganda about James's kingship, including political and theological messages. Translation into architecture of the ideas conceived by or for James was the responsiblity of his architects—who, it is now suggested, were his masters of works. James Murray, it is increasingly clear, was the driving force behind the new architecture of the second and third decades of the seventeenth century. Others must have contributed to design; masons and other tradesmen, of course, but presumably royal advisers and intellectuals, theologians and classicists, and surely—in enormous measure—James himself, at the Chapel Royal if not elsewhere. A significant input may have been made by Chancellor Dunfermline, who, reportedly, was skilled in architecture, building himself an astonishingly sophisticated classical villa at Pinkie (1613)—which, like the royal works, was crammed with imagery.[1] We have also seen similar work used in high-status, non-royal architecture, indicating the existence of a group of court designers and craftsmen being employed by others of high rank. The resident court had been generous in providing architectural patronage, and ready to exploit its allegorical potential; the absentee court similarly so.[2] Only with the Covenanting wars of the mid-century did this royal investment stall, and only after 1689 did it cease, until the nineteenth century.

1 M. Bath, 'Alexander Seton's painted gallery', in L. Gent (ed.), *Albion's Classicism* (New Haven, NY, 1995); Stevenson, *Freemasonry*, 29. Dunfermline is said to have designed old Somerville House (renamed Drum) part-incorporated within the existing pavilion. Architectural study was also a gentlemanly pursuit later in the century, as demonstrated by Sir William Bruce and the eleventh earl of Mar.

2 An important legacy of James's pre-1603 patronage would appear to have been Stuart commissions after 1603 to Inigo Jones, which for a time, through precocious buildings such as the Banqueting House, Whitehall (from 1619), placed England at the forefront of architectural accomplishment north of the Alps.

~ 10 ~

James VI and the General Assembly, 1586-1618

Alan R. MacDonald

James VI regarded himself as the benevolent 'nursing father' of the Kirk, supporting and nurturing religion in Scotland.[1] Recent historiography seems to support this to an extent, portraying the first six or seven years of his personal reign (which began in the last few months of 1585) as a period of 'peace' or 'harmony' between the crown and the Kirk, characterised by a lack of controversy over polity.[2] After 1592, however, a gradual deterioration of relations which culminated in open conflict in 1596 has been noted. The period between 1597 and 1610 is then seen as having experienced a unity of royal policy and mainstream clerical sentiment. The king is said to have gradually asserted his power over the Kirk, notably in general assemblies and through the reintroduction of episcopacy. This was done with the consent of the majority of the ministry and was made possible by the marginalisation of the 'Melvillians'.

This phase in the history of the Kirk has then been contrasted with the second decade of the seventeenth century in which a new royal policy, encompassing liturgical change rather than the form of ecclesiastical government, was pursued.[3] This new policy has been contrasted with that prior to 1610 by the assertion that it was resisted by most of the ministry, unlike its precursor which was concerned solely with changing the polity of the Kirk to shift the balance of power in favour of the episcopate. The years after 1610 have thus been portrayed as having witnessed the loss of clerical confidence in James VI's ecclesiastical policy, which had thus overstepped the bounds of acceptability.

The historiography of the Jacobean Kirk has long suffered from a concentration on the issue of the episcopate, and on the ideology, for want of a better term, known as Melvillianism.[4] These themes have commonly been portrayed as having acted in tandem: ecclesiastical

1 James VI, *Basilicon Doron*, i, 81.

2 M. Lee, *Great Britain's Solomon: James VI and I in His Three Kingdoms* (Urbana, Ill., 1990), 68; M. Lynch, *Scotland: a New History* (London, 1991), 233.

3 G. Donaldson, *Scotland: James V—James VII* (Edinburgh, 1965), 207; W.R. Foster, *The Church Before the Covenants, 1596-1638* (Edinburgh, 1975), 199-200; D.G. Mullan, *Episcopacy in Scotland: the History of an Idea, 1560-1638* (Edinburgh, 1986), 197.

4 Mullan, *Episcopacy*; Foster, *Church Before the Covenants*; Donaldson, *James V—James VII*; J. Kirk, 'The Development of the Melvillian Movement in Late Sixteenth-century Scotland' (University of Edinburgh Ph.D. thesis, 1972). None of these works deals solely with the Jacobean Kirk, all of them covering different timescales.

politics under James VI being envisaged as essentially a battle between entrenched episcopalian and presbyterian parties. The course of events, when looked at in strictly political and ideological terms, could be said to bear this thesis out. Superficially, the Kirk appears to have been dominated initially by presbyterians—commonly called Melvillians after their supposed leader Andrew Melville. There is, however, no firm evidence that Andrew Melville was the leader of an ecclestiastical faction nor that he was any more prominent in the Kirk than many others. His fame may derive largely from Thomas McCrie's view of him as the successor to John Knox who had been given a peculiarly pre-eminent role by general assemblies of the 1560s.[1] This 'Melvillian' dominance seems to have been followed by their loss of power in the face of royal intervention after 1596 and the ultimate triumph of an episcopalian polity in 1610. A detailed examination of the sources for the period, and of the relations between the king and the general assembly in particular, leads to the emergence of a very different picture.

I

There was, indeed, a marked deterioration in relations between the king and the Kirk in the years after 1592. It is difficult, however, to demonstrate that, during the preceding years, the relationship had been a harmonious one. Tension was clear and recurrent, most notably over the king's persistent reluctance to enforce anti-Catholic legislation. General assemblies between 1586 and 1589 repeatedly called for royal action against Catholic nobles, Jesuit missionaries and the alleged growth in grass-roots Catholicism. Rather than respond positively, the king used these demands, and consequent re-enactments of anti-Catholic legislation, as bargaining counters with the Kirk. In its calls for the laws against Jesuits to be enforced, the assembly of June 1587 illustrates this well. The king did not comply with the Kirk's request; instead he demanded a role in the trial of Patrick Adamson, archbishop of St Andrews, for having suppressed presbyteries while prominent in the government headed by the earl of Arran in 1584-5. James also insisted that the assembly should admonish two ministers who had refused to pray for Mary prior to her execution by Queen Elizabeth in February of that year; finally, he demanded that the Kirk should receive Robert Montgomery, the deposed archbishop of Glasgow, back into its bosom and annul the excommunication of the Catholic laird of Fintry. The assembly ignored the royal requests, just as he had ignored theirs, and renewed its calls for the persecution of Catholics.[2]

1 T. McCrie, *Life of John Knox* (Edinburgh, 1811) and *Life of Andrew Melville* (Edinburgh, 1819); A.R. MacDonald, *The Jacobean Kirk, 1567-1625: Sovereignty, Polity and Liturgy* (Aldershot, 1998), 2-3, 171-5.

2 *BUK*, ii, 697-701; Calderwood, *History*, iv, 627-32.

In 1589 and 1590, peace between the king and the Kirk prevailed for a brief spell. In February 1589, Richard Bancroft, later to become the archbishop of Canterbury, delivered a sermon at Paul's Cross in London which was extremely critical both of presbyterianism and of James's toleration of it.[1] What little affection for presbyterianism James may have had was kindled. The recently-failed, yet nonetheless alarming, Spanish Armada, combined with continued calls for action against the openly Catholic earl of Huntly, gave James an opportunity to demonstrate his Protestant zeal as well as his power within his own realm. Correspondence between Scottish Catholic nobles and Spain, and their open rebellion in March, led to the king undertaking a military expedition to the north-east. As a result, the earls of Huntly and Crawford were warded for treason.[2] James also reacted angrily to Bancroft's sermon, leading to some delicate diplomatic exchanges with England and an apology from Bancroft in the following year. All this endeared him to the Kirk as never before.[3] The prospect of a Protestant royal marriage, and James's absence in Scandinavia for it, aided this. In August 1590, the recently-returned, newly-married king addressed the general assembly, praising the Kirk for its doctrinal purity and comparing the English church unfavourably with it, saying that it had an 'evill said messe in English, wanting nothing but the liftings'.[4] James also promised augmentation of stipends and invited any minister who perceived personal shortcomings in his monarch to admonish him privately. The assembled ministers and laity gave him a fifteen-minute ovation.

Tensions, however, remained. The king's request for private admonition contained an implicit demand for the eradication of *public* criticism. James had also gone some way towards asserting royal supremacy by claiming a particular right, as monarch, to censure the Kirk. The assembly, for its part, clearly afraid to jeopardise this new-found and fragile understanding, had shelved proceedings against Patrick Adamson explicitly to avoid offence to James.[5] Royal failure to carry through the measures taken against Huntly and Crawford—they were not kept in ward for long—led to a renewal of demands for action from assemblies in 1590 and 1591.[6] The king's honeymoon with the Kirk had been short-lived.

1 Calderwood, *History*, v, 5-6.

2 Calderwood, *History*, v, 7-12, 14-36; Spottiswoode, *History*, ii, 390-8; see also R. Grant, 'The Brig o' Dee affair, the sixth earl of Huntly and the politics of the Counter Reformation', Chapter 5 above.

3 Robert Bowes to Lord Burghley, 24 Oct. 1590, same to same, 7 Dec. 1590, and same to same, 13 Jan. 1591, *CSP Scot.*, x, 409-10, 432, 448.

4 *BUK*, ii, 771.

5 *BUK*, ii, 762-78; Melville, *Diary*, 288.

6 *BUK*, ii, 772, 784; Bowes to Burghley, 26 July 1591, *CSP Scot.*, x, 547.

Early in 1592, this underlying unease erupted once more into vociferous opposition from the Kirk to royal lenience to Catholics. In February, the earl of Moray was murdered by the earl of Huntly's men and, in spite of the outcry from many pulpits, the king refused to punish him significantly. The general assembly, meeting in May, stepped up demands for action against Catholics and called for greater support for the Kirk from the state.[1] In an attempt apparently to placate this opposition, parliament, meeting at Edinburgh in June, passed what has become known as the Golden Act.[2] That name, however, was not a contemporary appellation. It was probably coined in seventeenth-century hindsight, contrasting it with the Black Acts of 1584, and harking back to a lost, and mythical, golden age.[3]

By recognising the presbyterian system of ecclesiastical government, the act acknowledged that the episcopate had virtually atrophied. The Golden Act can also, however, be portrayed convincingly as a reassertion of royal supremacy. It did not annul those of the Black Acts of 1584 which had asserted the supremacy of the king over all estates,[4] nor did it effectively supersede them. By the very fact that the civil authority had legislated on ecclesiastical matters, the act implicitly denied any separation or equality of the civil and ecclesiastical jurisdictions. It emphasised that the state could and would ratify ecclesiastical legislation and organisational structures with no reciprocal powers over civil legislation for the Kirk. The royal supremacy, asserted in 1584, remained in place; the only thing which was absent was the episcopate.

Perhaps the most significant provision of the Golden Act, indeed the English ambassador saw it as such at the time, was its assertion of the right of the king to name the time and the place for meetings of future general assemblies.[5] This had been a matter in dispute since the fall, in November 1585, of the Arran regime, which had passed the Black Acts and suppressed general assemblies. With the coming to personal rule of James VI, there was a Protestant monarch—a 'godly prince'—on the Scottish throne for the first time; a new relationship between the Kirk and the state was bound to be established. What that relationship was to be remained unclear, with the right to call general assemblies claimed by both the king and the assembly itself. Soon after the parliament of 1592 had risen, the privy council, in order to set the seal on the royal supremacy inherent in the Golden Act, formally proclaimed the date and place of the next general assembly.[6]

1 *BUK*, ii, 786-8; Calderwood, *History*, v, 156-8.

2 *APS*, iii, 541-2, c. 8.

3 The origins of the term are obscure; James Melville, David Calderwood, John Spottiswoode, John Row and William Scot do not appear to have used it in their works.

4 *APS*, iii, 292-4, cc. 2-6.

5 Bowes to Burghley, 6 June 1592, *CSP Scot.*, x, 685.

6 The council register left date and place blank and the record of the proclamation in the

Despite the ovation of 1590, and the apparent agreement signalled by the Golden Act, the predominant theme of the early 1590s was not a developing amity but continuing friction. Kirk and king held fast to their respective positions of demanding action against Catholics and refusing to respond positively. Between the last few months of 1594 and the beginning of 1596, however, another brief warming of relations occurred. After continued demands from general assemblies in 1593 and 1594, pressure from England and open rebellion by the earl of Huntly (now allied to Francis Stewart, earl of Bothwell, whom the king hated), decisive action was at last taken.[1] The parliament of June 1594 forfeited Huntly and his Catholic colleagues, the earls of Errol and Angus.[2] In September, after a number of procrastinations caused by postponements of the baptism of Prince Henry, the king undertook a military expedition to the north. Huntly and Errol fled to the Continent and were forbidden to return to Scotland without the king's permission, subject to the approval of the Kirk.[3] They would not, in other words, be allowed to come home unless they renounced their faith. The Kirk was satisfied, for the time being at least.

By the beginning of 1596, however, ecclesiastical dissatisfaction was emerging once more. On returning south after his action against Huntly and Errol, the king had left the duke of Lennox, Huntly's brother-in-law, as his lieutenant in the north. Instead of the forfeited property of the Catholic earls being broken up and distributed to others, as had happened to that of Bothwell, it had been given into the hands of their wives.[4] This aroused suspicion and resentment among the ministry, for it allowed for the full restoration of the earls to their lands at a future date. Added to this was the appointment, early in 1596, of a group of eight financial administrators—the Octavians. Their remit was to regularise and attempt to restore to order the disastrous financial situation of the crown but many of them, notably Alexander Seton (the future earl of Dunfermline and chancellor), were suspected of having Catholic sympathies. These suspicions regarding the king's favour to Catholics were confirmed in the eyes of many of the ministry in July, when the earl of Huntly returned to Scotland.[5] The permission of the Kirk had not been

treasurer's accounts does not give the information, so it is unknown what was actually proclaimed: *RPC*, iv, 753, 758; NAS, treasurer's accounts, 1590-2, E22/8, fo. 157r.

1 *BUK*, iii, 796, 821-2; Lord Zouche to Burghley, 15 Jan. 1594, Robert Cecil to Bowes, 23 Jan. 1594, and Cecil to Zouche, 1 Feb. 1594, *CSP Scot.*, xi, 263-5, 268-9, 274-6, and *passim*.

2 *APS*, iv, 56-61.

3 George Nicolson to Bowes, 19 Feb. 1595, *CSP Scot.*, xi, 536-7; Melville, *Diary*, 369, 371. Cf. M. Lynch, 'Court ceremony and ritual during the personal reign of James VI', Chapter 4 above.

4 Calderwood, *History*, v, 363, 416-17. Huntly's wife was Henrietta Stewart, Lennox's sister.

5 Bowes to Burghley, 18 July 1596, and Advices from Scotland, 9 Aug. 1596, *CSP Scot.*, xii, 282, 298-9. He would be formally reconciled to the church in June 1597, but doubts about

sought, let alone granted, and, in spite of the king's protestations to the contrary, it was widely suspected that he had been privy to Huntly's return. Errol soon followed. The Kirk demanded that the returned exiles should be banished once more until the original conditions for their return had been fulfilled. Although James asserted that these conditions would be adhered to, he did nothing to ensure their enforcement.

In the last three months of 1596, the mounting tension between the king and many in the Kirk exploded into open hostility. James VI was publicly criticised from the pulpit, and a standing committee of the Kirk, the commissioners of the general assembly, sat in Edinburgh repeatedly lobbying the king to persuade him to act against the Catholic earls. As hostility increased, David Black, one of the ministers of St Andrews, was accused of treason for having delivered a seditious sermon. He rejected the right of the privy council to judge his speeches from the pulpit, insisting that his presbytery should deal with any accusation the king had to make against him. The commissioners of the general assembly backed this rejection of civil jurisdiction and were banished from Edinburgh at the beginning of December. They refused to leave. When ordered to do so a second time they obeyed, leaving the task of carrying on the fight to the ministers of Edinburgh. On 17 December, a riot broke out after the king rejected some demands which they tried to hand to him in the tolbooth. James fled to Linlithgow and took the privy council with him.[1]

Whatever the exact circumstances of the riot were, as far as James was concerned it had been started by some over-zealous ministers who were, potentially, dangerous revolutionaries. It must thus have become clear to him that the Kirk could not be allowed the degree of freedom which it had enjoyed hitherto. He decided to begin to exercise what he clearly saw was his right to supremacy over all estates and take a firmer grip on the Kirk.

Subsequent events have been seen as the failure of the 'Melvillians' to maintain their grip on power, due to royal exploitation of divisions within their ranks and the coming to the fore of a more moderate majority of the ministry.[2] Analysis of the personnel of general assemblies from the surviving records of assemblies and from the records of the lower courts of the Kirk, however, suggests that some re-evaluation of this view is required. Many of those ministers who, after 1596, became noted moderates or favourers of the king's policy towards the Kirk had been regular attenders at general assemblies since 1586.[3] David Lindsay,

his sincerity continued: *Spalding Miscellany*, ii, pp. lx-lxii.

1 Melville, *Diary*, 371-2, 508-17; Calderwood, *History*, v, 443-515; Spottiswoode, *History*, iii, 9-33; NLS, 'A copy of the acts of the commissioners of the general assembly', Wodrow Quarto, xx, no. 18.

2 Lynch, *Scotland*, 231.

3 *BUK*, *passim*.

later bishop of Ross, and Peter Blackburn, later bishop of Aberdeen, had both been members of a smaller standing commission of the Kirk which had been set up in November 1596 by the commissioners of the general assembly to lobby the crown. Both had also been among those banished from the capital in December.[1] The vast majority of ministers who are known to have attended assemblies prior to 1596 appear to have continued to do so afterwards.[2] The explanation for the changes must therefore be that many ministers shifted their position from opposition to the king to acquiescence—perhaps because of the strength of the king's reaction to the riot, or because they themselves were shocked by the extremism unleashed in the last few months of 1596. Those who are now seen as noted radicals, such as Robert Bruce and James Melville, were the ones who did not change their minds. By maintaining their position, they were redefined as subversives in spite of the fact that, throughout the previous decade, they had been in the mainstream of clerical opinion, at least at general assemblies.

II

In general assemblies over the next few years James VI began to assert his paternal authority as the Kirk's 'nursing father'. He attended every assembly from 1597 until he left to take up the English throne in 1603. The first began at the end of February 1597. This, and the following assembly in May of the same year, met at the same time and in the same town as a convention of the estates, in Perth and Dundee respectively.[3] This was probably a deliberate act by James, making it clear that, as king, he wielded both swords, civil and ecclesiastical. It may even have been an attempt to threaten the Kirk by hinting that the general assembly might become something like the English houses of convocation, where the supreme courts of the church were more regularly subordinate to the civil legislature, meeting at the same time, under the authority of the crown.

At the assembly at Dundee in May, the king further emphasised his authority over the Kirk by nominating the commission of the general assembly.[4] The constitution and functions of this body prior to 1597 are unclear but it had commonly acted as one of the principal channels for conveying to the king the Kirk's views on royal policy, most notably in the last few months of 1596.[5] From May 1597 onwards, the direction of the traffic was reversed, with the commission becoming the medium through which the king dealt with the Kirk. In the words of the official

1 *RPC*, v, 332-3.

2 A.R. MacDonald, 'Ecclesiastical Politics in Scotland, 1586-1610' (University of Edinburgh Ph.D. thesis, 1995), 42, n.126, Appendix 1(a).

3 Calderwood, *History*, v, 607; Melville, *Diary*, 409; Bowes to Burghley, 11 May 1597, *CSP Scot.*, xii, 543.

4 *BUK*, iii, 927-9.

5 MacDonald, 'Ecclesiastical Politics', ch. 3.

record of its establishment, the commissioners were 'generally to give thair advyce to his Majestie in all affaires concerning the weill of the Kirk, and intertainment of peace and obedience to his Majestie within this realme'.[1]

During the general assemblies between 1597 and 1602, the king used a number of means to encourage the acceptance of his ecclesiastical policies. In the assemblies of 1597, 1598 and 1600, what could only be described as a whip system was operated: the king would call individual ministers to him to persuade them to vote in favour of one act or another.[2] Certain people were excluded from assemblies, most notably Andrew Melville and John Johnstone, academics from the university of St Andrews, who were feared by the crown as potential intellectual ringleaders of opposition.[3] Possibly the most significant move of all, however, was the passing of an act in the assembly of 1598 at Dundee which restricted the number of commissioners any presbytery could send to general assemblies. Previously, some presbyteries, most notably those of St Andrews and Edinburgh, had sent very large contingents to assemblies; henceforth each presbytery could send only three ministers and one baron.[4] This eminently reasonable act meant that it would be more difficult for assemblies to be packed by ministers and lairds favouring one particular position. It ensured that the vociferous minority of about twenty or thirty ministers who remained in opposition to the king would be unable to shake the new-found loyalty of so many of their brethren.

As well as attempting to achieve a more even representation of the ministry, James altered the time at which assemblies had been planned to meet. This resulted in there being no assembly at all in 1599, the first year without an assembly since 1585. Attempts during 1598 to reach an agreement between royal representatives and the ministers over a new system of parliamentary representation for the Kirk had failed. James wanted the assembly to set the seal on a final agreement and, because this had not yet been achieved, the assembly was prorogued until 1600.

James VI was attempting to act as a truly absolute monarch for the first time in his reign—endeavouring to wield supreme power over both civil and ecclesiastical spheres. Just as parliaments were held only if the king called them, now general assemblies of the Kirk met exclusively by royal decree. James's treatise on kingship, *Basilicon Doron,* written for his son Henry probably in the late summer of 1598, demonstrates this attitude. He advised Prince Henry that, when he became king, he should 'suffer

1 *BUK,* iii, 928.

2 Melville, *Diary,* 415-16, 530-1; Scot, *Apologetical Narration,* 100, 113; Calderwood, *History,* vi, 16.

3 Calderwood, *History,* v, 683; vi, 16; Melville, *Diary,* 440.

4 *BUK,* iii, 947.

na conventions nor meitings amongst kirkemen but [i.e. except] be youre knauledge & permission.'[1] The time at which this work was written was crucial to the expression of such a sentiment. The king would not have offered such advice at any time prior to the autumn of 1596, which witnessed a serious crisis in his relationship with the Kirk.

Since there appears to have been little opposition to the king's interventions in the operations and legislation of the general assemblies after 1597, the orthodox interpretation of royal power having been asserted in the last few years of the sixteenth century with the consent of most of the ministry must be accepted as valid. The act of the assembly of 1598 appears to have ensured that assemblies were truly representative. This, added to the moderation of clerical opinion resulting from the riot of 17 December 1596, meant that the assemblies of 1600, 1601 and 1602 were more amenable to the king's requests than ever before. In November 1602, an assembly met at the palace of Holyrood. Two of the new parliamentary bishops, David Lindsay of Ross and George Gledstanes of Caithness, were given powers of parochial visitation: hitherto they had had no ecclesiastical function *ex officio*. An annual thanksgiving for the king's delivery from an alleged attempt on his life in 1600 was instituted, and it was agreed that the next assembly should not meet until 1604.[2] The rump of ministers and others who maintained a hostile view of the king's attitude to the Kirk after 1596 had been pushed to the sidelines. Most of the clergy appear to have been satisfied with a royal policy which involved greater control of the Kirk by the crown and a revived parliamentary episcopate with very circumscribed powers.

It appears that, in this accommodation between the Kirk and the king, a *via media* between royal supremacy and ecclesiastical independence had emerged, with the emphasis being placed neither on pure presbyterianism nor on full-blown episcopacy. This was possible because the majority of ministers were not zealously committed to either. They were willing to accept a settlement in which the Kirk remained presbyterian in structure but which also included 'bishops' with some powers of visitation and the right to represent the Kirk in parliament. Some recent work on the English church in this period has attempted to shift the emphasis away from a portrayal of ecclesiastical politics as a clash between Arminians and Puritans—in tacit anticipation of the Laudian ascendancy and the Civil War—towards a perspective which recognises a moderate majority. The study of Scottish ecclesiastical politics might equally benefit from less of an emphasis on presbyterians and episcopalians.[3] If such a moderate majority existed in Scotland and a middle way

1 James VI, *Basilicon Doron*, i, 145-6; ii, 2.

2 *BUK*, iii, 1002, 1008; Calderwood, *History*, vi, 169, 185, 188.

3 P. White, 'The *via media* in the early Stuart Church', in K. Fincham (ed.), *The Early Stuart Church, 1603-1642* (London, 1993). White's work should be read in light of N. Tyacke,

was, indeed, emerging in the Kirk in 1602, it was stifled before it could flourish. King James had the opportunity to put ecclesiastical problems behind him but he was to squander it.

III

Historians appear to have missed the significance of the period between 1602 and 1606. The fact that the assembly of 1602 had been willing to allow nearly two years to pass between one general assembly and the next is crucial. Never before had the Kirk planned to do this. The norm was to hold one or two assemblies per year, and any previous failure to hold an assembly during a whole calendar year had been due to external pressures—their prevention by the Arran regime in 1585 or their prorogation by the king in 1599. At the beginning of April 1603, when James went south, he left a Kirk at peace, which trusted him sufficiently to have had no misgivings about the prospect of a year without an assembly.

In the summer of 1604, James's plans for an incorporating union between Scotland and England emerged and a parliament was called in Scotland to discuss them. Requests came from some quarters in the Kirk that the assembly should meet slightly earlier than had been planned—in May or June rather than in July—so that it could advise the parliamentary representatives of the Kirk as to how they should conduct themselves, as was enshrined in the 'caveats' imposed on the new parliamentary bishops. One of these 'caveats' had stated that the bishops could not vote in parliament without 'express warrant and direction from the church'.[1] The king declared that no assembly was necessary because the parliament would discuss only the plans for union, and any union would leave the Kirk inviolate.[2] The general assembly was then prorogued, indefinitely, until after the completion of an incorporating union with England.[3] It may even have been James's fear of opposition to his dearly-held plan for the union from the Kirk which caused him to prevent this and future assemblies from meeting. The notion certainly existed in November 1604. The earl of Huntly, perhaps wishing to postpone general assemblies to avoid their attentions regarding his religion, wrote to the king reporting that the ministry was 'fasting and preiching maliciouslie againis the union of the kingdomes'.[4]

The prospect of total exclusion from the discussions relating to union with a country which had a very different church alarmed many ministers. Calls for a general assembly grew. As a result, in early 1605, an

'Anglican attitudes: some recent writings on English religious history, from the Reformation to the Civil War', *Journal of British Studies*, xxxv (1996). Whatever the accuracy of White's claims, the interpretation seems to fit the period 1597-1603 in Scotland.

1 Spottiswoode, *History*, iii, 74; Melville, *Diary*, 555.

2 Melville, *Diary*, 555-6; Calderwood, *History*, vi, 264.

3 Melville, *Diary*, 560; Calderwood, *History*, vi, 264.

4 Huntly to James, 20 Nov.-10 Dec. 1604, *LP James VI*, 60-2.

assembly was scheduled for July—but it was then prorogued once more, until 1606. Faced with an unprecedented four years without an assembly, more than twenty ministers from fourteen different presbyteries defied this prorogation and held the assembly, as originally intended, at Aberdeen in July 1605. For thus defying the crown, six of them were convicted of treason by a packed assize and banished to the continent; eight more were internally exiled to remote parts of the realm. This was seen as extreme by many, including Archbishop John Spottiswoode of Glasgow, Bishop David Lindsay of Ross and the presbyteries of the north-east, who had hitherto been favourable to the king's ecclesiastical policy.[1] James had over-reacted.

In the summer of 1606, parliament passed the 'Act anent the restitution of the estate of Bischoppis' which restored all the episcopal revenues to the holders of the thirteen Scottish sees. The same parliament also received a number of petitions relating to the Kirk which it remitted to the general assembly—which, according to a proclamation by the privy council on 1 July, was to meet on the last Tuesday of May 1607.[2] Nearly four years had passed without a general assembly and now parliament appeared to be taking on responsibility for ecclesiastical legislation without giving the assembly the chance to comment. Eight prominent divines, including Andrew and James Melville, were called to the king at Hampton Court, ostensibly to discuss means of ironing out the problem of growing dissension within the Kirk. The two Melvilles were never allowed to return to Scotland and, when the other six obtained permission to go home, their freedom of movement was severely restricted. Not until those ministers involved in the Aberdeen assembly of 1605 who had refused to admit wrongdoing and the eight opposition leaders were safely out of the way did James feel ready to hold another national meeting of the Kirk.

In December 1606, a gathering of ministers who had been nominated entirely by the king, with the advice of his bishops, met at Linlithgow. Allegedly, financial incentives were offered to persuade the ministers there to approve the royal programme and, in the aftermath of the meeting, its acts were tampered with.[3] It had been advertised as a meeting between certain ministers and some nobles of the king's choice to discuss means to eradicate the disagreements, or 'eyelists', within the Kirk. It was explicitly described as a meeting which would lay the ground for a future general assembly. Not until after it had risen was it

1 *RPC*, vii, 105, 260; Spottiswoode to James, 26 Dec. 1605, *Eccles. Letters*, i, 24; NAS, register of the presbytery of Deer, CH2/89/1/1, fo. 62r; NAS, register of the presbytery of Ellon, CH2/146/1, fos. 134r, 136v; NAS, register of the presbytery of Aberdeen, CH2/1/1, fo. 177v.

2 *APS*, iv, 281-4, c. 2; Calderwood, *History*, vi, 492-3; *RPC*, vii, 218-19.

3 Balfour, *Works*, ii, 18; Calderwood, *History*, vi, 622-4; Melville, *Diary*, 685; Donaldson, *James V—James VII*, 205; Mullan, *Episcopacy*, 108; Foster, *Church Before the Covenants*, 112.

17. The Regent Morton or Portcullis Gate, Edinburgh Castle. It was built, like the Half Moon Battery, under the supervision of sir William Macdowell, king's master of works.

18. The Half Moon Battery, Edinburgh Castle. The eastern defences were reconstructed in 1573 after the 'lang siege'.

19. Mar's Wark, Stirling, an elaborate town house built in 1570–2 for John Erskine (d. 1572), 1st earl of Mar, regent of Scotland and hereditary keeper of Stirling Castle.

20. Chimney piece at Carnasserie Castle. The distinctive shafted decoration links this Argyll building with court architecture of the same period, like the Portcullis Gate and Mar's Wark.

21. Fyvie Castle, built *c.* 1596–99 for Alexander Seton (1556–1622), Octavian and later earl of Dunfermline, possibly by his 'true-hearted friend', William Schaw. Its castellated style contrasts with the sharper classicism of court architecture already characteristic by 1600.

22. Seton Palace, an eighteenth-century view by John Clerk of Eldin. The regular, classical block to the left, now demolished, was built by William Schaw after 1585 for Robert, sixth Lord Seton, elder brother of Schaw's friend Alexander Seton.

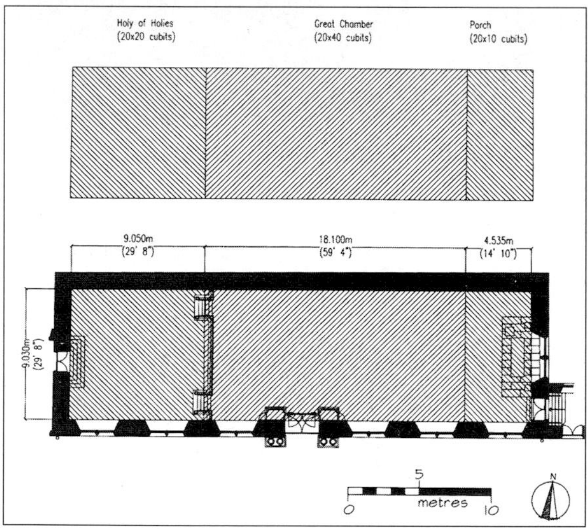

23, 24, 25. *Above:* The Chapel Royal, Stirling Castle, built in 1594 for the baptism of Prince Henry. Its design must have involved William Schaw as master of works. The original interior layout and furnishings are unknown. *Left:* The plan of the Chapel Royal followed Solomon's Temple in its proportions – 3.5 to 1. The interior of the Temple had three components: Porch (*'ulam*), Great Chamber (*hekhal* or *cella*) and Holy of Holies (*devir*). The floor plan is shaded to show how these were reproduced in the Chapel. The image of Solomon had featured in James's iconography since 1579. *Below left:* The Temple of Solomon, in a late fifteenth-century reconstruction by Koberger. The window arrangement, with groups of three paired round-arched lights in arched panels, is similar to the Chapel Royal and may have influenced its design.

26 (*left*). The Monument to William Schaw (d. 1602), king's master of works, in Dunfermline Abbey. It may reflect his links with Queen Anna. Its design may have involved his successor, Sir David Cunningham of Robertland.

27, 28. *Above right:* Baberton House. A small classical country house built by and for James Murray, king's master of works, in 1622–3. *Bottom:* Pitreavie House, built *c.* 1630 for Sir Henry Wardlaw, the king's receiver of rents and a friend of Murray. The close compositional similarities suggest that Murray designed both.

29. The north quarter of Linlithgow Palace, rebuilt in 1618 onwards by James Murray, king's master of works.

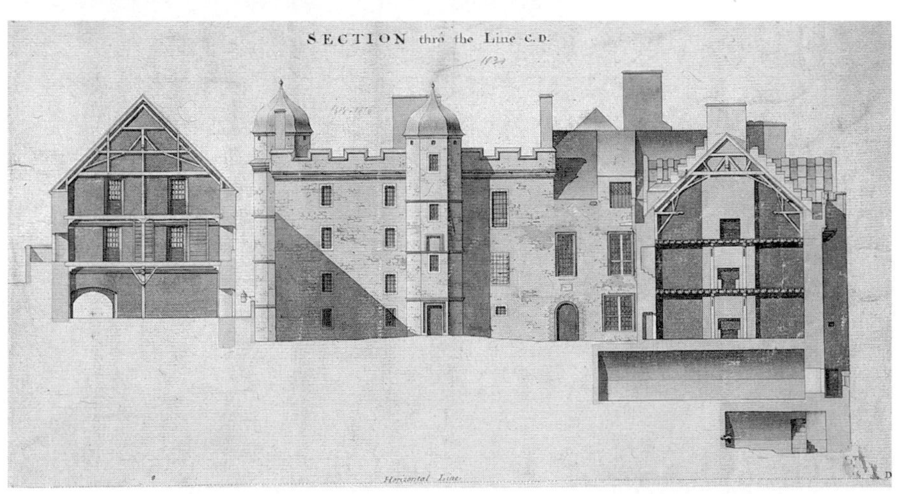

30. Edinburgh Castle: the palace block, in an eighteenth-century surveyor's drawing. The façade (since much altered) was reconstructed by James Murray as master of works and William Wallace, master mason, 1615–17.

31. Monument to John Byres of Coates (d. 1629), Edinburgh Greyfriars, executed by William Wallace, king's master mason. The master mason, unlike the master of works, was an operative.

32. In 1583 Sir Robert Drummond of Carnock, master of works, proposed that the palace at Stirling Castle have a high-level structure built on it, enjoying views of the kingdom in all directions.

33. View from Edinburgh Castle's palace roof platform, built for James's visit in 1617. It shows a historical townscape, involving nature, his 'heid burgh' and the symbolic structures of St Giles' and Holyroodhouse. The direct view into the courtyard at Holyroodhouse is particularly striking.

34. The birth room of James VI, Edinburgh Castle. Its interior was given its commemorative paintwork in preparation for James's visit in 1617. It had become a national shrine.

actually described as a general assembly. It seems that four years without assemblies, combined with heavy-handed treatment of ministers who had resisted royal policy, had pushed such a large number of the ministry into opposition to the crown's ecclesiastical policy that the king no longer felt that he could rely on the support of the majority of the clergy. Why else had he felt the need for such secrecy and deceit and why had he felt it necessary to renege on the act of 1598 for the representation of presbyteries at general assemblies? That act would have ensured that assemblies were as representative as possible—but an assembly which was broadly representative of the Kirk was something which, by this time, the king and his bishops were obviously not prepared to risk.

The 'assembly' at Linlithgow in December 1606 marked the beginning of an entirely new phase of royal intervention in the Kirk. In 1607 and 1609, no assemblies were allowed to meet because of widespread opposition to constant moderation of presbyteries and synods. This scheme, introduced in the aftermath of the 'assembly' at Linlithgow in 1606, involved a bishop or his appointee moderating presbyteries and synods indefinitely—previously both bodies had regularly elected their own moderators. Constant moderators for presbyteries had been approved at Linlithgow but, subsequently, the acts of the 'assembly' had been altered to make it appear that constant moderation of provincial synods, by bishops, had also been consented to. The assembly of 1608 was largely, if not entirely, nominated by the king and the bishops and James wrote to it threatening action against any who opposed the proposals sent up from court.[1] In February 1610, the general assembly, which had been continually postponed throughout 1609, was prorogued *sine die*.[2]

Soon afterwards, the power of the episcopate was further enhanced with the creation of two courts of high commission, one under each archbishop, which were to be supreme in all cases of ecclesiastical discipline. With no appeal to the general assembly, their establishment was designed to remove the necessity of frequent meetings of that body which was proving difficult to control. The king then decided that an assembly could be held, if only to give those new powers the appearance of the approval of the Kirk. As in 1606, the assembly which met in Glasgow in June 1610 was entirely nominated by the crown. Bribes totalling 10,000 merks (£6,666) were distributed among the ministers. The acts, including ones which recognised the new episcopal powers, ratified the royal supremacy and re-enacted constant moderators for synods (almost an admission of the falsification of the record of the 1606

1 Calderwood, *History*, vi, 705, 751; James to the provost of Glasgow, 14 June 1608, and James to the general assembly, 20 July 1608, *Eccles. Letters*, i, 142-5; Scot, *Apologetical Narration*, 202.

2 *RPC*, viii, 413.

assembly), were pushed through *en bloc*.[1] After the assembly had risen, a proclamation was issued by the privy council forbidding criticism of the acts of the assembly under pain of imprisonment.[2]

The techniques used by the crown to ensure consent in general assemblies hardly suggest that 'the vast majority' or the 'great majority' of the ministry accepted the legislation of 1610, nor can that assembly be said to have been the 'final completion of the task' as far as James's control of the Kirk was concerned.[3] If widespread consent had existed, there would have been no reason for the crown to go to such lengths to achieve success. The policy of the crown, the nature of general assemblies and the reactions of the ministry must cast strong doubts on the historiographical consensus that widespread opposition came only as a result of attempts at liturgical innovation after 1610. In the second decade of the seventeenth century, the fact that the king wanted to introduce liturgical change was new but the techniques he used to enforce the change and the incidence of opposition were not.

IV

In 1614, the liturgical innovations began. A proclamation was issued commanding that communion be held on Easter Sunday and this order was renewed in 1615.[4] The first assembly to meet after 1610 took place at Aberdeen in July 1616. Its membership, and that of the assemblies in 1617 and 1618, was manipulated by the episcopate through its power over the assignation of stipends (granted to it in 1607), and its moderation of diocesan synods. Constant moderators of presbyteries and the bishops could attend the assembly *ex officio*, while the lay contingent of the assembly was called to attend by personal letters from the king. John Spottiswoode, archbishop of St Andrews, moderated the assembly of 1616 without election. The newly unified court of high commission under the archbishop of St Andrews was given the assembly's *de facto* approval by being mentioned in an act against Catholicism. Confirmation of the young by bishops was instituted. It was agreed to draw up canons for the Kirk from the acts of previous assemblies, and to have a standard liturgy composed. The choice of which acts of previous assemblies would be included in these canons was to be made by ministers chosen by the king.[5]

1 James VI to the earl of Dunbar, 8 May 1610, *Eccles. Letters*, i, 425* (Additional Letters and Notes); *BUK*, iii, 1092-8; Calderwood, *History*, vii, 70, 95-101; Melville, *Diary*, 793.

2 *RPC*, viii, 616.

3 Foster, *Church Before the Covenants*, 29; Donaldson, *James V—James VII*, 207; Lee, *Great Britain's Solomon*, 81.

4 Scot, *Apologetical Narration*, 238; Row, *History*, 302; I.B. Cowan, 'The Five Articles of Perth', in D. Shaw (ed.), *Reformation and Revolution* (Edinburgh, 1967), 160.

5 Calderwood, *History*, vii, 233; viii, 67; Scot, *Apologetical Narration*, 240-4; Spottiswoode, *History*, iii, 235; James to Sir Andrew Murray of Balvaird, 18 July 1616, and James to the earl of Montrose, 27 Aug. 1616, *Eccles. Letters*, ii, 481-4.

King James's only visit to Scotland after 1603 took place in the summer of 1617. Some of the bishops and nobles attended a service at the palace of Holyrood and knelt to take communion in a service conducted according to the English liturgy. Choristers had been brought north by the king and an organ had been installed in the chapel—both absent from the Kirk's services since the Reformation.[1] In June, parliament met with the king present. He declared that 'the bishops must rule the ministers and the King rule both in matters indifferent', by which he meant ecclesiastical polity and liturgy, rather than doctrine. An act was then passed introducing the election of bishops by their chapters—thus removing the nominal role of the general assembly in their choice. The chapter was given the power formally to 'elect' the king's nominee.[2] Another proposed act, giving the king, with the advice of the bishops and any ministers whom he chose to consult, absolute power over the polity of the Kirk, proved so controversial that it had to be withdrawn. James, however, declared that the act was unnecessary because the royal prerogative endowed him with him such powers anyway.[3]

As was common, many ministers were in Edinburgh while parliament was meeting. A protestation was drawn up and signed by fifty-five of them.[4] The three who had been most prominent in its instigation, formulation and distribution were severely dealt with. Peter Hewat was deprived of his parish and warded, Archibald Simpson was warded, and David Calderwood was deprived and banished from the realm. King James was making it clear that opposition was unwelcome. In spite of, or perhaps because of, all these persuasive tactics, the assembly of November 1617 rejected the king's five articles—kneeling at communion, confirmation of children by a bishop, private baptism, private communion and the celebration of holy days (Christmas, Good Friday, Easter, Ascension and Whitsun or Pentecost).[5] The articles have become known as the Five Articles of Perth for it was there, at the general assembly in the following year, that they were passed.

James allowed the assembly at Perth in 1618 to meet only so that it could formally approve the articles. Epitomising his belief in his ability to govern Scotland with his pen, he addressed a letter to the assembly declaring that 'we will not be content with anything but a simple and direct acceptation of these articles'.[6] The royal guard was present, the king having told the privy council: 'It is Oure ... pleasoure that ye gif order to the Capitane of Oure guaird, with his horsemen, to attend Oure ... commissionaris during all the tyme of the said Assemblie'.

1 Calderwood, *History*, vii, 246-7; Scot, *Apologetical Narration*, 246; Row, *History*, 307.
2 *APS*, iv, 529.
3 Scot, *Apologetical Narration*, 246; Spottiswoode, *History*, iii, 241.
4 Scot, *Apologetical Narration*, 248-9; Row, *History*, 310-11; Calderwood, *History*, vii, 251-9.
5 Calderwood, *History*, vii, 284-6.
6 Spottiswoode, *History*, iii, 253.

The ministers attending the assembly were made to stand throughout its proceedings while the nobles, officers of state and bishops sat. Debate was restricted by the moderator, Spottiswoode; those who would oppose the articles were threatened with the loss of their stipends and banishment from the realm.[1] As had happened with the acts of the assembly at Glasgow in 1610, the Articles were not debated individually but pushed through *en bloc*. After that, no more assemblies met for another twenty years.

V

James VI was rarely on amicable terms with his Kirk, and this was strongly reflected in his turbulent relations with the general assembly. Between 1586 and 1596, there were moments of peace, but true concord did not prevail. As a result of the uncontrolled outburst of opposition in December 1596, the initiative passed to the king and it is clear that many ministers who had previously been happy to criticise him discovered a new loyalty, clearly not wishing to be associated with a minority of ministers who had come to be seen as politically subversive. By 1603, the opportunity for the establishment of effective royal control over the Kirk with the consent of most of the ministry appears to have been available. After James left Scotland, however, that opportunity was lost. Perhaps he concentrated too much on the government of his new realm, or on achieving an incorporating union to which he felt the Kirk would be opposed. He may also have been unable to accept the continuation of a polity in Scotland which would have precluded ecclesiastical union at some future point. Whatever the reason, the king's ecclesiastical policies in Scotland between 1605 and the end of his reign were unacceptable to the majority of ministers and had to be forced through. The enhancements of episcopal power after 1606 must thus be seen, along with the liturgical innovations, as unpopular aspects of crown policy and not contrasted with them in an attempt to portray the Kirk as amenable to Jacobean episcopacy.

In spite of the desire of most historians to talk of ecclesiastical politics in Jacobean Scotland in terms of two opposing parties,[2] absolute support either for episcopacy or presbytery appears to have been exhibited by no more than a handful of people. The form of ecclesiastical polity frequently changed, so it is hardly surprising that most people, both

1 Scot, *Apologetical Narration*, 255-63; Calderwood, *History*, vii, 307-32; James to the privy council, 27 July 1618, *Eccles. Letters*, ii, 567-8.

2 This is found in the works of most historians of the period: Mullan, *Episcopacy*, 86 ('the presbyterians'); Donaldson, *James V—James VII*, 200 'Melville's resolute party'); Foster, *Church Before the Covenants*, 17 ('the presbyterian party'); Lynch, 'Preaching to the converted?', devotes a section to 'The Melvillian Party'; J. Dawson, 'Anglo-Scottish Protestant Culture and Integration in Sixteenth Century Britain' in S.G. Ellis and S. Barber (eds.), *Conquest and Union: Fashioning a British State, 1585-1725* (London, 1995), 92, 89, 99, where emphasis is placed on 'two mutually antagonistic ecclesiastical parties'.

within and outwith the Kirk, did not take particular sides; rather there were frequent realignments. It was never really a question of a choice between two mutually exclusive systems, and so to describe an individual minister as either 'episcopalian' or 'presbyterian' (or 'Melvillian') is simplistic and unhelpful in a discussion of ecclesiastical politics; it begs too many questions. Moreover, it suggests that, in the period in question, there were clear-cut frames of reference to which these terms could be related, and this does not seem to have been the case. What was important to most of those Scottish ministers who took an interest in the politics of the Kirk in this period was not whether or not the Kirk should have bishops; rather it was a more subtle question of how powerful any individual in the Kirk ought to be and how much influence the state should have over the Kirk. It was sovereignty, rather than polity, which was the crucial issue, yet terms like 'presbyterian' and 'episcopalian' suggest the former rather than the latter. There was episcopacy in Scotland in 1550, in 1572, in 1602 and in 1610. At each of these dates, however, the form, powers and status of the episcopate were very different. In 1602, the vast majority of the ministry was happy to accept an episcopal element in the polity of what remained an essentially presbyterian Kirk. Yet the king began to interfere too much in the internal autonomy of the Kirk, by preventing the meeting of general assemblies after 1603, and by transferring control of such things as ordination and excommunication from presbyteries to bishops. Many ministers then joined the ranks of the opposition, long before any liturgical innovations were attempted. As early as 1606, the nursing father had a teenage rebel on his hands.

~ 11 ~

The Scottish State and its Borderlands, 1567-1625

Julian Goodare and Michael Lynch

> We should not study the frontier in itself. We should study and analyse it in relation to the state. Given a certain type of state we get a certain type of limit and, where necessary, a certain type of frontier in the military and political sense of the word.[1]

Gaelic bards looked back on the sixteenth century as the 'age of the forays'. To them, internal feuding had been overshadowed by the repeated and sometimes brutal interference inflicted on the Highlands by Stewart kings and their agents. For those monarchs, the image of the wild and barbarous Highlands became a 'worker by contraries', underlining the articulation of a sophisticated, new political culture, consolidating and promoting the status of the crown.[2] In the process, the king's realm was by the reign of James VI being redefined as the Scottish state. For the borderlands, all those marginal regions that had hitherto been cast as extras in national politics, the process of state formation gave them new and significant roles in government policy—as a frontier with a neighbouring but now friendly state, and as internal frontiers which had a cultural as well as political or military existence.

I

'Not very much of significance for the history of Scotland', it has been claimed, 'occurred more than 500 feet above Mean Tide Level'.[3] Yet how different the history of the first 500 feet would have been if Scotland had possessed no upland regions! Such regions, with their scattered, mobile, pastoral society, their almost egalitarian emphasis on kinship, and their readiness to fight—in short, with their refusal to fit the norms of the lowland—posed a challenge to the nation's rulers. The people of the uplands probably did not, among themselves, make any history of more than local significance. It is in their *interaction* with the low-lying core that their importance for the Scottish state lies.

In general, uplanders' challenge to the state is more a matter of image and potential than of action, since the uplands usually keep themselves

1 L. Febvre, '*Frontière*: the word and the concept', in P. Burke (ed.), *A New Kind of History from the Writings of Febvre* (London, 1973), 213.

2 A.H. Williamson, 'Scots, Indians and empire: the Scottish politics of civilization, 1519-1609', *Past and Present*, 150 (Feb. 1996), 56-66.

3 Lord Cooper, 'A historical atlas for Scotland', in his *Supra Crepidam* (Edinburgh, 1951), 13.

to themselves, and it is open to the government to do the same. Government is based in fertile plains that can supply the surplus necessary to support it. Even law courts need paperwork, education, and military force to back up their decisions; they have to be sustained from court fines and tribute. If the upland is poor, with long communications and a scattered population, it may literally not be worth governing.

Yet leaving the uplands to their own devices may be problematic for the rulers of the plains. Uplanders are warlike, partly in order to maintain their autonomy, and partly because their wealth consists of mobile livestock that is hard to defend. They may well raid the plains, causing damage and exposing the government to criticism from the victims. Even if they do not, their government-free existence may be taken as an affront—both by those who govern, and by the plains-dwellers who *are* obliged to submit to government. This becomes increasingly clear as government itself takes definite shape in the plains—that is, when a recognisably centralised state emerges. Interaction between plains and uplands then creates patterns that can be analysed using terms like 'core' and 'periphery'. The two may be complementary, for instance through trade—but it is more likely that they will come into conflict. The core may seek to exploit the periphery economically—so that it is not only poor, but forced to remain so. The periphery, remote from government agents, may become a refuge for freedom or dissidence.[1]

The Scottish Highlands form an obvious example of such a periphery. The distinctive nature of the Highlands has been a vital theme in Scottish history from the late middle ages to the present;[2] much of that theme grew out of the repositioning of the relationship between the Highlands and the state. The reign of James VI saw the Scottish state being reshaped. Political authority became more concentrated at the centre—giving more power to the crown itself, to the privy council, and to parliament.[3] This chapter suggests that in order to understand the shaping of the state, the shape of the state needs to be understood as well. Like a fitted carpet, the central authority of the state was now supposed to go right up to the edge.

From the 1590s onwards, three sets of borderlands were in course of being redefined. Firstly, boundaries were established, mostly in the minds of the king and his administrators, between the nearer Highlands, 'barbarous for the most part, and yet mixed with some shew of civilitie', and the further-flung western Highlands and Isles, which were 'alluterly

1 For a survey of interpretative models see P. Burke, *History and Social Theory* (Cambridge, 1992), 79-84.

2 Cf. E. Cameron, 'Embracing the past: the Highlands in nineteenth century Scotland', in D. Broun *et al.* (eds.), *Image and Identity: the Making and Remaking of Scotland through the Ages* (Edinburgh, 1998), 195-7.

3 J. Goodare, *State and Society in Early Modern Scotland* (Oxford, 1999), ch. 3.

barbares, without any shewe or sorte of civilitie'.[1] Secondly, the Border marches became a showpiece, the 'middle shires' of James VI and I's new British kingdom. Thirdly, another Anglo-Scottish frontier emerged in the north of Ireland with the Nine Years' War (1594-1603). Ulster had long been a crossroads of Gaelic society, and a theatre of rivalry between the MacDonald clan and their many enemies; the uprising there made it a vital strategic region to the English state. As part of the English campaign to suppress it, concerted efforts were made to halt the supply of West Highland mercenaries to the rebels. But in all three borderlands, perceptions—from the centre—were more significant than realities.

State formation in Scotland involved the restructuring of old habits of a feudal realm to accommodate a landed society widened by the secularisation of church lands. Political culture was recast around an interventionist but distinctly stationary monarch and royal court. After 1603, the construction of a new British state saw the quickening of a process already underway in both England and Scotland by the 1590s: the marginalisation of this state's enemies.[2] Edmund Spenser, in 1596, stigmatised most of Gaelic society, in Ireland (and, by implication, in Scotland), as barbarous. Robert Pont, veteran of the Reformation of 1560, branded papists, highlanders and borderers as obstacles to the civility and security promised by the union of crowns.[3]

There was an amount of self-deception at work here and some rearrangement of the facts of history over the previous century or so. A recent study of the borderlands of Tudor England has argued that 'the real test of Tudor government was its ability to uphold law and order in the borderlands', which comprised over half of the geographical area of the Tudor state, on the grounds that governing the core state, south-east England, was relatively easy. The important question was whether the state could command the loyalty of Cumberland or County Kildare.[4]

1 This passage in *Basilicon Doron*, i, 70, may owe something to Sir William Gerrard, lord chancellor of Ireland and a member of the royal council in Wales, who in 1578 had suggested that some of the Gaelic Irish would prove responsive to the rule of law while others would not, one of the main determining factors being location: C. Brady, 'Comparable histories? Tudor reform in Wales and Ireland', in S.G. Ellis and S. Barber (eds.), *Conquest and Union: Fashioning a British State, 1485-1725* (London, 1995), 78n, 81-2. By the 1590s, however, the distinction was commonplace in the case of Ireland.

2 Cf. J. Morrill, 'The British problem, c.1534-1707', in B. Bradshaw and J. Morrill (eds.), *The British Problem, c.1534-1707* (London, 1996), esp. 1-19; Ellis and Barber (eds.), *Conquest and Union*, 4-7, 9-13, 40-1.

3 Edmund Spenser, *A View of the Present State of Ireland*, ed. W.L. Renwick (Oxford, 1970), 38, 177-80; Robert Pont, *Of the Union of Britayne* (1604), in B. Galloway and B. Levack (eds.), *The Jacobean Union* (SHS, 1985), 18, 22.

4 S.G. Ellis, *Tudor Frontiers and Noble Power: the Making of the British State* (Oxford, 1995), 258; S.G. Ellis, 'Tudor state formation and the shaping of the British Isles', in Ellis and Barber (eds.), *Conquest and Union*, 42-4. Cf. also D.M. Loades, *Power in Tudor England* (London, 1997), 156: 'With the dangerous exception of Ireland, Tudor government worked.'

This contains important insights, but there are also difficulties with it. Firstly, government was as important to the people of Norfolk, for example, as it was to those of Kildare; it mattered just as much if your cow was stolen, wherever you lived. Secondly, it is not true that Norfolk would automatically be loyal. It usually was—but when it rebelled, as it did in 1549, this caused far more trouble than rebellion in the borderlands, and led to the downfall of an entire regime. Also, in Elizabethan England, loyalty to government and the established church went hand in hand, or was perceived to do so. In the darker corners of the Tudor lands, as a result, new heights of loyalty, in the form of religious conformity and the conversion of the marcher lords, were demanded as the reign of Elizabeth progressed.[1]

Similarly, in Scotland, it is often argued, the main threat to the government, in the century after the annexation of the Lordship of the Isles in 1493, came from the fringes of the realm which lay for the most part outside its direct control. Each reign between that of James III and James VI, it has been pointed out, faced at least one rebellion in the west.[2] Yet there is also exaggeration here. After the death of the last pretender to the Lordship of the Isles in 1545, the problem—if problem there was—consisted more of law and order than a threat to sovereignty. The government could tolerate with relative equanimity, for example, a rising which occupied the castle of Dunyveg in 1599;[3] far more fuss was made when rebels captured the castle of Stirling in 1584.

In practice, the state concentrated more of its firepower on potential rebellion in the Borders. Morton's regency saw intensive military and judicial action there: he personally led no fewer than seven judicial raids between 1573 and 1577, though ultimately to little effect. Plans devised in 1578 for a permanent commission to patrol the marches, which anticipated the creation of a mounted police force in 1605, fell away in the face of protests to the privy council about unconstitutional taxation.[4] Never in the Highlands, or indeed the eastern Border marches, did James face the threat of the invasion of a foreign army coupled with a rebellion at home orchestrated by a dissident regional noble. In the west march he did—with the pro-Spanish rebellion of Lord Maxwell in 1588. It is not surprising that the king went to the length of borrowing English artillery pieces to quell it.[5]

1 S.M. Keeling, 'The Reformation in the Anglo-Scottish Border counties', *Northern History*, xv (1979), 25.

2 M. Lynch, *Scotland: a New History* (London, 1991), 167-8.

3 *CSP Scot.*, xiii, I, 564.

4 G. Hewitt, *Scotland under Morton, 1572-1580* (Edinburgh, 1982), 130-6; *RPC*, iii, 56-7; M. Lee, *Government by Pen: Scotland under James VI and I* (Urbana, Ill., 1980), 45-7.

5 K.M. Brown, *Bloodfeud in Scotland, 1573-1625* (Edinburgh, 1986), 148; K.M. Brown, 'The making of a *politique*: the Counter Reformation and the regional politics of John, eighth Lord Maxwell', *SHR*, lxvi (1987), 161-7.

So violence and potential conspiracy at the court were more serious than any remote 'Highland problem'. Noble feud, whether spilling outwards from the court or escalating beyond its own local origins, was a far more serious problem—and certainly a greater threat to government—than violence on the marches or in the Highlands. There were a number of clan feuds in this period; they were often bloody affairs but they did not threaten the stability of the Lowland political system. Relatively few such feuds operated across the divide between Highlands and Lowlands.

II

Where exactly did the authorities think that the Lowlands ended and Highlands began? In the west, the outpost and symbol of royal power was the castle of Dumbarton, the favourite base camp of royal expeditions to 'daunt the Isles'. Beyond it, routine government ceased. When government extended its reach northwards from Edinburgh, it clung to the low-lying eastern coast of Scotland, and rarely headed inland. A messenger travelling north from Edinburgh would cross the Mounth—the easterly extension of the Grampian mountains in Kincardineshire—near the coast, usually at Stonehaven on the way to Aberdeen. If we follow one such messenger, Cuthbert Richardson, in 1581, 'passand of Edinburgh with the preceptis of parliament to all the erlis, lordis, schereffis, stewartis, bischoppis, abbottis, priouris and provestis and baillies of burrowis within the boundis of the scherefdomes of Fyiff, Kinrossschire, Perth, Forfair, Kincardin, Abirdene, Banff, Elgin and Fores, Narne, Innernes and Cromertie', we see that his itinerary took him across the Forth, then northwards to Perth where he crossed the Tay; at this point, instead of continuing northwards to Dunkeld and through the mountains to Blair Atholl (the route of the present A9), he headed north-east to Forfar and Aberdeen, finally turning west in Buchan to visit the burghs along the Moray Firth. Not once did he cross the Highland Line. Richardson, together with two colleagues who respectively visited the south-eastern and south-western shires (including, be it noted, the Borders), traversed only about half the land area of Scotland. They proclaimed the parliament at the market crosses of twenty-seven burghs. Those nearest to the Highlands were Dumbarton, Glasgow, Perth, Forfar, Aberdeen, Banff, Elgin, Forres, Nairn and Inverness.[1] The extensive progresses of Mary, queen of Scots covered almost exactly the same area, though she did once take the route through Atholl.[2] James VI was less ambitious with his progresses: during his first, in 1580, he turned back at Dunnottar. In his last, in 1617, he ventured only as far north as

1 *TA*, xiii, 201-2; *APS*, iii, 193.

2 P. McNeill and R. Nicholson (eds.), *An Historical Atlas of Scotland, c.400-c.1600* (Conference of Scottish Medievalists, 1975), 86-7, 198-9. Mary also once reached Inveraray, to the west.

Kinnaird, near Brechin. His route carefully skirted his 'middle shires': he entered Scotland at Berwick en route to Dunglass, and he left it on the route from Hamilton Palace via Sanquhar, Drumlanrig, Dumfries and Annan to Carlisle.[1]

Another tour through the political geography of Scotland, by pen rather than on horseback, is provided by one of those reports of which English statesmen were so fond, describing the counties and their leading nobles. It began conventionally in Berwickshire, moving westwards through the Border counties, then through Galloway, Ayrshire, Renfrewshire, Lennox (Dumbarton is as far west as we get, as it was for the messengers), followed by Stirlingshire, Lothian, Fife, Perthshire, Strathearn (again, this is our nearest approach to the central Highlands), then east and north across the Mounth and along the Moray Firth. This time we get as far as Caithness and Orkney, whereupon we jump abruptly to the southern Isles, where the English in Ireland were regularly interested in the doings of the MacDonalds.[2]

The coastal route across the Mounth was not just a convenient habit of royal messengers, but was enshrined in administrative documents and even in statute. Legal actions before the lords of council from north of the Mounth were postponed in 1501. An act of 1600 in favour of 'his majesteis subjectis inhabiting the north pairt of this realme' gave them fifteen days, rather than the normal six, to answer a summons to appear before the privy council—and the 'north pairt' was simply defined as 'benorth the watter of Die'.[3] This was clear enough to the people of Buchan, but what about those of Moidart?

The answer is, of course, that the people of Moidart would not be expected to compear before the privy council at all, or indeed to have any other significant dealings with central government, which was as little concerned with them as they were with it. Partly their dissociation sprang from topography. The firths and river crossings of the east coast, and still more the firths, lochs and islands of the west, were obstacles to government agents, who were landlubbers. Important messengers like Cuthbert Richardson went on horseback; routine letters were carried by servants running on foot. But to a seagoing people the water could be a link rather than a barrier—and this is what we find in the west Highlands and Islands, where lords possessed galleys as well as horses. The Scottish Highlands formed a single cultural region, linked with Ulster, within

1 McNeill and MacQueen (eds.), *Atlas*, 133; W.A. McNeill and P.G.B. McNeill, 'The Scottish progress of James VI, 1617', *SHR*, lxxv (1996).

2 BL, Cotton MSS, Caligula, B.v, fos. 152r.-161v. This MS dates from *c*.1590.

3 *ADC*, iii, 98; *APS*, iv, 239, c. 38. For a combination of the formula 'from the water of Dee north' with a more precise enumeration of sheriffdoms in 1616, see *RPC*, x, 618-19. Cf. the requirement in 1587 for Border pledges to be kept to the north of the Forth, Highland ones to the south: *APS*, iii, 465, c. 59, para 17. West of Stirlingshire, this was meaningless.

which the firths, the Minch and the North Channel facilitated communication.[1]

For the church, too, there were two main routes into the Highlands: one depended on the chain of Campbell holdings and patronage, stretching from southern Argyll into eastern Perthshire. This had been the basis of the initial impact made by John Carswell, former private chaplain to the fourth earl of Argyll, Protestant superintendent of the west from 1561 and bishop of the Isles from 1566. But the spread of a Protestant ministry had largely been confined to areas of Campbell influence.[2] Thereafter, in the Western Highlands and the Isles, progress would be slow and painstaking, depending on the traditional means of discourse and customs in Gaeldom rather than the standard weapons in evangelical ministers' armoury—catechism, bible and pulpit.[3]

A professional ministry in the west was rare until well into the seventeenth century: in 1609 only a third of the parishes in Argyll had a minister, and only one in fifteen in Skye and the Outer Hebrides.[4] What growth there was went largely unsupervised. Visitations organised by the general assembly in the 1580s and 1590s conspicuously avoided Argyll. No kirk sessions were set up in the Highlands until well into the seventeenth century, so that coercion was lacking; and records for the synod of Argyll date only from 1639. For the whole of the reign of James VI, the church in the west Highlands largely depended on Campbell centres of power, a largely itinerant ministry, and private patronage.[5]

The church's other route northwards followed the well-worn path of royal administrators: up the east coast, across the Mounth and into Moray. This was the basis of the early warning system set up by the general assembly in 1588 to chart the progress of the Armada; it extended no further north than the Black Isle and no further west than Inverness. Like the state, the kirk also detected an internal boundary separating the 'north parts' from Lowland Scotland. It would treat the coastal strip around the Moray Firth—basically Lowland, but remote—in the same way as the core of the state; but it would do it less frequently and less generously. A visitation of 1587, undertaken by three Edinburgh ministers,

1 J.E.A. Dawson, 'The origins of the "Road to the Isles": trade, communications and Campbell power in early modern Scotland', in R. Mason and N. Macdougall (eds.), *People and Power in Scotland* (Edinburgh, 1992); cf. J. Goodare, 'Economic history, people's history and Scottish history', *Scottish Economic and Social History*, xiii (1993), 78-9.

2 J. Kirk, 'John Carswell, superintendent of Argyll', in his *Patterns of Reform* (Edinburgh, 1989).

3 J. Dawson, 'Calvinism and the Gaidhealtachd in Scotland', in A. Pettegree *et al.* (eds.), *Calvinism in Europe, 1540-1620* (Cambridge, 1994), 236-8.

4 A.I. Macinnes, 'Crown, clans and *fine*: the "civilizing" of Scottish Gaeldom, 1587-1638', *Northern Scotland*, xiii (1993), 47.

5 *Minutes of the Synod of Argyll, 1639-1651*, ed. D.C. Mactavish (SHS, 1943); I.B. Cowan, *The Scottish Reformation* (London, 1982), 173; Kirk, *Patterns of Reform*, 305; Dawson, 'Calvinism and the Gaidhealtachd', 243-6.

was typical: it stretched from the Dee to the diocese of Caithness.[1] The progress of Protestantism along this route was patchy and preachers were much slower to travel it than a mere reading ministry. Optimistic analyses point to overall provision, of readers as well as ministers: by 1574, for example, only 23 per cent of parishes in Ross remained unfilled and about 11 per cent in Moray. Yet, by a more realistic measure, over 71 per cent of the ministry in both Ross and Moray were readers.[2] One result was a startling infrequency of communion: in 1608, it was complained that in many parts of Ross and Caithness—as in the south-west and the western Border marches—communion had never been celebrated since the Reformation.[3] Many of the difficulties of the church in the dark corners of the land sprang from lack of resources, which was not remedied much before the late 1620s or 1630s. In 1585, the eleven readers in Ross were paid somewhere between £20 and a miserable £4. These were sums which compared badly with stipends in the poorest parts of the church in Ireland.[4]

For the government, internal exile for dissident clergymen was sufficiently punitive north of the Mounth or the Dee rather than in the remote west: Robert Bruce, one of Edinburgh's ministers, had two spells in Inverness.[5] Here is a further example of the differential treatment meted out by a government which was able to reach some but not all of the 'dark corners of the land'.

When James VI began to intervene in the calling of meetings of the general assembly, an increasing voice was gained by the church north of the Tay, which comprised approximately 500 of the nation's 1,100 parishes. In the assembly of 1602, some 31 of the 91 ministers who attended were from the north. It was not until 1610 that northern ministers attended in anything like their appropriate numbers.[6] Progress, both in terms of the spread of a parish ministry and the quality of individual minsters, came distinctly earlier to Highland fringes rather than to the Highlands itself. Neither in the north nor in the west did the structure of the courts of the reformed church forge a new linkage between the centre and the furthest-flung localities.[7]

1 *BUK*, ii, 724; Calderwood, *History*, iv, 671-2.

2 *Wodrow Miscellany*, 396.

3 *BUK*, iii, 1061; Calderwood, *History*, vi, 774.

4 W.H. Makey, *The Church of the Covenant, 1637-1651* (Edinburgh, 1979), 107; Kirk, *Patterns of Reform*, 466; S.G. Ellis, 'Economic problems of the church: why the Reformation failed in Ireland', *Journal of Ecclesiastical History*, xli (1990), 254; M. Lynch, 'Preaching to the converted? Perspectives on the Scottish Reformation', in A.A. MacDonald *et al.* (eds.), *The Renaissance in Scotland* (Leiden, 1996), 311-12.

5 Calderwood, *History*, vii, 392-4, 450, 518, 624; Robert Bruce, *Sermons: with Collections for his Life*, ed. W. Cunningham (Wodrow Society, 1843), 132; *The Life of Mr Robert Blair*, ed. T. McCrie (Wodrow Society, 1848), 39n.

6 *BUK*, iii, 974-9, 1085-91; Lynch, 'Preaching to the converted', 315-16.

7 Cf. J. Wormald, *Court, Kirk and Community: Scotland, 1470-1625* (London, 1981), 40.

One of the most striking developments affecting Scotland in the century and a half after 1550 was the rapid improvement in a network of communications: by 1707 less than a fifth of the mainland was further than a dozen miles from a market centre or some kind of burgh.[1] Although the bulk of the growth was concentrated in the period after 1660, the long reign of James VI saw no fewer than seventy foundations of burghs of barony and regality, with forty-one of them coming after 1603.[2] Few if any of these burghs were in the Highlands: Inveraray, a fifteenth-century creation and focal point of Campbell power at a vital crossroads in the southern Highlands, was one exception but it remained a burgh of barony until 1648. Parliament was aware of the link between 'civilitie' and towns, which had informed much of English policy in Ireland. In 1597, it projected the building of three genuinely Highland royal burghs—Stornoway in Lewis, Gordonsburgh (now Fort William) in Lochaber, and Campbeltown in Kintyre.[3] They took three decades or more to materialise and, in the event, were outposts of Mackenzie, Gordon and Campbell influence rather than crown authority. More significant meantime were the increasing activities of frontier towns, such as Dumbarton, Stirling and Perth, each with extensive Highland trading hinterlands, and of Dingwall, Tain and Inverness in the north, reflecting the growth in demand for salted herring and live cattle.[4]

As trading contacts with the Highlands expanded, burghs of barony mushroomed, usually on the fringes of the Lowlands. About twenty were founded between 1587 and 1625. The largest group was in the shires of Banff, Nairn and Elgin: they included Geddes, Lochloy, Darnaway, Rothiemay and Fochabers. Meigle and Doune were two of a smaller group of Perthshire burghs. Gairloch was almost the only one in the south-western fringes. Three—including two of those projected in 1597—were further afield: Laggan on Islay, created for Campbell of Cawdor in 1614; Gordonsburgh; and Stornoway, a 'prettie town' begun by the Fife Adventurers in 1607 and taken over by Mackenzie of Kintail.[5] Stornoway rapidly became a base for Dutch fishing fleets, so that herring left the country without passing through the hands of Scottish middlemen—much to the annoyance of the convention of royal burghs.[6] All these towns functioned as transit points on a road not to the Isles but *from* it.

1 I. Whyte, *Agriculture and Society in Seventeenth Century Scotland* (Edinburgh, 1979), 178-94; McNeill and MacQueen (eds.), *Atlas*, 295.

2 G.S. Pryde, *The Burghs of Scotland: a Critical List* (Oxford, 1965), 60-8.

3 *APS*, iv, 139, c. 34; *Records of the Convention of Royal Burghs of Scotland*, 7 vols., eds. J.D. Marwick and T. Hunter (Edinburgh, 1866-1918), ii, 258-60; Macinnes, 'Crowns, clans and *fine*', 43.

4 Dawson, 'Road to the Isles', 82, 92; McNeill and MacQueen (eds.), *Atlas*, 244-7, 256-7.

5 Pryde, *Burghs*, nos. 238 (Gartmouth, 1587)—316 (Hatton of Fintray, 1625).

6 T. Pagan, *The Convention of the Royal Burghs of Scotland* (Glasgow, 1926), 221-4.

Towns also functioned as administrative centres, and those facing the Highlands had a special role to play. When the government wanted to communicate with the 'clannis of the Hieland' in 1552, a messenger was sent to issue a proclamation in Inverness and Elgin.[1] This was the equivalent of a proclamation being solemnly announced from the end of the pier at Leith to the distant shores where Scots merchants traded: the herald declaimed his message from the limits of active crown influence. Beyond, in the case of the Highlands, lay a conceptual wilderness, comparable to the frontier of nineteenth-century America.[2] Although some Highland chiefs did visit Inverness from time to time or sent their agents, and occasionally used the local sheriff and commissary courts, they played no role in the internal life or politics of the frontier burghs.[3] After 1610, when island chiefs had to report regularly to the privy council, they were obliged to appoint agents in Inverness or Rothesay, so that the council could serve summonses on them.[4] This was government at arm's length. The new burghs of barony were frontier posts in the literal sense.

Distinctions are also needed in the Borders. Tweeddale, in the east, was wealthier and more susceptible to outside influence than either the Scottish middle and west marches or any of the three English marches. The Tweed basin contained most of the Border towns and linked the east march and the north-eastern part of the middle march to Lothian and central Scotland. Beyond that, topography worked against a uniform system of Border administration; the frontier zone was crossed by a series of valleys or passes running north-south, leaving Liddesdale, Eskdale, Annandale and Nithsdale remote from the rest of the frontier as well as more inaccessible from Edinburgh. For the crown, there were, in effect, two Borders: one was a relatively settled frontier society; the other, like the Highlands, was seen as wilderness.[5] Although Tweeddale remained a sensitive issue because of its proximity to the English garrison

1 *TA*, x, 128.

2 Williamson, 'Scots, Indians and empire'.

3 Examples can be found in *The Mackintosh Muniments, 1442-1820*, ed. H. Paton (Edinburgh, 1903), and *Inventory of Chisholm Writs, 1456-1810*, ed. J. Munro (SRS, 1992). See also M. Lynch, 'The crown and the burghs, 1500-1625', in M. Lynch (ed.), *The Early Modern Town in Scotland* (London, 1987), 64-5, for nobles and Lowland towns.

4 J. Munro, 'When island chiefs came to town', *Notes and Queries of the Society of West Highland and Island Historical Research*, xix (Dec. 1982); J. Goodare, 'The Statutes of Iona in context', *SHR*, lxxvii (1998).

5 A.E. Goodman, 'The Anglo-Scottish marches in the fifteenth century: a frontier society', in R.A. Mason (ed.), *Scotland and England, 1286-1815* (Edinburgh, 1987), 20-2. Typically, different messengers were sent to the south-east and south-west. In 1583, for example, John Fraser was sent to the sheriffdoms of Lauder, Roxburgh, Selkirk and Peebles; he would have gone no further west than Jedburgh. John Adie went west to the sheriffdoms of Linlithgow, Stirling and Dumbarton before turning south into Renfrew, Lanark, Ayr, Wigton and Dumfries; his journey ended in the stewartries of Annandale and Kirkcudbright. *TA*, xiii, 201-2.

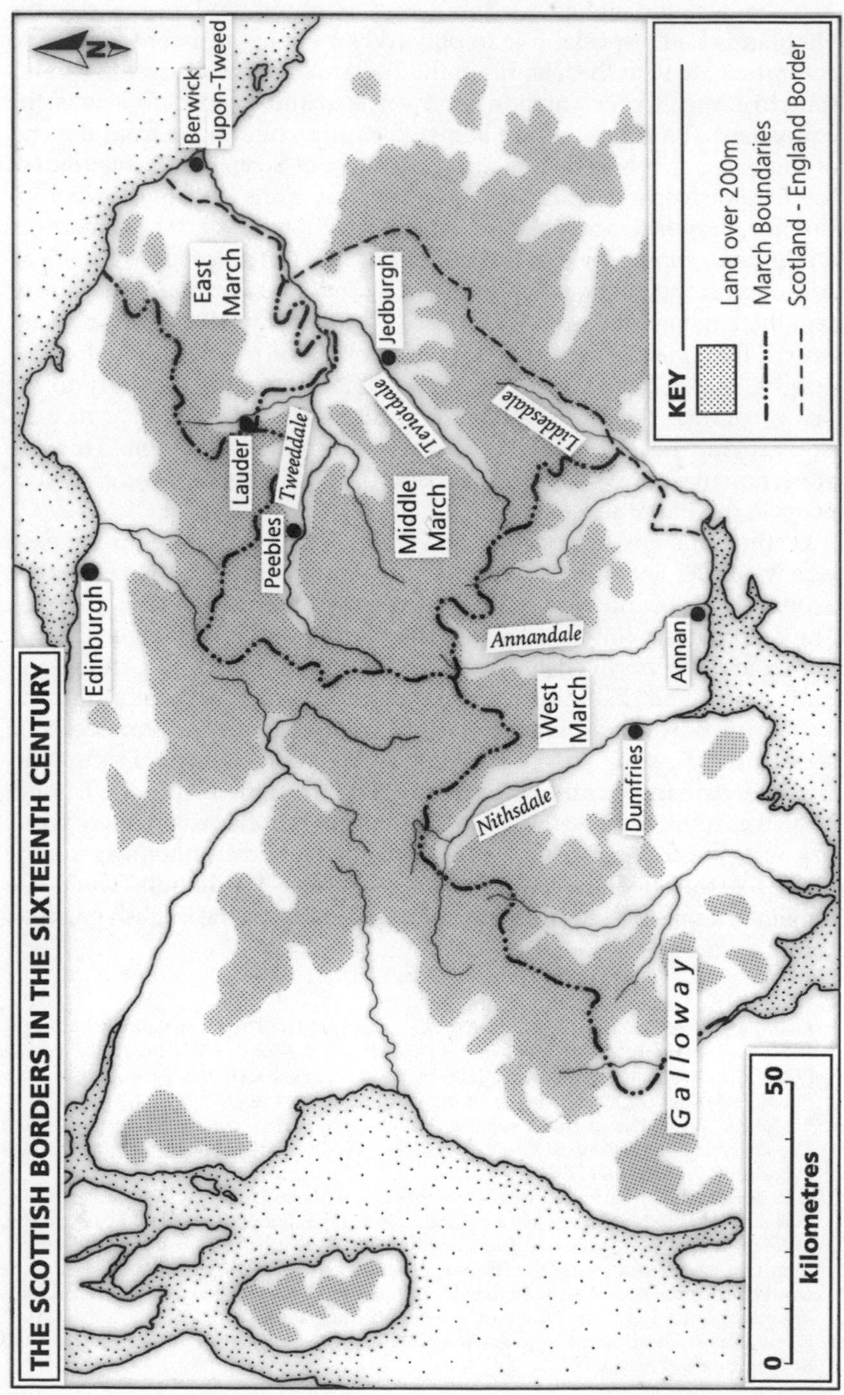
THE SCOTTISH BORDERS IN THE SIXTEENTH CENTURY
N
Berwick -upon-Tweed
East March
Jedburgh
Teviotdale
Liddesdale
Lauder
Tweeddale
Peebles
Middle March
Edinburgh
Annandale
Annan
West March
Dumfries
Nithsdale
Galloway
KEY
Land over 200m
March Boundaries
Scotland - England Border
0
50
kilometres

town of Berwick, the real challenge to authority lay west of Jedburgh. There, atrocity stories as shocking as any from the Highlands were commonplace, such as an account of mutilation of the dead and wholesale slaughter of prisoners in the west march in 1586. Stories like this would be used to justify official reprisals, including summary trial and execution on the spot, after 1605. Nowhere was the violence of the Scottish state more heavy-handed than in its south-western borderlands.[1]

III

Despite the increasing commerce between Highlands and Lowlands, contemporaries had no doubts about the uniqueness of the zone beyond the Highland frontier, and Scottish governments universally regarded the clans inhabiting it as a distinct nuisance. Historians, similarly, tend to discuss Highland clans in the confident belief that they can recognise a clan when they see one. Yet it would help to define the state's 'Highland problem' by looking more carefully at the definition of the Highlands. The difficulty is establishing where the Highlands began and ended. If Highlands and Lowlands differed qualitatively, it ought in theory to be possible to represent the Highland Line on a map in some way. Various attempts have been made to do this; they do not all agree in detail, but the basic criterion is almost always a linguistic one. The 'Highlands', defined as the area in which Gaelic was spoken, were increasingly sharply etched.[2] This may reduce the significance of topography, though in Aberdeenshire at least, the linguistic divide was also a topographical one, with Gaelic spoken in the moorland, forest and mountain areas.[3]

The problem was not primarily topographical but cultural. One important aspect of culture is language, and two main languages were spoken in Scotland: Middle Scots, one of the dialects of English, in the south and north-east, and Scots Gaelic, a Celtic language related to Irish, in the west. There was also a third language, Norn, a dialect of Norse, in the far north (Shetland, Orkney and parts of Caithness), which disappeared from usage early in the seventeenth century. The division between Scots and Gaelic—the 'Highland Line'—was by far the most significant cultural and political boundary in late medieval and early modern Scotland. By this period, Scots culture and Gaelic culture were not just different for they had always been that; they were hostile.[4]

1 Cf. McNeill and MacQueen (eds.), *Atlas*, 453; *RPC*, iv, 55-7.

2 A standard map for the late middle ages is McNeill and Nicholson (eds.), *Atlas*, map 74; cf. also maps 71-3 on the Lordship of the Isles. Additional studies of this period are shown in C.W.J. Withers, *Gaelic in Scotland, 1698-1981* (Edinburgh, 1984), 26, reproduced in McNeill and MacQueen (eds.), *Atlas*, 427, while the Gaelic-speaking area in 1698 is shown in Withers, *Gaelic in Scotland*, 47. All these studies attempt to define the *Gaidhealtachd*.

3 A. Watson and R.D. Clement, 'Aberdeenshire Gaelic', *TGSI*, lii (1980-2), 380.

4 D.D. Murison, 'Linguistic relationships in medieval Scotland', in G.W.S. Barrow (ed.), *The Scottish Tradition* (Edinburgh, 1974).

The language of government was Scots. Some records were kept, and documents issued, in Latin—mainly the registers of the great and privy seals, and the exchequer rolls; but these old-fashioned documents were mainly common form. Acts of parliament had adopted Scots in 1424. Central and local court proceedings were all recorded in Scots, as were royal letters under the signet. All these could perfectly well have been in Latin, which *was* used by local notaries; clerks *chose* to write in Scots. At least one judge, in the 1540s, had difficulty keeping his law reports in Scots, the official language of the court of session; he tended to lapse into the Latin legal phraseology with which he was more familiar.[1]

The Scots language in the fifteenth century was spreading in literary and official usage, and becoming more integrated in content; it could eventually have become the independent written language of an independent state. But it did not. In an important cultural shift, written Scots was slowly but steadily assimilated to standard English. The trend was already evident in 1520, thus antedating not only the union of crowns but the Reformation as well. The Reformation, or at least the widespread use of printing for religious literature, accelerated the process, but the union seems to have made little difference to it; religious texts were the quickest to become anglicised, central government records the slowest. By the mid seventeenth century the written language of Lowland Scotland differed but little from standard English.[2]

Meanwhile, Gaelic changed much less; it remained a free-standing language, with a culture that was central to people's lives, but developed no governmental role. There was less government in the Highlands; less of that was written down; and for what *was* written down, Latin sufficed—only one Gaelic charter, dated 1408, is known, and other legal documents in Gaelic are equally rare. Printing, too, passed Gaelic by—only one edition of one book was printed in it in all our period.[3] Gaelic retained its vitality and sophistication, but the main uses of written Gaelic were for poetry and medical treatises, neither relevant to government.

It was this lack of a governmental role for Gaelic which caused Gaelic-speaking society to be regarded as barbarous. Governments of later centuries, imbued with the spirit of modern nationalism, might

1 A.L. Murray, 'Sinclair's Practicks', in A. Harding (ed.), *Law-Making and Law-Makers in British History* (London, 1980), 96.

2 A.J. Devitt, *Standardizing Written English: Diffusion in the Case of Scotland, 1520-1659* (Cambridge, 1989), 16-17, 54-5, 62-7 and *passim*. Conscious anglicisation, with deliberate avoidance of Scotticisms, did not occur before the eighteenth century. See also J. Dawson, 'Anglo-Scottish Protestant culture and integration in sixteenth-century Britain', in Ellis and and Barber (eds.), *Conquest and Union*, 92-7.

3 J. Bannerman, 'Literacy in the Highlands', in I.B. Cowan and D. Shaw (eds.), *The Renaissance and Reformation in Scotland* (Edinburgh, 1983); R. Black (ed.), 'A Gaelic contract of lease, c.1603x1616', *Stair Society Miscellany*, ii (1984).

have regarded any form of cultural pluralism as suspicious. In the seventeenth century, a unified state did not require a single language or culture; it merely required that the local ruling classes should all recognise the state as the forum for politics and government. Either they had to learn the dominant language—such as Bohemians learning German after the Habsburg reconquest—or they had to possess provincial institutions which could use the local language without the royal court having to hear it—such as Catalans in the Spanish monarchy. That it was the Highland language that was anomalous is illustrated by the very term 'Highland Line'. No studies have been devoted to the problem of the 'Lowland Line'.[1]

The Scottish church's use of the vernacular in its *Gaidhealtachd* fell somewhere between the enthusiastic uptake by Welsh humanists, which had begun as early as the reign of Edward VI, and the reluctant, patchy usage by the Protestant Church of Ireland.[2] There was a fair amount of preaching in Scots Gaelic, at least in those parishes with ministers, although ministers ignorant of the language were sometimes found in Highland parishes. On the other hand, printing was neglected, with the lonely exception of John Carswell's free translation of the *Book of Common Order* (1567). Because of the formal nature of its language—classical Gaelic rather than the vernacular of the Scottish Highlands—and its ambiguous position in a predominantly oral culture, it would have been accessible to the clan elite rather than the people as a whole.

Highlanders who went to the royal court in the sixteenth century could presumably speak Scots, since it is unlikely that anyone there would have spoken Gaelic after the reign of James IV. In a sense, bilingualism was itself unimportant; plenty of people in early modern Europe were bilingual, as they are today. But bilingualism means different things in different contexts. In a context where a culture is under threat of annexation, people may be reluctant to learn the dominant culture's language, or if they do learn it, they may be reluctant to use it. In medieval Wales and Ireland, there were complex but well-defined frontiers, both between the native Welsh and the English and between the native Irish and the English. These frontiers were essentially local ones, and had dual functions: dividing one lordship from the next, and providing

1 With the possible exception of H.H. Speitel, 'The geographical position of the Scots dialect in relation to the Highlands of Scotland', in M. Benskin and M.L. Samuels (eds.), *So Meny People Longages and Tongs* (Edinburgh, 1981).

2 The Irish council had grudgingly allowed services in Gaelic in 1551; a Protestant catechism was printed in 1571 and a translation of the Bible, authorised in 1561, eventually appeared in 1613. T.W. Moody *et al.* (eds.), *Early Modern Ireland, 1534-1691* (New History of Ireland, vol. iii: Oxford, 1976), 511-12; S.G. Ellis, *Tudor Ireland: Crown, Community and the Conflict of Cultures, 1470-1603* (London, 1985), 202-12; H.A. Jeffries, 'The Irish parliament of 1560: the Anglican reforms authorised', *Irish Historical Studies*, xxvi (1988), 133-4, 136; Ellis, 'Economic problems of the church', 257-8. Ireland, however, lacked private Protestant patrons of Gaelic such as Argyll.

arrangements ('customs of the March' as they were often known) whereby people from different lordships and different cultures could co-exist as neighbours.[1]

In Scotland, by contrast, local definitions of the Highland-Lowland frontier seem to have been based less on territory than on family allegiance. One could not draw the frontier on a large-scale map, but one could say whether any particular member of the political elite was a highlander or lowlander, based on which family he belonged to. This, at least, is the impression given by Sir Robert Gordon's history of Sutherland; he seems to have perceived a clear distinction between Lowland families and Highland clans. He did not regard the Gordons, earls of Sutherland, or the Sinclairs, earls of Caithness, as clans. When he came to the Clan Gunn of Sutherland, he paused to give a description of their distinctive way of life; he later described their Highland custom of fosterage, noting the unusual fact that an earl of Caithness's brother had been fostered among the Gunns (so the line between Highland and Lowland customs could be crossed, even though it existed). He happily repeated derogatory remarks about 'the most pairt of all highlanders'. He persuaded one local clan to renounce its allegiance to another and to choose a chief of its own, something he would not have contemplated for a Lowland family such as his own with individual landed proprietors.[2]

Fosterage and other such links between Highland and Lowland families may have blurred the distinction between the two; some ruling families on the Highland Line were perhaps hybrids, and detailed local research on this might be illuminating. It was possible for families to convert from one to the other, as the Frasers seem to have done. Originally a feudal Norman family who settled in Strath Errick, they never intermarried with Highland families until 1512; but during the sixteenth century they gradually became assimilated into clan society.[3] On the whole, though, the Highland Line was a barrier to the integration of Scotland's elites. Lowland Scottish nobles at the Highland-Lowland frontier did not marry highlanders—except for close Campbell relatives of the earls of Argyll.[4] Indeed there were few marriages across the

1 R. Davies, 'Frontier arrangements in fragmented societies: Ireland and Wales', in R. Bartlett and A. Mackay (eds.), *Medieval Frontier Societies* (Oxford, 1989).

2 Gordon, *Sutherland*, 182, 188-9, 327, 374.

3 I.F. Grant, *Highland Folk Ways* (London, 1961), 18; G.W.S. Barrow, *The Anglo-Norman Era in Scottish History* (Oxford, 1980), 32. They apparently continued to emphasise their Norman descent, which indeed was no barrier to clanship; the Campbells even *invented* a Norman descent for themselves.

4 The *Scots Peerage* reveals, under the titles of Atholl, Caithness, Erskine, Drummond, Huntly, Lennox, Lovat, Mar and Menteith, for the fifteenth, sixteenth and early seventeenth centuries, only two marriages to non-Campbell highlanders. The eighth earl of Sutherland (d. 1508) *may* have married a daughter of Alexander MacDonald, lord of the Isles. John, master of Berriedale (father of the sixth earl of Caithness), married Jean Mackenzie, daughter of the first earl of Seaforth, in 1633-4; but the Mackenzies

Highland Line generally in the sixteenth and seventeenth centuries.[1] However, Lowland lords close to the Highlands might still possess lordship over clans, from whom they extracted such rent and services as they could—an example would be the Murrays in Highland Perthshire. This seems to have been common at the southern and eastern margin of the Highlands.

A further variant took the form of those branches of the Campbells who settled in the Lowlands during the fifteenth and sixteenth centuries; one episode of this, in Angus, has been described as 'the plantation of a Highland kindred in the Lowlands'.[2] The Campbells thus planted remained Campbells and loyal to their chief, Argyll; but it seems likely that in Angus the family took on more of the protective colouring of its surroundings, and perhaps even ceased to be a clan. The same probably happened to another remote branch, the Campbells of Loudoun, who as hereditary sheriffs of Ayr were well integrated into Lowland society despite their continuing family connection to the earls of Argyll. The Campbells were probably the main clan who expanded in this way, but there were others.[3]

IV

Language was no barrier between what contemporaries called the 'incuntrey' and 'outcuntrey', or the Borders. Apart from a pocket of Gaelic speakers in the uplands of Carrick, southern Scotland presented a society which had become, through the Wars of Independence, a more integral part of the Scottish realm.[4] Out of that experience came the need for more regular institutional contact between the king's administration and the Border marches. As a result, a distinctive system of executive machinery had grown up in the later fourteenth and fifteenth centuries. The Border wardens were the administrators of a society organised for war, permanently geared to the threat of the 'auld inemeyis of Ingland'. By the sixteenth century, however, wardens were being given a growing responsibility for serious domestic crime. From mid-century onwards, they were in effect acting as justiciars, empowered to try the four pleas of the crown—murder, robbery, rape and fire-raising. Alongside this growth of wardens' domestic duties was the 'general band' (by which landlords were obliged to find surety for crimes committed by their

collaborated with the government just as the Campbells did. For the Campbells' marriages from their point of view, see J. Dawson, 'The fifth earl of Argyle, Gaelic lordship and political power in sixteenth-century Scotland', *SHR*, lxvii (1988), 13-15.

1 I. Carter, 'Marriage patterns and social sectors in Scotland before the eighteenth century', *Scottish Studies*, xvii (1973); A.I. Macinnes, *Clanship, Commerce and the House of Stuart, 1603-1788* (East Linton, 1996), 8-9.

2 E.J. Cowan, 'The Angus Campbells and the origin of the Campbell-Ogilvie feud', *Scottish Studies*, xxv (1981), 26.

3 For the Alexanders of Menstrie in Clackmannan, descended from the MacDonalds, see A. Macdonald and A. Macdonald, *The Clan Donald*, 3 vols. (Inverness, 1896-1904), ii, 59-60.

4 Goodman, 'Anglo-Scottish marches', 29-30.

tenants and kinsmen), and, in more extreme cases, a system of 'pledges' or official hostages from suspect families.[1]

The Borders also lacked strong local lordship. The Tudors had a Dacre or Kildare in the north or Irish Pale to provide effective and cheap control, with a minimum of supervision from the centre.[2] Repeated harrying of the Scottish marches had prevented the establishment of similar magnates in the fourteenth century. Then when Border magnates did arise—the Black Douglases—they were destroyed by the crown in the 1450s. Their fall left a power vacuum: the result was a society in which lordship was fragmented as never before, especially in the middle and west marches, in both of which the Douglases had been the largest landowners.[3] This was the legacy with which the government of James VI had to contend 125 years later—a patchwork of local lairds and Lowland nobles drafted in to exercise some kind of supervision, either as lieutenant for the whole Borders or as a warden of the march in circumstances where authority had broken down. In November 1586, the eighth earl of Angus, who had held the office of lieutenant-general on the Borders under his uncle, Regent Morton, was reappointed at a sensitive moment in Anglo-Scottish relations, shortly after the beginning of the trial of Mary, queen of Scots.[4] After his death in 1588, a series of nobles were appointed to the post between 1592 and 1603 including Lord Ochiltree, the tenth earl of Angus and the sixth Lord Home. Their ineffectuality, especially in the strife-torn west march, can be judged by the success after 1606 of the more formidable team of the earl of Dunbar and Sir William Cranston.[5]

Landed society in the eastern Borders had more in common with Lowland Scotland than either the western Borders or its counterpart in the English east march. Lairds, the backbone of local society, could range from humble bonnet laird with barely fifty acres or two husbandlands to the heads of extensive kinship networks with vast acres under their control. The statistics of the structure of landholding in the eastern Borders are striking: fewer than 16 per cent were lesser or bonnet lairds. The bulk were comfortably well-off, having profited from the feuing of kirklands in the middle decades of the century. Often they had property in burghs or trading connections with merchants. Many had by the 1590s

1 Goodare, *State and Society*, ch. 8; T.I. Rae, *The Administration of the Scottish Frontier, 1513-1603* (Edinburgh, 1966), 64-6.

2 Cf. McNeill and MacQueen (eds.), *Atlas*, 111-13; Ellis, *Tudor Frontiers*, 261.

3 M. Brown, *The Black Douglases: War and Lordship in Late Medieval Scotland*, 1300-1455 (East Linton, 1998), 147-52, 166-75, 331.

4 *RPC*, iv, pp. xvi, 111; *Scots Peerage*, i, 194-6. A convention voted £15,000 to provide Angus with a force of 100 horse and 100 foot in Sept. 1586: *APS*, iii, 424-6. A further £10,000 was assigned in Nov. 1588: *RPC*, iv, 437; J. Goodare, 'Parliamentary taxation in Scotland, 1560-1603', *SHR*, lxviii (1989), 50.

5 *RPC*, vi, pp. xvvii, 122, 833; vii, pp. lxxx, 19; Lee, *Government by Pen*, 45-7.

invested in substantial houses, sometimes adapted from existing towers or monasteries. The greater lairds, of whom there were about forty, were conspicuous at court—notably the Homes of Wedderburn and Manderton. These were, in English terms, county gentry—to be distinguished from the petty proprietors, still living in fortified peels and towers, who typified the western marches on both sides of the Border.[1] Overpopulation was not a problem in Tweeddale; it was in Annandale.[2]

While the Highlands were frustratingly remote from the core of the state, the Borders were uncomfortably close. Border violence repeatedly spilled into the streets of the capital. Scotts and Kerrs fought a gun battle in Edinburgh in 1589; a struggle between different branches of the Kerrs for the provostship of Jedburgh resulted in the murder of the provost in an Edinburgh close in 1590.[3] With such outbursts of violence within sight of the royal court—and with similar episodes in other burghs[4]—it is not surprising that Border issues were tackled with vigour in the 1580s. It may well be that the crown was provoked, not by disorder, but by the multiple dangers posed by Lord Maxwell in Dumfriesshire and Galloway, whose disaffection provoked a raid on Dumfries led by the king in March 1587. By May 1588, Maxwell was in outright rebellion, resulting in a further royal expedition to capture Maxwell castles.[5] The success of such raids probably lay behind the king's announcement in 1587 that he would take 'some special paines' in the Highlands, as he had already done in the Borders.[6] A statute of that year codified a number of administrative devices familiar in the Borders, and applied them to the Highlands.[7] Yet this new interest in the Highlands marked no slackening in the campaign to bring the Borders under control. Even as late as 1607, it is clear that James himself attached a greater priority to the eradication of 'thift and oppressioun' in the Borders than to a 'perfyte setling' of the Highlands and Isles.[8]

One distinction to make between the government's treatment of Highlands and Borders is that the king took a personal role in the latter. For fifteen years after 1587, a publicity-conscious 'universal king' repeatedly employed two devices. One was a royal descent in person, with privy council, on a Border burgh, usually Dumfries. In November 1597 James

1 M.M. Meikle, 'The sixteenth century Border lairds: a study of the links between wealth and house building', *History of the Berwickshire Naturalists' Club*, xlvii (1993); Ellis, *Tudor Frontiers*, 257-8, 262.

2 Cf. Lee, *Government by Pen*, 74.

3 *CSP Scot.*, x, 122; K. Brown, 'Burghs, lords and feuds in Jacobean Scotland', in Lynch (ed.), *Early Modern Town*, 109, 112.

4 Brown, 'Burghs, lords and feuds', 108-10.

5 Brown, 'Making of a *politique*', 161-8.

6 Quoted in D. Gregory, *The History of the Western Highlands and Isles of Scotland, 1493-1625* (2nd edn., Edinburgh, 1881), 237.

7 *APS*, iii, 461-7, c. 59.

8 *RPC*, vii, 506-07.

spent a whole month there holding justice courts. The other was the calling of what might be called group therapy sessions to seek both a diagnosis of the ills of the Borders and a cure. In July 1600, thirty-five lairds from all three marches were summoned to confer with wardens and privy council at Falkland. Such sessions produced explanations which ranged from the naïve—an over-abundance of alehouses—to the acute—the tendency of Border lairds to spend more time in the 'incuntry', at court or elsewhere.[1] Both devices sought to find scapegoats for the recurrent breakdown of authority, and to force local elites into accepting primary responsibility for policing local society. In the process, administrative mechanisms were developed that could also be used for other remote regions. Consistently, and not only in 1587, Border policy anticipated and conditioned Highland policy.

The privy council first began to think about Borders and Highlands together in January 1585, when a number of Border and Highland landlords were summoned to advise on the ruling of their localities.[2] Perhaps this initiative was what prompted the statute of 1587 that established a common legislative framework for both regions. From then on, the government regularly bracketed its various troublesome frontiers together. In the west march it had become obsessed with 'broken men'—those without lords who would answer for them, and who were likely to live by violence; this obsession was transported into its Highland policy. Conversely, the increasing use of the Gaelic term 'clan' to describe disorderly elements in Border society concealed the complexity of power networks there. As well as 'surname' groups, who were primarily farmers, there were 'gangs', a contemporary term for loose associations of reivers.[3]

Once the Borders became the 'middle shires', the story of their policing is relatively well known. In 1605 a commission of justiciary was established. On the Scottish side, a police force was set up under the command of Sir William Cranston. In its first year of operations, it hanged thirty-two reivers, banished fifteen and outlawed a further 140. The long list of fugitives illustrated only too clearly the nature of the problem: less than thirty were drawn from the eastern Borders; the rest had disappeared into the wastes of Liddesdale, Nithsdale and Annandale. Cranston's force encountered a series of obstacles. Its numbers were modest—only 25, compared to the force of 200 raised for Angus in 1587. Its pay was usually in arrears in the first two years of its operations, and it even lacked a clerk.[4] By 1607, however, with fuller backing from Treasurer Dunbar, it began to come to grips with outlaws, even in the west march.

1 *RPC*, v, pp. lxv, 421-7; vi, 136-7; vii, 743.
2 *RPC*, iii, 718-19.
3 Cf. Rae, *Administration of the Scottish Frontier*, 6-8.
4 *RPC*, vii, pp. lxxxii, 709, 717, 724-7.

By 1609, the recent labours of Dunbar and Cranston were compared with the cleansing of the Augean stables. Even the formal minutes of the privy council, with the repeated exonerations issued to Cranston and his kinsmen for 'shooting with firearms, slaughter, mutilation and fire-raising', bring out some of the reality of the summary justice inflicted by the state in the period 1605-9.[1] Nowhere in the Highlands could the state act so ruthlessly. The problem of Maxwell power, which lay at the root of the volatility of the west march, was dealt with by internal exile: over thirty of the elite of the family and their allies were banished to Fife or north of the Tay. The extent of Maxwell influence in Dumfries and Annan is revealed by the numbers of leading burgesses exiled.[2] James himself sometimes urged dramatic solutions, such as the well-known transplantation of the notorious Graham network from the English west march to Connaught in 1606-7; the Scottish privy council was more cautious.[3] The story was not without its setbacks. The disbandment of the Border guard in 1611 may have been premature, but the copious details of judicial action on the frontier in 1622-3 reveal little more than sheep-stealing.[4] By then, the problem of the Border had been reduced to a minor one of provincial law and order.

V

A borderland, like a state, is an imaginary thing—or rather, it exists to the extent that people imagine it to do so.[5] In a Scottish state that was increasingly centralised, centrality and marginality were in flux—but they remained matters of perception. Some of the state's borderlands, in particular the Western Isles, had traditionally perceived themselves at the centre of their own world; they now began to realise that they were being firmly placed at the margin of someone else's. James himself described his British realm in 1604 as containing 'almost none but imaginarie bounds of separation', and possessing 'a communitie of language, the principall meanes of civil societie'. The message was clear: the 'Isle' over which he ruled was culturally homogeneous, or at least ought to be culturally homogeneous.[6] Those of his subjects who had a different culture were now anomalous.

1 Lee, *Government by Pen*, 73-4, 116, 163, 207-9; *RPC*, viii, 37, 278, 337n, 420, 846.

2 They included the commissary clerk and three other lawyers, a surgeon, glover and flesher: *RPC*, viii, 152-3. See also J. Wormald, *Lords and Men in Scotland: Bonds of Manrent, 1442-1603* (Edinburgh, 1985), 340, for Annan.

3 R.T. Spence, 'The pacification of the Cumberland borders, 1593-1628', *Northern History*, xiii (1977), 99-122; S.G. Ellis, *The Pale and the Far North* (Galway, 1988), 27-8.

4 Court Book of the Commissioners of the Middle Shires (May 1622-Apr. 1623), in *RPC*, xiv, 665-714.

5 Cf. B. Anderson, *Imagined Communities: Reflections on the Origin and Spread of Nationalism* (London, 1983).

6 *Stuart Royal Proclamations*, i (1603-1625), eds. J.F. Larkin and P.L. Hughes (Oxford, 1973), 95.

Yet culture is never wholly homogeneous. The king had himself divided the inhabitants of his largest Scottish borderland, the Highlands, into those who were totally barbarous and those who were only partly so. In fact the gradations in cultural, social, political and administrative practices could be far more subtle, and people could emphasise different aspects for different purposes. Highland chiefs, under pressure, agreed with the king that their own clansmen were partly barbarous;[1] probably they said something different to the clansmen themselves. The government, needing to categorise its anomalous people more precisely, faced increasing difficulties in applying the correct labels.

This can be illustrated from a remote but ambiguous region: Caithness. King James was informed in 1621 that the earl of Caithness had risen in rebellion. He exclaimed angrily that 'by the Godles and beastlie behavior of the said earle', the region had become 'so evill disordered, as no pairt of the Highlands, or most remote ilands of that our kingdome, wer ever more barbarous'. He ordered a military expedition to suppress the uprising, after which 'it is requisite that order be given, that (as the Ilesmen) everie landed man in that cuntrey shall, once or tuyse-a-yeir, compeir befor yow [the privy council], to ansuer to such complaints (iff any bee) as shall be maid against them'. The council replied smoothly that the earl was only at the horn for debt. He had not rebelled, and 'we haif hard als few complaintis or disordouris in that cuntrie as in ony other pairt of the Incuntrie'. Trade was not obstructed, and the 'landit men' were 'civile, peceable and answerable gentilmen'.[2]

Here we have at least two contrasting views of Caithness. Was it Highland or Lowland? Perhaps, like the Northern Isles, its Scandinavian antecedents placed it in a third category. The most prominent Caithness clan, the Gunns, claimed Danish descent.[3] The nearest James himself had ever been to Caithness may well have been on board the ship that took him to Norway to fetch his bride. He seems to have seen Caithness as *like* the Highlands, rather than as *part* of the Highlands. The Caithness elite, after all, spoke Scots. (The common folk may have spoken Scots, Gaelic or Norn, but they did not matter.) The council, by contrast, defined Caithness firmly as 'pairt of the Incuntrie'. Their view prevailed, even though the earl's bankruptcy had indeed caused a good deal of violence and disorder.[4] The point is that the 'barbarous' image, and the 'civile, peceable and answerable' one, were on the face of it equally credible.

1 Goodare, 'Statutes of Iona'.

2 Gordon, *Sutherland*, 368-9; NLS, council to James, 28 June 1621, Denmylne MSS, Adv. MS 33.1.1, vol. x, no. 12.

3 Gordon, *Sutherland*, 92-3, 182, 185.

4 Gordon, *Sutherland*, 366-71.

With the growth of state power, these official perceptions of the region *mattered*. If the earl of Caithness was labelled a highlander, he and his followers would be hauled before the council regularly to answer for their good behaviour. For an earl, this would probably be even more shameful than bankruptcy. In fact he escaped this fate through the privy council's good offices. Yet Caithness's son and heir, Lord Berriedale, was currently in gaol in Edinburgh because of his father's debts, and was trying to ingratiate himself with Sir Robert Gordon, tutor of Sutherland, his family's hereditary rival. Berriedale recognised that Gordon, a gentleman of the royal bedchamber, offered the court connection that was the only way to save his family's fortunes. Caithness himself preferred the life of a traditional magnate, surrounded by loyal kinsfolk and followers, but his contempt for the legal proceedings brought by his creditors was ill-judged. In 1623 he was forced into exile by a military expedition—led by Sir Robert Gordon.[1]

This episode illustrates two points. Firstly, there is the familiar picture of the growing power of the central state, able to impose its will on outlying regions more firmly than before. Nine years before his downfall, Caithness had himself commanded the royal expedition that destroyed the autonomous Stewart earldom of Orkney.[2] Secondly, we see the way in which the state was taking on new tasks—new burdens, even. The problem of Caithnesian barbarity that King James perceived in 1621 would not have troubled his predecessors. Nor had they possessed the distinctive means of dealing with barbarous regions that James's government had developed for the Isles—the system of supervision through annual summonses to the chiefs. That system required regular processing of information to ensure that the right chiefs were summoned. They had to be definable as barbarous, otherwise the summons would be unnecessary—but not *too* barbarous, otherwise tougher action would be more appropriate.

Closer contact with the borderlands had thus led to a need to develop more precise labels for them. A century earlier, no Scottish government would have imagined that it could or should define who was a highlander, any more than it could or should define religious doctrine. These had not been governmental concerns. Under James VI, that had now changed. Although his borderlands remained distinctive in their attitudes to state authority, their local elites had been forced into a closer relationship with the state. He regarded this as a success, but close relationships are not necessarily harmonious ones—as the subsequent history of the Highlands in particular would demonstrate.

1 Gordon, *Sutherland*, 375-82.

2 P.D. Anderson, *Black Patie: the Life and Times of Patrick Stewart, Earl of Orkney, Lord of Shetland* (Edinburgh, 1992), 113-24.

~ 12 ~

James VI and the 'Highland problem'

Michael Lynch

Images of the Highlands regularly enlivened the iconography of sixteenth-century kingship. In the celebrated tournaments of 1507 and 1508, James IV played a novel version of the 'knichtly game', taking on the role of the black knight who had recruited a band of 'wild men'; this pastiche had a clear political message, with the king usurping the role of Donald Dubh, pretender Lord of the Isles, who had been captured in 1505.[1] 'Wild men' were conventional in Renaissance humanist imagery but nonetheless real, threatening a wholesale subversion of the social order. They evoked dark and impenetrable woods, bogs and mountains. Yet there were tensions implicit within such imagery. The 'dark corners of the land' also promised fertility—and profit. And commentators, like Edmund Spenser, Elizabethan court poet and humanist, could often see in the figure of the wild man both the unredeemable barbarian, whether Gael or American Indian, and the potential convert to civilisation.[2] The distinction made by James VI in his *Basilicon Doron*, that some highlanders were capable of 'civilitie', was by then a commonplace.

A different kind of demonstration of kingly power was performed in 1540, when the first publication of a Scottish parliament's acts coincided with a spectacular show of military force by James V in a seaborne expedition to Orkney and the Western Isles.[3] The reasons for this circumnavigation of his kingdom are unclear and may have only partly been a reaction to the renewed activities in 1539 of a new generation of pretenders to the Lordship: the show of force—twelve ships with a formidable array of artillery pieces—seems disproportionate to the threat of a new pretender, who was a compromise candidate and as yet unestablished, or any associated problem of disorder. As was often the case in the crown's dealings in the Highlands, other circumstances were probably involved. One figure notable by his absence from the expedition was the

1 J. Dawson, 'The Gaidhealtachd and the emergence of the Scottish Highlands', in B. Bradshaw and P. Roberts (eds.), *British Consciousness and Identity: the Making of Britain, 1533-1707* (Cambridge, 1998), 287-8; L.O. Fradenburg, *City, Marriage, Tournament: Arts of Rule in Late Medieval Scotland* (Madison, Wis., 1991), 167-8. See also J. Goodare and M. Lynch, 'James VI: universal king?', Chapter 1 above.

2 P. Coughlan, '"Some secret scourge which shall by her come unto England": Ireland and incivility in Spenser', in P. Coughlan (ed.), *Spenser and Ireland: an Interdisciplinary Perspective* (Cork, 1989), 48, 50-3.

3 R.A. Mason, *Kingship and the Commonweal: Political Thought in Renaissance and Reformation Scotland* (East Linton, 1998), 133-4.

earl of Argyll, whose position as king's lieutenant in the west had been reduced to a shadow of its former self for much of the 1530s; the result had been a distinct faltering in the process of systematic exploitation by the Campbells of their official judicial powers which marked much of the sixteenth and early seventeenth centuries as well as the disorder which this brought in its wake. If the voyage was a demonstration of royal power, it was for the benefit of Campbell eyes as well as those MacDonald and Macleod networks which were attempting to revive the Lordship.[1]

James, whose father had created him 'Prince of Scotland and the Isles', probably conceived of the southern Isles as part of a wider political theatre in a period when relations with England were sharply deteriorating. English concerns in Ireland were mounting in the later 1530s. The issue was not simply the vacuum left after 1534 by the fall of the Fitzgeralds of Kildare—a reflection of a wider and longer-term problem of faltering Old English control of the areas beyond the Pale—which was eventually filled, at least temporarily, by the offer made in 1541 to Henry VIII of the crown of Ireland by the Irish parliament. The annexation of the Lordship had triggered migration across the North Channel of 'Scots Irish' settlers on an increasing scale; by the 1530s, in the mind of the Dublin authorities, their expulsion was an essential precondition of the extension of Tudor rule in Ulster. The mysterious offer of the kingship of Ireland to James V in 1540 was part of a war of nerves between England and Scotland, which preceded the outbreak of hostilities in 1542. Already, almost exactly a century before the 'war of the three kingdoms', the Highlands had become part of an elaborate, interwoven theatre of power and diplomacy involving the three kingdoms which bordered the Irish Sea; Ulster was their crossroads.[2] Disorder as well as novel varieties of 'civilised' order conceived by governments and their apologists, as part of the formalisation of a more unitary state, would result.[3]

In 1566, another point at which Anglo-Scottish relations were poor, a Renaissance triumph was staged outside Stirling Castle to mark the baptism of the queen's son, in which 'wild Hieland men' laying siege to a castle which represented the stability of the Stewart monarchy were

1 D. Gregory, *The History of the Western Highlands and Isles of Scotland from A.D. 1493 to A.D. 1625* (2nd edn., Edinburgh, 1881), 143-6.

2 J.E.A. Dawson, 'Two kingdoms or three? Ireland in Anglo-Scottish relations in the middle of the sixteenth century', in R.A. Mason (ed.), *Scotland and England, 1286-1815* (Edinburgh, 1987).

3 T.W. Moody *et al.* (eds.), *Early Modern Ireland, 1534-1691* (New History of Ireland, vol. iii, 1976), 47-8; H. Morgan, 'The end of Gaelic Ulster: a thematic interpretation of events between 1534 and 1610', *Irish Historical Studies*, xxvi (1988), 14-15; M. Lynch, 'National identity in Ireland and Scotland, 1500-1640', in C. Bjørn *et al.* (eds.), *Nations, Nationalism and Patriotism in the European Past* (Copenhagen, 1994), 55, 57-8.

repulsed, along with other stereotyped enemies of the state. It came after two failed coups, in 1565 and 1566. The first of these involved a high-level conspiracy at court and English backing for the fifth earl of Argyll in the west; this 'Chaseabout Raid', however, fizzled out in the wilds of Annandale. The restoration of order after the second, triggered by the Riccio murder, brought Mary again to the Borders with the result that, by the baptism in late 1566, English agents detected more disorder on this frontier than had occurred for a generation. Argyll, now restored to royal favour, was deeply resentful of being deserted by his English allies. London consequently feared intervention by Mary and Argyll in Ulster, where the rebellion led by Shane O'Neill now seemed out of control.[1] Campbell power, which had been promised by the Lords of the Congregation in 1560 to help the conversion of Ireland to Protestantism, now threatened to resist an English military conquest. By mid-1567, events, including the death of O'Neill and the deposition of Mary, had overtaken this English nightmare scenario, but the reigns of James V and Mary left a legacy for the reign of James VI: the borderlands of his realm became entangled with the twin issues of the 'amity' and the prospects of his succession to the English throne. The league with England, which the Scots expected to be concluded in 1573, took a further thirteen years to materialise.[2] The price of friendship levied by England escalated in the interim to include a settlement of disorder and violence in the borderlands of James's realm—in the Borders, Ulster and the southern Isles—which, to English eyes, so threatened the stability of the Tudor state.

Once the Anglo-Scottish league was finally concluded, in June 1586, both sides saw the Borders as the main threat to it. Three months later, £15,000 was voted by a convention to provide a force of 'wageit men' to police the frontier. And in April 1587, the king himself went to Dumfries on a justice ayre.[3] It was the first of a regular series of personal demonstrations of royal authority in the Borders. In contrast, the state's twofold 'Highland problem'—of internal disorder and trouble on the frontier which linked the Gaelic-speaking cultures on either side of the North Channel—seems to have eased in the late 1580s. Part of the elaborate entry conceived in 1590 to introduce James VI's Danish bride to her new kingdom included Highland dancing, staged as an entertainment in the streets of Edinburgh.[4] By then, the Highlands had apparently been reduced to a quaint, alien culture and no longer represented a threat,

1 M. Lynch, 'Queen Mary's triumph: the baptismal celebrations at Stirling, December 1566', *SHR*, lxix (1990).

2 *CSP Scot.*, iv, 463-6, 489.

3 D.L.W. Tough, *The Last Years of a Frontier* (Oxford, 1928), 241-9; *APS*, iii, 424-6; *RPC*, iv, 172.

4 M. Lynch, 'Court ceremony and ritual during the personal reign of James VI', Chapter 4 above.

either to law and order or to the authority of the crown. Yet the period between 1596 and 1617 would see a renewed vilification of Gaeldom and repeated attempts to conquer Highland society or beat it into civilisation. What provoked this renewed interest, even obsession, of James VI and his administration with the 'Highland problem'?

I

It is common to argue that the government of James VI first became concerned with a Highland 'problem' sometime in the 1580s (although the starting-point varies in different accounts) and that the experience of Highland disorder in the 1580s was uppermost in the king's mind when he composed the passage in *Basilicon Doron* which condemned part of Highland society as without 'civilitie'.[1] Certainly, conspicuously little attention was given by parliament to the Highlands before the 1580s. In the virtual absence of laws or statutes, it is difficult to maintain that the Scottish government had a Highland policy as such.[2] There is often added to this approach an overview of the shifting cultural identity of the Scottish state, increasingly reliant on Scots as the language of government, which had, in the work of John Mair and later commentators, seen a heightening of fears of the encroachment of highlanders and barbarity.[3] This phenomenon certainly existed. Both insiders and outsiders had since at least the 1520s recurrently tried to exploit the new vilification of the Highlands. A Maclean of Duart petition of 1517, which was composed against a background of a wider Campbell campaign to extend the judicial and political powers of the house of Argyll, spoke of the need of 'destroying the wicked blood of the Isles'.[4] Both of the classic cases which materialised in the last years of James VI's personal reign—the stigmatisation of the barbarities of the Western Isles immediately prior to the first expedition of the Fife Adventurers to conquer Lewis in 1598 and the outlawing of the MacGregors in 1603[5]—rested on a literature of propaganda which was almost a century old.

The argument that the 'Highland problem', in the sense of increasing breakdown of law and order, was getting worse in this period can be

1 J.M. Hill, *Fire and Sword: Sorley Boy MacDonnell and the Rise of Clan Ian Mor, 1538-1590* (London, 1993), 211; A.H. Williamson, 'Scots, Indians and empire: the Scottish politics of civilization, 1519-1609', *Past and Present*, 150 (Feb. 1996), 64, 66. Cf. Calderwood, *History*, v, 390, for the royal proclamation of Apr. 1596, anticipating the better-known passage in *Basilicon Doron* by some two years: James VI, *Basilicon Doron*, i, 70.

2 J. Goodare, *State and Society in Early Modern Scotland* (Oxford, 1999), ch. 8.

3 Williamson, 'Scots, Indians and empire', 59-62; Mason, *Kingship and Commonweal*, 53-5. See also J. Goodare and M. Lynch, 'The Scottish state and its borderlands, 1567-1625', Chapter 11 above.

4 Gregory, *History*, 119-22; cf. ibid., 136-7, for a similar offer by Argyll to destroy MacDonald power in Kintyre and the Isles 'root and branch' in 1531.

5 Gregory, *History*, 286-7, 290-3; cf. the later 'The ewill trowbles of the Lewes', *HP*, ii, 261-88; *RPC*, v, 558n. Ironically, the MacGregors had been a Campbell sept until the 1560s: M.D.W. MacGregor, 'A Political History of the MacGregors before 1571' (University of Edinburgh Ph.D. thesis, 1989).

challenged. Alternatively, it is suggested here that the state's agenda as regards the Highlands underwent three significant changes. The first came in the 1580s, as a result of the league with England. A high priority had now to be given in Scottish government policy to the quieting not only of the Borders but also the extended frontier between the two realms, stretching westwards and northwards from the North Channel separating Kintyre and the southern Isles from Ulster. The second change came in the mid-1590s, when the Highlands began to be seen as a escape route from the crisis which threatened to overwhelm the king's finances. By 1598, private entrepreneurs, ranging from nobles to novel consortia such as the Fife Adventurers, followed suit. The third change is more difficult to date precisely, for it is explained by a theme which permeates the reign of James VI from the later 1580s onwards. This was the general process of state formation, which redefined the internal frontiers within the king's realm.[1]

The first time that James VI's government was tempted to intervene in one of the potential flashpoints in the Highlands came early in 1581, when the power of Clan Donald South in Kintyre and Islay was already showing signs of waning.[2] Later that year, a statute castigated Highland clans as 'companeis of wikit men coupled in fellowschips be occasioun of thair surnames or neir duellings togidder'.[3] Another interpretation pinpoints the parliament of 1587 as defining a frontier problem which had three theatres of operation—on the Borders, across the Highland-Lowland divide and on the western seaboard with Ireland. The immediate result was a 'general band', citing 107 landlords, chiefs and leading clansmen. Such a device was the state's way of asserting its authority in a locality where it had few enforcement agents. The leading landlords were forced to sign a 'band' making them responsible for crimes committed by their tenants. It was thus hoped to isolate the 'broken men' or caterans, for whom no one would answer.[4] Early in 1588, the crown again seems to have considered the prospect of a coalition against Clan Donald South, led by Macleans and Campbells. If so, the scheme backfired and early in 1589 a series of remissions were granted by the crown to both Macleans and MacDonalds to settle their feud.[5]

1 Goodare and Lynch, 'The Scottish state and its borderlands', Chapter 11, above.

2 Hill, *Fire and Sword*, 182, 186, 211.

3 *APS*, iii, 218-19, c. 16.

4 *APS*, iii, 461-7. See A.I. Macinnes, 'Crown, clans and *fine*: the "civilizing" of Scottish Gaeldom, 1587-1638', *Northern Scotland*, xiii (1993), 31-2; A.I. Macinnes, *Clanship, Commerce and the House of Stuart, 1603-1788* (East Linton, 1996), 35, 51; Goodare, *State and Society*, ch. 8; Gregory, *History*, 234-7.

5 Hill, *Fire and Sword*, 211; Gregory, *History*, 238-41. The remissions had a price: some £6,000 arrears of royal rent was exacted from both Angus MacDonald of Dunyveg and Lachlan Maclean of Duart in 1591: *ER*, xxii, 17; *CBP*, i, 376; *CSP Scot.*, x, 463-4.

Each of these was a separate incident, with its own in-built dynamics, and they should not be collated to construct a general problem which did not exist. The statute of 1581 was probably prompted by two factors. One was the growing English concerns about the recruitment of Clan Donald mercenaries or 'redshanks' from Kintyre and Islay by Sorley Boy MacDonnell for Ulster.[1] The other may have been a reaction to short-term political rivalries at court: a split had opened up between the duke of Lennox and the chancellor, the earl of Argyll, which had induced Lennox to favour 'Macintosh, his adversary'.[2] If so, as in 1540, the cause was not Highland disorder but an anti-Campbell coalition at court.

The immediate concern of parliament in 1587, it is likely, was more with the effects of disorder on the Border, in the wake of the league with England.[3] The phrasing of the statute gives a clue to the reasoning behind it: 'the vicked inclinatioun of the disorderit subjectis, inhabitantis on sum pairtis of the Bordoures foiranent England, and in the Hielandis and Ilis, delyting in all mischeiffis ... takand occasioun of the leist truble that may occur in the inner pairtis of the realme'.[4] Although borderers and highlanders were barbarous by inclination, what worried the state was their potential to cause disorder closer to the heart of the realm. The tactic of a 'general band' had been used in the Borders since the 1520s and was now being extended to the realm's new-found internal frontiers.[5] The phenomenon of 'broken men' and tactics to deal with them were well known in the Borders; here both the diagnosis and the cure were being extended to the king's westernmost provinces, which formed a second, invisible frontier—with Ulster. Significantly, the northern Highlands were not subjected to the same treatment: here, all that happened was a precautionary letter sent in April 1587 by James VI to the earl of Huntly, still the customary king's lieutenant in the north, urging him to ensure that no disorder or feuds break out there.[6]

What had triggered this sudden appearance of a Highland problem in the minds of parliament and privy council? The answer may well lie in the death in September 1584 of the sixth earl of Argyll. He was succeeded by a minor, leaving a power vacuum in the west. Control passed to a council of six leading figures in the Campbell clan, but this opened up a series of internal divisions which were exacerbated by court politics. The

1 Hill, *Fire and Sword*, 186, 211.

2 *CSP Scot.*, vi, 94.

3 H. Morgan, 'British politics before the British state', in B. Bradshaw and J. Morrill (eds.), *The British Problem, c.1534-1707: State Formation in the Atlantic Archipelago* (London, 1996), 84; Hill, *Fire and Sword*, 208. Also at issue was a payment of some £3,000 sterling, James's English pension: J. Goodare, 'James VI's English subsidy', Chapter 6 above.

4 *APS*, iii, 461-7, c. 59.

5 T.I. Rae, *The Administration of the Scottish Frontier, 1513-1603* (Edinburgh, 1966), 212; Macinnes, 'Crown, clans and *fine*', 31-2, 34.

6 Gregory, *History*, 236-7.

Campbell empire in the west seemed about to splinter—an enticing prospect not only for the earl of Huntly, a familiar rival of Campbell expansionism, but also other courtiers, including the earls of Mar and Moray and the master of Glamis. No wonder both parliament and privy council were nervous.[1]

By 1589, however, the threatened crisis seems to have passed: precautionary arrangements were made to keep peace in the Borders but no special treatment was devised for the Highlands during the king's absence in Denmark.[2] There is nothing to suggest, when James and his Danish bride returned to Scotland in May 1590, that there was a serious Highland problem awaiting them. Indeed, matters had probably improved: the death of Sorley Boy three months earlier promised to ease the pressure put on Anglo-Scottish relations by the regular recruitment of Highland redshanks and to provoke internal divisions within Clan Donald South, on both sides of the North Channel. And a potentially serious feud in Islay involving MacDonalds and the Macleans of Duart had been settled (only temporarily as it happened) by the expedient of inviting three of the leading chiefs, who included Angus MacDonald of Dunyveg, to Edinburgh for a consultation, which took the form of locking them up in the Castle.[3] Yet in June 1590, scarcely a month after the king's return, a council for the Borders and Highlands, in effect a specialist sub-committee of the privy council, was established. It met regularly for barely eighteen months, but this provided sufficient momentum for the full council to give sustained attention to the Borders and Highlands for the rest of the decade, especially in the aftermath of the murders in 1592 of Sir John Campbell of Cawdor and the 'bonnie' earl of Moray.[4] By 1601-2, Highland business declined, seemingly because the government preferred to concentrate on the Borders.[5]

1 E.J. Cowan, 'Clanship, kinship and the Campbell acquisition of Islay', *SHR*, lviii (1979), 136-9; Gregory, *History*, 245-9. Cf. Macinnes, 'Crown, clans and *fine*', 35-6, for a similar argument about Clan Donald South and the Macleods of Lewis in the 1610s.

2 A special council for the Borders and Lanarkshire, headed by Lord Hamilton, was set up, with its headquarters at Jedburgh or Dumfries, but this was probably only precautionary for it never met. *RPC*, iv, pp. xlix, 423-30, esp. 426. No such arrangements were made for the Highlands, although a commission was later issued for the pursuit of Clan Gregor: ibid., 453-6.

3 Hill, *Fire and Sword*, 211-12; Cowan, 'Campbell acquisition of Islay', 133-4, 148.

4 *RPC*, iv, pp. liii-lvi, 781-814. Its Ordinance (pp. 790-2) referred only to the Borders, although clearly based on the act of 1587; but the title given to a special minute book included Highlands and Isles as well. A list of Highland landlords and clan chiefs on whose lands 'broken men' were located was drawn up in Dec. 1590; and the original 1587 list of troublesome clans was upgraded from 34 to 45 in June 1594, although there is a clear link between this measure and the forfeiture of the Catholic earls: *RPC*, iv, 802-3; v, 146; *APS*, iv, 71-3, c. 37. Even so, more attention was still being given in this period to the Borders.

5 *RPC*, vi, 824-34.

Sustained administrative attention to the Highlands would return in 1608, with the establishment of a commission for the Isles.[1]

When the royal administration next faced serious problems in the Highlands, in the years after 1592, it was against a very different background. The fall of Sir John Perrot, who had been Lord Deputy in Ireland 1584-8, culminating in a spectacular treason trial in April 1592, produced fresh recriminations within English circles about past failures in Ireland and threatened a fresh period of instability there. The outbreak of the Nine Years' War (1594-1603) brought such fears to fever pitch.[2] In Scotland, the crisis which had followed the murders, within days of each other, of Campbell of Cawdor and Moray had suggested a widespread conspiracy, orchestrated at court by Huntly and others; it provoked serious unrest throughout the Highlands, from Argyll to Sutherland.[3] The resultant warfare which broke out in 1593-4 between Campbells and Gordons, the traditional cornerstones of a royal presence in the Highlands, was on a new scale.[4] The instability stemming from the vacuum in the house of Argyll, which had marked the second half of the 1580s, was now replaced by a different kind of disorder, brought about largely by the increasingly aggressive gestures of a hyperactive teenager, the seventh earl.[5]

Against the background of a vacuum in policy in Dublin and the spectacular outbreak of old-style magnate rivalry, now linked to court faction, between the Scottish crown's traditional lieutenants in the west and north,[6] there was also, briefly, a prospect in 1593-4 of renewed cooperation across the North Channel between the Dunyveg and Antrim branches of Clan Donald South.[7] This was as unwelcome in Edinburgh as it was in Dublin. The reaction of each government was vigorous, embattled and at times histrionic. In 1596 James VI threatened personally to lead an expedition to the Isles. New heights of factionalism at the Elizabethan court over Irish offices, and stasis in Ireland itself under three successive viceroys, culminated in 1598 with the much-vaunted expedition of the earl of Essex and his even more spectacular failure after a mere six-month term as lieutenant.[8] The increasing

1 *RPC*, vii, pp. liii, 59-61, 737, 742-6; J. Goodare, 'The Statutes of Iona in context', *SHR*, lxxvii (1998).

2 H. Morgan, 'The fall of Sir John Perrot', in J. Guy (ed.), *The Reign of Elizabeth I: Court and Culture in the Last Decade* (Cambridge, 1995).

3 Cowan, 'Campbell acquisition of Islay', 140-1, 143; Gregory, *History*, 244-5.

4 Gregory, *History*, 254.

5 Cowan, 'Campbell acquisition of Islay', 138, 142-3, 146-7. Argyll was fourteen in 1590, when he received his act of curatory, and eighteen when he led 7,000 men to defeat at Glenlivet in 1594. Calderwood, *History*, v, 350, acidly summed it up: 'Argyll *puer* grat'.

6 Cf. R. Grant, 'The Brig o' Dee affair, the sixth earl of Huntly and the politics of the Counter Reformation', Chapter 5 above.

7 Hill, *Fire and Sword*, 211-12.

8 N. Mears, '*Regnum Cecilianum*? A Cecilian perspective of the court', in Guy (ed.), *Reign*

convergence of Tudor and Stewart aims over the need to close England's other 'postern gate', in Ulster, gave a new urgency to James VI's concerns in the Highlands. Yet these were largely problems of the state's own making or belonged to an expanded agenda, which recast links between the Scottish *Gaidhealtachd* and the Gaelic north of Ireland as a British theatre. If there was a 'Highland problem', it was not the Highlands that caused it.

II

The government of James VI was familiar with the nature of the Border problem, which it had inherited. It knew little of the Highlands. Against the web of complexities and ambiguities which permeated Highland society, it is hardly to be expected that an early modern government would follow a consistent line of policy. A series of factors, as has been seen, complicated the simple view of the Highlands, which, nevertheless, increasingly infused both official and more general Lowland opinion, as Scotland's equivalent of an alien territory beyond the Pale. Yet it is the natural instinct of historians to try to uncover the basic drift of government policy, chart deviations from it and highlight major turning points—such as in 1587 or in 1609, in the shape of the so-called Statutes of Iona. Such an approach will produce a picture of a bewildering series of apparent changes, contradictions and failures over the course of the two decades after 1596. What was happening, however, was more like a scatter-gun of official projects, some pet theories, private or quasi-official initiatives and *ad hoc* reactions by the royal administration to problems as they arose. It is not the case that the government had no policies towards the Highlands. It had a portmanteau of them, including direct conquest, colonisation or plantation, trading enterprises, dispossession or forfeiture, and the promotion of a local elite, usually as a means to subdue another.

A more fruitful approach is to consider, as should always be done in measuring the effectiveness of government which did not as yet have all the means or resources to govern, what comprised the instruments or agencies of royal rule. In such a partial vacuum, turning-points, or even benchmarks, are difficult to find. There was between 1596 and *c*.1617 not so much a see-sawing of royal policy as a jostling match by the different prospective agents of the state, each with its own solutions. This should not be seen as a feature of the unique factionalism of Scottish politics; very real analogies could be made with the 'labyrinth of caverns' of faction and conspiracy which made up the Elizabethan state of the 1590s.[1]

of Elizabeth, 59; C. Brady, 'England's defence and Ireland's reform: the dilemma of the Irish viceroys, 1541-1641', in Bradshaw and Morrill (eds.), *British Problem*, 102-4, 117; J. Guy, *Tudor England* (Oxford, 1988), 446-7.

1 Guy (ed.), *Reign of Elizabeth*, 18.

The promise of personal intervention by the king, in the shape of an expedition to the Isles, surfaced briefly in May 1596, 1598 and 1600 and in the winter of 1602-3.[1] It was, however, probably never a serious prospect. The promise of personal intervention was by this time a standard method used by James of calling attention to a problem, collecting the plaudits due to an interventionist 'universal king', and postponing dealing with it. The main check on such a show of military force was its cost. Various projects in this period were shelved because of what seems to have been a growing opposition to the rising burden of taxation. In 1600, James abandoned a third proposed personal expedition to the Isles because the burghs had proved unable, or unwilling, to furnish enough ships 'to insure his Majesty's safety'.[2] Yet the expedition of 1596, which was led instead by a lowly deputy, Colonel William Stewart, did achieve some results as did even, in a sense, the abandoned project of 1598. In 1596, Angus MacDonald of Dunyveg made a formal submission to his king and, more significantly, agreed to pay him more in rent.[3] This minor victory encouraged the notion, already present amongst some of James's council and particularly the Octavians, that one answer—and perhaps the only viable one—to the prospective bankruptcy of the crown was an increase in its rents from the Highlands. The supposed riches of the Highlands—in grain, fish, cattle and precious metals—became widely discussed from the mid-1590s onwards, driving both royal policy and private ambition.[4]

If the abortive 1598 expedition was the vehicle for James's new-found policy of plantation of parts of the Isles, it paved the way for others to implement it, beginning with the sporadic activities of the Gentlemen Adventurers of Fife in Lewis in 1598-1601, 1605-7 and briefly in late 1609. The Lewis expedition was seen as a harbinger of others. In 1598, a band of Lothian landowners were reported to be planning an expedition to Skye, although nothing came of it. And in 1600, when the first of the three Lewis expeditions was still going well, parliament anticipated the conquest of 'the remanent of his hienes Iyllis'.[5] Although it might be expected that official expeditions to daunt the Isles should have become more viable after 1603, when James had a pan-British agenda as well as English sea-power to call on, the separate agencies of the prototype

1 M. Lee, *Great Britain's Solomon: James VI and I in his Three Kingdoms* (Urbana, Ill., 1990), 199-200, 227n.

2 Eg. Gregory, *History*, 267, 293. A tax of £15,323 was raised for the 1596 expedition; the burghs alone paid £6,000 and the cost of three ships: J. Goodare, 'Parliamentary taxation in Scotland, 1560-1603', *SHR*, lxviii (1989), 42-5, 51.

3 Lee, *Great Britain's Solomon*, 199.

4 The prime resource which the Fife Adventurers thought could be extracted from Lewis was grain: their first contract, in 1598, included an obligation to pay 140 chalders of bere as part of the annual feu duty to the crown. By 1600, on closer acquaintance with the island, this was replaced by 3,600 fish. *APS*, iv, 248, c. 55.

5 *CSP Scot.*, xiii, I, 221; *APS*, iv, 248, c. 55.

British state—with councils of state in London, Edinburgh and Dublin, each with its own habits of government and separate political agendas—made the joint military task force the least frequented option of Jacobean policy. The main exception was in 1608, when Lord Ochiltree was joined by both Irish and English troops, in a well-planned raid on Islay. Yet even such a combined expedition was no guarantee of success: one of its main targets, the habitual figure of Angus MacDonald of Dunyveg, evaded it.[1]

Another government agency pushing on with its own agenda in the Highlands was the king's increasingly inquisitive team of lawyers and bureaucrats. It was undoubtedly their activities which lay behind the parliamentary statute of 1597, which threatened to invalidate all Highland land titles which were not registered with the exchequer within six months. Since few if any met the deadline and many would have had found it difficult to produce a valid parchment title, the quasi-legal basis for future, peremptory forfeitures was laid. In one sense, this was a Scots version of Henry VIII's tactic in Ireland of surrender and regrant, which also had been driven as much by a desire to raise money as to have the authority of the crown acknowledged.[2] Yet it was also no more than extending to the Highlands the sharp practice which James VI's lawyers were already inflicting on other sectors of Scottish society; clan chiefs, in effect, were being treated no worse than royal burghs.[3] In general, clan chiefs—like the burghs—bought their way out of trouble when it came, which was mostly after 1610. Some, however, fell foul of the trap and such was the fate of Hector Maclean of Duart, who (following his capture by Ochiltree) was threatened with forfeiture in 1609 on the basis of the failure of his father to register his title a dozen years before.[4]

Habitually over the course of the sixteenth century, royal commissions had been granted to (or extracted by) one or both of the traditional magnates in the west and the north—the earls of Argyll and Huntly. Such devices did not become extinct, but they were much rarer by the 1580s and 1590s, largely due, it is likely, to an increasing reluctance to invest in more Campbell or Gordon aggrandizement.[5] One such commission, in 1599, which condemned in more vitriolic terms than usual the murders and cruelties which had prevented the crown collecting

1 Gregory, *History*, 318, 322.

2 *APS*, iv, 138, c. 33; Gregory, *History*, 275-9, 281-2, 319.

3 The calling in of burgh charters and the demand that feu-ferm be paid in the original £ sterling, which was now worth eleven times the Scottish £, belongs to the same period: see M. Lynch, 'The crown and the burghs, 1500-1625', in M. Lynch (ed.), *The Early Modern Town in Scotland* (London, 1987), 68-70.

4 *RMS*, vii, 26.

5 This partial demotion of the Campbells continued until their consolidation of their position in Kintyre, against the opposition of a considerable part of the privy council, in 1607 by means of Argyll's reappointment as Justiciar and Lieutenant of the southern Isles. See Gregory, *History*, 310-12.

much of its rents and patrimony in Lewis, granted powers which included 'slauchter, mutilatioun, fyre-raising or utheris inconvenientis' to a familiar figure—the marquis of Huntly, in his old guise as a king's lieutenant. He was accompanied by a novel, mercurial figure—his brother-in-law, the twenty-seven year old cousin of the king, Ludovic Stewart, duke of Lennox.[1] Here was a combination of old practice and a new brand of favouritism, by which the crown sought to revive and, it hoped, more fully exploit to its own benefit the old device of lieutenancies. The focus in 1599 was on Lewis, so the commission extended only to the Highlands and Isles lying within the shire of Inverness.[2] In 1601, in another grant which lamented the loss of income to the crown, Huntly was given a commission for the northern Isles (excluding Lewis) and Lennox for the southern Isles, thereby supplanting Argyll.[3] By 1607, however, with Lennox comfortably settled as steward of the royal household in London, the tall order of having to 'extirpate the barbarous people of the Isles within a year' was entrusted once again to the traditional duo, Argyll and Huntly.[4] The following year, however, the king again turned to a Stewart kinsman, Lord Ochiltree, to wrench more income out of the southern Isles, in the operation which would eventually produce the Statutes of Iona.[5]

The privy council was inherently suspicious of the dangers inherent in the king's attempt to exploit the Lordship as a Stewart possession. Increasingly after 1603, Highland commissions and lieutenancies were vetted by the privy council. In 1607, it challenged the paltry £400 a year which Huntly had offered to pay to the exchequer for the extensive lands which he was due to receive in feu as part of his commission over most of the northern Isles.[6] In 1610 the council even blocked outright a commission in the Highlands sought by the son of an old crony of the king, the master of Tullibardine.[7] Such intervention by the council—blocking or refining initiatives which came either from outside it or from a faction within its own ranks—makes it all the more difficult to establish any consistency in policy. What has been termed 'government by pen'[8] was often government by veto.

In the 1590s, amidst the ceaseless quest for preferment and patronage which dominated the royal court, the Highlands were not being treated

1 *RPC*, vi, 8-10; Gregory, *History*, 286-7. Lennox had appeared briefly as lieutenant over the Isles, in effect as a notional replacement for the king, in the abortive expedition of 1598.

2 *RPC*, vi, 8-10; Gregory, *History*, 286.

3 Gregory, *History*, 293-4; *RPC*, vi, 254-6.

4 Gregory, *History*, 313-14.

5 *RPC*, viii, 93-5, 106, 110, 113-14; Goodare, 'Statutes of Iona'; Gregory, *History*, 321-4.

6 Gregory, *History*, 313-14; *HP*, iii, 119-20.

7 *RPC*, ix, 612; *Scots Peerage*, i, 468, 470-2.

8 M. Lee, *Government by Pen: Scotland under James VI and I* (Urbana, Ill., 1980), 80-1.

very differently from elsewhere. Indeed, the operation of outright favouritism came later to the Highlands than other spheres of the royal administration.[1] The king had to use the servants available to him and his first thought was usually to look no further than one or other of his 'two bodies'—his chamber and council. Kinsmen were naturally prominent in such a process. After 1603, however, the system of preferment began to work differently, with the privy council finding new ways to interpret—or thwart—the king's wishes in appointments. Crown servants, however, whether appointed in London or Edinburgh, often had their own agendas in the Highlands as well. The results, inevitably, were mixed.

The royal expedition to Kintyre in 1596 was led by Colonel William Stewart instead of the king himself. Stewart, a veteran of the Dutch wars, was the first example of a new breed of royal lieutenants, from outside the ranks of traditional magnates, in charge of what was explicitly a royal army.[2] As has been seen, the 1596 venture met with only limited success: a number of chiefs were captured and spent up to ten months in prison. Other military expeditions led by new-style lieutenants followed, in Kintyre again in 1605, and to Islay and Mull in 1608. Such direct intervention could be effective: it is no coincidence that the MacDonalds were deprived of Kintyre in 1607 and of Islay in 1612.[3] But the government was constrained by its reluctance to mobilise one part of the Highlands against another—unless it resorted to the old-style lieutenancies. The only real exception in the period was distinctly unusual: in 1602 the crown imposed a levy on Highland landowners to raise a force of 1,900 to help subdue the rebellion in Ireland.[4]

It should be no surprise that the new-style royal lieutenants from 1605 onwards were given new powers—to set feus and leases of crown lands.[5] It was a device especially focused on the estates within the old Lordship of the Isles. The first target was Islay, at the heart of the Lordship, and its rival clan chiefs—MacDonald of Dunyveg and Maclean of Duart.

1 The case of Patrick Stewart, younger cousin of the king and gentleman of the chamber when he was granted the earldom of Orkney in 1592 with what one witness called the 'most ampill commissioun of lieutenandrie and justiciarie ... that evir I saw', has a particular resonance. P.D. Anderson, *Black Patie: The Life and Times of Patrick Stewart, Earl of Orkney, Lord of Shetland* (Edinburgh, 1992), 15, 21-2, 88; *RPC*, xiv, 612.

2 Stewart of Houston, commendator of Pittenweem, had been a soldier in the employ of the Prince of Orange in the 1570s, and a crown servant and a minor figure in the privy council for well over a decade. *RPC*, v, 309-10; *Scots Peerage*, vii, 64-8; *DNB*, liv, 362-4; K.M. Brown, *Bloodfeud in Scotland, 1573-1625* (Edinburgh, 1986), 227; Gregory, *History*, 265.

3 Gregory, *History*, 263-9, 306-8; *HP*, iii, 72-85; *RMS*, vi, 1911.

4 *RPC*, vi, 343. The levy included even Clanranald and MacGregors. It specified: Campbells 300; Lennox 200; Atholl 100; MacGregors 50; Huntly 100; Mackintoshes 100; Grants 100; Lovat 100; Caithness 100; Sutherland 100; MacDonalds of Glengarry 100; MacDonalds of Clanranald 200; Mackenzies 100.

5 *RPC*, vii, 115-17.

Another new kind of royal agent appeared in the years after 1608—James's bishops. In 1610, James Law, bishop of Orkney, made his first appearance as a commissioner of the peace for the Northern Isles; by 1612 he was also an investigator and collector of royal revenues.[1] The first bishop to take on such a range of powers in the far-flung parts of the realm, however, was Andrew Knox, bishop of the Isles. Plucked from obscurity as minister of Paisley to his bishop's seat in 1605, Knox has come to be hailed as the architect of a new policy which materialised in 1609 as the Statutes of Iona, although there remains disagreement as to whether he was acting as an 'indefatigable servant' of his king or as the selfless agent of a privy council intent on achieving victory for its point of view.[2] What is more likely, however, is that both Knox and Ochiltree were acting on instructions from king and council working in concert; the evidence for separate agendas being pursued in London and Edinburgh is thin.[3] Viewed against the king's attempts for ten years or more to prise more income out of what he claimed to be his own estates in the Lordship, there should be little doubt that James himself viewed Knox, first and foremost, as another kind of debt collector.

Initially, when the expedition to the Isles was given its commission in the summer of 1608, it is clear that Ochiltree was regarded by James as the new lieutenant over the Isles—in effect, a counterpart of Lennox ten years before. Knox was cast in the role of loyal aide.[4] The detailed instructions, confirmed by parliament, also reflected the king's own agenda: the security of royal rents ranked above all other aims, including law and order, the surrender of alleged jurisdictions and a programme of drip-feed anglicisation through education of the children of the elite in the Lowlands.[5] By the standards of military adventures of the period, and despite the fact that a convention of estates flatly refused to make any contribution towards its cost, Ochiltree's much reduced expedition, numbering only 900 men, did remarkably well: it reached Skye as well as Mull and Islay, captured a handsome collection of clan chiefs and took possession of the castles of Dunyveg and Duart.[6] But Ochiltree had failed to do anything to secure the king's rents in Islay.

The second commission to the Isles, issued in May 1609 to Knox and the comptroller, Sir James Hay, also had clear instructions from James, which highlighted the need for a careful survey of the king's property

1 Anderson, *Black Patie*, 96, 100.

2 Cf. J. Kirk, *Patterns of Reform: Continuity and Change in the Reformation Kirk* (Edinburgh, 1989), 485-6: Lee, *Government by Pen*, 77-81; Lee, *Great Britain's Solomon*, 216-18.

3 Goodare, 'Statutes of Iona'.

4 Gregory, *History*, 321.

5 *APS*, iv, 404; *RPC*, viii, 59-61, 73; Gregory, *History*, 319-20.

6 *RPC*, viii, 173-5; Balfour, *Historical Works*, ii, 25-6; *APS*, iv, 404. Cf. Lee, *Government by Pen*, 77-8; Goodare, 'Statutes of Iona'; Gregory, *History*, 321-5; W.C. Mackenzie, *History of the Outer Hebrides* (Paisley, 1903), 237-9.

in the Isles. In the event, the comptroller, perhaps in failing health, never went. Knox, left to his own devices, ignored the main part of his instructions and composed his own provisional agenda—the distinctly loose and somewhat impractical agreement that has come to be known as the Statutes of Iona. Not surprisingly for a bishop deeply concerned at the slowness of the evangelisation in the Isles—in 1609 only a third of the parishes in Argyll had a minister and only one in fifteen in Skye and the Outer Hebrides[1]—Knox established as the first article the proper financing and plantation of the ministry, the rebuilding of ruinous churches, better keeping of the Sabbath, obedience to the clergy and an end to what he saw as superstitious marriage practices. Part of this was as much a petition to the king and his council as a laying down of the law to the men of the Isles. Knox must have been only too aware, in the spring and early summer of 1609, that Archbishop Spottiswoode had begun his visitation of the Borders and the earl of Dunbar had decided to confront Border lawlessness personally. The Statutes were an appeal for greater resources to be devoted to the problem of the Isles. What they were not was a policy laid down by either the king in London or his council in Edinburgh. In that one sense, the 'Statutes of Iona' may be well named; this was policy devised on the spot. The more precise reworking and extension of this programme by the privy council in 1616 was, by contrast, more of a landmark.[2]

Knox's next commission—as *steward* of the Isles in charge of royal rents in May 1610—reflected the fact that his royal master saw the Iona agreement only as a beginning.[3] In the same month, Knox was appointed to the bishopric of Raphoe in Ireland and he seems not to have done anything about his new commission as royal steward. Little, too, was done about the Statutes themselves, other than being registered by the privy council. Much had been left unsettled in the Iona agreement which had, in part, only been talks about future talks. When the chiefs came to Edinburgh en masse for the first time, late in June 1610, there seems to have been no discussion of the Statutes, nor any agreed set of measures.[4] Yet the fact that they had come and the deficiencies in the Iona conference brought about a new focus in the privy council's strategy.

The following years would see marked developments on two fronts—finances and the road trodden to Edinburgh from the Isles by the chiefs. In 1609, the crown's annual income from Islay stood at £1,000; but by 1615 it had risen to £6,000.[5] A combination of intermittent military force and a persistent litany of legal threats had done its work. Yet the delivery

1 Macinnes, 'Crown, clans and *fine*', 47.
2 For a fuller analysis, see Goodare, 'Statutes of Iona'.
3 *RPC*, ix, 16-18.
4 See Goodare, 'Statutes of Iona', for a fuller discussion of these points.
5 Goodare, *State and Society*, ch. 8.

of what were now royal rents was as significant as the sums themselves. By 1614, the chiefs had become used to delivering their rents, in person, to the privy council in Edinburgh, usually in July. In July 1616, this process was consolidated and enshrined in a new agreement, drawn up by the privy council, which spelled out, in precise terms, the other demands to be met by the chiefs. They included an explicit limit set on military retinues; the adoption of Lowland ways of agriculture and the English language, to the extent that a monoglot Gaelic speaker who was a chief's heir could not inherit; and the abandonment of the exaction of hospitality and cautions to obey the law. This was a real landmark, in a way which the Statutes of Iona had not been.[1] The road *from* the Isles, regularly tramped after 1610 by the clan elite, had become more important than the intermittent road to the Isles taken until 1610 by royal commissioners and other agents of government.

The same year of 1610 marked another turning-point for the Isles, which may well be linked, for it was then that the Fife Adventurers gave up their attempt to colonise Lewis.[2] The story is a tangled one, which does not wholly bear out the view that the enterprise was ill-conceived or hopeless from the outset. Despite a series of setbacks, which included a sharp, but minor defeat inflicted on an expedition dispatched late in 1609, the Adventurers were a more formidable force than before, at least in terms of political connections. The syndicate, when it was revamped in 1608, included Lord Balmerino, a secretary of state, and the ubiquitous entrepreneur, Sir George Hay of Netherliff. It survived the fall early in 1609 of Balmerino, whose share was gifted to Hay, and it did not give up until July 1610.[3] The attachment to Lewis was unlikely to have been sentimental: Hay had already amassed a business empire in glass making and iron. Nor was there as yet much sign of a general disenchantment with colonial enterprises. Huntly had intended to use the commission granted to him in 1607 to colonise Uist, 'not ... be agreement with the cuntrey people, but be extirpatioun of them'; the scheme was abandoned, but not because it was suddenly thought unviable.[4] Although plantation in the Isles fell away after 1610, it was not because it had been discredited as a money-spinner, either in Ulster or elsewhere.

The beneficiary in Lewis was Kenneth Mackenzie of Kintail, who in 1610 not only bought out the interests of Hay and the other remaining Adventurers but also profited from the crown's change of mind, which resulted in the disposal to him (rather than to Hay) of the third share of

1 According to R. Black, 'Colla Ciotach', *TGSI*, xlviii (1972-4), 214, 'Where the Statutes had been experimental and tentative, this Bond was precise and repressive'; Goodare, 'Statutes of Iona'.

2 This suggestion is more fully analysed in Goodare, 'Statutes of Iona'.

3 Lee, *Government by Pen*, 92-4, 162, 196. Hay became clerk register in 1616.

4 *RPC*, vii, 361; Gregory, *History*, 314-15.

Balmerino.[1] The shadowy activities of Mackenzie of Kintail explain much, not only about the difficulties of the Lewis venture, but also the workings of James's 'pen government'. Mackenzie first appeared on the privy council in 1596—the first Highland 'insider', apart from the Campbell earls or notables, to reach this position in James's reign.[2] It is unlikely that his appointment marked an immediate end to the century-old strategy of trying to control the Highlands through old-style magnates in favour of a new-style policy of cooperation with native elites.[3] His qualifications for office were impressive: he had a record of causing trouble, in Lewis and elsewhere, stretching back to 1594, had several times been chided by the council, latterly with regard to stirring up difficulties for the Fife Adventurers, and had been imprisoned in Edinburgh Castle in 1599.[4] Such regular troublemakers had a habit, in the personal reign of James VI, of being made an example of, either by victimisation or promotion. Further preferment, to a peerage in 1609—which in retrospect can be made to look like a significant, fresh departure, turning Highland chiefs into a new nobility—came at a point when Mackenzie's long campaign to undermine the Lewis Adventurers looked as if it had finally come to grief.[5] It was not that the new Lord Kintail had reached a unwonted prominence in affairs of state, for he played little formal part in the government's initiatives taken in the Highlands from 1610 onwards. Like any Lowland noble in such circumstances in the reign of James VI, he was being bought off, and he would have expected no less. If the episode has a wider significance, it is that Kintail was a pioneer in the general trend for many Highland chiefs in the seventeenth century to adopt more Lowland ways, which would distance them from their own clansmen.[6] The way forward, it was increasingly recognised, was through royal favour, loyal petition and regular settlement of their rents.[7] That route, it was already clear by the 1610s, also entailed conspicuous expenditure, massive lawyers' fees and chronic debt.[8]

1 Lee, *Government by Pen*, 93-4; *RPC*, ix, 13-15; *RMS*, vii, 341. Hay, presumably as a pay-off, established an iron foundry at Letterewe, in Mackenzie territory, in 1612: *RPC*, iv, 351; x, 22-3; xiv, 567; *LP James VI*, 365-6; S.G.E. Lythe, *The Economy of Scotland in its European Setting, 1550-1625* (Edinburgh, 1960), 44-5.

2 He had been recommended by parliament in 1592 for a seat on the privy council, but declined; his period of service dates from Feb. 1596. He was readmitted in 1602. *RPC*, v, 90, 273; vi, 497; *APS*, iii, 562.

3 Cf. Lee, *Great Britain's Solomon*, 201.

4 Gregory, *History*, 290-2, 298, 300-2; *RPC*, v, 161, 265, 364, 528-9; vi, 4-5, 101, 617, 624, 689.

5 *RPC*, ix, 13-15; *RMS*, vii, 341.

6 Cf. P. Burke, *Popular Culture in Early Modern Europe* (London, 1978), 270-81.

7 Cf. Goodare and Lynch, 'James VI: universal king?', Chapter 1 above.

8 K. Brown, 'Noble indebtedness in Scotland between the Reformation and the Revolution', *Historical Research*, lxii (1989); D. Watt, 'Chiefs, Lawyers and Debt: a Study of the Relationship between Highland Elite and the Legal Profession in Scotland, *c*.1550 to 1700' (University of Edinburgh Ph.D. thesis, 1998), ch. 8.

Office under the king from 1602 onwards certainly gave Mackenzie new opportunities to frustrate the Lewis enterprise. The episode in 1607, when he contrived the outright gift of Lewis under the great seal, only to see James veto it, reveals much about divisions within the privy council as well as the gulf of misunderstandings which regularly existed between it and the king. Huntly's appointment, as lieutenant in the north, was closely linked to the Lewis enterprise and the king's continuing support of it. Mackenzie's hostility to the Adventurers was put to a new use by Chancellor Dunfermline, with whom he had growing ties of interest. Yet any attempt by him to promote Kintail as an alternative government agent in the north, at the expense of Huntly, fell foul of James's continuing attachment to colonial ventures as well as to his kinsman by marriage.[1]

III

A survey of the years between 1603 and 1617 would show clear losers as well as gainers amongst Highland chiefs and clans. In 1603, the surname of MacGregor had been officially abolished and, after 1611, MacGregors could legally be killed by any and all simply for being MacGregors. Yet, by then the clan had been reduced to a fugitive band only two dozen strong.[2] Other vulnerable clans, such as the MacDonalds of Dunyveg and the Macleods of Lewis, both weakened by internal disputes, had been picked off. The argument, however, that weak or divided clans went to the wall because they were weak or divided can become a circular one.[3] The adoption of client clans, in order to extend the arm of the state, which became a growing feature of government strategy after 1607, when the Campbells acquired Kintyre, was a wild card thrown into Highland society and it had random results. Official clientage enjoyed by clan chiefs was sometimes unpopular with their clansmen and the heads of both ClanRanald and Mackinnon had to resort to seeking government commissions of justiciary against their own *fine*.[4] Clans were not necessarily as receptive to the process of civilising as their chiefs.[5] It is also difficult to draw a firm line showing that the victims were clans driven by internal feud or violence or that the winners were client clans marked by a unity of purpose. In 1615, for example, during the MacDonald uprising in Islay, Sir Roderick Macleod explained to the privy council that the composite force drawn from several clans acting

1 *RMS*, vii, 167-8; Lee, *Government by Pen*, 76; Lee, *Great Britain's Solomon*, 201, 213. Kintail's son, the future 1st earl of Seaforth, married a daughter of Dunfermline in 1614: *Scots Peerage*, iii, 372; vii, 507.

2 *APS*, iv, 550-1, c. 26; *RPC*, vi, pp. xxxiii-xlii, 558n; x, pp. xiv-xxv, 41.

3 Macinnes, *Clanship*, 37-8, 60.

4 *RPC*, viii, 445; ix, 324-5.

5 Cf. Macinnes, 'Crowns, clans and *fine*', 37.

on behalf of the government had had to be divided into 'thrie severall armyes and companyees' because of their mutual animosities.[1]

The overall results were mixed. In one sense, the years up to 1615, were marked by a succession of mostly *ad hoc* measures, in reaction to events, including one major rebellion. On the other hand, it is possible, from 1609 onwards, to point to the cumulative effect of a series of undertakings by clan chiefs, which were a mixture of coercion and agreement. The demand for proof of titles, first made in 1597, was reintroduced in 1608, in what was, in effect, a Henrician-style surrender and regrant. The Statutes of Iona, at best, set an agenda for discussion; the conference of leading chiefs and the government, which took place in June 1610, was inconclusive, but the bargaining continued, even during the MacDonald uprising in Islay in 1614.[2] By 1616, the full form of the agreement which had gradually emerged since 1608 or 1609, became explicit. Refinements, however, continued to be added: the most significant was the banning in 1617 of the taking of calps, or death duties, by chiefs.[3]

After 1616, the official view of the government increasingly was that the Highlands had been pacified, even if some highlanders still proved troublesome. Outbreaks of trouble, such as in Assynt in 1617 or Lochaber early in the 1620s, were treated as deviations from the norm. It was a line enthusiastically adopted by the elite's converts to King James's new-found peace. In 1622, Sir Roderick Macleod of Dunvegan, by then a regular visitor to Edinburgh to pay his dues, waxed lyrical about 'this delectable time of peace'.[4] Yet there were also suggestions for new kinds of direct government intervention, such as that made by Highland landlords in 1624 for the establishment of two twenty-man police forces, on the lines of Sir William Cranston's now disbanded force on the Borders. The scheme, however, foundered over disagreement as to who should pay for it.[5]

The government may in private have doubted its own propaganda. In 1615, Sir Alexander Hay, clerk register, reviewed the government's achievements following the suppression of the MacDonald uprising in Islay. His views have customarily been cited to give weight to the case against Campbell aggression in the west and factionalism at court.[6] For the crown, however, he saw little to celebrate: the expense of putting down the rising amounted to ten years of 'the rents of our whole Iyles'.[7] To a government which had for twenty years seen the Highlands as a potential economic bonanza, this was disappointing indeed. The

1 *HP*, iii, 243.
2 *RPC*, viii, 759-61; x, 698-700.
3 *APS*, iv, 548, c. 21.
4 *RPC*, xii, 744-5; Lee, *Government by Pen*, 145-6.
5 Lee, *Government by Pen*, 146.
6 E.g. Gregory, *History*, 289, 355.
7 *HP*, iii, 302.

crown's income from punitive fines had also failed to reach anything like its full potential: steadily, more and more went to its agents, and especially into Campbell coffers.[1] Amidst the welter of competing strategies offered by the servants of the crown from 1596 onwards—including settlement, occupation, plantation, trading ventures, official military expeditions and licensed private gangs of different kinds—it is difficult, and indeed fruitless, to pinpoint any uniformity of policy. There was only one consistent thread—the desire for the crown to profit from the Highlands before others did. The most accessible income, however, turned out to be that offered by clan chiefs in their annual excursion to Edinburgh. There was a price to pay for that, since the government, in effect, had found in such partly anglicised clan elites a new kind of devolved power, which, in turn, randomly produced both peace and disorder in different localities of the Highlands, depending on local circumstances. A government tough on Highland disorder but not on the root causes of disorder, which included the activities of some of its own agents, should have expected no less.

1 The 'Account Book of Fines for Reset of Clan Gregor, 1612-1624' (*RPC*, xiv, pp. xc-xcviii) shows that the crown received only 22.5 per cent of such fines, imposed on anyone who had helped MacGregors evade justice, the rest going to Argyll. The net sum collected was *c.*£44,665.

~ 13 ~

James VI and the Politics of South-West Scotland, 1603-1625

Sharon Adams

Although a scholar well versed in the history of the Old Testament, when James VI adopted the image of King Solomon the iconography was rather more apt than the king would have intended. As was made explicit in the entertainments for the entry of his queen into Edinburgh in 1590, James not only believed his reign to be divinely ordained by God, he also laid claim to the wisdom of Solomon and wished to believe that his kingdom was equally peaceful and well ordered.[1] Even more would James have liked to emulate the status and the fabulous wealth of a King Solomon. However, the parallels between the two monarchs run deeper, particularly in the realm of civil administration. James, like Solomon, inherited an enlarged kingdom over which he sought to exert his authority, adopting surprisingly similar methods in the process—Solomon, for example, had recognised the importance of employing crown-nominated officials in outlying areas and the levying of regular taxation. Both monarchs proved unable to pass on these benefits to posterity, which would, within a few years of their death, see a revolt in one half of the realm leading to civil war, the division of the kingdom and a breach within the national church.

Thus, for James as for Solomon, a key context for his reign was the relationship between his government and the regions of his kingdom. In a still largely decentralised state this relationship was, at the most basic level, the point of contact between governor and governed. The success—or failure—of this interaction between 'court and country' or 'centre and locality' becomes particularly pertinent after James's removal to London in 1603 when the concept of 'the centre' was itself in flux: was it Edinburgh or London, the king or his Scottish administration? For contemporaries, however, the relationship was more organic, a question of balance between a number of co-existing power bases. For James, his localities were a concern primarily when they interfered with the smooth course of royal government. Of course the converse was equally true; the monarch was often an issue for his subjects only when

[1] James VI, *Basilicon Doron*, i, 121; D. Stevenson, *Scotland's Last Royal Wedding: the Marriage of James VI and Anne of Denmark* (Edinburgh, 1997), 118-19. Cf. M. Lynch, 'Court ceremony and ritual during the personal reign of James VI', Chapter 4 above.

he threatened their way of life or vested interests, or when they required patronage.

Stewart monarchs have traditionally been judged as successes or failures according to criteria which incorporate these, sometimes contradictory, ideas of central power and local harmony. Effective monarchy meant a strong, centralised power base bolstering the authority of the crown in the localities. The relationship between centre and locality can be represented in various ways—by the institutional dynamics of power, the channels through which the crown implemented policy in the locality, or by the personal interaction between each sphere, such as the relationship between the king and his nobles. The connections between centre and locality were also affected by geography; by distance from the heart of the kingdom and ease of access from the localities to the centre of government. Thus the term locality tends to be associated with perceived problem areas such as the Highlands and the Borders. In practice, however, the serious political challenges facing the Stewart monarchy in the sixteenth, and certainly the seventeenth, centuries came from central Scotland—Ayrshire, Fife and Lothian. The question of how James and his government related to an area such as the south-west of his kingdom is, therefore, immediately relevant. How did royal government function in a specific locality? How successfully did James deal with local politics? Where did the levers of power lie? What did James want from his localities and, equally importantly, what did they want from him?

I

James VI's south-west—the area south of Glasgow and west of Annan—had many identities: on the one hand, Dumfries and Galloway, an area remote from the centres of government; on the other, North Ayrshire, a region immediately adjacent to central Scotland. In some aspects the south-west was a region governed more by proximity to Argyll, to the north of England and to Ulster than by distance from Edinburgh. Thus the south-west is in no sense a coherent political unit, but a broad geographical designation similar in context to 'the Highlands' or indeed to its antithesis, 'the north-east'. In administrative terms the south-west roughly corresponded to the sheriffdoms of Ayr, Wigtown and Dumfries and the stewartry of Kirkcudbright. The structure of local politics did not, however, fit neatly into administrative units. The ties of lordship, kinship and affinity and the exercise of power were more important, creating a complex pattern of overlapping networks and relationships.

While the role of central government may have become increasingly important in the reign of James VI, its success was still determined by the king's ability to govern his localities. Nor did the centre exist in and of itself, for its constituent parts—administrators, privy councillors, nobles in the king's favour—derived from the locality. Political success at all levels depended on the ability to operate effectively within both spheres of influence. This was particularly true of the greater and lesser nobility, who were both central and local, a fact which James himself recognised when he advised his son to remember that 'vertue followeth often noble blood', especially since 'it is they must be the armes and executers of your lawes'.[1] Influence at court ideally hinged on a strong power base in the locality, while royal favour was an equally important contributor to noble power. Influence at court, however, was not always compatible with influence in the locality; indeed the conflicting demands of the two environments could prove difficult to reconcile.

Of the three earls based in the south-west prior to 1603—Cassillis, Eglinton and Glencairn—the career of the seventh earl of Glencairn is an undeniably extreme example of sporadic involvement in government. A regular attender of the privy council in 1582-3, the period associated with the regime of the Ruthven raid, he spent most of the following years in comparative political obscurity, primarily in his local power base, the north of Ayrshire. Thus, in the two years prior to James's departure for London, Glencairn's rare attendance at meetings of the council was usually for a specific purpose, as in February 1601 when he brought a complaint or in March 1602 when the council met in Dumfries.[2] A contrasting pattern is provided by the second and third Lords Ochiltree, forced by financial embarrassment to pursue careers based at court and in the royal service. James employed the third Lord to perform a variety of services, such as pacifying the noble petitioners following the riot of December 1596, as an agent in the west Highlands and as a member of the 1609 commission anent the ravishing of women. Ochiltree also played a shadowy role in the feud between the sixth earl of Huntly and the earl of Moray. By 1615 when Ochiltree finally transferred his interests to Ireland, surrendering his lands and titles to his cousin 'by a kynd of succession alsweele as by purchase', he was declared to be 'as it wer deade in that oure kingdome'. Thus, for the Stewarts of Ochiltree, their family, name and connections were more important than their traditional locality.[3]

A more typical picture of the average noble, if such a person exists, is given by the career of the fifth earl of Cassillis.[4] The son of the so-called 'king of Carrick', the fifth earl presided over an extensive regional earldom and kin network, some members of which rivalled the earl

1 James VI, *Basilicon Doron*, i, 87.
2 *Scots Peerage*, iv, 243-4; *RPC*, vi, 203-4, 355-8; *RPC*, viii, 815.
3 R.R. Zulager, 'A Study of the Middle Rank Administrators in the Government of King James VI of Scotland, 1580-1603' (University of Aberdeen Ph.D. thesis, 1991), 169; K.M. Brown, *Bloodfeud in Scotland, 1573-1625* (Edinburgh, 1986), 222, 156-9; *APS*, iv, 454, c. 48; *RPC*, x, 334.
4 *Scots Peerage*, ii, 475-7.

himself in terms of prestige and influence. The earl's main power base lay in his locality but, like all successful or aspiring magnates, he required to combine this with influence at court, occasionally overreaching himself in the process. In 1597, he made a remarkable marriage to Jean Fleming, widow of Chancellor John Maitland of Thirlestane, which excited the attention of the court as she was a woman 'of good years, not like to bear children'. One commentator at court declared Cassillis to be 'clengit out of credit and estimation both here and at home with his own friends' since his marriage, a contemporary analysis which recognised that Cassillis operated in two distinct spheres.[1] It was largely as a result of this marriage that the earl entered into his brief and financially disastrous period as treasurer in 1599, when it was rumoured that James wished Cassillis to take the position so that 'his wifes purse should be opened for her rose nobles'.[2] Following his unsuccessful attempt at advancing himself through office-holding, Cassillis returned to a more traditional pattern of concentrating on his local power base while balancing this with attendance at court.[3]

The removal of the king to London had little immediate impact on the careers of men like Cassillis. Edinburgh remained for all practical purposes the centre of government and they continued to attend meetings of the privy council with more or less the same level of irregularity. There were a number of factors which might determine the reaction of provincial nobles to the departure of the king. The memory of the personal influence and authority of the monarch might remain strong enough to withstand his absence, at least in the short term. Equally the administration in Edinburgh might retain sufficient influence to counteract the king's absence. It is even possible that nobles whose primary interests lay in the locality might welcome absentee monarchy as giving them greater freedom of manoeuvre. Certainly, for Cassillis and others like him, the immediacy of the local community remained compelling. Amongst other factors, the striking number of noble and lairdly residences found in relatively small burghs bears testimony to the continuity of local society. It is perhaps not surprising that the earls of Eglinton and Glencairn, plus a dozen others, had identifiable residences in Irvine, or that a similar pattern can be found in Ayr. The small town of Maybole, however, boasted twenty-eight residences of Carrick lairds, including the impressive townhouse of the earls of Cassillis. Most of these lay in ruins by the end of the seventeenth century as attention turned away from the immediate locality to Ayr, or to Glasgow and Edinburgh.[4]

1 BL, Cotton MSS, Caligula, B. IV, fo. 244; *CSP Scot.*, xiii, I, 329.

2 *CSP Scot.*, xiii, I, 444.

3 K.M. Brown, 'A house divided: family and feud in Carrick under John Kennedy, fifth earl of Cassillis', *SHR*, lxxv (1996), 181-5.

4 J. Strawhorn, *The History of Irvine* (Edinburgh, 1989), 18; J. Strawhorn, *The History of Ayr* (Edinburgh, 1985), 35; J. Gray, *Maybole, Carrick's Capital* (Ayr, 1973), 16.

One potential source of friction lay in the appointment of justices of the peace from 1609-10. A potentially novel element of the justice system was the opportunity it gave for minor lairds to hold office—an opportunity they were able to exploit largely because of the lack of interest in these appointments. Few noblemen would have wished to concern themselves with matters such as the regulation of ferry prices between the south-west and Ulster.[1] While there may indeed have been little enthusiasm for the office of justice among the nobility, the lists of those appointed reflected the existing leadership of society: no other formula would have given the new office any chance of success. Thus confrontations which were alleged to have been caused by the new office were often merely old problems in a new guise. For example, David Calderwood recounts an apparent case of jurisdictional friction in which Cassillis and a Fife laird appeared before the privy council in 1612 accused of abuses in the conduct of their offices as JPs, and were offended 'because they perceived the council and noblemen crossed them in the execution of their office'. For their part, the noblemen on the council 'thought that this new office impaired their credite and freindship in the countrie'. This, however, was not a case of conflict between an upstart JP and established royal councillors; Cassillis was entitled to sit on the privy council and most of the councillors were themselves JPs. Further, the only case involving Cassillis brought before the council that year was an action by George Corrie of Kelwood, accusing the earl of forcing him from his bed at eight o'clock in the morning and imprisoning him for ten days. This might seem like a classic example of the abuse of power by a justice, but there is no indication that Cassillis was acting explicitly in the context of his position as JP, while Corrie of Kelwood himself appears on the list of JPs for Ayrshire in 1616.[2] In fact this was nothing more than old-fashioned local violence, perhaps camouflaged by the title of JP.

II

When James went south in 1603, relatively few key players from the locality were regularly involved in the royal administration and only three earls were based in the south-west, all in Ayrshire. One of James's policies which did, therefore, have a particular impact in the region was his creation of a number of new Scottish earldoms. With the creation of four new earls in Dumfries and Galloway, the picture would dramatically alter in the opening decades of the seventeenth century, largely as the result of a deliberate and planned royal policy.

The first of James's creations in the south-west was John, sixth Lord Fleming, raised to the dignity of earl of Wigtown in 1606. Although claiming descent from the fourteenth-century earls of Wigtown, his

1 M.M. Meikle, 'The invisible divide: the greater lairds and the nobility of Jacobean Scotland', *SHR*, lxxi (1992), 79-80; *RPC*, ix, 478.

2 Calderwood, *History*, vii, 178; *RPC*, x, 25, 619.

family had few direct links with the area; of more importance to James was its history of conspicuous loyalty to the crown. Wigtown was active in the king's service, undertaking many special commissions in addition to his appointment to the privy council and to the court of high commission.[1] His interests, however, were almost wholly located outwith the south-west, as were those of James's final creation in the locality, John Murray, earl of Annandale, a classic example of the consummate London-Scottish courtier. Murray, the second son of a Dumfriesshire laird, owed his advancement to a long and successful career in the king's household. He held substantial properties in the south-west and elsewhere, but his keen interest in Scottish affairs was expressed primarily within the context of his role as a conduit between the court and his extensive network of Scottish correspondents.[2]

While both Wigtown and Annandale can be seen as being intruded upon the region, the limited nature of their involvement in local affairs neutralised any negative impact created by their ennoblement. However, possibly the most interesting of James's creations, Robert, tenth Lord Maxwell, created earl of Nithsdale in 1620, successfully combined a career at court with influence in his locality. After the execution and forfeiture of his brother in 1613, Nithsdale saw that the key to preferment lay in favour at court. Following his rehabilitation in 1617, Nithsdale proved astonishingly successful at rapidly retrieving most of the forfeited lands as part of a long career of loyal and lucrative service to the crown.[3]

In one sense these ennoblements are not surprising. They were not made at the expense of existing magnates: James was acting to fill a local power vacuum, as well as to reward loyal service and ensure future loyalty in the region. No major regional magnate had held extensive lands for a prolonged period along the western border since the forfeiture of the Black Douglases in 1455. Local power had rested in the hands of substantial local kin networks, notably the Maxwells and the Johnstones, and with influential families such as the Crichtons of Sanquhar and the Agnews of Lochnaw. Thus, it was largely a historical and geographical accident that, in the first decades of the seventeenth century, so many families in the west borders were looking for advancement and saw the king's personal favour as the key to preferment. James took full advantage of this. William Crichton, ninth Lord Sanquhar, created Viscount Ayr in 1622 in return for his support in the parliament of 1621, was, like Nithsdale, the heir of an executed and forfeited predecessor.

1 *Scots Peerage*, viii, 545-6. Wigtown's seat was at Cumbernauld, the area in which his power base lay.
2 *Scots Peerage*, i, 226.
3 *Scots Peerage*, vi, 485-6.

What is surprising is the extent to which families like the Maxwells had become so successful, so loyal to the crown and so involved in government, virtually overnight. After 1606 James overwhelmingly used his new men to represent the south-west, as members of the privy council and the court of high commission. There is a definite parallel here between the western and eastern borders, where James similarly elevated and employed the Kerr earls of Roxburgh and Lothian and, the great success story of the seventeenth-century peerage, Scott of Buccleuch. It was not so much that James's new creations alienated an existing nobility in the south-west, but that his use of his new nobles militated against the successful involvement of other magnates in royal government. James did not make equally sure of the loyalty of his established nobility.

III

One sphere in which James employed his newly created nobles was in establishing firm control over the institutions of the church. Like the nobility themselves, the church operated at both central and local levels. Of the sixteen peers whom James appointed as commissioners to the general assemblies of 1606, 1608 and 1610, seven had been elevated since 1603.[1] Appointments to bishoprics were also an issue of central control, representing attempts by the crown to establish an additional channel for royal authority in the localities. The same issue of control arose in other areas of religious policy. The right to nominate a parish minister, for example, was as much an item of property as a heritable jurisdiction or a local office and interference with it an invasion of personal privilege. Perhaps it was fortunate for James that for most nobles ecclesiastical issues were not significant enough, or did not promise sufficient personal advantage, to risk disagreement with the king and loss of royal favour.

The situation in towns, where the most vocal ministers and the most influential pulpits were to be found, was much more sensitive. The burgh of Ayr offers a striking example of the way in which the king's wishes became enmeshed with the intricacies of local politics. John Welsh, minister at Ayr from 1600, was exiled to France in 1606 following his attendance at the proscribed Aberdeen general assembly.[2] Welsh's replacement, George Dunbar, was himself removed from the charge by order of the privy council in October 1611 and ordered to be imprisoned in Dumbarton for 'seditious praying' on behalf of the 'banischit brethren', who included his predecessor. In addition the provost and bailies of Ayr were to be imprisoned for 'assisting and not correcting the said prayer'. Their replacements were named and charged with choosing a

1 A.R. MacDonald, 'Ecclesiastical Politics in Scotland, 1586-1610' (University of Edinburgh Ph.D. thesis, 1995), 45.

2 Scott, *Fasti*, iii, 5.

council of 'most conformable and discreit men' in a letter from James to the chancellor on 20 September.[1]

James's fears of the magistrates' non-conformity were not unfounded. The town council had continued to provide financial support to the exiled John Welsh for several years. Hugh Kennedy, the provost for 1610-11, voted against the Five Articles of Perth in the parliament of 1621 while his son, also Hugh Kennedy, would be active in the opposition to Charles I and a commissioner to the radical-dominated parliament of 1649.[2] However, James's letter of 1611 arrived too late and the Michaelmas election had already taken place, creating an impasse between the crown and the burgh. The burgesses of Ayr further complained that, in James's leet, a craftsman, George Bell, was chosen as a bailie 'which never was thair permittit'. Not only was this a valid objection representing a serious area of contention in urban politics at the time, but Bell appears to have been a relatively minor figure—who does not, for example, feature greatly in the accounts of the burgh. In the event a compromise was reached: two of James's nominations stood and Bell was replaced by a merchant 'who hes promisit grit reformation of matteris there'—exactly as the election appears in the burgh court book which betrays no suggestion of any disputed nominations.[3]

One of the agents who effected this compromise was John Spottiswoode, archbishop of Glasgow, and the controversy over the election of magistrates in Ayr illustrates the extent to which Spottiswoode operated both as the superior of the diocese and as the king's secular representative. James's original charge had stipulated that the privy council deal only with the magistrates, leaving the further punishment of the minister to the church. In practice, Spottiswoode's remit appears to have been more extensive, allowing him to comment on the issue of the magistrates. The diocesan synod held at Irvine in 1612 to deal with dissident ministers certainly received petitions on behalf of the burgh, requesting Spottiswoode to intercede with the king on their behalf.[4]

This was a satisfactory outcome for the burgh of Ayr, which had already successfully resisted the appointment of a royal nominee as provost in 1587.[5] The matter was not concluded so easily for Spottiswoode, who pronounced himself 'sollist for a Minister to the town ... I

1 *Eccles. Letters*, i, 279-81; *RPC*, ix, 252-3, 630-1.

2 *Ayr Accounts*, 227, 231, 235, 243, 249-50; M.D. Young (ed.), *The Parliaments of Scotland: Burgh and Shire Commissioners*, 2 vols. (Edinburgh, 1992-3), i, 388.

3 A George Bell purchased a licence to sell his goods 1609-10 and a cooper, possibly the same George Bell whose election was disputed in 1611, received payment for making slate pins for the church roof 1615-16: *Ayr Accounts*, 246, 263; *Eccles. Letters*, i, 281; Ayr Carnegie Library, B6/12/5, Ayr Burgh Court Book 1607-1612, entry for 'magistrates at Michaelmas 1611'.

4 *RPC*, ix, 631; *Eccles. Letters*, i, 279.

5 Strawhorn, *Ayr*, 25.

hold it no way sure to commit that flock to that Shepheard that hes teachit tham far to stray. Men ar heir very hardly found that hes curage or witt to cary tham selfis with suche ane affectit people, and I wold glaidly haif sum Englishe man to reside thair for a season'.[1] George Dunbar, however, was allowed to return as minister of the second charge of Ayr in 1613, and served as minister of the first charge from 1619, before he was finally deprived by the court of high commission in 1622 for non-conformity to the Five Articles of Perth. His successor, William Annand, was imposed upon the reluctant burgh, which paid £426 to Thomas Foster 'quha suld haif bene minister here'. Annand would be an enthusiastic supporter of Charles I's liturgical changes and was himself to be deposed from the ministry, this time by the general assembly of 1638 on the grounds of erroneous doctrine.[2]

George Dunbar's experience may have been part of a wider trend. Three of his colleagues, the ministers of Kilwinning, Irvine and Ochiltree, are also known to have been cited by the high commission for non-conformity to the Five Articles.[3] In the south-west, however, the real significance of the Five Articles was the impetus they gave to galvanising lay opinion in the region. The opposition to the Articles signalled a new phase in the continuing opposition to James's religious policy. Whilst non-conformist elements of the ministry had already opposed the king over the imposition of episcopacy and the authority of the general assembly, the Articles, especially the requirement to kneel at communion, were the primary catalyst for lay opposition. This should not be surprising: changes in liturgy and worship affected everyday parish life in a way that changes in the ecclesiastical structure never had. Equally, it was much easier to question James's authority to prescribe for the church in matters of theology than his right to assume executive control over the institutions of the church. The timing of the Articles was also unfortunate. They came at a period in James's reign when the moderately disaffected welcomed an issue to express their dissatisfaction; opposition to the Five Articles became linked with opposition to other issues, such as increased taxation. Additionally, the length of James's absence in England made opposition to the king a practicable option. Would it have been possible for so many to vote against a king permanently resident in Scotland?

At first glance, the voting patterns of the south-west in 1621 on the issue of the Five Articles seem curious for an area which, from its later record, would appear to have been more inclined to presbyterianism than to episcopalianism. In practice, the parliament of 1621 illustrates

1 *Eccles. Letters*, i, 281.
2 *Ayr Accounts*, 280-1; Scott, *Fasti*, iii, 6.
3 P.H.R. MacKay, 'The reception given to the five articles of Perth', *RSCHS*, xix (1975), 195, 199.

the political faultlines in the locality. James's new men—the earls of Wigtown and Nithsdale, Crichton of Sanquhar, Stewart of Garlies (created earl of Galloway in 1623)—voted for the Articles, as did the commissioners for the localities associated with these magnates: Wigtownshire, Dumfriesshire and the burghs of Wigtown, Dumfries, Annan and Sanquhar. The sixth earl of Cassillis contrived to be absent, but the earl of Eglinton, the commissioner for Ayrshire and the burghs of Ayr, Irvine and Kirkcudbright all voted against the Articles.[1] Thus the geographical pattern of opposition to the Five Articles in the parliament of 1621 anticipated the future distribution of radical opposition to Charles I in the 1630s and 1640s.[2]

This geographical demarcation—representatives from Ayrshire tended to vote against the Articles, those from further south for the Articles—can be explained in terms of patterns of loyalty to the king but was also, arguably, a result of the religious map of the area. The Reformation in Ayrshire had proved relatively successful, most parishes being filled by the 1580s at the latest. In contrast, many of the parishes along the western border remained vacant until the seventeenth century.[3] The key issue here was not patronage but finance—the presbytery of Dumfries, where the influence of the pro-Catholic Maxwells was strongest, was if anything filled faster. Few of these parishes could afford to provide a suitable building for worship or a stipend sufficient to sustain a minister. Thus the parliament of 1609 passed an 'Act for Uniting Certain Kirkis in Annandale' affecting a total of twenty-three parishes, and recognised that the burgh of Annan was 'miserablie impoverisheit sa as they are not able to build ane kirk to them selffis'.[4] These were the kind of parishes which attracted the attention of the Commissioners for the Augmentation of Stipends: in 1618 the stipend of the parish of Anwoth, near Kirkcudbright, was raised from 163 merks to 520 merks.[5] While the Reformation was longer in taking effect in some areas of the south-west, reformed service when it did come was provided by younger, more partisan men whose agenda had been honed by the lessons of the preceding years. The first incumbent of the newly financially independent parish of Anwoth, disjoined from its neighbour in

1 Calderwood, *History*, vii, 498-501; J. Goodare, 'The Scottish parliament of 1621', *Historical Journal*, xxxvii (1995), 39, 48-51.

2 S. Adams, 'The making of the radical south-west: Charles I and his Scottish kingdom, 1625-49', in J. Young (ed.), *Celtic Dimensions of the British Civil Wars* (Edinburgh, 1997), 55, 64.

3 See e.g. Scott, *Fasti*, ii, *passim*; M.H.B. Sanderson, *Ayrshire and the Reformation: people and change, 1490-1600* (East Linton, 1997), 120-44, 158-76; M. Lynch, 'Preaching to the converted? Perspectives on the Scottish Reformation', in A.A. MacDonald *et al.* (eds.), *The Renaissance in Scotland* (Leiden, 1994), 309, 333, 338.

4 *APS*, iv, 441, c. 23, 24.

5 W.R. Foster, *The Church Before the Covenants, 1596-1638* (Edinburgh, 1975), 162.

1627, was Samuel Rutherford, one of the most outspoken critics of Charles I.

In the long term, however, it would be the shape which opposition to the Articles took which would prove most damaging. The desire to avoid unpopular forms of worship led the religiously disaffected to seek alternative ministries and organise 'private meetings', in effect the first Protestant alternative to the establishment since 1560.[1] These allowed the disaffected to make contact and were the forerunners of the networks which would prove so effective in co-ordinating opposition to Charles I. George Dunbar of Ayr finally settled in Ireland, one of the first of many Scottish ministers who would find a parish in Ulster where their services were so urgently required as to make their exact theological positions less important.

All of these men retained contact with Scotland, particularly with the south-west. Robert Blair, who joined Dunbar in Ulster in 1625, had already carried out an itinerant preaching ministry in Ayrshire and would return to preach in the south-west on several occasions. John Livingstone, who entered into the ministry at Killinchy in Ireland, is typical of the younger generation of James VI's dissident ministers. Born in 1603, he described himself as being 'from my infancy bred with aversnes from Episcopacy and ceremonies', the first practical example of which was his refusal to kneel to receive communion while a student in Glasgow. By 1626, during a visit to Galloway, Livingstone would be able to describe how he preached at a communion 'where was many good people that came out of Kirkcudbright' and held private meetings with many 'worthy experienced Christians'.[2] Religious life, at least in the south-west, entered the reign of Charles I 'uneasily stretched between the Established Church and the underground conventicle'.[3]

IV

The south-west was the region of Scotland which exhibited the most consistent pattern of opposition to James's son and grandsons. As the areas in which James's policy *vis-à-vis* the local community can be measured—relations with the nobility, the church and interference with the mechanisms of local society—are traditionally the areas in which the government of Charles I has been found deficient, comparison between the policies of the two monarchs is unavoidable. There are a number of possible verdicts—that Charles took a radically different approach to government, or that the difference was simply one of degree—but, with regard to the south-west, the key word would seem to be *development*.

1 *The Life of Mr John Livingstone*, in *Select Biographies*, ed. W. Tweedie, 2 vols. (Wodrow Society, 1845-47), i, 136.

2 *Autobiography and Life of Mr Robert Blair*, ed. T. McCrie (Wodrow Society, 1848), 19; *Life of Livingstone*, 133-6.

3 D. Stevenson, 'Conventicles in the kirk, 1619-37: the emergence of a radical party', *RSCHS*, xvii (1973); M. Lynch, *Scotland: a New History* (London, 1991), 243.

Many of the issues relevant to the reign of Charles I stemmed directly from the precedents already set by James and the reactions to his initiatives. The policies of Charles show a clear continuity with those of James. Charles continued and extended the pattern of creating earldoms along the western border, while using first- and second-generation earls such as Wigtown and Nithsdale as agents of royal government. Apologists for James credit him with having the political sense not to enforce an unpopular piece of legislation, such as the Five Articles of Perth, in contrast to his more headstrong son Charles. However, having established the principle behind his wide-ranging and deeply unpopular revocation of 1625, Charles never attempted to employ the full implications of his act. Similarly, it is perhaps surprising that the equally autocratic and uncompromisingly episcopalian reign of Charles saw far fewer set-piece confrontations with the church, at least in its first decade. In this, as in other areas, Charles quite simply did not have to act—James had already done it. It was not until Charles tried to escalate the process of liturgical change that major conflict ensued.

It has been suggested that the key to local society in early modern England was the need to find 'ways of co-operating and resolving differences at a local level', using the institutions of the shire.[1] The principle remains true for Scotland but the practice takes a different form. While the case for the importance of the institutions even of English local government should not be overstated, there were fewer such institutions in Scotland. The mechanisms of local co-operation in the reign of James VI remained grounded in personal contacts, networks and that near-impossible quality to define, influence—often styled 'credit'—which might or might not coincide with jurisdiction. At least initially, the newly appointed justices of the peace operated within the confines of this informal system. Bodies such as baron and bailie courts did play a role in resolving issues at a local level but were firmly grounded within local society rather than a structure imposed upon it. Did, for example, the earl of Cassillis have status because he was the bailie principal of Carrick, or did he hold the post because of his pre-existing status as the premier magnate in the region? In fact such appointments were important to the earl, confirming and enhancing his status; for anyone else to hold such a post in his area of influence would have undermined his authority. Possible scenarios for the relationships between centre and locality must, therefore, reflect the realities of what was possible. A strongly interventionist approach to local politics would lead to disaster. The king and his primary agents in the locality—the greater and lesser nobility—were facing a shifting situation in which neither side was precisely sure of the role which was expected of them.

1 J. Morrill, 'County communities and the problem of allegiance in the English civil war', in his *The Nature of the English Revolution* (London, 1993), 185.

This was, in a sense, a no-win situation for all but the most territorially secure or the most politically astute. As a result of the intensely personal nature of relationships, both in the local community and between centre and locality, the potential for tension or political dislocation was considerable.

How successful was James VI in his dealings with the local community? This is one area of James's reign where it is perhaps feasible to argue that the king took a balanced approach in his policies. While James was certainly intrusive, he worked within the framework of local politics and was careful not to interfere with the existing mechanisms of power, at least with regard to the nobility. The lists for the appointment of JPs, for example, precisely mirrored the existing elite structures. Nowhere is this conservatism more clearly seen than in what was potentially one of the most destabilising policies, the inflation of the peerage after 1603. None of James's new creations rivalled the long established nobility of Ayrshire: all served to fill the power vacuum among the greater nobility along the western border and the majority came from powerful and well-established local families. Their relevance lies rather in the circumstances surrounding these elevations and in the way in which James used his newly-created earls. Significantly James did not elevate lords and lesser nobles of a similar standing in, for example, the north-east where this could have alienated the existing magnates.

The developing faultlines in the relationship between the king and the south-west were, however, already apparent in the interaction between James and the burgh of Ayr; in his dealings with the church in the locality, and in his inability to integrate long-established nobles with a strong local power base effectively into his government. In the last analysis it was perhaps what James *failed* to do which proved most significant. While there was in James's reign no immediate conflict between, for example, old and new nobles, or courtiers and locality-based nobles, he proved unable to arrest the growing rift between the two spheres caused by the changing nature of power and the absence of the king. Whether any monarch could have done so is a moot point and, at least in the short term, James's policies made good political sense. An apt motto for James's reign might well be 'new problems, short-term solutions'; James shelved problems rather than solving them. However, given the complexity of local relationships and the level of vested interest involved, maintaining political stability for so long was in itself no mean feat.

~ 14 ~

'Tis True I am a Cradle King': the View from the Throne

Jenny Wormald[1]

> 'Tis true I am a cradle king
> yet doe remember every thinge
> That I have heretofore put out
> and yet begin not for to doubt.

These lines have a haunting effect, written as they were at the end of his life by a king whose achievements were by any standards stupendous and yet whose reign was running down into disarray and failure. The poem in which they appear was written in late 1622 or early 1623; its immediate context was the mounting tension over James's insistence on bringing what became the horrific Thirty Years' War in Europe to an immediate end through negotiations underpinned by Anglo-Spanish friendship, and his refusal to take up arms as the leader of Protestant Europe on behalf of his son-in-law Frederick Elector Palatine, whom he rightly regarded as a dangerous fool. The libel to which his poem was an answer has not survived; but the content of the poem gives us a fair clue to its contents. It seems to have referred to Magna Carta, that document so beloved—and so often misused—by the English; for the poem contains the tart lines 'The Charter which you great doe call / came first from Kings to stay your fall / ffrom an uniust rebellion moved / by such as Kingdomes little loved ...' Rumours were clearly circulating about the religious position of a man who upheld Spanish friendship, and so: 'yet you that knowe me all soe well / why do you push me down to hell / by makeing me an Infidell.' And if the poem does not quite go so far as Charles I's famous 'A subject and a sovereign are clean different things', it certainly presages it; it is for the king to make laws, call parliaments, settle religious matters, determine foreign policy, choose his councillors—'And to no use were Counsell Tables / if State affaires were publique bables'. The king was answering a wide-ranging attack on his kingship.[2]

More than twenty years earlier, he had used the same imagery:

> As I being a King by birth ...
> & laiking parents, brethren, bairns or any neir of kinn

[1] This is a version of an article published in *Dictionary of Literary Biography*, vol. 172: *Sixteenth-Century Non-Dramatic Writers*, ed. D.A. Richardson (Cleveland, 1996). I am grateful to Gale Publishers for allowing me to use the material.

[2] James VI, *Poems*, ii, pp. 182-91, ll. 134-7, 118-21, 131-3, 78-9.

inkaice of death or absence to suplee my place thairin
& cheiflie in so kittill a lande quhaire feu remember can
for to have seine governing thaire a king that vas a man.

These lines appear in an unfinished poem on his journey to Denmark in 1589-90 to claim his bride Anna. But here the image of the royal orphan is used in a quite different context; the poem is one of serene confidence, depicting the man whose destiny does not depend on the chancy turning of fortune and the stars, but on God's fixed and unchanging plan for his creation, and contrasting those who 'wandered here and there/ by gess vith groaping stummelling oft but vist not hou or quhaire' with himself. 'I may affirme that in my self I proved it to be treu'. The contrast could not be more complete.[1]

What, then, had happened in the intervening years to introduce the profound note of bitterness of the later poem? We are offered a unique insight into the reasons because of one remarkable source: the king's own writings. They are not, of course, an open book, any more than is the endless stream of memoirs by modern politicians, but they are much better written and much more interesting than the modern and already often tired genre. And they were, in his own day, a matter for admiring comment, from the probable reference in Philip Sidney's *Defense of Poesie* (although Sidney might possibly have been referring to James I) to rather less felicitous praise:

The King of Scots (now living) is a Poet
As his *Lepanto* and his *Furies* shoe it.

Thus in 1598 Richard Barnefield recorded—'passing well', according to one of his poetic friends—his tribute to the poet-king of Scotland. This is hardly inspiring. Nevertheless, James VI, likely successor to Elizabeth and therefore observed with an exceedingly watchful eye by English politicians, did indeed have a unique claim to fame, recognised and lauded by a host of English writers, Sidney, Jonson, Taylor and others. And to Gabriel Harvey, James was not just a poet; he was 'the soveraine of the divine art', 'a Homer to himselfe'.[2]

Early modern English and Scottish monarchs were, of course, expected to be cultured creatures, like their European counterparts, presiding over distinguished courts, patronising writers, and even, in some cases, penning their own poems or translating classical authors in addition to invoking the rhetoric of power in their speeches and letters. And in the past, I have equated James VI and I with Alfred, as the only kings in the British Isles who wrote their own accounts of their kingship. I would now argue that Alfred, remarkable though he was, cannot be so

1 ibid., ii, pp. 147-9, ll. 31, 33-6, 22-3, 30.
2 ibid., i, 274-5, 278.

equated, nor can other possible candidates like Henry VIII or Elizabeth. James, unlike Henry VIII, was his own polemicist. James, unlike Alfred, wrote his own accounts of kingship instead of incorporating them into translations. Like Alfred—and like Elizabeth—he was a translator, but he was far more than that. The sheer quantity of his output is staggering, and so is its range: James the poet-king and writer of poetic theory; James the new David, with his translation of the Psalms; James the theologian; James the political theorist as well as practising politician; James the speech- and letter-writer on a vast scale. What other monarch has left us such an amazing corpus of material about himself?

It should make life easy for the historian. Of course, it does not. I would not go as far as the modern literary critic Jonathan Goldberg in depicting a king obsessed with the *arcana mysterii,* not least because Goldberg's discussion is based more heavily on Jonson and Donne, and Tacitus, than on James's own statements. Coming down to earth, James did have a strong sense of matters properly reserved to himself. 'Mell not with that', he snapped at his ambassadors going to Denmark after his mother's execution, when they asked how they should respond to questions about his intentions towards England; foreign policy was ultimately the king's business in 1587, just as it was in 1621 when the English House of Commons trespassed on the forbidden territory of the prince's marriage. But James was arguably less obsessed than Elizabeth about reserving all matters of foreign policy; and the declared intention of a great deal of his writing was to demystify and explain his kingship, so that the hidden should be open as he said in his preface to the reader in *Basilicon Doron*. Nevertheless, the measured verse of the youthful poet catches an echo in the description of the fifteen-year old king by Henry, Lord Hunsdon as 'the greatest dissembler that ever was heard of for his years', or, even more succinctly, Elizabeth's outburst againt 'that false Scots urchin'; and the theme of dissimulation was taken up again in the hostile account of James by Anthony Weldon, who attributed to him not only the motto *beati pacifici* ('blessed are the peacemakers'), but also Tiberius's *Qui nescit dissimulare, nescit regnare* ('Whoever knows not how to dissimulate, knows not how to rule'). The Machiavellian in James does not prompt me to suggest direct dissimulation in his writings as such, as opposed to his political actions. But political demands on a political theorist meant that he was certainly able to confuse—as he did his faithful Commons of England, kept always on the jump by a king who could soothe them with the most acceptable account of the relationship between king and law, and then, when he seemed to have been pinned down, promptly make claims for his power and prerogative which immediately revived their fears, as he did in the 1610 parliament in his speeches of 21 March, which delighted his hearers, and then of 21 May which manifestly did the reverse.[1]

The ability to confuse goes back to the days of his Scottish rule. The sources of English confusion, the great political works, *The Trew Law of Free Monarchies* and *Basilicon Doron*, were written in Scotland in 1598-9. But we can get much earlier indications of the nature and aspirations of James's kingship; for they can be viewed not only through the major works on kingship but through his earliest writings, which brought him initial fame as an author: his poetry. It was, of course, fairly fashionable for kings to pen the odd verse. But that is not an adequate account of the phenomenon that was James VI. What, then, explains the commitment to poetry, to its style, its rules, as well as its expression? The answer can be sought in a mixture of personal inclination, morale-boost, political pride—and sheer fun. James's bleak childhood is very well known; whose childhood would not have been bleak with George Buchanan as a tutor? But Buchanan was not only the harsh mentor and exponent of unacceptable resistance theory. He was also a poet and playwright, and his metrical paraphrase of the Psalms was a work of great quality and success. No wonder, then, that James remembered his tutor with both fear and admiration to the end of his life. And Buchanan's international distinction was the one claim to fame which the Scottish court had in the dismal years after Mary's deposition; her sole achievement, a notable court culture, exemplified in the dazzling ceremonies devised for the baptism of Prince James in December 1566, had been lost with her fall. Thereafter, the 'court' was no more than the young king and his attendants in Stirling, with Buchanan, and his gentler tutor Peter Young, building up the wide-ranging library whose contents, rather oddly, included bows, arrows, a shooting glove and golf clubs.[2]

But in 1579, James came from Stirling accompanied by several of the leading nobility and a vast train, and made his first state entry into Edinburgh, where—neatly encapsulating the tensions in Scottish society between the sacred and the profane—he was met by Dame Music and her scholars as well as by Dame Religion, and a sermon and the singing of the 20th Psalm were followed by a meeting with Bacchus, sitting with

1 J. Goldberg, *James I and the Politics of Literature* (Baltimore, 1983), especially ch. 2; see also K. Sharpe, 'Private conscience and public duty in the writings of James VI and I', in J. Morrill *et al.* (eds.), *Public Duty and Private Conscience in Seventeenth-Century England* (Oxford, 1993), 77-100; *Warrender Papers*, ii, 44; James VI, *Basilicon Doron*, i, 12-22, where in the 1603 edition the king explains his reasons for making public a work originally written for the private instruction of his son; *CSP Scot.*, vi, 35; *CSP Spain, 1580-6*, 207-8; *The Secret History of the Court of James I*, ed. Walter Scott (Edinburgh, 1811), i, 32; James I, *Political Works*, 306-25; James VI and I, *Political Writings*, 179-203; and *Proceedings in Parliament, 1610*, ed. E.R. Foster, 2 vols. (New Haven, 1966), ii, 100-7.

2 M. Lynch, 'Queen Mary's triumph: the baptismal celebrations at Stirling in December 1566', *SHR*, lxix (1990), 1-21; 'The library of James VI, 1573-1583', ed. G.F. Warner, *SHS Miscellany*, i, pp. xi-lxiv.

his puncheons of wine at the market cross. But what was there when he had passed by the shows and pageants, and arrived at Holyrood? One court poet, Patrick Hume of Polwarth, languishing alone in the bardic chair in the chimney nuik. Thereafter, the transformation was instant. James's first favourite, Esmé Stewart, came to Edinburgh from France, bringing with him the most distinguished of the Jacobean poets, Alexander Montgomerie; and James himself judged the flyting with which Montgomerie and Polwarth recreated the great age of the court of James IV, and the famous flyting of Dunbar and Kennedy, when Montgomerie challenged Polwarth for pride of place, and was declared the winner by the king.[1]

From then on, Montgomerie was the focal point of a circle of poets, one of whom was the king. Buchanan's pupil gave way to the self-styled 'Prentise in the Divine Art of Poesie'; and in the early years of the 1580s, James displayed a talent for sheer light-hearted enjoyment, which is deeply attractive, and was never really repeated. Here he is, teasing his greatest poet:

> geif patient eire to sumthing I man say
> Belovit sandirs maister of oure airt
> the mous did help the lyon one a daye
> sa I protest ye tak it in guid pairt
> my admonition cumming from a hairt
> that wishis veill to you & all youre craft
> quha vald be sory for to see you smairt
> thocht uther poetes trowis ye be gain daft

And he warns Montgomerie that Polwarth 'countis you done and hopes but ony maire/ his time about to winn the chimlay nuik' and that all the other poets 'hope for till out flyte you'. All of which was because Montgomerie had been boring everyone by boasting all night of his brown horse, but when the test came, poet and horse were left so far behind in the race that they were not even spattered by the mud thrown up by the horses in front. Bacchus appears again when the young poet confesses that he had, after supper, 'with pen and drinke compiled yow this propine/ I gatt it ended long before the dawing/ Such pith hade Bacchus ou'r me God of wine.' And he is invoked finally in a poem which begins as a serious address to the Gods, runs into trouble and saves itself by turning to Bacchus, who had helped Alexander the Great, and has now ensnared 'our maister poete' of the same name, whose epitaph would be: 'Here lyis whome Bacchus by his wyne/ Hath trapped first, and made him render syne.'[2]

1 H.M. Shire, *Song, Dance and Poetry at the Court of Scotland under King James VI* (Cambridge, 1969), ch. 4.

2 James VI, *Poems*, ii, pp. 120-9, ll. 1-8, 15-16, 24, 113-15; pp. 113-14, ll. 44-5.

The art of which Montgomerie was the master was, of course, far more than flyting or teasing. The king's court poets called themselves the Castalian Band, the name taken from the spring on Mount Parnassus dedicated to the Muses; the king himself represented Apollo. They exchanged sonnets, using them as introductory compliments to the work of others; James's *Poeticall Exercises at Vacant Houres* (1591), the cycle which contained the major poem *Lepanto* and his translation of du Bartas' *Les Furies*, for example, was prefaced by a number of admiring sonnets, by William Fowler and others. They also wrote longer works; the other major collection of James's poetry, *The Essayes of a Prentise in the Divine Art of Poesie* (1584), included, along with a number of sonnets and other short pieces, another translation of du Bartas, the *Uranie*, in which he experimented with heroic couplets, and what was probably the best and most moving of his poems, the *Phoenix*, a long allegory on the exile and death of Esmé Stewart, from whose 'ashes' would come the new Phoenix, his son Ludovic. James's translations broke his own rule, which was to advise against translation because it denied 'Inventioun'. His poets followed his example rather than his advice; Stewart of Baldynneis produced a version of Ariosto's *Orlando Furioso*, Thomas Hudson of du Bartas' *Judith*, and Fowler of Petrarch's *Trionfi* as well as the first translation into 'English'—Scots—of Machiavelli's *Il Principe*. The impact of what was now happening in the Scottish court can be seen in the fact that du Bartas himself paid James the great compliment of translating his *Lepanto*.[1] And it is easy to sense the confidence and pleasure which James derived from his Castalian Band, fellow-poets, gentlemen of the court, men who shared also in his political life as royal servants. For now, surrounded by them, he was emerging as a man who could take pride in his kingship.

King and scholar as well as poet: it is not surprising that the 'Prentise' in poetry also showed an early taste for being master. Thus the *Essayes of a Prentise in the Divine Art of Poesie* contained one prose work: *Some Reulis and Cautelis to be observit and eschewit in Scottish Poesie*. This was not a plagiarism of the English *Certayne Notes of Instruction* by George Gascoigne, as has been dismissively suggested. James's library showed a huge preponderance of French over English works, and much more probably the *Reulis and Cautelis* drew on Ronsard and du Bellay, whose works on poetry were on his bookshelves. But the most important point about it is that it was a work—the only work—intended to lay down rules for the glory of *Scottish* poetry, an assertion, in other words, of the importance and value of Scottish culture, as exemplified by the court of James VI. He justified his work on two grounds. First, 'lyke as the tyme is changeit sensyne, sa is the ordour of Poesie changeit ... Thairfore, quhat

1 J.D. McClure, 'Translation and transcreation in the Castalian period', *Studies in Scottish Literature*, xxvi (1991), 185-98.

I speik of Poesie now, I speik of it, as being come to mannis age and perfectioun, quhair as then [in the past], it was bot in the infancie and chyldheid.' Second, 'that as for thame that hes written in it of late, there has never ane of thame written in our language. For albeit sindrie hes written of it in English, quhilk is lykest to our language, yit we differ from thame in sindrie reulis of Poesie, as ye will find be experience.' Thus he offers his work not

> To ignorants obdurde, quhair wilfull errour lyis,
> Nor yit to curious folkis, quhilkis carping dois deject thee,
> or yit to learned men, quha thinkis thame onelie wyis,
> But to the docile bairns of knawledge I direct thee.[1]

In other words, those willing to follow the king's rules would create, with him, the Scottish Renaissance.

Thus formal rules were laid down for the writing of Scots poesie, using terms unique to James: *Troilus Verse*, to be used 'for tragicall materis, complaintis, or testamentis'; *Rouncefallis* or *Tumbling Verse*, 'for flyting or Invectives'; *Ballad Royal*, for 'any heich and grave subjectis, specially drawn out of learnit authouris'; *Commoun verse*, 'in materis of love'; and each of these was illustrated by the king's own verse, or those of his Castalians. Above all were the rules for the new form now being taken up by James and his poets, the sonnet. It came late to Scotland. But the 700 written between the 1580s and 1630 show its popularity and its endurance. In subject matter, it was to be much more wide-ranging than the English sonnet:

> For compendious praysing of any bukes, or the authouris thairof, or ony argumentis of uther historeis, quhair sindrie sentences, and change of purposis are requyrit, use *Sonet* verse, of fourtene lynis and ten fete in every lyne.

Love was not even mentioned, though love sonnets were of course written. And under Montgomerie's influence, the sonnet form consistently used by James, as illustrated in his two introductory sonnets in the *Reulis and Cautelis*, and prescribed for his poets, was that normally associated with Spenser, but in fact anticipating him: ababbcbccdcdee.[2]

In form and range of subject matter, James's poets did follow the king's rules, from philosophy and religious themes to Montgomerie's use of the sonnet to demand a pension from the king. The *Reulis and Cautelis* did indeed provide the guidelines for the new culture of the Scottish court. And what other king in Europe could rival the king who was the motivating force for that culture, not by buying, importing, commissioning

1 James VI, *Poems*, i, 65-83, xxviii-xliv, 66 (quotation).
2 ibid., i, 80-2; R.J. Lyall, '"A new maid channoun"? Redefining the canonical in medieval and Renaissance Scottish literature', *Studies in Scottish Literature*, xxvi (1991), 13-15.

artists and architects, but by creating it—and 'legislating' for it? That kings came before parliaments, and were the first law-makers, would be a note sounded by the mature king James in his analysis of divine-right kingship, the *Trew Law of Free Monarchies* of 1599. The first law he ever made, when emerging from his minority in 1584, was the law for Scottish poesie.

Yet from the mid-1580s, the beginnings of change are detectable. James continued for another decade and more to write poetry, on a wide variety of subjects, from sonnets to Anna of Denmark, which were fairly flat, to rather more lively satires on women, sonnets to Tycho Brahe and du Bartas, on the attack on him in Holyrood by the earl of Bothwell, and so on. Thereafter, he wrote rarely, although he continued to the end of his life with his translation of the Psalms. His poems after 1603 include a complaint about the cold in January 1616, into which not even the most industrious literary critic could read anything other than frustration with weather which, as the last line says, 'kills all creaturs and doth spoile our sport'; a dignified but again uninspired work on the death of Queen Anna; inevitably a poem to his greatest favourite, the duke of Buckingham; and little else, apart from the long and bitter political diatribe of 1622-3.[1] The change may be significant. The teenager who had come out of his study to enjoy the new poetic life of his court inevitably became the king caught up in politics.

Thus in the later 1580s, the luxury of the writing game was increasingly overtaken by political events: the threat posed by the extreme presbyterians in the kirk, the Melvillians, the final crisis over his mother, and the Armada. Montgomerie left Scotland in 1586, on a mission which has not yet been properly explained. When he returned in 1590, it was not to royal favour; there was no place for this strenuous Catholic and covert supporter of Mary, although on his death in the late 1590s, James wrote a genuinely moving epitaph for him.[2] Other influences were coming in. To his religious poetry the king now added theology, with his first biblical commentary, on Revelation, published in 1588, and having as its imprimatur not a sonnet by a fellow Castalian, but a preface by a minister of the kirk. It brings us sharply up against a problem. For it launches into a vitriolic attack on Antichrist:

> hee shall bee head of a false and hypocriticall Church; hee shall claime a supreme power in earth; he shall usurp the power of God; he shall deceive men with abusing locusts; he shall persecute the faithfull ... In the end, feeling his kingdome decay, and the trew Church beginning to prosper, he shall by a new sort of deceiving spirits, gather together the Kings of the earth ... and by joyning or at least suffering of that other great open enemy, he shall ... encompasse the campes of the faithfull ...[3]

1 These are all printed in James VI, *Poems*, i and ii.
2 ibid., ii, 107-8.
3 James VI, *A Fruitefull Meditation ... of the 7. 8. 9. and 10. verses of the 20 chap. of the Revelation*

The interest of this diatribe lies not in any novel ideas, but in the identifications James made. Antichrist was the pope; his new deceiving spirits were the Jesuits, the great enemy the Turk, with whom the pope was now at truce. Within twenty years, James would be writing his attacks on Bellarmine and the theory of the indirect deposing power of the papacy in equally flamboyant language, and sending his *Premonition* round the crowned heads of Europe, Catholic and Protestant alike. But by that time, James had fallen naturally and habitually into the role of the king who himself provided the defence for kingly power; and Bellarmine and Paul V were an all-too-obvious target.

These works do not, therefore, necessarily conflict with the image of James the non-persecutor of Catholics, expressed dramatically in a letter written to Robert Cecil in 1601-3, proclaiming that 'I protest to God I reverence their Church as our mother church although clogged with many infirmities and corruptions, besides that I ever did hold persecution as one of the infallible notes of a false church', an attitude which the kirk in Scotland complained about, but which the Catholics in England after the Gunpowder Plot welcomed with immense relief—though James had some fiery things to say about the Plot in his writings. But the choice of the verses in Revelation which produced the impassioned anti-papalism of 1588 cannot be so readily explained. Politically, it was not particularly appropriate for a king who was keeping open diplomatic options which would enable him to indulge in some shady negotiations with Philip II and the papacy in the mid-1590s. Surely, therefore, it marks the moment when James began to carve out a new role for himself: the most cultured king in Europe was beginning the ascent to becoming the most Protestant king in Europe; the poet-king was becoming the theologian-king. Catholics might be tolerated, provided they kept quiet; Jesuits—Antichrist's minions—were more to be feared; and the Pope was the great enemy of God and the king. Even the poet played his part. James's *Lepanto*, the great epic of the decisive victory by the Christian over the Turkish fleet in 1571, was clearly a poem in which he took distinct pride. It is not in fact a great work, though it sweeps along in a lusty narrative, showing the king who would become 'Rex Pacificus' caught up and excited by the drama of battle. But he was very careful not to leave it as a victory for a Catholic hero over the infidel Turk. It was God who joined forces against Satan.[1]

By the time *Lepanto* was published, Satan had not only been defeated in the east. He was a very present figure in Scotland. For in 1590 the coven of witches at North Berwick had confessed to James that their diabolic pact was aimed directly against him, the king whom Satan regarded—

(London, 1603), B3; James I, *Political Works*, 110-68.

1 James VI, *Letters*, 205; James VI, *Poems*, i, 197-257.

with some flattery—as 'the greatest enemie he hath in the world'. This began the first of the great Scottish witch-hunts, which lasted until 1597, the particularly intensive periods being 1590-2 and 1596-7. James was undoubtedly fascinated and terrified; and he took a prominent part in the trials. But in 1597, he did two things. He revoked the standing commissions of the privy council which had provided the judicial machinery for the persecution; and he wrote his tract on witchcraft, the *Daemonologie*. It is a short work, much shorter than the works of those great sceptics Johann Weyer and Reginald Scot, whom he was setting out to refute; it is almost entirely unoriginal; it is unusually turgid for a man who would show himself in later writings to be a master of vivid and compelling prose. And it was done in a hurry, as the fragments of the first draft indicate; they are much cleaner than James's usual first drafts, which are full of erasures and rewriting. Almost certainly it was written for self-reassurance by a king who still believed in witchcraft and diabolic power, but who found it increasingly impossible to believe that the hundreds of women condemned in the 1590s had all been witches. The preface tells us that his intention was to resolve doubting hearts. Perhaps the most doubting heart was that of the author.[1]

His theological works give us not only his views about Catholics and witches, but—sometimes strikingly—his view of the godly. He had some very pointed things to say about the puritans in *Basilicon Doron*. But back in 1589, at one of his weaker points in his struggle with the Melvillians, he turned to write his *Meditation on ... 1 Chronicles, ch. 15*; and here, one passage of obvious relevance leaps from the page. Describing those who accompanied David in bringing the Ark of the Covenant to Mount Sion, the Elders, Captains, and Priests and Levites, he had this to say about the third:

> this is to be marked well of Princes, and of all those of any high calling or degree that hath to do in God's cause. David did nothing in matters appertaining to God without the presence and speciall concurrence of God's ministers, appointed to be spiritual rulers in his Church.[2]

James was certainly not writing to please the Melvillians. His future attitude might harden. But here we get a glimpse of the king in his study, away from the public glare of the dramatic collisions with Melville and his associates, where extreme positions were taken up. And here we see the moderate, who could offer an appeal to more moderate ministers in the kirk, with results which were already visible in the late 1580s, and very clear a decade later.

1 *Newes from Scotland*, in Pitcairn, *Trials*, i, III, 217; Bodleian Library, Oxford, MS 165; James VI, *Prose Works*, xvii-xxi, 1-56; R. Dunlap, 'King James and the witches: the date and text of the *Daemonologie*', *Philological Quarterly*, liv (1975), 40-6.

2 James I, *Works*, 84.

By that time, what mainly interested him was political theorising. By then he was well on the way to winning his battle for control of the kirk with the Melvillians, whose strenuous assertion of the separation of church and state and denial of royal control had made them his most dangerous opponents in the 1590s. If the *Daemonologie* was written for reassurance, the next two works, *Basilicon Doron* and *The Trew Law of Free Monarchies*, written in 1598-9, are a clear and confident statement of the kingship he was now exercising. Now he was indeed using his writing to demystify and explain his kingship. The explanation is certainly comprehensive. There is a vast difference between the two works. *The Trew Law*, setting out the theory of divine right kingship, is a full-scale demolition of the contractual and resistance theory of the Huguenots and James's own tutor George Buchanan, and of the Melvillian theory of the two swords, church and state. *Basilicon Doron*, by contrast, is a practical manual of kingship, written for James's son Henry. Its scathing diatribes against the puritans gave no more comfort to the Melvillians than the *Trew Law*, and predictably they howled about it; but there was much less in it to upset secular politicians. The Scottish nobility might have felt collectively affronted by the assertion that 'The naturall sicknesse that I have perceived this estate subject to in my time, hath been, a fectlesse arrogant conceit of their greatnes and power', or the comment on their feuding: '(without respect to God, King, or Commonweale) to bang it out bravelie, hee and all his kinne, against him and all his'. But at least they had the consolation that the king advised his son that it was to his honour to make use of them, and to 'consider that vertue followeth oftest noble blood'. For the 'phanaticke spirits', the puritans, 'verie pestes in the Church and Common-weale', there was no such compensation. *Basilicon Doron* was to make far more impact than the more theoretical *Trew Law*, perhaps because it was clearly the book in which James took most pride; as late as 1620, two decades after he had written and revised it, he was dragging it into his *Meditation on the Lords Prayer*, when describing the care he took with dedications: *Basilicon Doron* had been his dead son Henry's, and this must now therefore belong to Charles—and a note of nostalgia, perhaps not only for his dead son but for a happier past when the book was written, is surely detectable. The king's own enthusiasm for this splendid, fast-moving, witty piece of prose had its effect in the vast number of copies which flooded the London market in the spring of 1603, and the subsequent translations; the *Trew Law* was a poor second best.[1]

Yet there is some doubt about how far *Basilicon Doron* was actually read; and it was all too easy for those who did glance at it to discern, if only from the introductory sonnet, the theme of divine right informing

1 James VI, *Basilicon Doron*, i, 83, 87, 79; James VI, *Prose Works*, 57-82; James VI and I, *A Meditation upon the Lords Prayer* (London, 1619), A4.

the writings of a divine-right monarch, especially after 1603 when the monarch was all too inclined to charge enthusiastically into constitutional debates which only served to confirm such perceptions of him. To that extent, the sheer down-to-earth practicality of *Basilicon Doron* creates a problem. Not only does it differ from the *Trew Law*. It differs so markedly from his later, increasingly tortuous writings that it forces the question whether it actually does represent a king at ease with his kingship at the end of the 1590s, in a way in which he would never be again; a king confident enough to be able to encompass great theory as a useful political weapon against a very specific threat to his power without feeling the need endlessly to assert it personally and individually. In other words, James's divine-right kingship was developed in the Scottish context of the great European debate where it was the answer to resistance theory and ideas of contractual kingship. Buchanan and Melville brought it out. But when not directing his brilliant pen at these great opponents, what was 'divine right'? Was society itself not ordered by divine right, in the Great Chain of Being where every man had his place, king, noble, commoner, all with their obligations to the God who had given them that place? And in that context, there was no need to emphasise divine right—until James went south, and the whole issue was thrown up again by the English, with their obsession with privilege, precedence and the common law, which brought them straight into conflict with a master of Continental and Scottish theory.

In Scotland, the move to theology, demonology and political writing was never allowed to crowd out the culture of the court; a distinguished court, as much as the need to overcome his presbyterian opponents and rid his land of witches, was the basis for a kingship which would impress Europe. But there was another consideration. James's *Reulis and Cautelis* extolled Scottish poetry; and it had its postscript when after 1603 he unfairly trounced William Alexander, one of the younger Castalians who followed him to England, and followed his lead in Anglicising his writings, for his 'harshe vearses after the Inglishe fasone'. But he was the future king of England, and not wholly averse to English culture, despite the heavy Scottish emphasis on French influence. He himself had indeed tried to bring French influence to bear not just on his present but on his future kingdom, explaining his translation of du Bartas' *Uranie* on the grounds that 'I could not do so well, as by publishing some work of his to this yle of Brittain (swarming full of quick ingynes,) aswell as they ar made manifest already to France'. But equally some of these 'quick ingynes' from south Britain were being invited to make an impact in the north. He had inherited an English family of musicians, the Hudsons, from his mother; but they had become absorbed into the Castalian Band. 1589, however, saw a new departure. In 1588 he himself had written a masque, which has not survived, for the wedding of his second great favourite, George, earl of Huntly, to the daughter of his first, Esmé Stewart, and apparently took a leading part in it. But when preparing for his own forthcoming marriage, he asked Elizabeth for six masquers and six torch-bearers, and for English actors. English actors—comedians—seem to have been invited again in 1594, presumably for the baptism of his first son, Henry; certainly Laurence Fletcher was known to the king by this time. And Fletcher and his men were back in 1599, causing a furious row between James and the Edinburgh clergy—which the king won. They may, indeed, have stayed on in Scotland; for they turn up again in 1601, when they went on tour to Dundee and Aberdeen. And Fletcher's name heads the list, with Shakespeare's second, in the Letters Patent to the King's Men in May 1603. Scottish culture had begun it all. 'British' culture was being introduced in the north well before James became king of Britain.[1]

In 1603, therefore, England got a king who, from uncertain and even weak beginnings, had built up a confidence, an expertise, of unusual range. As king, as poet, as theologian, as political theorist, he had made his emphatic mark. He could justifiably take pride in his achievements, and look forward to the future when the successful king of Scotland would bring two nations long hostile to one another together in peace as the new kingdom of Great Britain. It all went wrong.

Explanations for this based on an apparent rush to divine-right monarchy, an absolutist ideology, miss an essential point. An immediate and better clue to what happened lies in the quick and hostile reaction by his English subjects to a king who disliked public processions and spectacle. That is a well-known fact, taken for granted. But why? In Scotland, James had certainly been observed to like solitude. But equally he had taken part with no lack of enthusiasm in public spectacles, acting in his masque, taking the part of one of the Christian knights who fought in the tournament during the baptism celebrations of 1594, appearing publicly in procession in Edinburgh. Indeed, his own devising of appropriate robes for members of the Scottish parliament to process through Edinburgh does not suggest a king unaware of the importance of royal show.[2] And his journey south in 1603 was not marked by royal hostility or indifference; far from it.

What surely went wrong was that this man, with justifiable pride in his own achievements, suddenly found that the sheer scale of the English court and its culture, and indeed the sheer scale of English government, was not amenable to the control which he had imposed in Scotland, and which had made him the easy and confident author of *Basilicon Doron*. The intimacy which was so much the flavour of his Scottish court was

1 James VI, *Poems*, ii, 114; i, 16; R. Dunlap, 'King James's masque', *Philological Quarterly*, xli (1962), 249-56.

2 *APS*, iii, 443.

profoundly different from the formality of Elizabeth's. The state entry into London in 1604 was far more glorious than anything devised in Scotland; it was also infinitely more chaotic—and it is a nice irony that the same would be true of King James's own funeral. The surviving Castalians came south with him; but there was no longer a Castalian Band. Poets flattered; but perhaps only Jonson recreated the relationship which with his Scottish poets had given him a society. Wherever one looks, one finds the same problem of scale; pressure of suitors is an obvious example. The sureness of touch of *Basilicon Doron* and the *Trew Law* gave way to rhetorical jostling, as the man grounded in resistance theory came up against the unreal ideal of what the English chose to call harmonious politics, and as king was told by English common lawyers how to play by the rules.

And, as the years wore on, tiredness and disillusion had their part. The early years of his English rule saw the frustration and failure of his dream of union. But he still had his Scots with him. From about 1612, that was much less the case. There was no second earl of Dunbar, and even in the Bedchamber, Scottish dominance was no longer complete after 1617.[1] James wrote less in England—certainly less for recreation and pleasure. And the works of his last years are a sad decline. He had never been a great poet; but he had been a master of taut, pithy prose. Now, he rambled, shoving great and small matters together in an increasingly ill-judged mishmash. His preface to the *Counterblaste to Tobacco*, for example, is far too grand for a treatise on what he himself called mere smoke. His *Meditation upon the Lords Prayer*, written in 1620, wanders all over the place. Some of the old bite is still there: 'And lead us not into temptation' produces 'The Arminians cannot but mislike the frame of this Petition; for I am sure they would have it, *And suffer us not to be ledde into temptation*, and Vorstius would adde, *as farre, Lord, as is in thy power, for thy power is not infinite*'. But it begins with a vitriolic digression on puritans and Brownists, which takes him far from their attitude to prayer; and it includes a couple of hunting stories, a pious reference to his father-in-law, and an invocation of 'Tobacco-drunkardes' as the epitome of sinners. The same rambling informs his amazing choice of subject on which to create a discourse on the inauguration of kings—the passion of Christ; he is frankly boring on the question of the lost recipe for the purple dye of the ancients—and it is something of a shock to find King James a bore.[2] Perhaps the loss of judgement symbolises a king floundering in the excessive complexity of English ideology, English

1 N. Cuddy, 'The revival of the entourage: the bedchamber of James I in administration and politics, 1603-1625', in D. Starkey (ed.), *The English Court from the Wars of the Roses to the Civil War* (Harlow, 1987), 173-225.

2 James VI, *Prose Works*, 84-6; *Meditation upon the Lords Prayer*, 116-17, 15, 83-8, 96, 76; *A Meditation upon the 27. 28. 29 Verses of the xxvii Chapter of St Matthew, or A paterne for a Kings inauguration* (London, 1620).

style, English government, that government now so overblown and elaborate, so maddeningly inefficient and ineffective to a king from Scotland. Comparison between his rule in Scotland before 1603 and his dual monarchy thereafter highlights the difference between the sureness of touch in his dealings with his northern kingdom, the confidence of familiarity, and the sense of control slipping away as the reign neared its end in England.

Of his three last poems, his demand that court ladies should leave London and go to the country retains some of the old vigour; James could still be quite amusing in his attitude to women. The final one, appealing for the safe return of 'Jack and Tom' (Buckingham and Charles), has a certain grace and pathos. But his lengthy 'Answere to the Libell called the Comons teares' is a tragic poem. Like the much earlier poem on his journey to Denmark, it shows his strong sense of the peculiar nature of his kingship, and the background which had dictated so much of his struggle for success: 'Tis true I am a cradle king'. It contains one of the most effective lines he ever wrote: 'God and Kings doe pace together'. He had little else left to pace with. As the foreign policy which he had followed so consistently, as Rex Pacificus, throughout his reign in England, was falling apart, so he invoked not the language of love, but of threat: 'If once I bend my angry brow ...' 'Hold you the publique beaten way/ wonder at kings and them obey.' Royal love would only be given for obedience. It was a very unequal contract. It was also the despairing cry of a man whose style of kingship had changed, had been impoverished by the demands made on him in England. Eleven years earlier, he had been described in a hostile letter by Lord Thomas Howard to Sir John Harington as talking 'of his subjects fear and subjection', where the old queen had talked of their love; already in 1611, the pressures and the scale of English rule had had their effect on a king known for intimate dealings and affection in Scotland.[1] And the poem looks forward also to the last speech he ever made to the English parliament, in 1624. His foreign policy was now in ruins, the war-party in full cry; and this master of rhetoric was reduced to complaining that he had been presented with two scrolls of grievances, 'wheras I expected you rather should have presented your thankes unto me that you had soe little cause of grevance, for I dare bouldly say never commons had lesse'. This is not the bouncy confidence which prompted him to write, in *Lepanto*, that 'it becomes not the honour of my estait lyk a hyrling to penn the praise of any man'. In these last words of a king of such ability and such achievement, there is only the echo of the sad whingeing of his mother, when her world

1 James VI, *Poems*, ii, pp. 178-81, 192-3; p. 183, l. 9, p. 191, l. 165, p. 183, ll. 15-16. J. Harrington, *Nugae Antiquae* (London, 1769), 126.

crashed about her in 1567 as his was doing now in 1624: the whinge that her subjects did not appreciate her.[1]

In May 1624 that indefatigable letter-writer Thomas, earl of Kellie wrote to John, earl of Mar an account of this parliament; a contemporary Scotsman identified the problems of English government in a quite different way from later historians of the so-called 'early Stuart' kings. 'I did never see since his Majestie did cume to this crooun onye Parlament lyke to it, whitche dois evrye daye grate upone the Kings prerogateve soe mutche as I doe mutche dout hardlye it shalbe recovered', he said. Seven months earlier, he had told Mar: 'You can not imagin how the world is possessed of the vexatione his Majestie hes in his mynd. It maye cume that young folks shall have their world. I know not if that wilbe fitt for your Lordshipe and me.'[2] That haunting refrain of the recognition of an age coming to an end recurs again and again in Kellie's letters. Perhaps those short-lived creatures, James's Scottish predecessors, had been more fortunate than we sometimes think, in not outliving the days of their energy and power. But James's sadness is the sadness of an old and tired man—who still had enough life in him to drag a reluctant French ambassador out hunting at four in the morning in 1624, and still had enough grasp of political reality to prophesy with absolute accuracy what his son and his favourite were bringing down on themselves by turning from peace to war. And at least when the aged king looked back, he could look back on a reign which had been in many ways such a triumphant success—a success the extent of which we are last getting closer to appreciating, as the source of it, the great political ability of a Scottish king, is increasingly recognised.

1 For various versions of this speech, *Journals of the House of Lords* (London, 1846), iii, 424; J. Rushworth (ed.), *Historical Collections* (London, 1721), i, 146-7, and Folger Shakespeare Library, Folger MS V.b.303, 255; James VI, *Poems*, i, 201; *RPC*, i, 512, 514-15.

2 HMC, *Mar & Kellie*, ii, 200, 183.

CHRONOLOGY OF THE REIGN OF JAMES VI

DATE	IN SCOTLAND	BEYOND SCOTLAND
1566	James born.	Beginnings of Dutch revolt against Spanish rule.
1567	Queen Mary deposed; James crowned by a faction.	
1568	Mary defeated in bid to recover crown; flees to England and is imprisoned.	
1570	Factional strife degenerates into civil war between king's and queen's parties.	Pope excommunicates Queen Elizabeth.
1572	Earl of Morton becomes regent.	Alliance between England and France. St Bartholomew Massacre in France. Spanish reconquest of Netherlands collapses.
1573	King's party wins civil war, aided by English military task force.	
1578	James declared of age; factional struggles renewed.	
1579	James's formal entry into Edinburgh.	
1580	Ascendancy of Esmé Stewart, who becomes duke of Lennox. Full royal court established; 'Castalian Band' of poets. Royal progress through kingdom. Fall of Morton (executed 1581).	
1581	Parliament first legislates on Highlands.	
1582	James kidnapped in Ruthven Raid. Buchanan's *History* published.	
1583	James escapes from Ruthven Raiders. Ascendancy of Captain	John Whitgift becomes archbishop of Canterbury; crackdown on English presbyterians.

	James Stewart, who becomes earl of Arran.	
1584	'Stirling Raid' against Arran fails. Parliament passes 'Black Acts' asserting royal control over church.	
1585	Arran overthrown by noble coalition. James takes full responsibility for government, with John Maitland of Thirlestane as chief minister.	English military intervention in the Netherlands leads to open war with Spain.
1586	Treaty between England and Scotland (June).	Babington Plot against Elizabeth revealed; Mary queen of Scots convicted of complicity (October).
1587	Major reforming parliament. Maitland becomes chancellor. Pro-Catholic revolt by Maxwells in the south-west.	Mary executed (February).
1588	Presbyterians gain influence in the church. Second Maxwell revolt.	Spanish Armada defeated.
1589	Huntly's rebellion at Bridge of Dee, backed by Spain. James marries Anna of Denmark and spends winter in Denmark.	Henry III of France assassinated; accession of Protestant Henry IV leads to civil war. Spain intervenes to support Catholic League; England supports Henry.
1590	Coronation of Anna, and her formal entry into Edinburgh.	
1591	Earl of Bothwell falls out with James and is outlawed.	
1592		Henry IV converts to Catholicism, winning support.
1594	Prince Henry born (Feb.); baptised (Aug.). Huntly rebels again, but surrenders and is temporarily exiled.	
1595	Maitland dies. Bothwell finally exiled.	
1596	Octavians take over financial administration. Military expedition to Highlands. Princess Elizabeth born. Riot in Edinburgh	Second Spanish Armada scattered by storm.

	(Dec.) leads to political eclipse of presbyterians.	
1597	General assembly of church at Montrose accepts greater royal control.	
1598	Octavians displaced by courtiers. 'Act anent feuding': submission of noble feuds to royal justice. James writes *Basilicon Doron*. Attempt to colonise island of Lewis with lowlanders: ultimately defeated (1609).	Peace of Vervins in France: victory for royalists against Spain and Catholic League.
1599	James makes military preparations, fearing disputed English succession. Tax scheme to fund this devised.	Disgrace of earl of Essex, who James had hoped would further his succession claim.
1600	Tax scheme rejected by convention of estates. Some bishops appointed, but have few powers. 'Gowrie conspiracy' apparently attempts to kidnap or assassinate James. Prince Charles born.	
1601	Major currency debasement.	James reaches understanding with Sir Robert Cecil, Elizabeth's leading minister, about succession.
1602		English victory in Ireland.
1603	Government outlaws MacGregor clan.	James succeeds to English throne.
1604	Union scheme discussed in Scotland and England. Alexander Seton (earl of Dunfermline 1605) becomes chancellor, and governs with earl of Dunbar, treasurer.	Peace between England and Spain.
1605	Presbyterian party holds unauthorised general assembly in Aberdeen. Six ministers later convicted of treason for this (1606).	Gunpowder Plot: Catholic plot against James.
1606	Bishops given some powers in church. Andrew Melville imprisoned in Tower of London and later exiled.	

1607	MacDonalds forfeit Kintyre.	English parliament rejects union.
1608	Military expedition to Islay. Dunbar takes initiative against lawlessness in Borders.	James launches pamphlet war with pope, claiming pope has no power to depose kings.
1610	Bishops given full powers in church.	Failure of 'Great Contract', scheme for English fiscal stability.
1611	Treasurer Dunbar dies.	
1612	Parliament confirms bishops' powers but scales down government tax proposal. MacDonalds forfeit Islay.	Prince Henry dies. Princess Elizabeth marries Frederick, Elector Palatine.
1614	MacDonalds' uprising in Islay defeated.	
1615		Ascendancy of new favourite, George Villiers, later duke of Buckingham.
1616	Agreement between privy council and clan chiefs.	
1617	James visits Scotland and unveils plan to alter church worship.	
1618	Five Articles of Perth, introducing new religious ceremonies.	Elector Palatine accepts Bohemian crown, launching war with Habsburgs in Germany.
1619	Open resistance to Five Articles' implementation begins.	
1621	Five Articles face serious opposition in parliament.	Spanish troops invade Palatinate in support of Austrian Habsburgs. Breakdown of relations between James and English parliament.
1622	Chancellor Dunfermline dies.	Collapse of James's attempts to mediate peace in Germany.
1623		Prince Charles and Buckingham visit Spain and take over English foreign policy.
1624	Scots reject royal scheme to export their wool only to England.	War between England and Spain.
1625	MacDonalds' uprising in Ardnamurchan defeated.	James dies.

FURTHER READING

The following is intended as a critical guide to further reading in the areas covered by this book.

1. James VI: Universal King?

James has never received a full-length biography since D.H. Willson, *King James VI & I* (London, 1956), still worth consulting although set in an older tradition of disparagement of the king. M. Lee's valuable *Great Britain's Solomon: James VI and I in his Three Kingdoms* (Urbana, Ill., 1990) is a series of interconnected essays rather than a biography. Jenny Wormald is working on an eagerly-awaited new biography. There are good textbook treatments of the reign in G. Donaldson, *Scotland: James V—James VII* (Edinburgh, 1965), part 2, a pioneer revaluation of James's abilities; J. Wormald, *Court, Kirk and Community: Scotland, 1470-1625* (London, 1981), part 3; and M. Lynch, *Scotland: a New History* (London, 1991), ch. 14.

2. Scottish Politics in the Reign of James VI

The works on this subject by Maurice Lee are essential reading for a full understanding of the reign. In M. Lee, *John Maitland of Thirlestane and the Foundation of the Stewart Despotism in Scotland* (Princeton, NJ, 1959), he provided a detailed and stimulating study of the politics of the 1580s and early 1590s, based on the career of James VI's first great minister. He also launched a debate, still continuing, about the nature of James's regime. The story was continued in M. Lee, *Government by Pen: Scotland under James VI and I* (Urbana, Ill., 1980), a narrative of how Scotland was governed after the union of 1603. This book was also built round the careers of leading politicians, one of whom, the earl of Dunfermline (chancellor 1604-22), was further discussed in M. Lee, 'James VI's popish chancellor', in I.B. Cowan and D. Shaw (eds.), *The Renaissance and Reformation in Scotland* (Edinburgh, 1983). The greatest politician of all, and one whom Professor Lee much admired, was the king himself, the central subject of his *Great Britain's Solomon*.

The nature of James's regime in Scotland has been much debated. Professor Lee, in *Maitland*, argued that the king and his minister created new laws and institutions that were able to bring the semi-independent nobility under central control and turn them into law-abiding courtiers, while introducing a new class of lairds to an independent role in government. This thesis was criticised by J. Brown (now Wormald), 'Scottish politics, 1567-1625', in A.G.R. Smith (ed.), *The Reign of James VI and I* (London, 1973); she argued that James ruled in an entirely traditional way, by co-operation with the nobles. A vigorous but inconclusive debate followed: M. Lee, 'James VI and the aristocracy', *Scotia*, i (1977), 18-23; J. Wormald, 'James VI: new men for old?', *Scotia*, ii (1978), 70-6.

The subject received fresh impetus from K.M. Brown, *Bloodfeud in Scotland, 1573-1625* (Edinburgh, 1986): this book showed in detail that the allegedly lawless nobility did in fact have sophisticated codes of behaviour, and were able to settle their own disputes. But it also showed that the bloodfeud, under pressure from the king, gradually faded away between about 1590 and 1625. This might appear to have supported the Lee thesis, but Professor Brown instead chose to highlight the continued co-operation between crown and nobility, and aristocratic continuity was the main theme of his survey of seventeenth-century Scottish politics: K.M. Brown, *Kingdom or Province? Scotland and the Regal Union, 1603-1715* (London, 1992). Crown-noble co-operation was a common feature of the absolutist states of the Continent, although it was often achieved only after a struggle. J. Goodare, 'The nobility and the absolutist state in Scotland, 1584-1638', *History*, lxxviii (1993), 161-82, offered a modified version of the Lee thesis, using fiscal evidence to show that the crown began to make large payments to the nobility in the early seventeenth century. Perhaps the nobles were simply bought off. The functioning of the absolutist state has been further discussed in J. Goodare, *State and Society in Early Modern Scotland* (Oxford, 1999), especially ch. 3.

That the regime was increasingly built on taxation—regular from the 1580s, heavy from the 1590s—was shown in J. Goodare, 'Parliamentary taxation in Scotland, 1560-1603', *SHR*, lxviii (1989), 23-52. This may have alienated those outside the charmed circle, and there were frequent clashes in parliament over taxation. The unique voting record of the 1621 parliament was analysed in J. Goodare, 'The Scottish parliament of 1621', *Historical Journal*, xxxviii (1995), 29-51, to show a marked divide between those with court connections voting for the Five Articles of Perth, and those with none—particularly below the level of the nobility—voting against.

Brown's *Kingdom or Province?* was not, despite the title, primarily a study of the union. Here the essential work is B.P. Levack, *The Formation of the British State: England, Scotland and the Union, 1603-1707* (Oxford, 1987). Also relevant is R.A. Mason (ed.), *Scots and Britons: Scottish Political Thought and the Union of 1603* (Cambridge, 1994), including chapters by Wormald, Lee and Brown among others. One contributor to this collection was Arthur Williamson, whose detailed and complex study, *Scottish National Consciousness in the Age of James VI* (Edinburgh, 1979), discussed intellectual contributions to the political culture of the period. James was himself an intellectual, and the relationship of his ideas on kingship to those of the radical presbyterians (including his celebrated tutor George Buchanan) is the focus of J.H. Burns, *The True Law of Kingship: Concepts of Monarchy in Early Modern Scotland* (Oxford, 1996), chs. 5-8.

3. James VI and the Sixteenth-Century Cultural Crisis and 4. Court Ceremony and Ritual during the Personal Reign of James VI

Comparatively little has been written on the royal court as such in James VI's reign in comparison with the three which preceded it, although aspects of its literature, music and architecture are well served. H.M. Shire's delightful *Song, Dance and Poetry of the Court of Scotland under James VI* (Cambridge, 1969) is still the starting-point for court culture. Also useful and informative is R.D.S. Jack (ed.), *The History of Scottish Literature, vol. i: Origins to 1660* (Aberdeen, 1988), which contains Jack's own article on 'Poetry under King James VI'. There are also important articles by J. Derrick McClure: 'Translation and transcreation in the Castalian period', *SSC*, xxvi (1991), and '"O Phoenix Escossois": James VI as poet', in A. Gardner-Medwin and J. Hadley Williams (eds.), *A Day Estivall: Essays on the Music, Poetry and History of Scotland and England ... in honour of Helena Mennie Shire* (Aberdeen, 1990). But there lingers on in these works the idea that James's fame as a poet rests more on his kingship than his talent; and the most positive views are still those of J. Craigie in his introductions to *The Basilikon Doron of King James VI*, 2 vols. (STS, 1944-50), *The Poems of James VI of Scotland*, 2 vols. (STS, 1955-8) and, with A. Law, *Minor Prose Works of King James VI and I* (STS, 1982).

The court has received little attention from historians. One chapter is devoted to it in Lee, *Great Britain's Solomon*. The index to K.M. Brown, *Bloodfeud in Scotland, 1573-1625* (Edinburgh, 1986), under 'court' reveals much. Useful, though brief, is N. Cuddy, 'The revival of the entourage: the bedchamber of James I, 1603-1625', in D. Starkey (ed.), *The English Court: from the Wars of the Roses to the Civil War* (London, 1987), 173-96. Much information is contained within C.J. Burnett, 'The Officers of Arms and Heraldic Art under King James the Sixth and First, 1567-1625' (University of Edinburgh, M.Litt. thesis, 1992).

The specialised subject of royal entries is dealt with in D. Gray, 'The royal entry in sixteenth-century Scotland', in S. Mapstone and J. Wood (eds.), *The Rose and the Thistle: Essays on the Culture of Late Medieval and Renaissance Scotland* (East Linton, 1998); in D.M. Bergeron, *English Civic Pageantry, 1558-1642* (London, 1971), despite its title; and in M.M. Bartley, 'A Preliminary Study of the Scottish Royal Entries of Mary Stuart and Anne of Denmark', (University of Michigan Ph.D. thesis, 1981). The Danish account of the coronation and entry of 1590 is reprinted and translated in D. Stevenson, *Scotland's Last Royal Wedding: the Marriage of James VI and Anne of Denmark* (Edinburgh, 1997). The banquet after the baptism of 1594 is treated by J. Fergusson, 'A ship of state', in his *The White Hind and Other Discoveries* (London, 1963). An essential source remains A.J. Mill, *Mediaeval Plays in Scotland* (Edinburgh, 1927).

5. The Brig o' Dee Affair, the Sixth Earl of Huntly and the Politics of the Counter-Reformation

There is little modern literature on the Counter-Reformation in Scotland before the seventeenth century. T.G. Law, *Collected Essays and Reviews*, ed. P.H. Brown (Edinburgh, 1904), covers a range of topics, from studies of individuals to events such as the Spanish Blanks in 1592. W. Forbes-Leith (ed.), *Narratives of Scottish Catholics under Mary Stuart and James VI* (Edinburgh, 1885), is a collection of contemporary correspondence with editorial text interspersed, providing insights into the role of Scottish mission priests. K.M. Brown, 'The making of a *politique*: the Counter-Reformation and regional politics of John, eighth Lord Maxwell', *SHR*, lxvi (1987), 152-75, shows that the Catholic nobility used the Counter-Reformation to further their own local position as much as the Catholic faith. The following articles are insightful commentaries on the Scottish Jesuit mission: J. Durkan, 'William Murdoch and the early Jesuit mission in Scotland', *Innes Review*, xxxv (1984), 3-11; J. Durkan, 'Sidelights on the early Jesuit mission in Scotland', *Scottish Tradition*, xiii (1984-5), 34-48; J. Durkan, 'Edinburgh in 1611: Catholic sympathisers', *Innes Review*, xl (1989), 158-61.

For the European context of the Counter-Reformation, see A.O. Meyer, *England and the Catholic Church under Queen Elizabeth*, trans. J.R. McKee (London, 1916), a seminal work with significant Scottish references; M.J. Rodriguez-Salgado and S. Adams (eds.), *England, Spain and the Gran Armada* (Edinburgh, 1991); J.D. Mackie, 'Scotland and the Spanish Armada', *SHR*, xii (1914-15); and R. MacKenney, *Sixteenth Century Europe: Expansion and Conflict* (London, 1993), chs. 8, 12.

6. James VI's English Subsidy

H.G. Stafford, *James VI of Scotland and the Throne of England* (New York, 1940), is an exhaustive and reliable general account of James's foreign relations, though inevitably dated in some of its assumptions. A recent overview of Anglo-Scottish relations as seen from Lord Burghley's desk is W.T. MacCaffrey, *Elizabeth I: War and Politics, 1588-1603* (Princeton, NJ, 1992), ch. 15. W. Ferguson, *Scotland's Relations with England: a Survey to 1707* (Edinburgh, 1977), ch. 5, is lively but sees the issues almost entirely in religious terms; for a more rounded view, see M. Lee, *Great Britain's Solomon: King James VI and I in his Three Kingdoms* (Urbana, Ill., 1990), ch. 4. None of these works pursues the issue of money far.

The suggestion that the search for subsidies dominated James's foreign relations was advanced in R.S. Brydon, 'The Finances of James VI, 1567-1603' (University of Edinburgh Ph.D. thesis, 1925), ch. 4—a work to be used with caution. K.M. Brown, 'The price of friendship: the "well affected" and English economic clientage in Scotland before 1603', in

R.A. Mason (ed.), *Scotland and England, 1286-1815* (Edinburgh, 1987), complements the present study by focusing on subsidies to the Scottish nobility (mainly before 1586). Finally, the English subsidy cannot be studied in isolation from the man who administered it for most of the 1590s, the goldsmith and financier Thomas Foulis; for him, see J. Goodare, 'Thomas Foulis and the Scottish fiscal crisis of the 1590s', in W.M. Ormrod *et al.* (eds.), *Crises, Revolutions and Self-Sustained Growth: Essays in Fiscal History, 1130-1830* (Stamford, 1999, forthcoming).

7. A Meddlesome Princess: Anna of Denmark and Scottish Court Politics, 1589-1603

There is only one published biography of Anna: E. Carleton Williams, *Anne of Denmark* (London, 1970), which concentrates more on the period after 1603. Agnes Strickland overlooked Anna as a Scottish queen by including her in *Lives of the Queens of England*, 8 vols. (London, 1844), vol. vii. L. Barroll, 'The court of the first Stuart Queen', in L.L. Peck (ed.), *The Mental World of the Jacobean Court* (Cambridge, 1991), refers to Anna's Scottish years. There had, however, been many Stuart queens before Anna so this title typically ignores the relevance of Scottish history. M.H. Fink, 'Anne of Denmark: the Character and Political Influence of James I's Queen Consort' (University of Mississippi M.A. dissertation, 1977) again gives more attention to the years after 1603 and does not acknowledge James as VI of Scotland and I of Great Britain. Finally, see B. Keifer Lewalski, *Women Writing in Jacobean England* (Cambridge, Mass., 1993), ch. 1.

8. The Personal Letters of James VI

There is a discussion of the letters as a group in the introduction to *Letters of King James VI and I*, ed. G.P.V. Akrigg (Berkeley, Calif., 1984).

James can also be studied through his other writings, particularly the splendid and readable *Basilicon Doron* ('The Royal Gift'), a manual of advice on kingship for his son. This is the first item in King James VI & I, *Political Writings*, ed. J.P. Sommerville (Cambridge, 1994). Writings about James by those who knew him—mainly in England but including comments on his early reign in Scotland—are collected in R. Ashton (ed.), *James I by his Contemporaries* (London, 1969).

9. James VI's Architects and their Architecture

The most exhaustive text for the architecture of this period remains D. MacGibbon and T. Ross's magisterial *Castellated and Domestic Architecture of Scotland*, 5 vols. (1887-92). R. Fawcett, *Scottish Architecture from the Accession of the Stewarts to the Reformation, 1371-1560* (Edinburgh, 1994), and D. Howard, *Scottish Architecture: Reformation to Restoration, 1560-1660* (Edinburgh, 1995), are the most comprehensive and authoritative recent works; see also M. Glendinning, R. MacInnes and A. MacKechnie, *A History of Scottish Architecture* (Edinburgh, 1996), ch. 2. Published primary material essentially consists of official records, including the crucial *Accounts of the Masters of Works*, vol. i (1529-1615), ed. H. Paton (Edinburgh, 1957), and vol. ii (1616-1649), eds. J. Imrie and J. Dunbar (Edinburgh, 1982), where also are contained biographical accounts of the various officers. Other documentation is collected in R.S. Mylne, *The Master Masons to the Crown of Scotland* (Edinburgh, 1893).

10. James VI and the General Assembly, 1586-1618

The church has received more attention than most other aspects of the reign. Gordon Donaldson, in *The Scottish Reformation* (Cambridge, 1960), insisted that contemporaries had a 'preoccupation ... with church order, with systems of administration, with organisation and even with finance', and that historians should follow that agenda. That book and his *James V—James VII* are basic texts, written from a resolutely episcopalian standpoint. Numerous other useful pieces are collected in his *Scottish Church History* (Edinburgh, 1985); one that is not is his chapter, 'The Scottish church, 1567-1625', in A.G.R. Smith (ed.), *The Reign of James VI and I* (London, 1973). His ambitious *The Faith of the Scots* (London, 1990) sets out a new agenda but devotes surprisingly little space to the reign.

The work of James Kirk, mostly drawn together in his *Patterns of Reform: Continuity and Change in the Reformation Kirk* (Edinburgh, 1989), mostly offers a presbyterian perspective on Donaldson's administrative agenda, and also adds two provocative chapters on the Highlands. His editions of *Stirling Presbytery Records, 1581-1587* (SHS, 1981), *The Second Book of Discipline* (Edinburgh, 1980) and *The Books of Assumption of the Thirds of Benefices: Scottish Ecclesiastical Rentals at the Reformation* (Oxford, 1995) are essential source material. W.R. Foster, *The Church before the Covenants, 1596-1638* (Edinburgh, 1975), continues Donaldson's episcopalian perspective but discusses the role of ministers in society as well as matters ecclesiastical. M. Lee, 'James VI and the revival of episcopacy in Scotland, 1596-1600', *Church History*, xliii (1974), 50-64, is characteristically succinct but its description of 1597 as the moment when James, stripped of his options by the kirk's intransigence, was forced to turn to the remedy of bishops, has effectively been rebutted. I.B. Cowan, 'The Five Articles of Perth', in D. Shaw (ed.), *Reformation and Revolution: Essays presented to Hugh Watt* (Edinburgh, 1967), and P.H.R. Mackay, 'The reception given to the Five Articles of Perth', *RSCHS*, xix (1977), 185-201, are standard works. T. McCrie, *Andrew Melville* (3rd edn., Edinburgh, 1855), with its copious appendices, is still essential reading. Melville himself, however, remains something of an enigma.

A fresh look at the reign is provided in D.G. Mullan, *Episcopacy in Scotland, 1560-1638* (Edinburgh, 1986), which critically examines both polity and theology from a standpoint which eschews conventional party lines. A.R. MacDonald's *The Jacobean Kirk, 1567-1625: Sovereignty, Polity and Liturgy* (Aldershot, 1998) offers a series of challenges to accepted interpretations, notably in its distrust of the convenient label of 'Melvillianism'. The same author also provides useful correctives in his 'David Calderwood: the not so hidden years, 1590-1604', *SHR*, lxxiv (1995), 69-74, and 'The subscription crisis and church-state relations, 1584-1586', *RSCHS*, xxv (1994), 222-55. James's bishops await further study but a particularly useful analysis of them, which deserves wider attention, is J. Wormald, 'No bishop, no king: the Scottish Jacobean episcopate, 1600-1625', *Miscellanea Historia Ecclesiasticae*, viii (1987), 260-7.

W.H. Makey, *The Church of the Covenant, 1637-1651: Revolution and Social Change in Scotland* (Edinburgh, 1979) is much more widely cast in period than its title suggests, providing insights into the phenomenon of the rise of the ministers as a new, formidable social grouping and the growth of religious radicalism, especially in Edinburgh, from the 1580s onwards. A sceptical view of the progress of evangelising and catechising during this reign and beyond is given in M. Lynch, 'Preaching to the converted? Perspectives on the Scottish Reformation', in A.A. MacDonald *et al.* (eds.), *The Renaissance in Scotland* (Leiden, 1994). J. Dawson, 'Anglo-Scottish Protestant culture and integration in sixteenth-century Britain', in S.G. Ellis and S. Barber (eds.), *Conquest and Union: Fashioning a British State, 1485-1725* (London, 1995), usefully explores the difficult question of why a largely common British Protestant culture failed to produce, despite James VI's efforts, closer relations between its churches.

11. The Scottish State and its Borderlands, 1567-1625

The realms of James VI and I contained numerous marginal regions. Most works discuss them separately, but a good overview is provided by J. Morrill, 'The British problem, *c*.1534-1707', in B. Bradshaw and J. Morrill (eds.), *The British Problem, c.1534-1707* (London, 1996). A detailed comparison of state power in the English Borders and the Irish Pale is made by S.G. Ellis, *Tudor Frontiers and Noble Power: the Making of the British State* (Oxford, 1995). Policies towards the Scottish Borders and Highlands are evaluated together in J. Goodare, *State and Society in Early Modern Scotland* (Oxford, 1999), chs. 7-8. Contemporary ideas about them are placed in a broad context by M. Lynch, 'A nation born again? Scottish identity in the sixteenth and seventeenth centuries', in D. Broun *et al.* (eds.), *Image and Identity: the Making and Re-making of Scotland through the Ages* (Edinburgh, 1998), and A.H. Williamson, 'Scots, Indians and empire: the Scottish politics of civilization, 1519-1609', *Past and Present*, 150 (Feb. 1996), 46-83.

Comparatively little has been written on government in the Borders. The standard work is T.I. Rae, *The Administration of the Scottish Frontier, 1513-1603* (Edinburgh, 1966). G.R. Hewitt, *Scotland under Morton, 1572-1580* (Edinburgh, 1982), devotes a chapter to it. D.L.W. Tough, *The Last Years of a Frontier: a History of the Borders during the Reign of Elizabeth* (Oxford, 1928) provides some extra information. The problem of the English north is discussed in R.T. Spence, 'The pacification of the Cumberland borders, 1593-1628', *Northern History*, xiii (1977), 99-122. For works on the Highlands, see Chapter 12 below.

12. James VI and the 'Highland Problem'

Neither D. Gregory, *The History of the Western Highlands and Isles of Scotland, 1493-1625* (2nd edn., Edinburgh, 1881), nor W.C. Mackenzie, *History of the Outer Hebrides* (Paisley, 1903), have been superseded on the political history of the Highlands. J. Goodare, 'The Statutes of Iona in context', *SHR*, lxxvii (1998), 31-57, challenges the traditional idea that the Statutes (1609) marked a turning-point in the Highlands' relationship with the state.

The clan system has recently been discussed by A.I. Macinnes, *Clanship, Commerce and the House of Stuart, 1603-1788* (East Linton, 1996), and in three papers by Jane Dawson: 'The origins of the Road to the Isles": trade, communications and Campbell power in early modern Scotland', in R. Mason and N. Macdougall (eds.), *People and Power in Scotland* (Edinburgh, 1992); 'Calvinism and the Gaidhealtachd in Scotland', in A. Pettegree *et al.* (eds.), *Calvinism in Europe, 1540-1620* (Cambridge, 1994); and 'The Gaidhealtachd and the emergence of the Scottish Highlands', in B. Bradshaw and P. Roberts (eds.), *British Consciousness and Identity: the Making of Britain, 1533-1707* (Cambridge, 1997). D. Stevenson, *Alasdair MacColla and the Highland Problem in the Seventeenth Century* (Edinburgh, 1980), touches on this period, as does I.F. Grant and H. Cheape, *Periods in Highland History* (London, 1987).

The nature of Campbell power is discussed in E.J. Cowan, 'Clanship, kinship and the Campbell acquisition of Islay', *SHR*, lviii (1979), 132-57. The MacDonald network, in both Scotland and Ulster, is discussed in J.M. Hill, *Fire and Sword: Sorley Boy Macdonnell and the Rise of Clan Ian Mor, 1538-1590* (London, 1993) and in G. Hill, *The Macdonells of Antrim* (Belfast, 1873). For links with Ireland, G.A. Hayes-McCoy, *Scots Mercenary Forces in Ireland* (Dublin, 1937) has not been superseded. Other, general overviews are listed above, under Chapter 11.

13. James VI and the Politics of South-West Scotland, 1603-1625

There is no recent history of the south west, or indeed of any Scottish locality, in this period. Ayrshire is ably catered for in M.H.B. Sanderson, *Ayrshire and the Reformation: People and Change, 1490-1600* (East Linton, 1997), while studies of other localities, such as F.D. Bardgett, *Scotland Reformed: The Reformation in Angus and the Mearns* (Edinburgh, 1989), provide a useful comparison. Older works such as G. Robertson, *A Genealogical Account of the Principal Families of Ayrshire* (Irvine, 1825) and P. M'Kerlie, *History of the Lands and their Owners in Galloway*, 5 vols. (Edinburgh, 1870-79) are still helpful. Most parishes in the south west have their own histories, as do individual burghs, including J. Strawhorn, *A History of Ayr* (Edinburgh, 1989) and *A History of Irvine* (Edinburgh, 1985), and W. McDowall, *History of Dumfries* (4th edn., Dumfries, 1986). Useful analyses of the relationship between centre and locality can be found in K.M. Brown, *Bloodfeud in Scotland, 1573-1625* (Edinburgh, 1986), and J. Wormald, *Court, Kirk and Community: Scotland, 1470-1625* (London, 1981).

14. 'Tis True I am a Cradle King': the View from the Throne

Reading on court culture is discussed above, at Chapters 3 and 4. On James in England, the most extensive treatment is the dense and unnecessarily *recherché* J. Goldberg, *James I and the Politics of Literature* (Baltimore, Md., 1983), and the more readable and lively K. Sharpe, 'Private conscience and public duty in the writings of James VI and I', in J. Morrill *et al.* (eds.), *Public Duty and Private Conscience in Seventeenth Century England* (Oxford, 1993). On the political writings, there are extremely valuable introductions to *The Political Works of James I*, ed. C.H. McIlwain (New York, 1965) and King James VI & I, *Political Writings*, ed. J.P. Sommerville (Cambridge, 1994). It is interesting that the English works tend to 'mystify' James's attitude to his kingship to a much greater extent than the Scottish ones, which may itself reflect a shift in the king's approach and his subjects' aspirations after 1603.

CONTRIBUTORS

SHARON ADAMS is a postgraduate student in the Department of Scottish History, University of Edinburgh. She is the author of 'The making of the radical south west: Charles I and his Scottish kingdom, 1625-1649', in J. Young (ed.), *Celtic Dimensions of the British Civil Wars* (John Donald, 1997).

JULIAN GOODARE is Lecturer in the Department of Scottish History, University of Edinburgh. He is author of *State and Society in Early Modern Scotland* (Oxford University Press, 1999), and of a number of articles on early modern Scottish history. He is Publication Secretary of the Scottish History Society and an Associate Editor of the *New Dictionary of National Biography*.

RUTH GRANT is Educational Development Adviser, Centre for Learning and Professional Development, University of Aberdeen, and a postgraduate student in the Department of Scottish History, University of Edinburgh. She is the author of 'Politicking Jacobean aristocratic women: Lady Fernihurst and the countesses of Arran and Huntly, *c*.1580-1603', in E.L. Ewan and M.M. Meikle (eds.), *Women in Scotland, c.1100-c.1750* (Tuckwell Press, 1999).

RODERICK J. LYALL is Professor of English Literature in the Vrije Universiteit, Amsterdam. He is author of numerous articles on early Scottish literature, and has edited several texts including William Lamb, *Ane Resonyng of ane Scottis and Inglis Merchand Betuix Rowand and Lionis* (Aberdeen University Press, 1985) and Sir David Lindsay of the Mount, *Ane Satyre of the Thrie Estaitis* (Canongate Publishing, 1989). He is working on a full study of Alexander Montgomerie.

MICHAEL LYNCH is Sir William Fraser Professor of Scottish History and Palaeography at the University of Edinburgh. He is author of *Edinburgh and the Reformation* (John Donald, 1981) and *Scotland: a New History* (Pimlico, 1991), and has edited several books on Scottish history, most recently (with Dauvit Broun and R.J. Finlay) *Image and Identity: the Making and Remaking of Scotland through the Ages* (John Donald, 1998). He is general editor of the forthcoming *Oxford Companion to Scottish History*.

ALAN R. MACDONALD is Postdoctoral Research Fellow with the Scottish Parliament Project in the Department of Scottish History, University of St Andrews. He is author of *The Jacobean Kirk, 1567-1625: Sovereignty, Polity and Liturgy* (Ashgate, 1998), and of a number of articles on early modern Scottish history.

AONGHUS MACKECHNIE is Principal Inspector of Historical Buildings, Historic Scotland. He is co-author (with Miles Glendinning and Ranald MacInnes) of *A History of Scottish Architecture from the Renaissance to the Present Day* (Edinburgh University Press, 1996) and *Building a Nation: the Story of Scotland's Architecture* (Canongate Books, 1999).

MAUREEN M. MEIKLE is Senior Lecturer in History in the School of Humanities and Social Sciences, University of Sunderland. She is co-editor (with Elizabeth Ewan) of *Women in Scotland, c.1100-c.1750* (Tuckwell Press, 1999), and has published several articles on early modern British history. She is working on a biography of Anna of Denmark's Scottish years.

GRANT G. SIMPSON was formerly Reader in Scottish History at the University of Aberdeen and is now a Heritage Consultant in Aberdeen. He is the author of *Scottish Handwriting, 1150-1650* (Aberdeen University Press, 1973) and (with the late Lionel Stones) of *Edward I and the Throne of Scotland, 1290-1296*, 2 vols. (Oxford University Press, 1978). He has edited numerous books on Scottish history, most recently *Scotland and the Low Countries, 1124-1994* (Tuckwell Press, 1996).

JENNY WORMALD is Fellow and Tutor in Modern History at St Hilda's College, Oxford. She is author of *Court, Kirk and Community: Scotland, 1470-1625* (Arnold, 1981) in the 'New History of Scotland' series of which she was general editor; *Lords and Men in Scotland: Bonds of Manrent, 1442-1603* (John Donald, 1985); and *Mary Queen of Scots: a Study in Failure* (George Philip, 1988). She is editor of the forthcoming *Oxford Illustrated History of Scotland*, and is working on a biography of James VI and I.

INDEX